Data Engineer with Google Cloud Platform

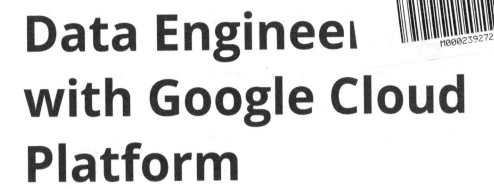

A practical guide to operationalizing scalable data analytics systems on GCP

Adi Wijaya

BIRMINGHAM—MUMBAI

Data Engineering with Google Cloud Platform

Copyright © 2022 Packt Publishing

Publishing Product Manager: Devika Battike

Senior Editor: David Sugarman

Content Development Editor: Sean Lobo

Technical Editor: Devanshi Ayare

Copy Editor: Safis Editing

Project Coordinator: Aparna Ravikumar Nair

Proofreader: Safis Editing

Indexer: Hemangini Bari

Production Designer: Jyoti Chauhan

Marketing Coordinator: Priyanka Mhatre

First published: March 2022

Production reference: 2100322

Published by Packt Publishing Ltd.
Livery Place
35 Livery Street
Birmingham
B3 2PB, UK.

ISBN 978-1-80056-132-8

www.packt.com

Contributors

About the author

Adi Wijaya is a strategic cloud data engineer at Google. He holds a bachelor's degree in computer science from Binus University and co-founded DataLabs in Indonesia. Currently, he dedicates himself to big data and analytics and has spent a good chunk of his career helping global companies in different industries.

About the reviewer

Fajar Muharandy has over 15 years' experience in the data and analytics space. Throughout his career, he has been involved in some of the largest data warehouse and big data platform designs and implementations. Fajar is a strong believer that every data platform implementation should always start with business questions in mind, and that all stakeholders should strive toward defining the right data and technology to achieve the common goal of getting the answers to those business questions. Aside from his professional career, Fajar is also the co-founder of the Data Science Indonesia community, a community of data science enthusiasts in Indonesia who believe that data should be the foundation to push and drive actions for the greater good.

Table of Contents

Section 2: Building Solutions with GCP Components

3

Building a Data Warehouse in BigQuery

4

Building Orchestration for Batch Data Loading Using Cloud Composer

5

Building a Data Lake Using Dataproc

6

Processing Streaming Data with Pub/Sub and Dataflow

7

Visualizing Data for Making Data-Driven Decisions with Data Studio

8
Building Machine Learning Solutions on Google Cloud Platform

Section 3: Key Strategies for Architecting Top-Notch Data Pipelines

9
User and Project Management in GCP

10
Cost Strategy in GCP

11
CI/CD on Google Cloud Platform for Data Engineers

12
Boosting Your Confidence as a Data Engineer

Index

Other Books You May Enjoy

Preface

There is too much information; too many plans; it's complicated. We live in a world where there is more and more information that is as problematic as too little information, and I'm aware that this condition applies when people want to start doing data engineering in the cloud, specifically **Google Cloud Platform** (**GCP**) in this book.

When people want to embark on a career in data, there are so many different roles whose definitions sometimes vary from one company to the next.

When someone chooses to be a data engineer, there are a great number of technology options: cloud versus non-cloud; big data database versus traditional; self-managed versus a managed service; and many more.

When they decide to use the cloud on GCP, the public documentation contains a wide variety of product options and tutorials.

In this book, instead of adding further dimensions to the data engineering and GCP products, the main goal of this book is to help you narrow down the information. This book will help you narrow down all the important concepts and components from the vast array of information available on the internet. The guidance and exercises are based on the writer's experience in the field, and will give you a clear focus. By reading the book and following the exercises, you will learn the most relevant and clear path to start and boost your career in data engineering using GCP.

Who this book is for

This book is intended for anyone involved in the data and analytics space, including IT developers, data analysts, data scientists, or any other relevant roles where an individual wants to gain a jump start in the data engineering field.

This book is also intended for data engineers who want to start using GCP, prepare certification, and get practical examples based on real-world scenarios.

Finally, this book will be of interest to anyone who wants to know the thought process, have practical guidance, and a clear path to run through the technology components to be able to start, achieve the certification, and gain a practical perspective in data engineering with GCP.

What this book covers

This book is divided into 3 sections and 12 chapters. Each section is a collection of independent chapters that have one objective:

Chapter 1, Fundamentals of Data Engineering, explains the role of data engineers and how data engineering relates to GCP.

Chapter 2, Big Data Capabilities on GCP, introduces the relevant GCP services related to data engineering.

Chapter 3, Building a Data Warehouse in BigQuery, covers the data warehouse concept using BigQuery.

Chapter 4, Building Orchestration for Batch Data Loading Using Cloud Composer, explains data orchestration using Cloud Composer.

Chapter 5, Building a Data Lake Using Dataproc, details the Data Lake concept with Hadoop using DataProc.

Chapter 6, Processing Streaming Data with Pub/Sub and Dataflow, explains the concept of streaming data using Pub/Sub and Dataflow.

Chapter 7, Visualizing Data for Making Data-Driven Decisions with Data Studio, covers how to use data from BigQuery to visualize it as charts in Data Studio.

Chapter 8, Building Machine Learning Solutions on Google Cloud Platform, sets out the concept of MLOps using Vertex AI.

Chapter 9, G User and Project Management in GCP, explains the fundamentals of GCP Identity and Access Management and project structures.

Chapter 10, Cost Strategy in GCP, covers how to estimate the overall data solution using GCP.

Chapter 11, CI/CD on Google Cloud Platform for Data Engineers, explains the concept of CI/CD and its relevance to data engineers.

Chapter 12, Boosting Your Confidence as a Data Engineer, prepares you for the GCP certification and offers some final thoughts in terms of summarizing what's been learned in this book.

To get the most out of this book

To successfully follow the examples in this book, you need a GCP account and project. If, at this point, you don't have a GCP account and project, don't worry. We will cover that as part of the exercises in this book.

Occasionally, we will use the free tier from GCP for practice, but be aware that some products might not have free tiers. Notes will be provided if this is the case.

All the exercises in this book can be completed without any additional software installation. The exercises will be done in the GCP console that you can open from any operating system using your favorite browser.

You should be familiar with basic programming languages. In this book, I will focus on utilizing Python and the Linux command line.

If you are using the digital version of this book, we advise you to type the code yourself or access the code from the book's GitHub repository (a link is available in the next section). Doing so will help you avoid any potential errors related to the copying and pasting of code.

This book is not positioned to replace GCP public documentation. Hence, comprehensive information on every single feature of GCP services might not be available in this book. We also won't use all the GCP services that are available. For such information, you can always check the public documentation.

Remember that the main goal of this book is to help you narrow down information. Use this book as your step-by-step guide to build solutions to common challenges facing data engineers. Follow the patterns from the exercises, the relationship between concepts, important GCP services, and best practices. Always use the hands-on exercises so you can experience working with GCP.

Download the example code files

You can download the example code files for this book from GitHub at `https://github.com/PacktPublishing/Data-Engineering-with-Google-Cloud-Platform`. If there's an update to the code, it will be updated in the GitHub repository.

We also have other code bundles from our rich catalog of books and videos available at `https://github.com/PacktPublishing/`. Check them out!

Download the color images

We also provide a PDF file that has color images of the screenshots and diagrams used in this book. You can download it here: `https://static.packt-cdn.com/downloads/9781800561328_ColorImages.pdf`.

Conventions used

There are a number of text conventions used throughout this book.

`Code in text`: Indicates code words in the text, database table names, folder names, filenames, file extensions, pathnames, dummy URLs, user input, and Twitter handles. Here is an example: "Mount the downloaded `WebStorm-10*.dmg` disk image file as another disk in your system."

A block of code is set as follows:

```
html, body, #map {
  height: 100%;
  margin: 0;
  padding: 0
}
```

When we wish to draw your attention to a particular part of a code block, the relevant lines or items are set in bold:

```
[default]
exten => s,1,Dial(Zap/1|30)
exten => s,2,Voicemail(u100)
exten => s,102,Voicemail(b100)
exten => i,1,Voicemail(s0)
```

Any command-line input or output is written as follows:

```
$ mkdir css
$ cd css
```

Bold: Indicates a new term, an important word, or words that you see on screen. For instance, words in menus or dialog boxes appear in **bold**. Here is an example: "Select **System info** from the **Administration** panel."

> **Tips or Important Notes**
> Appear like this.

Get in touch

Feedback from our readers is always welcome.

General feedback: If you have questions about any aspect of this book, email us at `customercare@packtpub.com` and mention the book title in the subject of your message.

Errata: Although we have taken every care to ensure the accuracy of our content, mistakes do happen. If you have found a mistake in this book, we would be grateful if you would report this to us. Please visit `www.packtpub.com/support/errata` and fill in the form.

Piracy: If you come across any illegal copies of our works in any form on the internet, we would be grateful if you would provide us with the location address or website name. Please contact us at `copyright@packt.com` with a link to the material.

If you are interested in becoming an author: If there is a topic that you have expertise in and you are interested in either writing or contributing to a book, please visit `authors.packtpub.com`.

Share Your Thoughts

Once you've read *Data Engineering with Google Cloud Platform*, we'd love to hear your thoughts! Scan the QR code below to go straight to the Amazon review page for this book and share your feedback.

`https://packt.link/r/1-800-56132-6`

Your review is important to us and the tech community and will help us make sure we're delivering excellent quality content.

Section 1: Getting Started with Data Engineering with GCP

This part will talk about the purpose, value, and concepts of big data and cloud computing and how GCP products are relevant to data engineering. You will learn about a data engineer's core responsibilities, how they differ from those of a data scientist, and how to facilitate the flow of data through an organization to derive insights.

This section comprises the following chapters:

- *Chapter 1, Fundamentals of Data Engineering*
- *Chapter 2, Big Data Capabilities on GCP*

1
Fundamentals of Data Engineering

Years ago, when I first entered the **data science** world, I used to think data was clean. Clean in terms of readiness, available in one place, and ready for fun data science purposes. I was so excited to experiment with **machine learning** models, finding unusual patterns in data and playing around with clean data. But after years of experience working with data, I realized that data science in big organizations isn't straightforward.

Eighty percent of the effort goes into collecting, cleaning, and transforming the data. If you have had any experience in working with data, I am sure you've noticed something similar. But the good news is, we know that almost all processes can be automated using proper planning, designing, and engineering skills. That was the point where I realized that data engineering will be the most critical role from that day to the future of the data science world.

To develop a successful data ecosystem in any organization, the most crucial part is how they design the **data architecture**. If the organization fails to make the best decision on the data architecture, the future process will be painful. Here are some common examples: the system is not scalable, querying data is slow, business users don't trust your data, the infrastructure cost is very high, and data is leaked. There is so much more that can go wrong without proper **data engineering** practice.

In this chapter, we are going to learn the fundamental knowledge behind data engineering. The goal is to introduce you to common terms that are often used in this field and will be mentioned often in the later chapters.

In particular, we will be covering the following topics:

- Understanding the data life cycle
- Know the roles of a data engineer before starting
- Foundational concepts for data engineering

Understanding the data life cycle

The first principle to learn to become a data engineer is understanding the data life cycle. If you've worked with data, you must know that data doesn't stay in one place; it moves from one storage to another, from one database to other databases. Understanding the data life cycle means you need to be able to answer these sorts of questions *if you want to display information to your end user*:

- Who will consume the data?
- What data sources should I use?
- Where should I store the data?
- When should the data arrive?
- Why does the data need to be stored in this place?
- How should the data be processed?

To answer all those questions, we'll start by looking back a little bit at the history of data technologies.

Understanding the need for a data warehouse

Data warehouse is not a new concept; I believe you've at least heard of it. In fact, the terminology is no longer appealing. In my experience, no one gets excited when talking about data warehouses in the 2020s. Especially when compared to terminologies such as **big data**, **cloud computing**, and **artificial intelligence**.

So, why do we need to know about data warehouses? The answer to that is because almost every single data engineering challenge from the old times to these days is conceptually the same. The challenges are always about moving data from the data source to other environments so the business can use it to get information. The difference from time to time is only about the how and newer technologies. If we understand why people needed data warehouses in historical times, we will have a better foundation to understand the data engineering space and, more specifically, the data life cycle.

Data warehouses were first developed in the 1980s to transform data from operational systems to decision-making support systems. The key principle of a data warehouse is combining data from many different sources to a single location and then transforming it into a format the data warehouse can process and store.

For example, in the financial industry, say a bank wants to know how many credit card customers also have mortgages. It is a simple enough question, yet it's not that easy to answer. Why?

Most traditional banks that I have worked with had different operating systems for each of their products, including a specific system for credit cards and specific systems for mortgages, saving products, websites, customer service, and many other systems. So, in order to answer the question, data from multiple systems needs to be stored in one place first.

See the following diagram on how each department is independent:

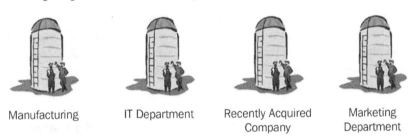

| Manufacturing | IT Department | Recently Acquired Company | Marketing Department |

Figure 1.1 – Data silos

Often, independence not only applies to the organization structure but also to the data. When data is located in different places, it's called **data silos**. This is very common in large organizations where each department has different goals, responsibilities, and priorities.

In summary, what we need to understand from the data warehouse concept is the following:

- Data silos have always occurred in large organizations, even back in the 1980s.

- Data comes from many operating systems.

- In order to process the data, we need to store the data in one place.

What does a typical data warehouse stack look like?

This diagram represents the four logical building blocks in a data warehouse, which are **Storage**, **Compute**, **Schema**, and **SQL Interface**:

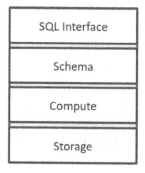

Figure 1.2 – Data warehouse main components

Data warehouse products are mostly able to store and process data seamlessly and the user can use the SQL language to access the data in tables with a structured schema format. It is basic knowledge, but an important point to be aware of is that the four logical building blocks in the data warehouse are designed as one monolithic software that evolved over the later years and was the start of the **data lake**.

Getting familiar with the differences between a data warehouse and a data lake

Fast forward to 2008, when an open source data technology named **Hadoop** was first published, and people started to use the data lake terminology. If you try to find the definition of data lake on the internet, it will mostly be described as *a centralized repository that allows you to store all your structured and unstructured data.*

So, what is the difference between a data lake and a data warehouse? Both have the same idea to store data in centralized storage. Is it simply that a data lake stores unstructured data and a data warehouse doesn't?

What if I say some data warehouse products can now store and process unstructured data? Does the data warehouse become a data lake? The answer is no.

One of the key differences from a technical perspective is that data lake technologies separate most of the building blocks, in particular, the storage and computation, but also the other blocks, such as schema, stream, SQL interface, and machine learning. This evolves the concept of a monolithic platform into a modern and modular platform consisting of separated components, as illustrated in the following diagram:

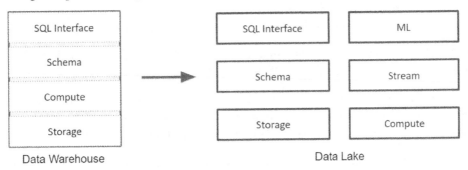

Figure 1.3 – Data warehouse versus data lake components

For example, in a data warehouse, you insert data by calling SQL statements and query the data through SQL tables, and there is nothing you can do as a user to change that pattern.

In a data lake, you can access the underlying storage directly, for example, by storing a text file, choosing your own computation engine, and choosing not to have a schema. There are many impacts of this concept, but I'll summarize it into three differences:

Data Lake	Data Warehouse
Schema is not mandatory	Schema is mandatory
Possibility to compute using different technologies for the same underlying storage	With all access using SQL, the developer doesn't have control over how to compute and store the data
First focus is to store as much data as possible. Business relevancy and data model are defined later	First focus is business relevancy and data models. Only store data based on the business needs

Figure 1.4 – Table comparing data lakes and data warehouses

Large organizations start to store any data in the data lake system for two reasons, *high scalability* and *cheap storage*. In modern data architecture, both data lakes and data warehouses complete each other, rather than replacing each other.

We will dive deeper and carry out some practical examples throughout the book, such as trying to build a sample in *Chapter 3, Building a Data Warehouse in BigQuery*, and *Chapter 5, Building a Data Lake Using Dataproc*.

The data life cycle

Based on our understanding of the history of the data warehouse, now we know that data does not stay in one place. As an analogy, data is very similar to water; it flows from upstream to downstream. Later in this book, both of these terms, upstream and downstream, will be used often since they are common terminologies in data engineering.

When you think about water flowing upstream and downstream, one example that you can think of is a waterfall; the water falls freely without any obstacles.

Another example in different water life cycle circumstances is a water pipeline; upstream is the water reservoir and downstream is your kitchen sink. In this case, you can imagine the different pipes, filters, branches, and knobs in the middle of the process.

Data is very much like water. There are scenarios where you just need to copy data from one storage to another storage, or in more complex scenarios, you may need to filter, join, and split multiple steps downstream before the data can be consumed by the end users.

As illustrated in the following diagram, the data life cycle mostly starts from frontend applications, and flows up to the end for data users as information in the dashboard or ad hoc queries:

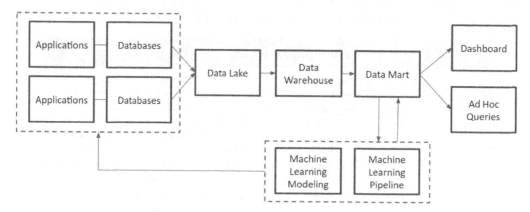

Figure 1.5 – Data life cycle diagram

Let's now look at the elements of the data life cycle in detail:

1. **Apps and databases**: The application is the interface from the human to the machine. The frontend application in most cases acts as the first data upstream. Data at this level is designed to serve application transactions as fast as possible.

2. **Data lake**: Data from multiple databases needs to be stored in one place. The data lake concept and technologies suit the needs. The data lake stores data in a file format such as a CSV file, Avro, or Parquet.

   The advantage of storing data in a file format is that it can accept any data sources; for example, MySQL Database can export the data to CSV files, image data can be stored as JPEG files, and IoT device data can be stored as JSON files. Another advantage of storing data in a data lake is it doesn't require a schema at this stage.

3. **Data warehouse**: When you know any data in a data lake is valuable, you need to start thinking about the following:

   A. What is the schema?

   B. How do you query the data?

   C. What is the best data model for the data?

   Data in a data warehouse is usually modeled based on business requirements. With this, one of the key requirements to build the data warehouse is that you need to know the relevance of the data to your business and the expected information that you want to generate from the data.

4. **Data mart**: A data mart is an area for storing data that serves specific user groups. At this stage, you need to start thinking about the final downstream of data and who the end user is. Each data mart is usually under the control of each department within an organization. For example, a data mart for a finance team will consist of finance-related tables, while a data mart for data scientists might consist of tables with machine learning features.

5. **Data end consumer**: The last stage of data will be back to humans as information. The end user of data can have various ways to use the data but at a very high level, these are the three most common usages:

   A. Reporting and dashboard

   B. Ad hoc query

   C. Machine learning

Are all data life cycles like this? No. Similar to the analogy of water flowing upstream and downstream, in different circumstances, it will require different data life cycles, and that's where data engineers need to be able to design the data pipeline architecture. But the preceding data life cycle is a very common pattern. In the past 10 years as a data consultant, I have had the opportunity to work with more than 30 companies from many industries, including financial, government, telecommunication, and e-commerce. Most of the companies that I worked with followed this pattern or were at least going in that direction.

As an overall summary of this section, we've learned that since historical times, data is mostly in silos, and it drives the needs of the data warehouse and data lake. The data will move from one system to others as specific needs have specific technologies and, in this section, we've learned about a very common pattern in data engineering. In the next section, let's try to understand the role of a data engineer, who should be responsible for this.

Knowing the roles of a data engineer before starting

In the later chapters, we will spend much of our time doing practical exercises to understand the data engineering concepts. But before that, let's quickly take a look at the data engineer role.

The job role is getting more and more popular now, but the terminology itself is relatively new compared to other job roles, such as accountant, lawyer, doctor, and many other well-established job roles. The impact is that sometimes there is still a debate of what a data engineer should and shouldn't do.

For example, if you came to a hospital and met a doctor, you know for sure that the doctor would do the following:

1. Examine your condition.
2. Make a diagnosis of your health issues.
3. Prescribe medicine.

The doctor wouldn't do the following:

1. Clean the hospital.
2. Make the medicine.
3. Manage hospital administration.

It's clear, and it applies to most well-established job roles. But how about data engineers?

This is just a very short list of examples of what data engineers should or shouldn't be responsible for:

- Handle all big data infrastructures and software installation.

- Handle application databases.

- Design the data warehouse data model.

- Analyze big data to transform raw data into meaningful information.

- Create a data pipeline for machine learning.

The unclear condition is unavoidable since it's a new role and I believe it will be more and more established following the maturity of data science. In this section, let's try to understand what a data engineer is and despite many combinations of responsibilities, what you should focus on as a data engineer.

Data engineer versus data scientist

A data engineer is someone who designs and builds data pipelines.

The definition is that simple, but I found out that the question about the different between a data engineer versus a data scientist is still one of the most frequently asked questions when someone wants to start their data career. The hype of *data scientists* on the internet is one of the drivers; for example, up until today people still like to quote the following:

"Data scientist: the sexiest job of the 21st Century"

– Harvard Business Review

The data scientist role was originally invented to refer to groups of people who are highly curious and able to utilize big data technologies for business purposes back in 2008. But since the technologies are maturing and becoming more complex, people start to realize that it's too much. It's very rare for a company to hire someone who knows how to do all of the following:

- How to handle big data infrastructure

- Properly design and build ETL pipelines

- Train machine learning models

- Understand deeply about the company's business

Not that it's impossible, some people do have this knowledge, but from a company's point of view, it's not practical.

These days, for better focus and scalability, the data scientist role can be split into many different roles, for example, data analyst, machine learning engineer, and business analyst. But one of the most popular and realized to be very important roles is data engineer.

The focus of data engineers

Let's map the data engineer role to our data life cycle diagram *Figure 1.5* from the previous section.

In the diagram, I added two underlying components:

- **Job Orchestrator**: Design and build a job dependency and scheduler that runs data movement from upstream to downstream.

- **Infrastructure**: Provision the required data infrastructure to run the data pipelines.

  And on each step, I added numbers from 1 to 3. The numbers will help you to identify which components are the data engineer's main responsibility. This diagram works together with *Figure 1.7*, a data engineer-focused diagram to map the numbering. First, let's check this data life cycle diagram that we discussed before with the numbering on it:

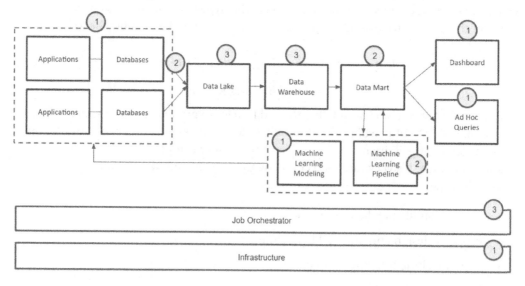

Figure 1.6 – Data life cycle flows with focus numbering

After seeing the numbering on the data life cycle, check this diagram that illustrates the focus points of a data engineer:

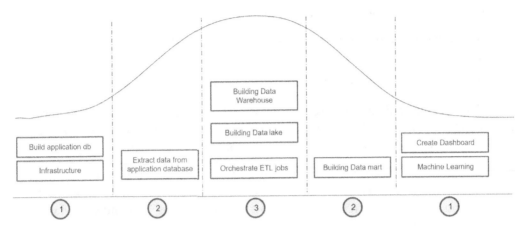

Figure 1.7 – Data engineer-focused diagram

The diagram shows the distribution of the knowledge area from the end-to-end data life cycle. At the center of the diagram (number **3**) are the jobs that are the key focus of data engineers, and I will call it the core.

Those numbered **2** are the *good to have* area. For example, it's still common in small organizations that data engineers need to build a data mart for business users.

> **Important Note**
>
> Designing and building a data mart is not as simple as creating tables in a database. Someone who builds a data mart needs to be able to talk to business people and gather requirements to serve tables from a business perspective, which is one of the reasons it's not part of the core.

While how to collect data to a data lake is part of the data engineer's responsibility, exporting data from operational application databases is often done by the application development team, for example, dumping MySQL tables as CSV in staging storage.

Those numbered **1** are the *good to know* area. For example, it's rare that a data engineer needs to be responsible for building application databases, developing machine learning models, maintaining infrastructure, and creating dashboards. It is possible, but less likely. The discipline needs knowledge that is a little bit too far from the core.

After learning about the three focus areas, now let's retrospect our understanding and vision about data engineers. Study the diagram carefully and answer these questions.

- What are your current focus areas as an individual?

- What are your current job's role focus areas (or if you are a student, your study areas)?

- What is your future goal in the data science world?

Depending on your individual answers, check with the diagram – do you have all the necessary skills at the core? Does your current job give you experience in the core? Are you excited if you could master all subjects at the core in the near future?

From my experience, what is important to data engineers is the core. Even though there are a variety of data engineers' expectations, responsibilities, and job descriptions in the market, if you are new to the role, then the most important thing is to understand what the core of a data engineer is.

The diagram gives you guidance on what type of data engineers you are or will be. The closer you are to the core, the more of a data engineer you are. You are on the right track and in the right environment to be a good data engineer.

In scenarios where you are at the core, plus other areas beside it, then you are closer to a full-stack data expert; as long as you have a strong core, if you are able to expand your expertise to the *good to have* and *good to know* areas, you will have a good advantage in your data engineering career. But if you focus on other non-core areas, I suggest you find a way to master the core first.

In this section, we learned about the role of a data engineer. If you are not familiar with the cores, the next section will be your guidance to the fundamental concepts in data engineering.

Foundational concepts for data engineering

Even though there are many data engineering concepts that we will learn throughout the book by using **Google Cloud Platform** (**GCP**), there are some concepts that are basic and you need to know as data engineers. In my experience interviewing in data companies, I found out that these foundational concepts are often asked to test how much you know about data engineering. Take the following examples:

- What is **Extract-Transform-Load** (**ETL**)?

- What's the difference between ETL and **Extract-Load-Transform** (**ELT**)?

- What is big data?

- How do you handle large volumes of data?

These questions are very common, yet very important to deeply understand the concepts since it may affect our decisions on architecting our data life cycles.

ETL concept in data engineering

ETL is the key foundation of data engineering. All things in the data life cycle are ETL; any part that happens from upstream to downstream is ETL. Let's take a look at the upstream to downstream flows that has an ETL process in between here:

Figure 1.8 – ETL illustration

ETL consists of three actual steps that you need in order to move your data:

- What is *extract*? This is the step to get the data from the upstream system. For example, if the upstream system is an RDBMS, then the extract step will be dumping or exporting data from the RDBMS.

- What is *transform*? This is the step to apply any transformation to the extracted data. For example, the file from the RDBMS needs to be joined with a static CSV file, then the transform step will process the extracted data, load the CSV file, and finally, join both information together in an intermediary system.

- What is *load*? This is the step to put the transformed data to the downstream system. For example, if the downstream system is BigQuery, then the load step will call BigQuery load job to store the data into BigQuery's table.

Back in *Figure 1.5, Data life cycle diagrams*, each of the individual steps may have a different ETL process. For example, at the application database to data lake step, the upstream is the application database and the data lake is the downstream. But at the data lake to data warehouse step, the data lake becomes the upstream and the data warehouse as its downstream. So, you need to think about how you want to do the ETL process in every data life cycle step.

The difference between ETL and ELT

ETL is extract, transform, load and ELT is extract, load, transform. From the acronym itself, the difference between ETL and ELT is only the ordering of the letters T and L. Should you transform first and then load the data to the downstream or load the data to the downstream first and then transform the data inside the downstream system?

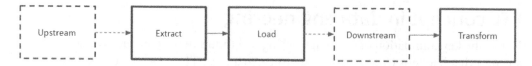

Figure 1.9 – Extract load transform

Easy! What's the big deal?

Even though it's a very simple difference in the acronym, deciding on the method can really affect your choice of technology products, system performance, scalability, and cost. For example, not all downstream systems are powerful enough to transform large volumes of data; in this case, ETL is preferred since using the ELT pattern will introduce issues in your downstream system.

In other cases, the downstream system is a lot more powerful compared to any intermediary system, so you want to choose the ELT pattern. This mostly happens after the data lake era where the downstream are products such as Hadoop, BigQuery, or other scalable data processing products. But this is not the absolute answer; depending on your available choice of technology, you may change your ETL versus ELT strategy.

You will understand this better after running through the content of this book with a lot of ETL and ELT examples, but at this point, the important thing to keep in mind is, as a data engineer, you have two options of where to transform your data: *in an intermediary system* or *in the target system*.

What is NOT big data?

After learning about ETL and ELT, the other most common terminology is **big data**. Since big data is still one of the highly correlated concepts close to data engineering, it is important how you interpret the terminology as a data engineer. Note that the word big data itself refers to two different subjects:

- The data itself is big.
- The big data technology.

With so much hype in the media about the words, both in the context of data is getting bigger and big data technology, I don't think I need to tell you the definition of the word big data. Instead, I will focus on eliminating the non-relevant definitions of big data for data engineers. Here are some definitions in media or from people that I have met personally:

- All people already use social media, the data in social media is huge, and we can use the social media data for our organization. That's big data.

- My company doesn't have data. Big data is a way to use data from the public internet to start my data journey. That's big data.

- The five Vs of data: volume, variety, velocity, veracity, and value. That's big data.

All the preceding definitions are correct but not really helpful to us as data engineers. So instead of seeing big data as general use cases, we need to focus on the *how* questions; think about what actually works under the hood. Take the following examples:

- How do you store 1 PB of data in storage, while the size of common hard drives is in TBs?

- How do you average a list of numbers, when the data is stored in multiple computers?

- How can you continuously extract data from the upstream system and do aggregation as a streaming process?

These kinds of questions are what are important for data engineers. Data engineers need to know when a condition (the data itself is big) should be handled using big data or non-big data technology.

A quick look at how big data technologies store data

Knowing that answering the *how* question is what is important to understanding big data, the first question we need to answer is how does it actually store the data? What makes it different from non-big data storage?

The word *big* in big data is relative. For example, say you analyze Twitter data and then download the data as JSON files with a size of 5 GB, and your laptop storage is 1 TB with 16 GB memory.

I don't think that's big data. But if the Twitter data is 5 PB, then it becomes big data because you need a special way to store it and a special way to process it. So, the key is not about whether it is social media data or not, or unstructured or not, which sometimes many people still get confused by. It's more about the size of the data relative to your system.

Big data technology needs to be able to distribute the data in multiple servers. The common terminology for multiple servers working together is a cluster. I'll give an illustration to show you how a very large file can be distributed into multiple chunks of file parts on multiple machines:

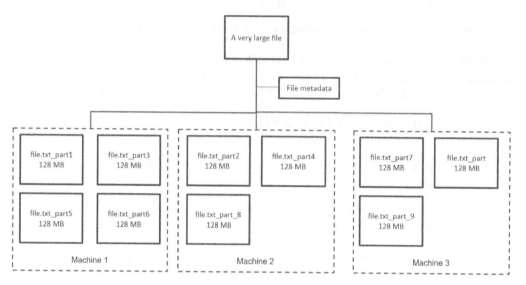

Figure 1.10 – Distributed filesystem

In a distributed filesystem, a large file will be split into multiple small parts. In the preceding example, it is split into nine parts, and each file is a small 128 MB file. Then, the multiple file parts are distributed into three machines randomly. On top of the file parts, there will be metadata to store information about how the file parts formed the original file, for example, a large file is a combination of file part 1 located in machine 1, file part 2 located in machine 2, and more.

The distributed parts can be stored in any format that isn't necessarily a file format; for example, it can be in the form of data blocks, byte arrays in memory, or some other data format. But for simplicity, what you need to be aware of is that in a big data system, data can be stored in multiple machines and in order to optimize performance, sometimes you need to think about how you want to distribute the parts.

After we know data can be split into small parts on different machines, it leads to further questions:

- How do I process the files?
- What if I want to aggregate some numbers from the files?
- How does each part know the records value from other parts while it is stored in different machines?

There are many approaches to answer these three questions. But one of the most famous concepts is MapReduce.

A quick look at how to process multiple files using MapReduce

Historically speaking, **MapReduce** is a framework that was published as a white paper by Google and is widely used in the Hadoop ecosystem. There is an actual open source project called MapReduce mainly written in Java that still has a large user base, but slowly people have started to change to other distributed processing engine alternatives, such as **Spark**, **Tez**, and **Dataflow**. But MapReduce as a concept itself is still relevant regardless of the technology.

In a short summary, the word MapReduce can refer to two definitions:

- MapReduce as a technology
- MapReduce as a concept

What is important for us to understand is MapReduce as a concept. MapReduce is a combination of two words: map and reduce.

Let's take a look at an example, if you have a file that's divided into two file parts:

Figure 1.11 – File parts

Each of the parts contains one or more words, which in this example are fruit. The file parts are stored on different machines. So, each machine will have these three file parts:

- File **Part 1** contains two words: **Banana** and **Apple**.

- File **Part 2** contains three words: **Melon**, **Apple**, and **Banana**.

- File **Part 3** contains one word: **Apple**.

How can you write a program to calculate a word count that produces these results?

- **Apple** = 3

- **Banana** = 2

- **Melon** = 1

Since the file parts are separated in different machines, we cannot just count the words directly. We need MapReduce. Let's take a look at the following diagram, where file parts are *mapped*, *shuffled*, and lastly *reduced* to get the final result:

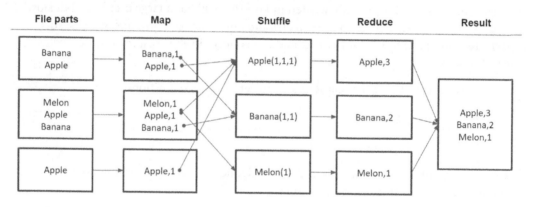

Figure 1.12 – MapReduce step diagram

There are four main steps in the diagram:

1. **Map**: Add to each individual record a static value of 1. This will transform the word into a key-value pair when the value is always 1.

2. **Shuffle**: At this point, we need to move the fruit words between machines. We want to group each word and store it in the same machine for each group.

3. **Reduce**: Because each fruit group is already in the same machine, we can count them together. The **Reduce** step will sum up the static value 1 to produce the count results.

4. **Result**: Store the final results back in the single machine.

The key idea here is to process any possible process in a distributed manner. Looking back at the diagram, you can imagine each box on each step is a different machine.

Each step, **Map**, **Shuffle**, and **Reduce**, always maintains three parallel boxes. What does this mean? It means that the processes happened in parallel on three machines. This paradigm is different from calculating all processes in a single machine. For example, we can simply download all the file parts into a pandas DataFrame in Python and do a count using the pandas DataFrame. In this case, the process will happen in one machine.

MapReduce is a complex concept. The concept is explained in a 13-page-long document by Google. You can find the document easily on the public internet. In this book, I haven't added much deeper explanation about MapReduce. In most cases, you don't need to really think about it; for example, if in a later chapter you use BigQuery to process 1 PB of data, you will only need to run a SQL query and BigQuery will process it in a distributed manner in the background.

As a matter of fact, all technologies in GCP that we will use in this book are highly scalable and without question able to handle big data out of the box. But understanding the underlying concepts helps you as a data engineer in many ways, for example, choosing the right technologies, designing data pipeline architecture, troubleshooting, and improving performance.

Summary

As a summary of the first chapter, we've learned the fundamental knowledge we need as data engineers. Here are some key takeaways from this chapter. First, data doesn't stay in one place. Data moves from one place to another, called the data life cycle. We also understand that data in a big organization is mostly in silos, and we can solve these data silos using the concepts of a data warehouse and data lake.

As someone who has started to look into data engineer roles, you may be a little bit lost. The role of data engineers may vary. The key takeaway is not to be confused about the broad expectation in the market. First, you should focus on the core and then expand as you get more and more experience from the core. In this chapter, we've learned what the core for a data engineer is. At the end of the chapter, we learned some of the key concepts. There are three key concepts as a data engineer that you need to be familiar with. These concepts are ETL, big data, and distributed systems

In the next chapter, we will visit GCP, a cloud platform provided by Google that has a lot of services to help us as data engineers. We want to understand its preposition and what the services are that are relevant to big data, and lastly, we will start using the GCP console.

Now let's put the knowledge from this chapter into practice.

Exercise

You are a data engineer at a book publishing company and your product manager has asked you to build a dashboard to show the total revenue and customer satisfaction index in a single dashboard.

Your company doesn't have any data infrastructure yet, but you know that your company has these three applications that contain TBs of data:

- The company website

- A book sales application using MongoDB to store sales transactions, including transactions, book ID, and author ID

- An author portal application using MySQL Database to store authors' personal information, including age

Do the following:

1. List important follow-up questions for your manager.

2. List your technical thinking process of how to do it at a high level.

3. Draw a data pipeline architecture.

There is no right or wrong answer to this practice. The important thing is that you can imagine how the data flows from upstream to downstream, how it should be processed at each step, and finally, how you want to serve the information to end users.

See also

- Learn more about Hadoop and its distributed filesystem: https://hadoop.apache.org/docs/r1.2.1/hdfs_design.pdf.

- Learn more about how MapReduce works: https://static.googleusercontent.com/media/research.google.com/en//archive/mapreduce-osdi04.pdf.

- Key facts about data engineers and why the role is getting more popularity than data scientists in 2021: https://www.kdnuggets.com/2021/02/dont-need-data-scientists-need-data-engineers.html.

2

Big Data Capabilities on GCP

One of the most common scenarios when people start using **Google Cloud Platform** or **GCP** is getting lost because there are too many products and services. GCP offers a very broad range of services for multiple disciplines, for example, for application development, microservices, security, AI, and of course, one of them is **Big Data**. But even for big data products, there are multiple options that you can choose.

As an analogy, GCP is like a supermarket. A supermarket has almost everything that you need to support your daily life. For example, if you plan to cook pasta and go to a supermarket to buy the ingredients, no one will tell you what ingredients you should buy, or even if you know the ingredients, you will still be offered the ingredients by different brands, price tags, and producers. If you fail to make the right decision, you will end up cooking bad pasta. In GCP it's the same; you need to be able to choose your own services yourself. It is also important to know how each service is dependent on the others, since it's impossible to build a solution using only a single service.

In this chapter, we will learn about the products and services of GCP. But instead of explaining each product one by one, which you can access from public documentation, the focus in this chapter is to help you narrow down the options. We will map the services into categories and priorities. After finishing this chapter, you will know exactly what products you need to start your journey.

And on top of that, we will start using GCP! We will kick off our hands-on practice with basic fundamental knowledge of the GCP console.

By the end of the chapter, you will understand the positioning of GCP products related to big data, be able to start using the GCP console, and be able to plan what services you should focus on as a data engineer.

Here is the list of topics we will discuss in this chapter:

- Understanding what the cloud is
- Getting started with Google Cloud Platform
- A quick overview of GCP services for data engineering

Technical requirements

In this chapter's exercise, we will start using the GCP console, **Cloud Shell**, and **Cloud Editor**. All of the tools can be opened using any internet browser.

To use the GCP console, we need to register using a Google account (Gmail). This requires a payment method. Please check the available payment method to make sure you are successfully registered.

Understanding what the cloud is

Renting someone else's server: this definition of the **cloud** is my favorite, very simple, to the point, definition of what the *cloud* really is. So as long as you don't need to buy your own machine to store and process data, you are using the cloud.

But increasingly, after some leading cloud providers such as Google Cloud having gained more traction and technology maturity, the terminology is becoming representative of sets of architecture, managed services, and highly scalable environments that define how we build solutions. For data engineering, that means building data products using collections of services, APIs, and trusting the underlying infrastructure of the cloud provider one hundred percent.

The difference between the cloud and non-cloud era

If we want to compare the cloud with the non-cloud era from a data engineering perspective, we will find that almost all the data engineering principles are the same. But from a technology perspective, there are a lot of differences in the cloud.

In the cloud, computation and storage are configured as services, which means that as engineers, we can control them using code and make them available on demand.

If you're starting your data journey directly with cloud services, maybe it's a bit difficult for you to imagine what non-cloud looks like. As an illustrative example of a non-cloud experience, I once helped a company to implement a **data warehouse** before the cloud era. The customer had data in **Oracle** databases and wanted to store the data in an on-premises data warehouse. How long do you think it took before I could store my first table in the data warehouse? 4 months!

We needed to wait for the physical server to be shipped from the manufacturer's continent to our continent. And after the server arrived, we waited for the network engineer to plug in cables, routers, power, the software installation, and everything, which again took months before the data engineers could access the software and store our first table in it.

How long do you need to store your file in a table in **BigQuery**? Less than 1 minute.

The on-demand nature of the cloud

Another important aspect of the cloud is the ability to *turn on*, *turn off*, *create*, and *delete* services based on your actual usage.

For example, it's common for organizations to have different infrastructure environments. Common examples are production, development, and testing. Imagine that in the cloud, you can create the testing environment when testing happens and entirely delete the service when there are no tests running. In a non-cloud environment, this action would be like selling the entire machine to other companies and then repurchasing it again when you need it.

Another example involves a Hadoop pattern. The usual Hadoop usage in on-premises is to have a giant cluster that consists of tens to thousands of server nodes to store data in the **Hadoop File System (HDFS)** and process thousands of jobs in Spark. In GCP, it's common to create a **Spark cluster** for each individual job.

Since it's very easy and fast to create a Hadoop cluster in GCP, a common practice is to create a dedicated cluster to run one Spark job at a time and delete the cluster after the job is finished. The reason? Dedicated resources and the fact that you only want to pay for the cluster when the job runs. If you don't use it, you don't need to pay for the idle nodes. This concept is called an **Ephemeral cluster**, which we will practice later, in *Chapter 5, Building a Data Lake Using Dataproc* .

Getting started with Google Cloud Platform

OK, let's start! Let's take the first step and try GCP.

Chances are you already registered or have created your own project in GCP before reading this book. But in case you haven't, these steps are mandatory to follow:

1. Access the GCP console from this link from any browser: `http://console.cloud.google.com/`
2. Log in with your Google account (for example, Gmail).
3. With the Google account, register for GCP.

At this point, I won't write many step-by-step instructions, since it's a straightforward registration process. You can check on the internet if you have doubts about any step, at this link: `https://cloud.google.com/free`.

A common question at this point is, *am I going to pay for this?*

When you initially register for GCP, you will be asked for a payment method, but you won't be charged for anything at that point. So, when will you get charged?

You will be charged after the following:

-   Using any services
-   Using the service more than the free tier allows
-   Using GCP for longer than the free trial

I'll explain. You will get charged after you use a service, but not until you pass the free tier limits. Some products have free tiers, some do not.

For example, if you use BigQuery, you won't be charged until you store more than 10 GB a month or query tables more than 1 TB per month. If your usage in BigQuery is less than that, your bill will be zero. But it is different when you use Cloud Composer – you will be charged when you start Cloud Composer instances.

Check the GCP pricing calculator if you are interested in simulating costs: `https://cloud.google.com/products/calculator`.

It must be confusing at this point about the cost aspect because every single service in GCP has its own pricing mechanism. But on the cloud, the cost is one of the major factors to be considered and needs to be strategized, so we will have a special section for that in a later chapter. But my suggestion is not to think about it for now. It's better to focus on the *how-to* aspect of the services and we will learn about the pricing mechanisms while learning about the services.

In later chapters, when we do hands-on exercises, I will always warn you if costs are unavoidable. You may choose to continue the exercise or not.

Another question that might pop up in your mind is whether there are any free trials.

Yes, if you are a new GCP customer, then you will get a free $300 to try any services within a 90-day period. The $300 is applied on top of the free tiers of each product.

Introduction to the GCP console

After you finish registration, you will be directed to the GCP console. GCP centralizes every single user interaction in this single console, as shown in the following screenshot:

Figure 2.1 – GCP console main page

From enabling services, configuring user access, monitoring billing, checking logs, and much more, you can even build an entire end-to-end data ecosystem without leaving the console. So, the GCP console is very powerful. Let's start by clicking the navigation menu (the hamburger button) at the top left of your screen. After the menu has expanded, you should see the list of services available on GCP in the **Navigation** menu.

Scroll down and see what services are available there. Check how GCP categorizes products, for example, **COMPUTE**, **STORAGE**, and **DATABASES**:

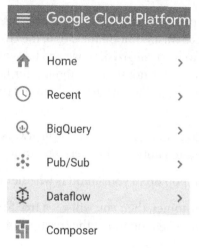

Figure 2.2 – Navigation menu on the GCP console

You will see a long list of services in the **Navigation** menu. The list is basically all the services that you can use in the entire GCP.

Practicing pinning services

You will be a little bit overwhelmed at first since there are so many services in the list. Let's make it simpler by pinning products that are relevant for us.

For example, let's pin BigQuery:

1. Find **BigQuery** under the **Big Data** section.
2. Find the pin button on the right of the **BigQuery** text and click it.
3. Back at the very top of the navigation menu, **BigQuery** will be pinned there:

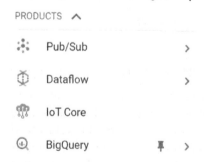

Figure 2.3 – Pinning the BigQuery service

Let's practice by pinning other services, listed as follows:

- **IAM & Admin (PRODUCTS)**
- **Cloud Storage (STORAGE)**
- **Composer (BIG DATA)**
- **Dataproc (BIG DATA)**
- **Pub/Sub (BIG DATA)**
- **Dataflow (BIG DATA)**

Once you've done that, you will have all services at the top of your navigation menu.

Creating your first GCP project

Follow these steps to create your first GCP project:

1. If you check, on the top bar, you will see **My First Project**. This is your project name. We want to change this default project name to a new one. So, click the text **My First Project**. I will call this button project menu for simplicity in later steps:

Figure 2.4 – Top bar

2. After you are in the project menu, click **NEW PROJECT** at the top right:

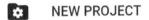

Figure 2.5 – NEW PROJECT button

3. After that, you will find a form to be filled in with the project details. Enter your new project name in the form. There are two pieces of project information in GCP:

    - **Project Name**: A user-friendly name – it doesn't need to be unique.
    - **Project ID**: Needs to be unique globally, which means you cannot use a project ID that's already being used by other users.

    The project name can be the same as the project ID as long as it's globally unique.

    I usually use the initial of my name or my company in front of the project name followed by the project purpose. This, most of the time, will help with uniqueness and standardization.

For example, I could use the following:

- **Project Name**: `packt-gcp-data-eng`

- **Project ID**: `packt-gcp-data-eng` (The same with project name since no other GCP users use the project ID globally).

- If the **Project ID** is already used by other user, GCP will automatically generate unique **Project ID** for you. You can check this under the **Project name** form.

4. After deciding on your new project name, click **CREATE**:

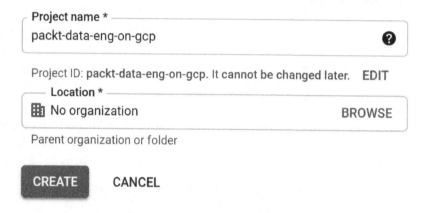

Figure 2.6 – Creating a new project

5. After successfully creating your project, click on the **Project** menu again, and follow these two steps:

A. Search for your newly created project here.

B. Click your project name from the list.

This way, you will work on your own project, not the default **My First Project**:

Figure 2.7 – Choosing the new project

The project is a very important aspect of GCP that you need to design and strategize, for example, to answer these kinds of questions:

- How many projects should I create?

- When should I create a new project?

- Can I use one project for all of my tasks?

We will learn about projects later, in *Chapter 9, User and Project Management in GCP*. But at this stage, let's not worry much about that and focus on how to use individual services first.

Using GCP Cloud Shell

I want to introduce one important feature in GCP that will help a lot with our practice later, which is the terminal and editor tool. You can access a Linux terminal in the GCP console. This is a standard Linux environment preinstalled with all the necessary libraries, for example, the `gcloud` command. Let's try to use it:

1. Open the terminal by clicking the top-right button in the GCP console:

Figure 2.8 – Cloud Shell button at the top right

2. Wait for a few seconds and you will see your terminal is ready for you:

Figure 2.9 – Cloud Shell user interface

3. Still in the terminal, if you check the bar, you will see the **Open Editor** button. Let's try that:

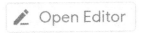

Figure 2.10 – Open Editor button at the top right

4. The terminal will change into a simple text editor. The text editor is not designed to replace an IDE such as **IntelliJ** or **Eclipse**, but this is good enough to edit your code in the Linux system:

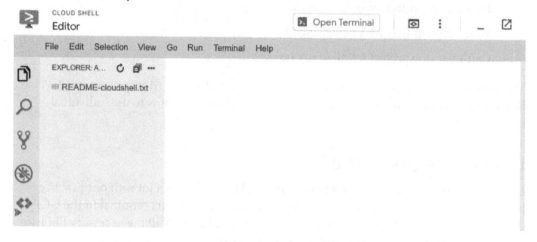

Figure 2.11 – Cloud Editor user interface

Now that we have the system ready for writing some commands, let's warm up by creating a Hello world Python script:

1. Go to **File | New File** and then name the file hello_world.py.

2. In the editor, add the following command:

```
print("Hello world")
```

Just to check what you should have on your screen, your Cloud Editor should look like this:

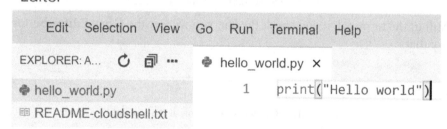

Figure 2.12 – Using the Cloud Editor for Python code

The Editor will automatically save your file, so you don't need to click a save button.

3. Now let's run the Python script from the terminal by clicking the **Open Terminal** button and run the following Python command:

```
#python hello_world.py
```

Your Cloud Shell should look like this:

Figure 2.13 – Running the hello world script in Cloud Shell

The terminal will show you the **Hello world** text from the Python file, and that's it.

Let's summarize what we've done up until this point. We've learned how to use the GCP console and how to create and use a new project. And in this section, we learned how to use Cloud Shell. We will use this tool a lot in this book to run `gcloud` commands and to write and run Python scripts.

In the next section, we will learn what services are available in GCP and how to focus on specific services for data engineering use cases.

A quick overview of GCP services for data engineering

As you can see in the GCP Console navigation bar, there are a lot of services in GCP. The services are not only limited to data and analytics. They also cover other areas such as application development, machine learning, networks, source repositories, and many more. As a data engineer working on GCP, you will face situations when you need to decide which services you need to use for your organization.

You might be wondering, who in an organization should decide on the services to use? Is it the CTO, IT manager, solution architect, or data engineers? The answer depends on the experience of using GCP of each of them. But most of the time, data engineers need to be involved in the decision.

So how should we decide? In my experience, there are three important decision factors:

- Choose services that are serverless.
- Understand the mapping between the service and the data engineering areas.
- If there is more than one option in one area, choose the most popular service in the market.

Choosing a serverless service or, to use another common term, a fully managed service, **Software as a Service** (**SaaS**), can also mean choosing services that are the easiest. The easiest in terms of Google manages everything for us, so we can just use the tool.

On top of that, to choose the right service, you need to be able to understand the service positioning in data engineering areas. You can go back to *Chapter 1, Fundamentals of Data Engineering*, and the section *The focus of the data engineer*. Each service in GCP can be mapped to the data flow diagram in that section.

And lastly, if there are multiple options in the same area, I suggest you choose the most popular one. Not because of **FOMO** (**Fear of Missing Out**), but this is often a good indicator to choose a product in the IT industry. There are a couple of good reasons for this, such as you know that the products or services will still be there in the long run, the support from both Google and the community will be a lot better, and lastly, from the company perspective, you will be able to hire an expert more easily compared to less popular products.

Now let's discuss these three factors in more detail in the following subsections.

Understanding the GCP serverless service

Before going into the **serverless service** or **fully managed service**, if this is the first time you have heard of a *managed service*, it is a term for products that are literally managed, or in other words, configured and maintained by the service provider. This was a breakthrough in the IT industry in the early 2010s. Before that era, if you wanted to use an IT product, you needed to buy a computer, install the OS, install the software, configure the software, and use it.

In the managed service era, if you want to use an IT product, you just simply use it. And that's the new normal in the IT industry. But the question is how easy is it to *simply use it*. This varies widely, depending on the service provider, and even in Google Cloud, it varies depending on the services. Some services are a lot easier compared to others.

To simplify, I will introduce three approaches to using managed services in GCP. In general, there are three groups of services in GCP:

- **VM-based**
- **Managed services**
- **Serverless (fully managed services)**

VM-based means you, as a user, use a Google-managed **Virtual Machine** (**VM**) (in GCP, the service is called Compute Engine). You don't need to buy your own machine and install an OS, but you need to install the software yourself. This is still an option because not all software is available in GCP. As an example from my own experience, Google doesn't have a managed service for the Elasticsearch database, so what I need to do is to create VMs in **Google Compute Engine** (**GCE**) and install Elasticsearch on top of the VMs.

Managed service means Google manages the software for you. Not only do you not need to install an OS but you don't need to install software dependencies either, or carry out maintenance. For another real example, the first time I used GCP was because I wanted to use Hadoop in the cloud. At the time, I took the VM-based approach. I installed Hadoop from an open source installer on some VMs, until I realized that is not the best practice. The best practice if you want to use Hadoop on GCP is to use **Dataproc**. Using Dataproc, we don't need to install Hadoop ourselves; Google manages it for us. But as a user, I still need to configure the machine size, choose the networks, and other configurations.

A *serverless service* means *simply use it*. You just use the software instantly. You don't need to set up anything to use the software, for example, BigQuery. In BigQuery, we can instantly create tables and trigger SQL queries without configuring anything. But on the other hand, we also have zero visibility of the underlying infrastructure. We will discuss this a lot in *Chapter 3, Building a Data Warehouse in BigQuery*.

The following table shows you the key differences between the three groups and on-premises for comparison:

	Manage physical infrastructure	Manage virtual machines	Manage application service	Develop solution on top of the service
On-premises (non-cloud)	O	O	O	O
VM-based	X	O	O	O
Managed service	X	X	O	O
Fully managed service	X	X	X	O

Figure 2.14 – Comparison metrics for managed services

Let's see what **X** and **O** in the preceding table mean:

- **(X)** means: You as a developer don't need to do it. Google manages it for you.
- **(O)** means: You as a developer need to do it. Google gives you flexibility.

Let's take a look at a practical example. As a GCP data engineer, you are requested to store and process CSV data. The file size is 1 TB and your end user wants to access it in table format using SQL. How do you solve the request?

For sure you need a big data service to handle this amount of data, and there are three possible scenarios:

Scenario 1 – VM-based:

1. Provision multiple VM instances in GCP using Compute Engine. Then configure the VM networks, OS, packages, and any infra requirements.

2. Install the Hadoop cluster on top of the Compute Engine instances. You can choose any Hadoop version that you like.

3. Store data in HDFS and create a hive table on top of the Hadoop cluster.

Scenario 2 – Managed service:

1. Provision a Hadoop managed service cluster (Dataproc).

2. Store data in HDFS and create a hive table on top of the Hadoop cluster.

Scenario 3 – Fully managed service:

1. Store data in a BigQuery table, which is a fully managed service for a data warehouse.

Scenario 3 only has one step; it shows you that fully managed service products, in general, are the best choice for simplicity since you can jumpstart directly to the development stage without worrying about setting up the infrastructure and software installation.

What is the drawback? Flexibility. In scenario 1, you can install any software and its version as you like, you have full control of your infrastructure, but you need to take care of its scalability, availability, logging, and other management stuff yourself.

In scenario 2, when using Dataproc, you don't need to create each VM instance manually; Google will set the underlying Hadoop infrastructure for you, but you need to choose the version that is available.

In general, use a fully managed service if one is available and suits your needs. Unless you have issues with compatibility, have specific feature requirements, or the cost doesn't meet your budget, then you may consider scenarios 1 and 2.

Service mapping and prioritization

So, what products should we focus on first? As described before, there are two aspects that I use to decide what to focus on:

- How close is the service to the core of data engineering? (Check *Chapter 1, Fundamentals of Data Engineering*, in the section *The focus of Data Engineers*.)

- The number of adoptions by companies across industries.

To understand service categorization in GCP, let's take a look at the following figure:

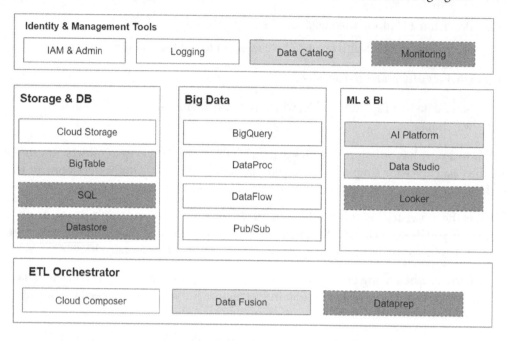

Figure 2.15 – Big data service mapping and priority

The GCP services are mapped to their main categories. There are five main categories, and in each category, there are service options that are represented by three different box colors:

- **White**: Priority 1
- **Light gray**: Priority 2
- **Dark gray**: Priority 3

Take your time to check each service in the figure and its priority. The reason we want to use the two aspects to decide on our first focus is we want to make sure we start with the data engineer's main responsibility, as discussed in *Chapter 1, Fundamentals of Data Engineering*.

And on top of that, if there are options in the same category, I would prefer to start with services that have been adopted the most by GCP customers. The reason is, when many GCP customers use services, it gives us confidence that the services are proven both in scalability and maturity. And on top of that, the service will be highly supported by the product team at Google in the long-term future, and this is a very important aspect of choosing products.

If you are wondering why there are so many products, the answer is because each product is meant for specific purposes. Unlike most traditional IT products that tried to provide full stack products as one bundled product, in GCP each service usually has one specific purpose. And as data engineers, we need to combine them together to build solutions.

Now that we know the categorization of each prioritized product from the previous section, we want to quickly look at each product's main position in data engineering.

Big data

Here is the list of services under **big data**:

1. **BigQuery**: A fully managed data warehouse service

2. **Dataproc**: A Hadoop-managed service including HDFS, MapReduce, Spark, Presto, and more

3. **Dataflow**: A fully managed distributed processing framework service, very suitable for streaming jobs

4. **Pub/Sub**: A fully managed service messaging system, to publish and subscribe data

Storage and DB

Here is the list of services under **storage and database**:

1. **Cloud Storage**: A fully managed service for storing large files

2. **Bigtable**: A fully managed NoSQL database service

3. **SQL**: A managed service for application databases, for example, MySQL, PostgreSQL, and SQL Server

4. **Datastore**: A fully managed NoSQL document database service

ETL orchestrator

Here is the list of services under **ETL orchestrator**:

1. **Cloud Composer**: An Airflow-managed service. Airflow is a Python-based job orchestration tool.

2. **Data Fusion**: A UI-based orchestration tool to run Hadoop jobs on Dataproc.

3. **Dataprep**: A UI-based data wrangling tool. While data wrangling is similar to the ETL process in general, Dataprep has unique features, for example, checking data distribution in histograms and checking missing values. Dataprep is managed by a third party, **Trifacta**, which means that GCP customers need to have separate legal agreements with Trifacta.

Identity and management tools

Here is the list of services under **Identity and management tools**:

1. **IAM & Admin**: User and project management for all GCP services
2. **Logging**: A logging system for all GCP services
3. **Monitoring**: A monitoring system with dashboards driven by data from Cloud Logging
4. **Data Catalog**: A metadata system that stores data from GCS, BigQuery, and PubSub

ML and BI

Here is the list of services under **machine learning and BI tools**:

1. **Vertex AI**: All the tools that you need to build ML and MLOps, for example, notebook, pipeline, model store, and other ML-related services
2. **Looker**: A full-fledged BI tool to visualize data in reports and dashboards
3. **Data Studio**: A simple visualization tool to visualize data

At this point, I have only added very short and simple descriptions for each service. The reason is what is important for now, at this stage, is for us to know the services' positioning. A detailed explanation of each service can be found easily on the internet. In this book, we will try the services with hands-on exercises, and at the end of the book, you will understand the services completely by having done those exercises.

The concept of quotas on GCP services

Another fundamental terminology that we need to be aware of is **quotas**. When we talk about limitations in the cloud ecosystem, one of the most common boundaries that people usually think of is cost. It's very common to think that, as long as you have an unlimited budget, then you can store and process any amount of data as you need.

That is partially true, but there is another important boundary, which is quotas. Quotas are sets of limitations on each GCP service as a default rule that applies to all GCP users.

For example, in BigQuery, you cannot have more than 10,000 columns in a table. Another example is the maximum size limit of individual objects stored in Cloud Storage is 5 TB.

Each service has its own quotas, and the most important thing is that you are aware of this and know where to check. You can check the Cloud Storage quotas here: `https://cloud.google.com/storage/quotas`.

And BigQuery quotas here:

`https://cloud.google.com/bigquery/quotas`.

You can check quotas for other products following the same URL pattern. There are two main reasons why quotas are in place:

- To make sure services are highly available. Even though you don't need to worry about physical servers in GCP, the services are running on top of actual Google Cloud giant clusters that are shared with many customers. Quotas prevent uncontrolled usage by one customer that affects other customers.

- The second reason is that quotas can act as a reminder of bad practices. If you develop a solution and exceed the quotas, you might need to review your solution design. For example, from the previous BigQuery example, you might need to review your table if your table has more than 10,000 columns because that indicates that, in general, that's not a common practice.

Quotas are something that are gradually updated based on GCP customers' usage and needs. You don't need to remember all the quotas; the important takeaway from this section is you just need to be aware of what a quota is and where to check them.

User account versus service account

The last terminologies that we need to be aware of before we continue the hands-on practice in the following chapters are **User Account** and **Service Account**:

- **User Account** is your personal account as a human user.
- **Service Account** is an account that will be used by non-humans.

What are non-humans? In many cases, we want to automate our solutions, and in order to do that, we want machines to do the tasks, for example, triggering jobs, building Docker images, running Python scripts, and much more. We need service accounts for this instead of personal user accounts.

For example, if an organization has the email address `domain @company.com` and has three employees, Agnes, Brian, and Cory, then the typical user accounts would be as follows:

- `agnes@company.com`

- `brian@company.com`

- `cory@company.com`

The company uses **Cloud Composer** to orchestrate an ETL load from GCS to BigQuery. Then, what they need is a service account for Cloud Composer, for example, `service-composer@company.iam.gserviceaccount.com`.

This Cloud Composer service account will have access to the GCS bucket and BigQuery datasets. In this case, the company doesn't need to use one of the employee's personal emails to run these automated jobs. In this way, the company has the flexibility to limit the employees' access to sensitive datasets and let the service account handle the jobs.

Understanding the difference between a user and a service account is very important in GCP. We will use both a user account and a service account in our exercises, and you will get more of an idea of how to use them properly.

Summary

We've learned a lot of new things in this chapter about the cloud and GCP – let's summarize it. We started this chapter by accessing the GCP console for the first time. We then narrowed things down to find our first priority GCP services for data engineers to focus on.

And we closed the chapter by familiarizing ourselves with important features and terminologies such as quotas and service accounts.

In the next chapter, we will do a lot more step-by-step, hands-on exercises with practical use cases using the services that we introduced in this chapter to build data solutions. So, make sure you've set up the GCP console properly and are ready for the exercises. In the next chapter, we will start by practicing developing a data warehouse. As we've learned in this chapter, the cloud data warehouse in GCP is BigQuery. We will start by learning about this very famous service – and one of the most important – for GCP data engineers.

Section 2: Building Solutions with GCP Components

This part will talk about leveraging GCP products to support storage systems, pipelines, and infrastructure in a production environment. It will also cover common operations, such as data ingestion, data cleansing, transformation, and integrating data with other sources. By the end of this part, you will have acquired the practical knowledge to build efficient ETL data pipelines via GCP.

This section comprises the following chapters:

- *Chapter 3, Building a Data Warehouse in BigQuery*
- *Chapter 4, Building Orchestration for Batch Data Loading Using Cloud Composer*
- *Chapter 5, Building a Data Lake Using Dataproc*
- *Chapter 6, Processing Streaming Data with Pub/Sub and Dataflow*
- *Chapter 7, Visualizing Data for Making Data-Driven Decisions with Data Studio*
- *Chapter 8, Building Machine Learning Solutions on Google Cloud Platform*

3
Building a Data Warehouse in BigQuery

The power of a **data warehouse** is delivered when organizations combine multiple sources of information into a single place that becomes the single source of truth. The utopia of data analytics will be when every single business aspect in an organization relies on data. That condition will be met when all business decision makers know how to access data, trust the data, and can make decisions based on it.

Unfortunately, most of the time, utopia is far removed from reality. There are many challenges along the way. Based on my experience, there are three main challenges – *technology bottlenecks*, *data consistency*, and the *ability to serve multiple business purposes*.

The preceding challenges are natural when we build a data warehouse. It's not limited to certain technologies and organizations. In this chapter, we will learn those challenges through two hands-on scenarios. We will mainly use **BigQuery** as the **Google Cloud Platform (GCP)** Data Warehouse cloud service. And along with that, we will also use **Google Cloud Storage (GCS)** and **Cloud SQL** to demonstrate their dependencies.

I will tell you in advance that this book will not be the most complete explanation of BigQuery, nor of the data warehouse theories. The BigQuery public documentation on the internet is the best place to find the most complete, detailed documentation, and there are books out there that explain data warehouse theories in great detail. So, what are we going to do in this chapter?

In this chapter, rather than explaining all the detailed features one by one, we will learn how to build a data warehouse by doing it using BigQuery. And by doing it, you will know the exact path and the order of importance for both the technology and the principles.

We will begin the chapter by introducing three services: BigQuery, GCS, and CloudSQL. In the later sections, we will utilize two scenarios to design and build a data warehouse.

After finishing this chapter, you will be familiar with how to use BigQuery and GCS, how to load data into BigQuery, and the principle of data modeling in BigQuery.

In particular, we will cover the following topics in this chapter:

- Introduction to Google Cloud Storage and BigQuery
- Introduction to the BigQuery console
- Preparing the prerequisites before developing our data warehouse
- Practicing developing a data warehouse

Technical requirements

In this chapter's exercises, we will use the following GCP services: **BigQuery** and **GCS**. If you have never opened any of these services in your GCP console, open them and enable the APIs.

Make sure you have your **GCP console**, **Cloud Shell**, and **Cloud Editor** ready.

Before starting, you must have a basic knowledge of Python programming, SQL, Linux commands, and Git.

All the example Python scripts are developed using Python 3. Make sure you run the Python commands using Python 3 instead of Python (Python 2) from Cloud Shell.

Download the example code and the dataset here: `https://github.com/PacktPublishing/Data-Engineering-with-Google-Cloud-Platform/tree/main/chapter-3`.

Introduction to Google Cloud Storage and BigQuery

Google Cloud Storage (**GCS**) is object storage. It's a service that is fully managed by GCP, which means we don't need to think about any underlying infrastructure for GCS. For example, we don't need to think about pre-sizing the storage, the network bandwidth, number of nodes, or any other infrastructure-related stuff.

What is object storage? **Object storage** is a highly scalable data storage architecture that can store very large amounts of data in any format.

Because the technology can store data in almost any size and format, GCS is often used by developers to store any large files, for example, images, videos, and large CSV data. But, from the data engineering perspective, we will often use GCS for storing files, for example, as dump storage from databases, for exporting historical data from **BigQuery**, for storing machine learning model files, and for any other purpose related to storing files.

BigQuery is a fully managed data warehouse in the cloud. BigQuery allows users to store and analyze data immediately without needing to think about infrastructure.

And on top of that, using BigQuery gives you a high degree of confidence regarding scalability in terms of both storage and processing power. BigQuery has been shown to be able to store and process petabytes of data in many organizations around the world.

Going a little bit deeper into what is under the hood of BigQuery, BigQuery consists of four data warehouse main parts, as discussed in *Chapter 1, Fundamentals of Data Engineering*:

- Storage
- Processing
- Metadata
- SQL interface

BigQuery *stores* data in a distributed filesystem called **Google Colossus**, in columnar storage format. Colossus is the successor to Google File System, which is the inspiration for **Hadoop File System** (**HDFS**). As users, we can't access Google Colossus directly. We access the data using tables (metadata) and the **SQL interface** to process the data.

BigQuery *processes* data in a distributed **SQL execution engine** inspired by **Dremel SQL**. Dremel SQL is a Google internal SQL analytics tool. The main purpose of Dremel is to interactively query large datasets. But BigQuery is a product in its own right. Many improvements and adjustments have been made to BigQuery compared to Dremel. The reason is, of course, to serve broader GCP customer requirements around the world. By way of a simple example, the SQL language is different in Dremel (legacy SQL) to BigQuery (standard SQL).

As BigQuery users, we don't need to know what happens under the hood (**Colossus** and **Dremel**). However, as a GCP data engineer, it's good to be aware of this. We sometimes encounter situations when we need to improve the performance of BigQuery, troubleshoot table issues, or any other issues. Knowing Colossus and Dremel SQL at a high level might help. You can read in more detail about how both technologies work in their white publications on the internet.

One final topic that it is good to know in relation to BigQuery is *data location*. When people start using cloud technologies, sometimes they may wonder where the data is stored. Is the data stored in a private place? Is it going to meet certain data locality regulations? We will discuss this in the next section.

BigQuery data location

BigQuery is physically located in different countries and cities. The different locations are grouped into regions, and each region has different zones. For example, in the country where I live, the closest region is *asia-southeast*. There are two zones in the region: *Singapore* and *Jakarta*. When I choose *Singapore* as the BigQuery dataset region, the data will be stored and processed in *Singapore* clusters.

The data is stored in a GCP cluster in the specified region, and no user, including Google internal, can access the data. You can decide for yourself whether this satisfies your organization's regulations. At the same time, as a data engineer who, most of the time, is responsible for creating BigQuery objects, you need to pay attention to the location configuration for each GCP service (not only BigQuery) to make sure you choose the correct location. As an additional note, not every GCP service is available in every region, so you need to check the public documentation regarding availability.

BigQuery is very good at storing large volumes of data and performing analysis and processing immediately using the SQL interface. And on top of that, there are two main features that I think excel compared to other similar products in the market, which are **streaming** and **machine learning**. BigQuery allows you to insert streaming data. BigQuery also allows you to perform machine learning using BigQuery SQL directly in the console at scale. This is very useful for organizations that need to quickly gain access to machine learning capability.

Given all the advantages of BigQuery, keep in mind that BigQuery is not a transactional database. BigQuery is not designed for millisecond query latency. It can process 1 TB of data in 5 seconds, but this doesn't mean you can process 1 MB of data in 0.0005 seconds. It is simply not designed for that purpose.

Having got to grips with the basic principles of BigQuery, in the next section, let's start using it from the BigQuery console.

Introduction to the BigQuery console

The best way to understand BigQuery is by using it, so let's start with a simple exercise. This first exercise will focus on understanding the BigQuery console. The BigQuery console is your main user interface for developing and using BigQuery. In this exercise, we will create a dataset and table and query the table using the BigQuery console.

Let's start our exercise by opening the BigQuery console from our browser:

1. Open your GCP console.

2. Go to the navigation bar and choose **BigQuery**. This is the BigQuery main page, called the BigQuery console.

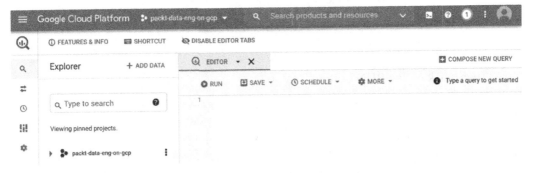

Figure 3.1 – BigQuery console

3. As you can see, there are a multitude of buttons and panels in the BigQuery console. I recommend that you quickly scan through the console to familiarize yourself with the menus. As the first step, let's look at the left panel, **Explorer**.

You can find your project name in **Explorer** as a default, but later you can add datasets, tables, views, and any other BigQuery objects under **Explorer**.

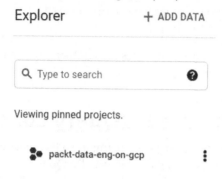

Figure 3.2 – BigQuery Explorer section

In the center panel, you may already have guessed that this is the query element. You can write your query in here and run it either using the **RUN** button or using keyboard shortcuts. I recommend you use the latter option for agility.

Check the shortcuts button and look for the **Run Queries** and **Run selected queries** shortcuts, as these will be helpful for us. These will depend on your operating system – in Windows, for example, this will be *Ctrl + E*.

4. Now let's try our first `hello world` query by typing the following in the editor:

```
SELECT "hello world";
```

Then, click on the **RUN** button.

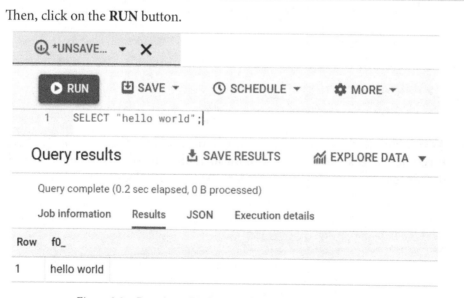

Figure 3.3 – Running a BigQuery query in the Editor section

5. After running the query, you can see the result shown at the bottom as tables, and there are three other sections: **JOB HISTORY**, **QUERY HISTORY**, and **SAVED QUERIES**.

Take a look at all of them and become familiar with how to read the information there. In the next section, we will learn how to create a dataset in BigQuery.

Creating a dataset in BigQuery using the console

The terminology *dataset* in BigQuery is used to abstract groups of tables. By calling it a dataset, BigQuery tries to influence users to create meaningful data groups compared to only thinking about technical purposes.

For example, if we have data from banking systems, we can name our datasets as follows:

*   `Layer_1`
*   `Layer_2`
*   `Reference data`

Or, we can name our datasets as follows:

*   `Customer saving`
*   `Website logs`
*   `Customer loan`

Which one do you think is better? For me, the latter is far more meaningful for humans.

Some other data technologies often use the term *database* for the table group abstractions, which often leads data engineers to group tables for technical purposes. On the other hand, *the term dataset* is often used by data scientists, which drives one's thinking to design the table groupings based on business representations, so try to think from the business perspective when you want to design your datasets.

Let's now try to create our first BigQuery dataset:

1. Click the action button. The action button is an icon alongside the project name, like this:

Figure 3.4 – Action button

After clicking the **Create dataset** button, proceed to the next step.

2. Choose a name for the dataset. Any name will do.

3. Choose the data location. Any location will suffice.

4. Set everything else as the default settings for now and then click **CREATE DATASET**.

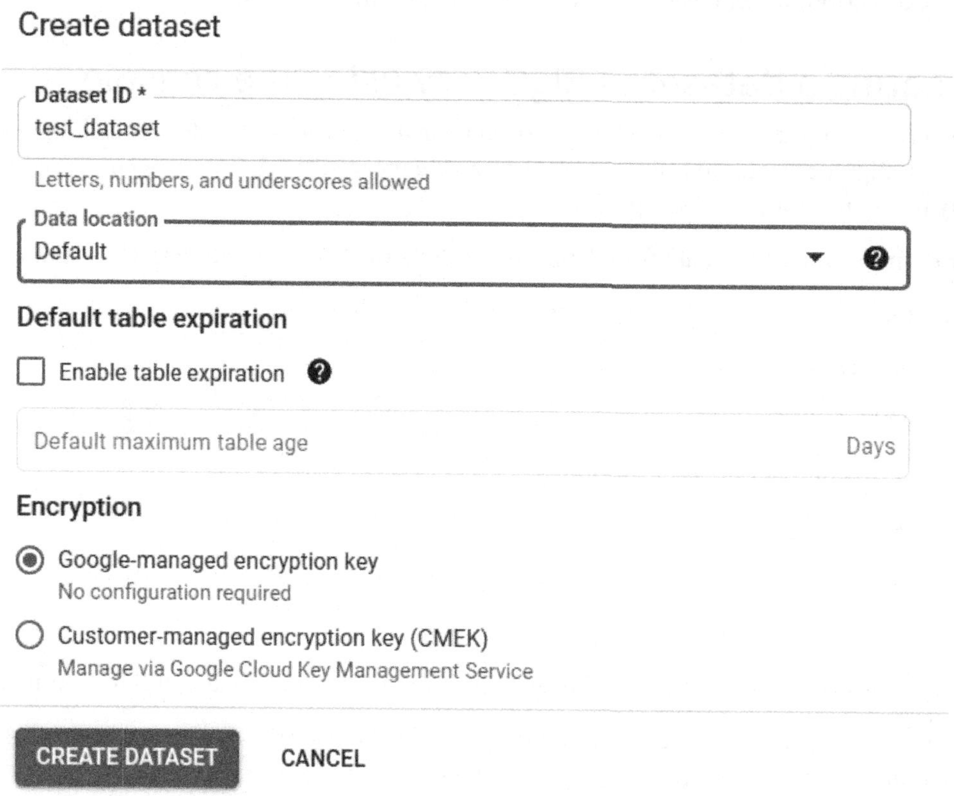

Create dataset

Dataset ID *

test_dataset

Letters, numbers, and underscores allowed

Data location

Default   ▼   ❓

Default table expiration

☐ Enable table expiration   ❓

Default maximum table age   Days

Encryption

◉ Google-managed encryption key
No configuration required

○ Customer-managed encryption key (CMEK)
Manage via Google Cloud Key Management Service

CREATE DATASET   CANCEL

Figure 3.5 – Creating a BigQuery dataset using the console

After finishing, you can see your dataset under the project name in the **Explorer** panel. In the next section, we want to create a table from a CSV file using the BigQuery console.

Loading a local CSV file into the BigQuery table

There are many ways in which to load data into BigQuery, and one of the simplest and most user-friendly for early users is to use the BigQuery console.

Do that by clicking the action button alongside the dataset name. This differs from the previous section. The action button is situated next to the dataset name, and not the project name, like this:

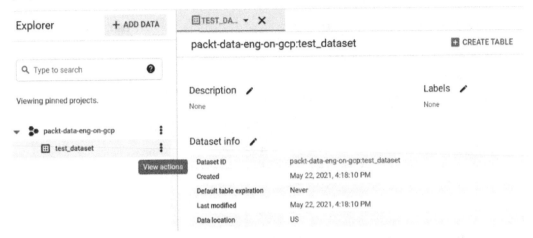

Figure 3.6 – Finding the dataset action button alongside the dataset name

You can find the **CREATE TABLE** button in the top-right corner of the screen. Let's create a table by completing the form as per the following details:

- **Create table from**: Upload.

- **Select file**: Find any CSV files that you have.

- **Table name**: Any name.

- **Schema**: Click the **Auto detect** checkbox.

This is demonstrated in the following screenshot:

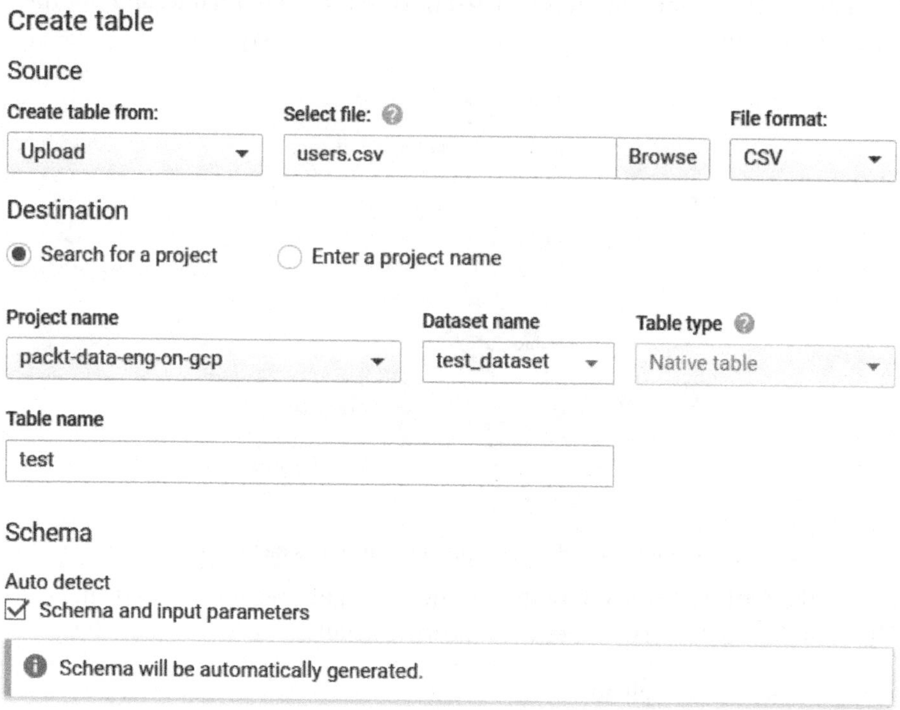

Create table

Source

Create table from:	Select file: ❓		File format:

Upload ▾ | users.csv   Browse | CSV ▾

Destination

◉ Search for a project   ○ Enter a project name

Project name   **Dataset name**   **Table type** ❓

packt-data-eng-on-gcp ▾   test_dataset ▾   Native table ▾

Table name

test

Schema

Auto detect
☑ Schema and input parameters

ℹ Schema will be automatically generated.

Figure 3.7 – Creating a BigQuery table from the console

If you don't yet have CSV files on your local computer, you can find one on the internet; for example, download any public dataset from a Google dataset search:

`https://datasetsearch.research.google.com/search?query=csv.`

After completing the steps, you can see your table under the dataset. Then, you can access the table using the SELECT statement in the editor or choose **PREVIEW** after clicking the table name in **Explorer**.

We have now completed the first example of loading data into BigQuery using local files, so you can delete your table and the dataset. We will create new ones for later sections. In the next section, we will try to use public data from BigQuery.

Using public data in BigQuery

The easiest approach to loading data into BigQuery, as shown in the previous section, is to upload a local file directly into the BigQuery table. This is straightforward when it comes to experimentation as an early user.

If we are talking about the most common approach, loading data from local files is not the most common data engineering practice. The most common is to load data from GCS files into BigQuery, which we will do in a later section.

However, if you are new to BigQuery, sometimes you will be wondering what data you can use for practice. In my experience, looking for public data for the purpose of learning data engineering on the internet is difficult. You can find a lot of *data*, but most of it is ready-made data and not representative of an actual database schema, which should consist of multiple tables, inconsistent values, unclear column names, and other real challenges that always happen in databases.

A good resource for finding such data is BigQuery public datasets. BigQuery comes up with a lot of example data in the public datasets. Even though there is also a lot of small data there, they provide some real raw datasets. For example, later you can check the dataset names, such as `stackoverflow`, `crypto_ethereum`, `github_repos`, and many others that are pretty good at representing real databases.

Let's try to access one of them by following these steps:

1. From the BigQuery console, click **Add data**.
2. Choose **Pin a project**.
3. Then, choose **Enter project name** (do not search for the project).
4. Enter the project name: `bigquery-public-data`.

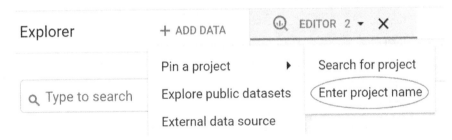

Figure 3.8 – Finding the Enter project name button in Explorer

Now you can see that `bigquery-public-data` is pinned under **Explorer** and you can access any table under this project.

For this exercise, find the following:

*   A dataset named `baseball`
*   A table named `schedules`

Regarding the cost of BigQuery, be mindful of the table size. If you want to explore data in public data, always check the table size first before querying it. As a rule of thumb, as long as the table is under 1 GB in size, in general, you are safe. Remember that the free tier is limited to 1 TB query size per month.

To quickly check the table size, perform the following steps:

1. Click on **table name**.
2. Three option bars will appear: **SCHEMA**, **DETAILS**, and **PREVIEW**.
3. Click on **DETAILS**.

Following the preceding steps will show you the table details, and you can see the table size here.

For example, as regards the `baseball.schedules` table, the size is **582.81 KB**, as shown in this figure:

schedules	Q QUERY	+⦿ SHARE	�📋 COPY
SCHEMA	DETAILS	PREVIEW	

Table info

Table ID	bigquery-public-data:baseball.schedules
Table size	582.81 KB
Long-term storage size	582.81 KB
Number of rows	2,431
Created	Oct 25, 2016, 4:43:18 AM UTC+8
Last modified	Oct 25, 2016, 4:43:18 AM UTC+8
Table expiration	NEVER
Data location	US
Description	

Figure 3.9 – BigQuery table info

Given the small table size, it's good for our first practice. Therefore, let's access this table: `baseball.schedules`.

Run the query in the editor, for example:

```
SELECT * FROM `bigquery-public-data.baseball.schedules` LIMIT
1000;
```

You will see the query result under the **Editor** panel. Take your time to play around with other tables and functionalities in the BigQuery console. Following the exercises, let's spend time understanding some of the principles and features of BigQuery.

Data types in BigQuery compared to other databases

One of the things that you can check regarding the table metadata is data types. For example, try to click the baseball.schedules table and check the **Table schema** pane. You can see the field data types there:

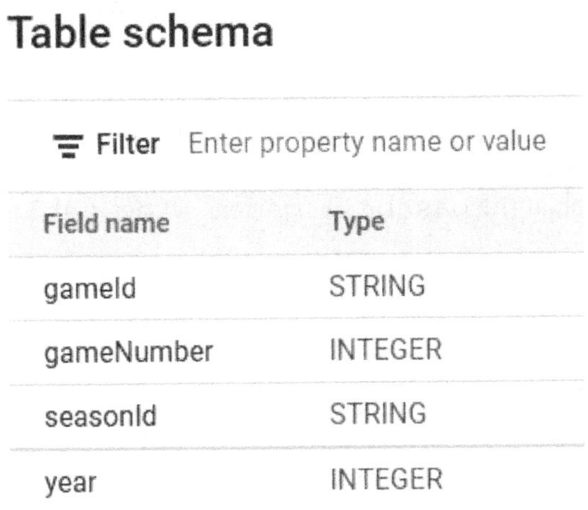

Table schema

Field name	Type
gameId	STRING
gameNumber	INTEGER
seasonId	STRING
year	INTEGER

Figure 3.10 – BigQuery table schema

One of the most common attributes in every database is data types. In principle, data types in BigQuery are similar to any other database. However, I want to highlight something about data types in this section.

BigQuery has a very simple list of data types. For example, for storing text in BigQuery, you simply use the STRING data type, while for storing numbers, you simply use INTEGER. This might seem odd if your background is in other database technologies. In traditional data warehouse systems such as Teradata, Oracle, or perhaps a simple PostgreSQL database, you need to think about the expected data size. For example, for text columns, you might need to choose between char, varchar, text, and varchar(n). If you want to store numbers, you also need to choose between smallint, int, int8, int32, and int64, but in BigQuery, all round numbers are INTEGER.

There are, of course, other data types, including `decimal`, `timestamp`, `date`, and `boolean`, and other data types that you can check in the following public documentation:

`https://cloud.google.com/bigquery/docs/reference/standard-sql/data-types`

As you can see from the documentation, the list is very short and simple, but don't be confused by the simplicity in BigQuery. As the user, you don't need to think about the data type memory and efficiency in BigQuery. BigQuery will handle all of that under the hood. For example, when storing one character, *I*, or some long text, *I really enjoy reading books almost all the time*, in the `STRING` BigQuery, both have the exact same efficiency.

After learning about BigQuery data types, in the next section, we will take a look specifically at the timestamp data type.

Timestamp data in BigQuery compared to other databases

The last, but by no means least, fundamental aspect of BigQuery that I want to highlight is timestamp data. Timestamp data stores information about the date and time in detail. For example, take a look at the `baseball.games_wide table`, specifically at the `startTime` column.

games_wide

SCHEMA	DETAILS	PREVIEW				
Row	gameId		seasonId	seasonType	year	startTime
	dc42dfe7-d6dd-4831-a9ad-c1dcfc8f62af		565de4be-dc80-4849-a7e1-54bc79156cc8	REG	2016	2016-05-11 19:10:00 UTC
	dc42dfe7-d6dd-4831-a9ad-c1dcfc8f62af		565de4be-dc80-4849-a7e1-54bc79156cc8	REG	2016	2016-05-11 19:10:00 UTC
	dc42dfe7-d6dd-4831-a9ad-c1dcfc8f62af		565de4be-dc80-4849-a7e1-54bc79156cc8	REG	2016	2016-05-11 19:10:00 UTC

Figure 3.11 – The startTime column contains timestamp data

You will notice according to the timestamp postfix that the time is stored in UTC format. In BigQuery, you can't store timestamp data in non-UTC format. BigQuery wants you to always store timestamps in UTC format. The reason for this is data consistency. This is very useful for organizations that conduct business in multiple countries or regions that have time differences. Using the UTC-only format, the data engineer will be forced to transform the local time format to UTC before loading to BigQuery.

As a user, if you need to convert back to your local timezone in your query, you can always use the time function like this:

```
SELECT DATETIME(startTime,"America/Los_Angeles")  as startTime
FROM `bigquery-public-data.baseball.games_wide`;
```

This query will give you the `startTime` column data in the `Los Angeles` timezone.

To summarize our first BigQuery exercise, what we've done up to this point is as follows:

- We've learned that in BigQuery, we can group tables into datasets.
- One method for loading data into BigQuery is to upload a file from your local machine.
- For experimentation purposes, BigQuery offers public datasets that you can use and access from your project.
- BigQuery has unique prepositions pertaining to data types.

This is the most basic information that you need to know in order to start using BigQuery. However, using BigQuery doesn't mean we are creating a data warehouse. In the next section, we will practice creating our simple data warehouse and, more importantly, go through the thinking process for designing one.

But before that, we need to set out some prerequisites for preparing our credentials using `gcloud` commands.

Preparing the prerequisites before developing our data warehouse

Before starting our practice exercise, let's carry out these small but important steps for authentication purposes. In this section, we will do the following:

1. Access Cloud Shell
2. Check our credentials using `gcloud info`
3. Initialize our credentials using `gcloud init`
4. Download example code and datasets from `git`
5. Upload data to GCS from `git`

Let's look at each of these steps in detail.

Step 1: Access your Cloud shell

Revisit *Chapter 2, Big Data Capabilities on GCP*, if you haven't accessed your cloud shell in the GCP console.

Step 2: Check the current setup using the command line

We want to check our current setup in Cloud Shell. To do that in Cloud Shell, type the following:

```
#gcloud info
```

Click **authorize** if prompted.

This command will give you information about installed components, Python versions, directories, and much more information besides. But what we want to check for now are the account and project, written in this format:

```
Account : [your email]
Project : [your project]
```

Check the account and project. Make sure it's your email and the project you created.

Step 3: The gcloud init command

After checking the environment, we want to configure a new environment using the `gcloud init` command. In Cloud Shell, run the following command:

```
#gcloud init
```

This command will show lists of configurations that have been created, but we want to try to create a new one, so choose the following option:

```
[2] Create a new configuration
```

Then, give this configuration a name, for example, `personal-config`. Choose the option to use your existing email:

```
[1] your email
```

Alternatively, if you need to log in with another email address, choose the following option:

```
[2] Login in with a new account
```

Lastly, choose your project number. You can see the number alongside your project name:

```
[number] project name.
```

The last option relates to configuring the default region and zone. Just choose n (no).

You can check using gcloud info again to confirm that the gcloud init steps work; for example, check whether the project name and your email are as intended.

Step 4: Download example data from Git

The final prerequisite is to download the example codes and dataset from Packt's Git repository. To do that, in Cloud Shell, clone repository from your GitHub repository:

```
https://github.com/adiwijaya/Data-Engineering-with-Google-
Cloud-Platform
```

For example, use this command to clone the repository:

```
git clone https://github.com/adiwijaya/Data-Engineering-with-
Google-Cloud-Platform.git
```

Each chapter will contain individual codes and datasets. Make sure the repository is properly cloned to Cloud Shell since we will use all of them throughout the book.

Step 5: Upload data to GCS from Git

After getting our dataset in Cloud Shell, let's upload the file to our GCS bucket using the GCP console.

There are three steps involved in this:

1. Create a GCS bucket.
2. Enter the bucket information.
3. Upload a local file to the GCS bucket using gsutil.

Let's look at each of these in detail.

Create a GCS bucket

Go to the **Navigation** menu and choose **Cloud Storage**. You will see the GCS console like this:

Figure 3.12 – GCS main page

Click the **CREATE BUCKET** button.

Enter the bucket information

Fill in the bucket name: `[your own project name]-data-bucket`.

Keep in mind that the bucket name in GCS should be unique globally, so using your project name as a prefix is a way to ensure uniqueness.

You may notice that you can choose the location for the GCS bucket on the page, but for this practice exercise, we will use **Default** to make sure that we don't have a location issue when loading data to BigQuery.

> **Important Note**
> Loading data from GCS to BigQuery requires data to be stored in the same location. For example, files in a GCS bucket located in the `asia-southeast2` region can't be loaded to the BigQuery dataset's `us-central1` location. By using **Default**, this means that we store the data in the multi-region US location.

Upload a local file to the GCS bucket using gsutil

Now, let's upload our files to the newly created GCS bucket using the `gsutil` command.

In Cloud Shell, enter the following commands:

```
#export DESTINATION_BUCKET_NAME=packt-data-eng-on-gcp-data-bucket
```

```
#gsutil cp -r Data-Engineering-with-Google-Cloud-Platform/* gs://$DESTINATION_BUCKET_NAME/from-git/
```

Please check your bucket by going to the `/from-git/chapter-3/dataset` bucket. You will see the three dataset folders there, `regions/`, `stations/`, and `trips/`, as in the following screenshot:

packt-data-eng-on-gcp-data-bucket

| OBJECTS | CONFIGURATION | PERMISSIONS | RETENTION | LIFECYCLE |

Buckets > packt-data-eng-on-gcp-data-bucket > from-git > chapter-3 > dataset ⏍

UPLOAD FILES   UPLOAD FOLDER   CREATE FOLDER   MANAGE HOLDS   DOWNLOAD   DELETE

Filter by name prefix only ▼   ☰ Filter Filter objects and folders

	Name	Size	Type	Created
☐	📁 regions/	—	Folder	—
☐	📁 stations/	—	Folder	—
☐	📁 trips/	—	Folder	—

Figure 3.13 – The three folders should be in the GCS bucket

We will use these datasets and code for our practice exercise in the next sections.

Practicing developing a data warehouse

Now we are set and ready to build our first data warehouse. We will proceed with the help of two scenarios. Each scenario will have different learning purposes.

In the first scenario, we are going to focus on how to use the tools. After understanding the tools, in the second scenario, we will focus on the principles. Principles here mean that even though we know how to use the tools, there are many possibilities for using them. If we are talking about principles, there is no right or wrong answer. What we can do is to learn from common patterns and a number of theories.

We will use the San Francisco bike-sharing dataset. The dataset relates to a bike-sharing company. The company records the trip data of its members. Each bike trip contains information about the stations, and lastly, each station is located in certain regions. This dataset is very simple compared to a real-world data warehouse, but for practice purposes, this is a good representation of real database tables from application databases.

In each scenario, the starting point is *requirements* and *business questions*. In the real-world scenario, it's the same. You will satisfy end user requirements and business questions, and these two aspects are the ingredients for designing and building a data warehouse.

The second step is the *thinking process*. After reading the requirements and business questions, I suggest you think for yourself first in terms of how you want to do it. However, I will also share my thoughts on the steps and planning, so you can compare them with yours. After that, we will build the *solutions* in BigQuery. Follow the steps in the next section.

Data warehouse in BigQuery – Requirements for scenario 1

In this scenario 1, we met with business users, and here are their requirements:

1. As a regional manager user, I want to know the top two region IDs, ordered by the total capacity of the stations in that region.

2. As a regional manager, I want to download the answers to my questions as CSV files to my local computer.

3. The data source table is the station table, which is located in the `CloudSQL-MySQL` database.

4. There will be more data sources in the future besides the station table.

Given the requirements, I suggest you take a moment to imagine yourself in this situation:

-   What will you do?

-   What GCP services will you use?

-   How will you do it?

> **Important Note**
>
> By way of a reminder, CloudSQL is a managed service for application databases, for example, MySQL, PostgreSQL, and SQL Server. As a managed service, you don't need to worry about VM creation and software installation. However, you will still need to decide the VM machine type, software versions, and other configurations that you can find when you create an instance.

In the next section, we will use the requirements to plan and decide how we want to build our solution.

Steps and planning for handling scenario 1

Given the first and second statements, we understand that the business user wants to be able to download the results as a CSV file from a very specific business question.

Planning:

1. Since there is a very specific business rule, we need some transformation. The rule seems doable in SQL, and BigQuery is a good system for handling such jobs.

2. The BigQuery table can easily be downloaded into CSV files from the console. So, storing the results as a BigQuery table or view will be great.

From the second and third requirements, we learned that the source data is in a MySQL database and may potentially come from another database in the future.

Planning:

Since the data sources come from multiple systems, this is a data warehouse situation.

The data is in the `CloudSQL-MySQL` database, so we need to find a way to extract the `station` table from the MySQL database and load it into BigQuery.

There are options for doing the extract and load from MySQL to BigQuery. For standardization and scalability, we will use GCS as our staging layer from MySQL. This extraction method applies to almost any data source. On top of that, GCS is also very scalable when it comes to handling the incoming data in terms of volume, variety, and velocity.

Loading data from GCS to BigQuery is very straightforward, and we can use the BigQuery console for this.

So, here are the overall steps:

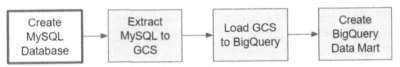

Figure 3.14 – The four steps of our data pipeline

Note that in this practice, we don't want to learn about MySQL databases in depth, but we will still try to create a CloudSQL instance for MySQL. The goal is for us to really try to understand what *Extract* in *ETL* really means, and how to do it.

Step 1: Create a MySQL database in CloudSQL

The first step is to prepare our CloudSQL-MySQL environment. This step is not part of building a data warehouse. However, to simulate table extraction from application databases to GCS, this will be very helpful. So, let's start by creating the Cloud SQL instance. Here are the steps:

1. Create a CloudSQL instance.
2. Connect to the MySQL instance.
3. Create a MySQL database.
4. Create a table in the MySQL database.
5. Import CSV data into the MySQL database.

Let's look at each of the steps in detail in the following sections.

Create a CloudSQL instance

You can create a CloudSQL instance from the GCP console by choosing **SQL** under the database section in the navigation bar. You can follow the **Create Instance** steps, but for simplicity, we will run it using the `gcloud` command in Cloud Shell.

Run the following command in Cloud Shell:

```
gcloud sql instances create mysql-instance-source  \
--database-version=MYSQL_5_7 \
--tier=db-g1-small \
--region=us-central1 \
--root-password=packt123 \
--availability-type=zonal \
--storage-size=10GB \
--storage-type=HDD
```

Wait for around 5 minutes. After it's finished, refresh your browser or go back to your Cloud SQL home page and you will see that your MySQL instance is ready.

> **Warning**
> Is it going to cost us? Yes.

CloudSQL instances will cost us based on instance hours. But since we will be using the smallest instance tier for development (db-g1-small) across a short period, the cost will be $0.035/hour. If you still have a $300 free tier, then you don't need to pay the costs, but don't forget to delete the instance after this practice exercise.

Connect to the MySQL instance

Return to Cloud Shell and run this gcloud command to connect to your mysql instance using a MySQL shell:

```
# gcloud sql connect mysql-instance-source --user=root
```

When prompted for a password, the password is packt123. This is stated in the gcloud command in the *Create a CloudSQL instance* step. However, if you have changed the password, use your password for logging in. After successfully logging in, you will see the MySQL shell.

Create a MySQL database

Let's create a MySQL database named apps_db.

Run this script in the MySQL shell:

```
CREATE DATABASE apps_db;
```

After creating the database, you can verify that your database has been created by running the following command:

```
SHOW DATABASE;
```

Create a table in the MySQL database

While still in the mysql shell, we need to create the table using a **Data Definition Language** (**DDL**) statement.

You can create the table by running the following DDL:

```
CREATE TABLE apps_db.stations(
station_id varchar(255),
name varchar(255),
region_id varchar(10),
capacity integer
);
```

The `create table` script will create the `stations` table in `apps_db`. Next, we want to import data using a CSV file.

Import CSV data into the MySQL database

In the real-life scenario, the tables will be used by applications, and the data will be inserted based on user interactions with the database. We will not go back too far to build a sample application that writes records to our table. We will just load CSV files to our tables from GCS.

In a later section, we will export the MySQL table back to GCS, and you may be wondering why. The reason why we are doing this is to simplify the data generation the MySQL database. But for the later steps, given that the MySQL database is a genuine example of a data source, we will use it for simulating the *Extraction* step in an ETL process.

To import the CSV data from GCS to MySQL, we can use the Cloud SQL console.

Don't close the MySQL shell yet, since we want to check our imported data later using the SELECT statement. Just minimize Cloud Shell if necessary.

To upload the data, go to the Cloud SQL console:

1. Click the created `mysql-instance` source, and then find and click the **Import** button.

2. Choose the name of the data file in our GCS bucket under bucket-name/file-name:

    ```
    gs://[your project name]-data-bucket/from-git/chapter-3/
    dataset/stations/stations.csv
    ```

3. Change the **File format** option to **CSV**.

4. Input the destination database, apps_db, and the table name, `stations`.

5. The configuration is as shown in the following screenshot:

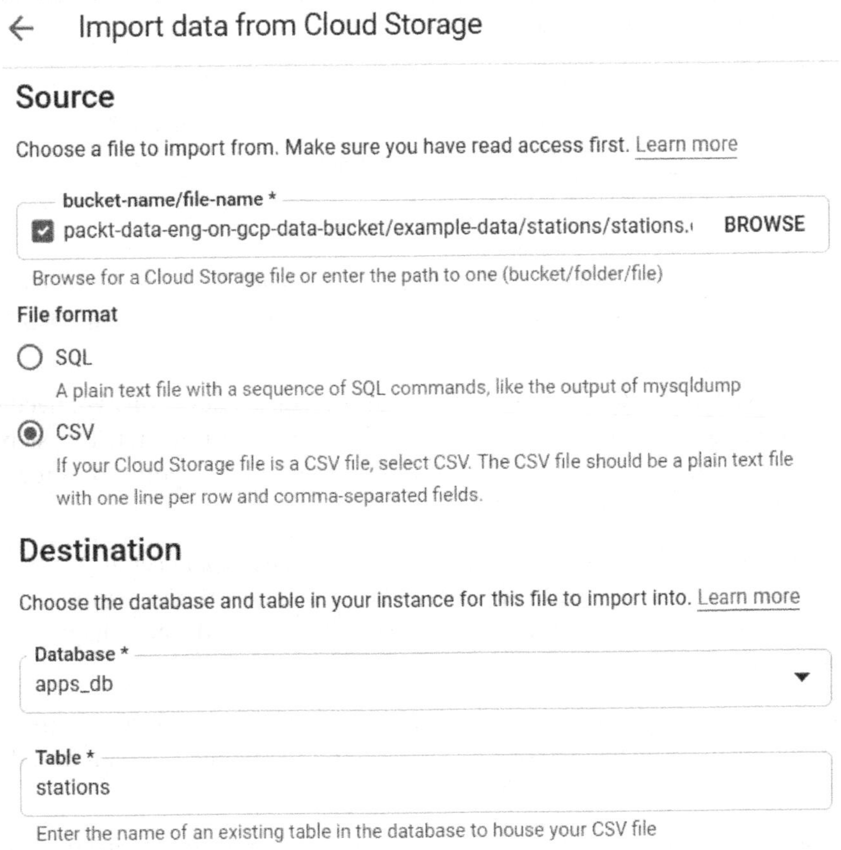

Import data from Cloud Storage

Source

Choose a file to import from. Make sure you have read access first. Learn more

bucket-name/file-name *

☑ packt-data-eng-on-gcp-data-bucket/example-data/stations/stations.   **BROWSE**

Browse for a Cloud Storage file or enter the path to one (bucket/folder/file)

File format

○ SQL

A plain text file with a sequence of SQL commands, like the output of mysqldump

◉ CSV

If your Cloud Storage file is a CSV file, select CSV. The CSV file should be a plain text file
with one line per row and comma-separated fields.

Destination

Choose the database and table in your instance for this file to import into. Learn more

Database *

apps_db   ▼

Table *

stations

Enter the name of an existing table in the database to house your CSV file

Figure 3.15 – Import data from Cloud Storage

6. Once everything is complete, click the **Import** button.

7. Now we will return to Cloud Shell and try to access the `stations` table. In the
    MySQL shell, run the following query:

```
mysql> SELECT * FROM apps_db.stations LIMIT 10;
```

Make sure you see some data there. Repeat the process if you can't see any records.
If successful, exit from the MySQL shell by typing `exit`, as shown in the following
code block:

```
mysql > exit
```

Now we have a simulation MySQL database as our data source. In the next section, we will
do the extraction from MySQL to GCS.

Step 2: Extract data from MySQL to GCS

In *step 2*, we want to extract data from the MySQL database to GCS.

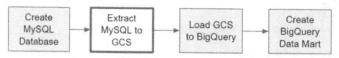

Figure 3.16 – Step 2: Extract MySQL to GCS

Since we are using CloudSQL, we can use the `gcloud` command to dump tables into GCS files, but you can do the same thing in self-managed MySQL without using the `gcloud` command.

First of all, we need to handle **Identity and Access Management (IAM)**. We need to assign the **CloudSQL service account** a **Storage Object admin** role first. This step will be a little bit confusing if you are new to IAM, but it's a good starting point for understanding IAM without going into too much depth.

IAM is a broad concept by itself, and GCP uses IAM to manage all user authentication and authorization for all services. IAM needs to be viewed holistically organization-wide, across projects, services, groups, and users. So, we will have a dedicated chapter later to talk about this in more detail.

At this point in time, let's break down what we need just for the purposes of this scenario. CloudSQL automatically generated one service account to operate. You can find the service account in your CloudSQL console.

From the CloudSQL console, go to your MySQL instance, for example, **mysql-instance-source**, and click on it.

Scroll down a little bit, and you can find the service account somewhere in the middle, like this:

Figure 3.17 – Copying the service account from the CloudSQL console

The service account will be in this format:

`[any text]@gcp-sa-cloud-sql.iam.gserviceaccount.com`.

Your service account will be different from what's shown in the preceding code. The service account is autogenerated and different each time you create a CloudSQL instance.

Copy that service account to any text editor because we want to add an IAM role to it.

To add the new role to the service account, follow these steps:

1. Go to the navigation bar.
2. Choose **IAM & Admin** -> **IAM**.
3. Click +**Add**.
4. Paste the CloudSQL service account into **New principals**.
5. Then, select a role.

Type `gcs object` and you will be able to choose **Storage Object Admin** (not **Storage Admin**).

The screen will look like this:

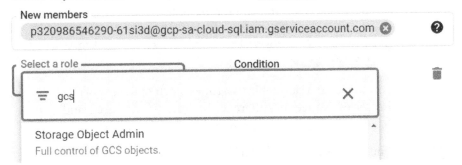

Add members, roles to "packt-data-eng-on-gcp" project

Enter one or more members below. Then select a role for these members to grant them access to your resources. Multiple roles allowed. Learn more

New members

p320986546290-61si3d@gcp-sa-cloud-sql.iam.gserviceaccount.com

Select a role ——————————— Condition

gcs

Storage Object Admin
Full control of GCS objects.

Figure 3.18 – Finding the Storage Object Admin role in IAM

After finishing the process, your CloudSQL service account will have permission to write and delete file objects in all GCS buckets in your project.

To summarize, the preceding steps are necessary to grant the CloudSQL service account the **Storage Object Admin** role. The role is to allow the service account to load data to your GCS bucket. Next, we want to load the data.

Access your Cloud Shell again and trigger a `gcloud` command to export the MySQL query results to a CSV file using a shell script from our Git repository.

The file is available here: `Data-Engineering-with-Google-Cloud-Platform/ chapter-3/code/gcloud_export_cloudsql_to_gcs.sh`.

We need to edit some variables, so open the file using **Cloud Editor**. If you have forgotten what Cloud Editor is, it is a simple text editor that you can access from Cloud Shell. Click the **Open Editor** button in the top-right corner.

Find the file and then change the `bucket_name` variable to that of your variable:

```
bucket_name=[your gcs bucket name]
gcloud sql export csv mysql-instance-source \
gs://$bucket_name/mysql_export/stations/20180101/stations.csv \
--database=apps_db \
--offload \
--query='SELECT * FROM stations WHERE station_id <= 200;'
gcloud sql export csv mysql-instance-source \
gs://$bucket_name/mysql_export/stations/20180102/stations.csv \
--database=apps_db \
--offload \
--query='SELECT * FROM stations WHERE station_id <=400;'
```

Once finished, return to Cloud Shell and run the script by running this command:

```
#sh Data-Engineering-with-Google-Cloud-Platform/chapter-3/code/
gcloud_export_cloudsql_to_gcs.sh
```

The script will export the `stations` table two times. Each of the exports will be stored in two different directories. Notice the difference between `/20180101` and `/20180102`. The latter (`/20180102`) is for our data warehouse exercise scenario 2.

For each export command, wait around 5 minutes for completion.

Once finished, you can check in your GCS bucket under the `mysql_export` folder. Your station CSV file should be there. If not, recheck every step.

In a real-world scenario, most of the time, the extractions happen from the clone instance. Application databases usually have a clone instance for providing high availability. Hence, it's good to extract data from there. That way, we won't interrupt the production database.

Summarizing this step regarding moving data fromCloudSQL to GCS, it is designed to demonstrate the *E* in *ETL*, which is to extract data from a data source into a GCS bucket. The method is pretty much the same for other database types, but every database might have a different command for dumping (exporting) table data to files.

For the exercises throughout this chapter, we will assume that the data is already in the GCS bucket. You can delete the MySQL instance for now.

You can delete the MySQL instance by running the following command:

```
#gcloud sql instances delete mysql-instance-source
```

Check the CloudSQL home page to ensure that the instance is deleted.

Step 3: Load GCS to BigQuery

In *step 3*, we will load data from GCS to BigQuery using the BigQuery console.

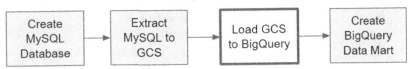

Figure 3.19 – Step 3: Load GCS to BigQuery

Let's go back to the BigQuery console.

Create a new dataset named `raw_bikesharing`.

Just as a reminder, for this exercise, let's use the default (multi-region US) dataset location. In scenario 2 later, we will want to use some tables from public datasets, which are located in the US.

In the `raw_bikesharing` dataset, let's create a new table from the BigQuery console:

1. Click on the Create table icon (+).

2. In the **Create table from** option, choose **Google Cloud Storage**:

    ```
    Browse Select file from GCS bucket:
    [your bucket name]/mysql_export/stations/20180101/
    stations.csv
    ```

3. For **Table name**, select `stations`.

    Note that the BigQuery table name is case-sensitive. We use lowercase letters in this instance.

4. In the **Schema** option, choose **Edit as text**.

5.   Write the following in the **schema** textbox:

```
station_id:STRING,name:STRING,region_
id:STRING,capacity:INTEGER
```

6.   Click on **Create table**.

Important Note

There is another alternative for defining the schema. You can try to enter your field names yourself. However, don't use the autodetect schema since the CSV file exported from MySQL doesn't provide headers.

You can check the `stations` table and see that the data is already in the BigQuery table. We have four columns here: `station_id`, `name`, `region_id`, and `capacity`.

station_id	name	region_id	capacity
6	The Embarcadero at Sansome St	3	0
64	5th St at Brannan St	3	0
133	Valencia St at 22nd St	3	0
79	7th St at Brannan St	3	3

Figure 3.20 – Stations table in BigQuery

If you can see the preceding table, we are good to go regarding the final step of this scenario.

Step 4: Create a BigQuery data mart

Depending on company regulations, most companies don't allow business users to access raw tables directly. Business users usually access data from data marts.

Technically, you can use BigQuery or other databases as the data mart. In this example, we will use BigQuery as our data mart, which is a very common practice.

Let's create a new dataset with the name `dm_regional_manager`.

Now, at this point, let's revisit what the business question is.

As a business user, I want to know the top two region IDs, ordered by the total stations' capacity in that region.

As the final step, we want to create a table or view in our BigQuery data mart based on the query result:

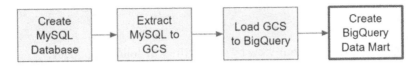

Figure 3.21 – Step 4: Create BigQuery Data Mart

Now we have two options for the query results:

- Create a table.

- Create a view.

Both tables and views have advantages and disadvantages. There are two advantages to using a view. First, the view costs no additional storage. If you create a view, the data won't be stored anywhere; it will just save the SQL formula. The second advantage is real time; if you access the view, then every time the underlying table changes, the view will get the latest update.

However, there are reasons as to why you would want to avoid using too many views physicalized into a new table. Sometimes, views can be heavy, and when the underlying tables are large and there are many joins and aggregations in the view's query, you may end up having very heavy processing.

> **Important Note**
> A physicalized table means using the query result to create a new table.

Imagine you have 5 upstream raw tables, each 1 PB in size, and your downstream consists of 1,000 views accessing the 5 tables. You may end up processing the PBs of data repeatedly, and that's bad in terms of both cost and performance.

In this scenario, however, since the `stations` table is small, we will use a view in the data mart.

Create a view based on the query using this SQL script:

```
CREATE VIEW `[your project id].dm_regional_manager.top_2_
region_by_capacity`
AS
SELECT region_id, SUM(capacity) as total_capacity
FROM `[your project id].raw_bikesharing.stations`
```

```
WHERE region_id != ''
GROUP BY region_id
ORDER BY total_capacity desc
LIMIT 2;
```

And that's it. You can access your view by submitting the following query:

```
SELECT * FROM `[your project id].dm_regional_manager.top_2_
region_by_capacity`;
```

This will produce results such as this:

Row	region_id	total_capacity
1	3	2903
2	12	849

Figure 3.22 – The query result

After checking the results, let's carry out the final steps:

1.   Click **SAVE RESULTS**.

2.   Take a moment to see what the available export options are.

3.   Finally, choose CSV (local file).

Done! We've practiced running an end-to-end ELT process on GCP. We extracted data from MySQL into a GCS bucket, loaded it into BigQuery, and transformed the table into a data mart table. The key takeaway from this scenario 1 is the hands-on experience using all the important components. But this is not yet a data warehouse, since we are only using one table, and we haven't thought much about what we should do with the data model. In scenario 2, we will try to load transaction data and start thinking about how we should reload and model the tables.

Data warehouse in BigQuery – Requirements for scenario 2

In the second scenario, we are going to load two more tables – bike trips and regions. In this scenario, we want to simulate how to handle new data loading and think about data modeling.

Here are some requirements:

1. As an operational business user, I need to access the following information:

    - How many bike trips take place daily?

    - What is the daily average trip duration?

    - The top five station names as the starting station that has the longest trip duration.

    - The top five region names that have the shortest total trip durations.

2. The bike trips data is in the GCS bucket, and each bucket folder contains daily data.

3. The regions data is from the BigQuery public dataset.

4. New data will be updated daily in the GCS bucket for `stations` and `trips` tables.

Similar to scenario 1, I suggest you take a moment to imagine yourself in the situation:

- What will you do?

- What services will you use?

- How will you do that?

In this scenario, we will start using the **Python** API instead of using the GCP console. Using a GCP console is still the best way to start learning GCP services, but it's not scalable from an engineering perspective; for example, when you need to create multiple ETL pipelines, it's better to have a loop in the pipelines using code. Using code also makes you able to implement proper testing and deployment. So, we will perform all the steps in this scenario using Python code.

Steps and planning for handling scenario 2

Now, the business users have more complex business questions. To answer the questions, we need to use the `JOIN` operation from multiple tables in our queries.

Here are some initial thoughts and planning:

1. Since the user is interested in daily measurements, we will create a layer to provide daily aggregation to the user.

2. There will be new data daily, so we need to plan how to handle the incoming data from GCS directories.

3. If you imagine our three main tables, stations, regions, and trips in real life, they are different entities. Stations and regions are static objects, while trips are events. We will get clearer information after checking the data later, but at this point, we should think how to handle both types of information differently.

4. The data mart is similar to scenario 1. We can use the same datasets to store the result there.

So, here are the overall steps:

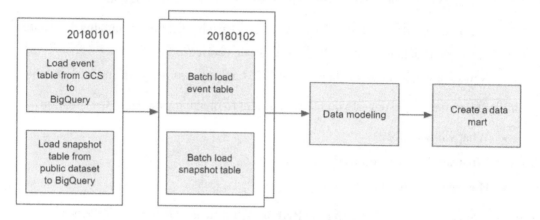

Figure 3.23 – The overall steps for scenario 2

There are five principal steps involved here:

1. Create the required datasets.

2. Load the initial trips and region tables to BigQuery:

    - Trips from GCS

    - Regions from the BigQuery public dataset

3. Handle the daily batch data loading:

    - For the `trips` table

    - For the `stations` table

4. Design data modeling for BigQuery.

5. Store the business questions result in tables.

There are two dates for our experiment. The initial load is using 2018-01-01, and we need to be able to handle the new data from 2018-01-02 and the upcoming days without any issues, for example, duplication.

Step 1: Create the datasets using Python

Let's create our datasets using Python. We want to add a new dataset called dwh_
bikesharing. But since its code-based, it's very easy to add the other datasets. So, we'll
also add raw_bikesharing and dm_bikesharing to the list just to make sure you
don't miss the datasets from scenario 1.

> **Important Note**
> You can run the Python script from your local computer if you have already
> installed the Python Google Cloud SDK, or use Cloud Shell. I recommend
> using Cloud Shell for simplicity.

To do that, check our code example from our repository.

The file is located here:

```
Data-Engineering-with-Google-Cloud-Platform/chapter-3/code/
bigquery_scenario_2_step_0_create_datasets.py
```

The file contains Python code that will create our required datasets:

1. Let's look at the code example. First, we will use the bigquery Python client line
    as follows:

    ```
    from google.cloud import bigquery
    client = bigquery.Client()
    ```

2. The BigQuery Python library is installed by default in Cloud Shell, so you don't
    need to install it manually. We will loop the datasets_name list to check whether
    the datasets exist. If they don't, create new ones:

    ```
    datasets_name = ['raw_bikesharing','dwh_bikesharing','dm_
    regional_manager', 'dm_operational']
    ```

    You don't need to change anything in the code. Let's run it using Cloud Shell.

3. Go to the chapter 3 directory:

    ```
    # cd Data-Engineering-with-Google-Cloud-Platform/
    chapter-3/code
    ```

    Then, run the Python script using the python3 command, like this:

    ```
    # python3 bigquery_scenario_2_step_0_create_datasets.py
    ```

After running the code, check your BigQuery console and make sure the three datasets have been created in your project. Note that BigQuery Explorer won't refresh automatically, so you need to refresh your internet browser to view the changes.

Step 2a: Initial loading of the trips table into BigQuery

The first step is to load the initia trips data from GCS into BigQuery.

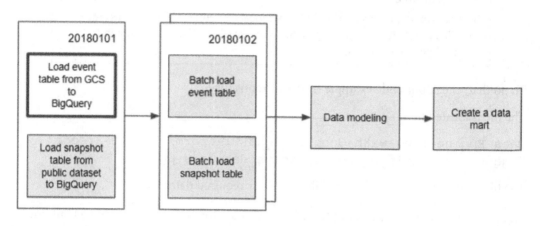

Figure 3.24 – Load event table from GCS to BigQuery

The dataset is in our GCS bucket, inside this directory: `packt-data-eng-on-gcp-data-bucket/from-git/chapter-3/dataset/trips`.

Notice that there are two folders there with the date information. This is a common directory format for storing daily batch data in GCS.

To load the data into BigQuery, let's look at the code in our repository. The filename is as follows:

```
bigquery_scenario_2_step_1a_load_trips_data.py
```

The script will load trips data from gcs to BigQuery. There are a few things that you need to pay attention to in the code.

The GCS file path contains date information, for example, `20180101`. We will use the folder name in our `gcs` file path like this:

```
gcs_uri = "gs://{}-data-bucket/from-git/chapter-3/dataset/
trips/20180101/*.json".format(project_id)
```

The data stored in `NEWLINE DELIMITED JSON` is compressed in `gzip` files. The

BigQuery load job config accepts the `NEWLINE_DELIMITED_JSON` file format, and not standard JSON. In case you have standard JSON, you need to transform it first to the correct JSON format. In the code, we need to define the format like this:

```
source_format=bigquery.SourceFormat.NEWLINE_DELIMITED_JSON,
```

The write disposition is `WRITE_APPEND`. This won't matter during the initial load, but is an important configuration for handling new data. We will revisit this later in the next steps:

```
write_disposition = 'WRITE_APPEND'
```

Lastly, you will need to change the `project_id` variable to that of your `project_id` variable, since you want to load data from your own GCS bucket. See the following line:

```
project_id = "packt-data-eng-on-gcp"
```

Run the Python script from Cloud Editor using this command:

```
# python3 bigquery_scenario_2_step_1a_load_trips_data.py
```

After running the Python script, you will see that the new table has been created in your `raw_bikesharing` dataset. Check the table preview to familiarize yourself with the data:

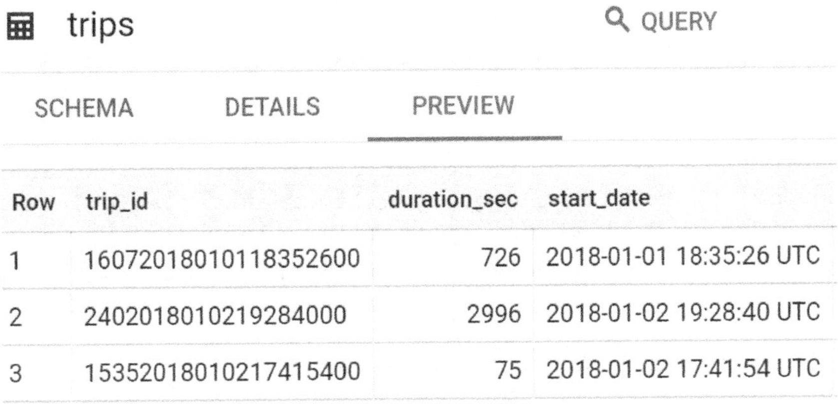

Row	trip_id	duration_sec	start_date
1	16072018010118352600	726	2018-01-01 18:35:26 UTC
2	2402018010219284000	2996	2018-01-02 19:28:40 UTC
3	15352018010217415400	75	2018-01-02 17:41:54 UTC

Figure 3.25 – BigQuery table PREVIEW feature

Check your `trips` table in the **PREVIEW** table. We will load another table in the next section.

Step 2b: Initial loading of the regions table into BigQuery

Still in *step 2*, we want to load another table, the `regions` table, from the BigQuery public dataset. This is to illustrate the nature of the data warehouse, where you can combine data from different data sources.

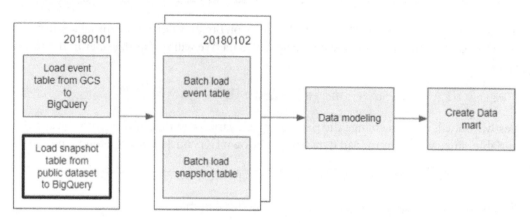

Figure 3.26 – Load table from the BigQuery public dataset

To do that, let's look at the code example:

```
bigquery_scenario_2_step_1b_load_regions_data.py
```

The script will run a query to access data from the `bigquery-public-data` dataset:

```
public_table_id = "bigquery-public-data.san_francisco_
bikeshare.bikeshare_regions"
```

```
sql = "SELECT * FROM `{}`;".format(public_table_id) But instead
of showing the result, the query will create a table in our
project. Take a look at this particular line:
job_config = bigquery.QueryJobConfig(destination=target_table_
id)
```

Run the Python script using the `python3` command:

```
# python3 bigquery_scenario_2_step_1b_load_regions_data.py
```

After running the script, the `regions` table will be available in your `raw_bikesharing` dataset.

regions

	SCHEMA	DETAILS	PREVIEW

Row	region_id	name
1	12	Oakland
2	14	Berkeley
3	3	San Francisco

Figure 3.27 – Example result from the regions table

As a summary of *step 2*, we added two new tables to our `raw_bikesharing` dataset. The next step is to load additional data into our existing tables and make sure that the loading doesn't mess with the existing data.

Step 3a: Handle the daily batch data loading for the trips table

In *step 3*, we will add new records to our existing tables:

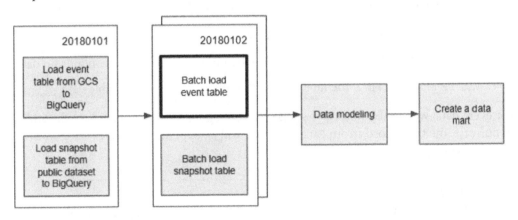

Figure 3.28 – Loading data for the next date

We will load data from the same bucket, but a different date directory, for example, `20180102`.

How about the code? You can use the same code as in *Step 2a: Initial loading of the trips table into BigQuery*:

```
File : bigquery_scenario_2_step_1a_load_trips_data.py
```

But we need to change the code a little bit. Let's adjust the date by changing this line:

```
gcs_uri = "gs://{}-data-bucket/example-data/trips/20180101/*.
json".format(project_id)
```

To the following code:

```
gcs_uri = "gs://{}-data-bucket/example-data/trips/20180102/*.
json".format(project_id)
```

Or, as an alternative, you can use the code that has already been modified:

File : bigquery_scenario_2_step_1a_load_trips_data_20180102.py

Before running the script, let's understand first what will happen with our data.

The code will append new records to the `trips` table. This kind of data is called events. In events data, every new record is a new event, which won't affect any existing data. The nature of an event, once it happens, can't be updated and deleted. This is similar to the real world; you can't change something that has happened.

Technically, BigQuery has three `write_disposition` variables. This configuration is to determine what the intended data writing behavior is. Here are the three options:

- `WRITE_APPEND`: If the table exists, BigQuery appends the data to the table.
- `WRITE_EMPTY`: Only write to the table when the table exists and contains no data.
- `WRITE_TRUNCATE`: If the table exists, BigQuery overwrites the table data.

For event data, we can use `WRITE_APPEND` to keep appending new records to the table. In our case, the trip records from `2018-01-02` will be appended to the existing `2018-01-01` record.

> **Important Note**
>
> In a later chapter, we will revisit this matter for data orchestration purposes, but for now, `WRITE_APPEND` is a natural way to load event data.

Now, after changing the date in our Python variable, let's run the Python script and do some checking. Run the Python script as usual:

```
# python3 bigquery_scenario_2_step_1a_load_trips_data.py
```

Let's check whether we have data from both 2018-01-01 and 2018-01-02 by using this SQL query on the BigQuery console:

```
SELECT distinct(date(start_date))
FROM `[your project id].raw_bikesharing.trips`;;
```

The query should produce two records:

- 2018-01-01

- 2018-01-02

And finally, we want to make sure that no records have been duplicated by using this SQL query:

```
SELECT count(*) cnt_trip_id, trip_id
FROM `[your project id].raw_bikesharing.trips`
GROUP BY trip_id
HAVING cnt_trip_id > 1;
```

The query will return no records. Retry and review the overall steps in case your results are incorrect.

Step 3b: Handle the daily batch data loading for the stations table

In this section, we want to simulate loading data for our stations table. We will load data from 2018-01-02.

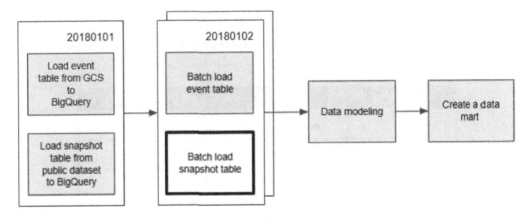

Figure 3.29 – Loading stations data for the next date

For the `stations` table, the approach will be different compared to the `trips` table. This kind of table may have new records (`INSERT`), updated records (`UPDATE`), and removed records (`DELETE`) records. Imagine a real-world bike station; a new bike station can be demolished, capacities or the station name may change, or a new station may be established in the region. So, this kind of data is called a snapshot. Snapshot data is not event data. Snapshot data is an object or entity in the real world; it doesn't happen, it's just there.

Let's use an illustration by way of example in our station table. Just for illustration, we will have the **DAY 1** and **DAY 2** data.

The **DAY 1** data has two records, `station_1` and `station_2`, as shown in the following table. But for **DAY 2**, for a variety of business reasons, `station_1` gets additional capacity (`UPDATE`), `station_2` no longer exists (`DELETE`), and there is a new station, `station_3` (`INSERT`).

DAY 1	station_id	name	region_id	capacity
	501	station_1	3	10
	504	station_2	5	10

DAY 2	station_id	name	region_id	capacity
	501	station_1	3	20
	505	station_3	5	15

Figure 3.30 – Stations table illustration

Then, if you use `WRITE_APPEND`, after loading the **DAY 2** data, the table will look like this:

station_id	name	region_id	capacity
501	station_1	3	10
504	station_2	5	10
501	station_1	3	20
505	station_3	5	15

Figure 3.31 – Stations table after WRITE_APPEND

This is invalid because there are duplications for station_1, and station_2 should no longer be in the table. If the end user wants to count how many stations are in the table, SELECT count(*) FROM stations won't give the correct answer.

There are a number of approaches for handling this condition, so let's start with the easiest one, by using write disposition: WRITE_TRUNCATE. Look at the following code example:

```
bigquery_scenario_2_step_2b_load_stations_data.py
```

As you may have noticed, the write_disposition variable is WRITE_TRUNCATE:

```
write_disposition = 'WRITE_TRUNCATE'
```

Before running it, make sure you change the project_id variable.

If the script results in an error because it can't find the file, recheck the section in scenario 1, *Extract MySQL to GCS*.

The GCS directory, bucket/mysql_export/stations, should look like this:

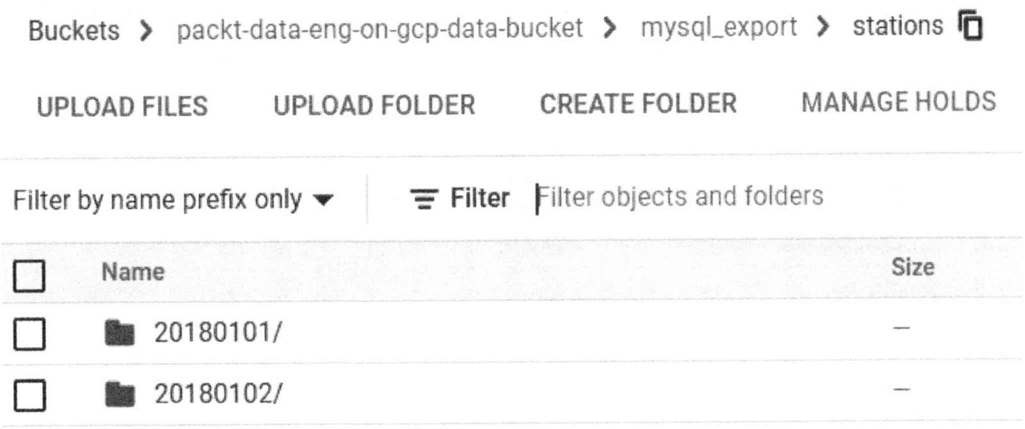

Buckets ❯ packt-data-eng-on-gcp-data-bucket ❯ mysql_export ❯ stations 🗐

UPLOAD FILES   UPLOAD FOLDER   CREATE FOLDER   MANAGE HOLDS

Filter by name prefix only ▼   ☰ Filter Filter objects and folders

	Name	Size
☐	📁 20180101/	—
☐	📁 20180102/	—

Figure 3.32 – Inside the GCS bucket stations folder

Now, let's check whether there are any duplicated records by using a SQL query:

```
SELECT
station_id, count(*) as cnt_station
FROM `[your project id].raw_bikesharing.stations`
GROUP BY station_id
HAVING cnt_station > 1;
```

The query should give you no records, which means there are no duplicated stations in our records, and that is good enough. In some cases, however, you may want to keep your historical data. Using the preceding method, you will lose your historical information.

In the next section, we will learn how to keep historical records while maintaining valid information.

Handle loads using snapshot

Since, in our scenario, there is no requirement for maintaining historical data, we won't do this section as part of our exercise, but let's quickly get an idea of how to do it conceptually by looking at this figure:

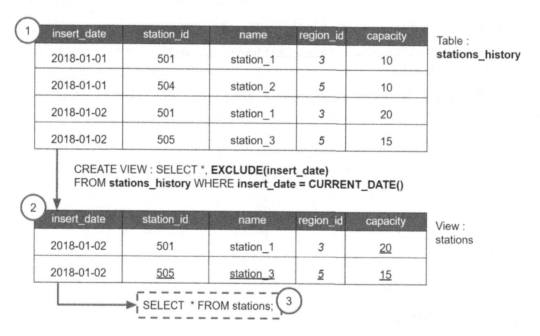

Figure 3.33 – General concept of the snapshot table

There are three additional steps compared to simply using the WRITE_TRUNCATE approach:

1. After loading to our table in raw_bikesharing, we will create another table that adds an insert_date column (or you can add it as an ETL process, before loading to BigQuery). The table will keep appending the new data daily. There will be duplication at the station_id level, but since we have the insert_date column, we can use the date information to get just the latest data snapshot.

2. Create a view that excludes the `insert_date` column and filter `insert_date` using the `CURRENT_DATE()` function, which returns today's date.

3. The later user will access the view instead of the raw or historical tables. The user experience will still be the same since they can use the common query `SELECT * FROM stations` and obtain just today's station version.

With this mechanism, any time business users have requests for data from historical periods, you can always access the `stations_history` table.

What is the drawback? Naturally, it will affect storage and performance. That's why it always goes back to the requirements.

There are two other common approaches that I will not cover in this book, but I suggest you look at the concepts on the internet:

1. Incremental load using the `MERGE` BigQuery operation. `MERGE` is a unique operation in BigQuery. It's a combination of `INSERT` if it does not exist, and `UPDATE` if there are changes.

2. **Slowly Changing Dimensions**, or **SCDs** for short. SCDs are methods that you can follow to handle dimension data. Dimension data is equal to snapshot data in our context here, but I chose not to use dimension data since it's tightly related to the data modeling techniques that we will visit in the next section.

Let's summarize our overall progress so far by checking our three tables. Now your tables should have this number of records:

- Regions: 6 records
- Stations: 342 records
- Trips: 4,627 records

If you don't have the same result, I suggest a number of options:

1. Revisit all the previous steps.

2. In case there are tables with 0 records, I strongly suggest revisiting all the previous steps.

3. In case all the tables have records, but different numbers of records, you may continue to *step 4*. You may overlook some small detail steps, but this won't prevent you from continuing the practice exercise.

Step 4: Design data modeling for BigQuery

In this section, we want to start thinking about whether there any better ways to reshape our table's schema to better represent our business user needs. Just to summarize, this is the second-to-last step in our plan here.

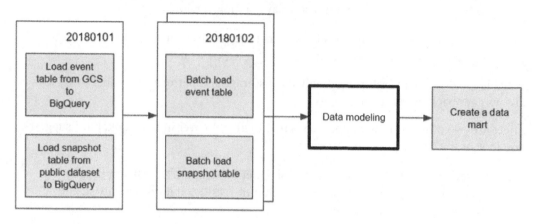

Figure 3.34 – The data modeling step

I will give you a heads-up here before we continue our practice exercise. We will spend more time in this section to understand some theories and principles compared to the other steps.

When this book was written, I felt there was a big gap between how far the data technologies have evolved (in general, and not limited to BigQuery) compared to the common theories, for example, data warehouse modeling. For example, the concern about the storage size and the computational power of a data warehouse differs enormously from 30 years ago compared to today's technologies, yet the data warehouse modeling principles that we often use today are based on theories from the 1990s.

There are two concerns here. The first one is that some of the old design principles that used to handle storage and process efficiency may no longer be relevant in modern technologies. Secondly, since modern data engineers realize the non-relevancy of the old principles and, at the same time, the demand to insert any data in data warehouses is growing tremendously, they tend to skip the data modeling steps, and that's bad. Skipping the data warehouse principles means ignoring the fact that we need to maintain data consistency. This fact may lead to some bad results. Take the following common example:

- Data is duplicated in many locations.
- Some values are not consistent across different users and reports.
- The cost of processing is highly inefficient.

- The end user doesn't understand how to use the data warehouse objects.
- The business doesn't trust the data.

In my opinion, a modern data warehouse is still a data warehouse. The objective of a data warehouse is to build a centralized and trustworthy data storage that can be used for business. Data engineers need to take more time to do proper data modeling in data warehouses compared to the data lake concept in order to meet this objective.

Introducing data modeling

What is data modeling? **Data modeling** is a process for representing the database objects in our real-world or business perspective. Objects in BigQuery can be datasets, tables, or views. Representing the objects as close as possible to the real world is important because the end users of the data are human. Some of the most common end users are business analysts, data analysts, data scientists, BI users, or any other roles that require access to the data for business purposes.

This is the main difference between designing a data model in a data warehouse and designing an **OLTP** database (transactional database) for applications. In the application database, the end users of the database are applications, not humans. In the data warehouse, you serve humans. So, as data engineers, we need to think from their perspective.

Let's look at this example. We want to represent people in a table object. Which of the following two tables, A or B, do you think better represents people? Here is People table A:

name	age	hair color	gender
Mona	20	black	Female
Oscar	35	black	Male
Adam	56	white	Male
Barb	34	red	Male
Hazel	25	brown	Female

Figure 3.35 – People table A

Try and compare this with People table B:

name	gender	postal code	wealthy
Mona	Female	111111	yes
Oscar	Male	232323	no
Adam	Man	423333	no
Barb	Man	NULL	yes
Hazel	Woman	452222	yes

Figure 3.36 – People table B

If we look back at the objective, we want to represent people. Then I think we can all agree that *People table A* is better at representing people because this table represents people clearly. It's very natural to imagine people having names, ages, hair colors, and genders. A good data model is self-explanatory, like *People table A*. This means that even without anyone explaining to you how to read the table, you already know what the table is about.

Now, why is *table B* bad? There are a few reasons:

- The lists of attributes don't really represent people; for example, `postal code`. Even though we know people may have houses, and houses have postal codes, it's difficult to imagine people as entities having a postal code as part of them.

- What is `NULL` in relation to `postal code`? Does that mean Barb doesn't have a house? Or maybe he forgot his postal code? Or perhaps this is just a bug. The table can't really tell you that.

- Still on the subject of the postal code, how about if one of the people here has more than one house? Should we add new records to this table? It will become complicated.

- Gender is inconsistent. `Female` and `Woman`, and `Male` and `Man`, may have the same meanings, but may not.

- The wealthy column has `yes` and `no` values. What does this mean? How can this column be justified?

It is not that the information is wrong – we often need to store such information. Now the question is, can we store the same information, but with a better data model?

Let's take another example. Perhaps this better represents the real world for the required information:

Salary

name	Salary
Mona	1000000
Oscar	2000
Adam	3000
Barb	100000
Hazel	100000

People

name	gender
Mona	Female
Oscar	Male
Adam	Male
Barb	Male
Hazel	Female

Address

name	postal code
Mona	111111
Oscar	232323
Adam	423333
Hazel	452222

Figure 3.37 – Alternative C using multiple tables

Maybe this *Alternative C* is better. We still have the people table, but only with people-related attributes, for example, `gender`. Then, `postal code` is part of the `Address` table. It may have other address information, but in this example, we will keep it simple with just the postal code. And if someone such as `Barb` doesn't have a postal code, then we don't need to put the `NULL` record there. And lastly, we may assume that wealth is driven by salary (just for example purposes), so we had better just store the salary information, and later use queries to put the `wealthy` logic on top of the salary information. This is more natural and closer to the real world.

What could happen with a bad data model? It is often the case that the end user will have too much dependency on the data engineering team. Unable to understand the table shapes, end users need to keep posing the following questions to the data engineering team, for example:

1. What does `NULL` mean?
2. How should I join the tables?
3. Why are there duplications?
4. Why do some records have the attribute X while others don't?

In the worst-case scenario, the end user doesn't trust the data in the data warehouse, so the goal of using the data for a business impact has failed.

In the best-case scenario, a perfect data model is where the end user doesn't need to put any questions to the data engineering team. They can answer any business questions just by looking at the table structures and trust the data 100%. And that's our goal as data engineers.

But, at the end of the day, it's very difficult to design a perfect data model because there are other aspects that a data engineer needs to think about when designing a data model.

Other purposes of the data model

Besides representing data in a real-world scenario, there are three other reasons why we require a data model in a data warehouse:

- **Data consistency**
- **Query performance**
- **Storage efficiency**

Let's start with the latest point first: *Storage efficiency*. How can we improve storage efficiency by the data model?

Take a look at this example again. Which one is more storage-efficient? Perhaps a table with name and gender, where gender is written in a string data type as Man or Woman:

People

name	gender
Mona	Female
Oscar	Male
Adam	Man
Barb	Man
Hazel	Woman

Figure 3.38 – Storage efficiency option A

Or perhaps *option B*? We create a gender reference table, and the main table will only store one character, gender_id, as a reference. The user can later join both tables for the same result as *option A*.

People

name	gender_id
Mona	1
Oscar	2
Adam	2
Barb	2
Hazel	1

Gender

gender_id	gender
1	Female
2	Male

Figure 3.39 – Storage efficiency option B

Option B is definitely better, as we don't need to repeat storing Female and Male strings in our storage. It looks like a small difference, but the same technique applies to all categorical string attributes, and that can have a significant impact.

Using the same technique, we can also improve data consistency. For example, we can use the gender reference table for other tables, as in the following example user table:

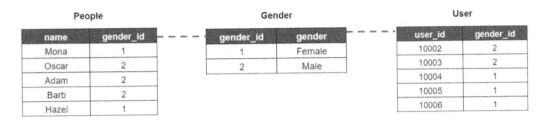

Figure 3.40 – Storage efficiency option B with an additional table

With that, we avoid data inconsistency; for example, the People table uses Female-Male, and the User table uses Man-Woman. This is a very common practice, and the common terminology in the data warehouse world to refer to this is normalized and denormalized.

Storage efficiency option A is a denormalized table, while *Storage efficiency option B* is a normalized table.

Last but not least, one reason why we need a data model is for query performance. In a big data system where data is stored in distributed storage, there is a general rule of thumb regarding which operation is the most resource-intensive, which is JOIN. JOIN in general is a very expensive operation, especially when we need to join multiple large-volume tables. And if you look back at the normalized and denormalized approaches, you will realize that even normalized data is good for storage efficiency and data consistency, but it's bad for performance because you require a lot of Join operations.

At the end of the day, we need to find a balance between all the factors. There will be no right or wrong answer for a data model in a complex data warehouse. In a complex data warehouse, this may involve thousands to millions of tables. So, everyone will have a different approach for designing the data model. However, there are some theories that we can use as reference.

Inmon versus the Kimball data model

If you look at the internet, there will be many references to data modeling, but two of the most famous approaches are the **Inmon** method (data-driven) and the **Kimball** method (user-driven).

We will take a quick look at these methods, but we won't spend much time or go into too much detail in this book since there are so many details to explain regarding the framework. I suggest you do some more in-depth research from other resources regarding these two methods to better understand the step-by-step approaches and the frameworks. What we want to learn from them are the differences and the thinking processes behind them.

At a very high level, the Inmon method focuses on building a central data warehouse or single source of truth. To achieve that, the data model must be highly normalized to the lowest level, so the data can be highly consistent. The Inmon data model follows a top-down approach, which means the data warehouse is built as the central data source for all the downstream data marts, sometimes referred to as the **Enterprise Data Warehouse**. The downstream data marts need to follow the rules from the data warehouse, as in this figure. Imagine the gray boxes are tables.

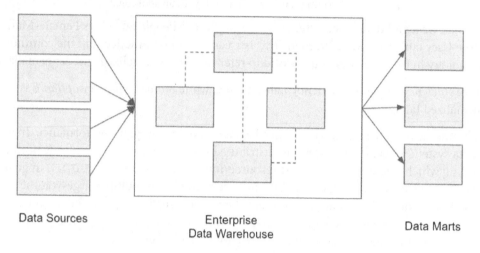

Data Sources   Enterprise
                               Data Warehouse   Data Marts

Figure 3.41 – Inmon data model illustration

Compared to the Inmon method, the Kimball method focuses on answering user questions and follows a bottom-up approach. This method keeps end user questions in mind and uses the questions as a basis to build necessary tables. The goal is to ease end user accessibility and provide a high level of performance improvement.

The tables may contain the entity's basic information and its measurements. This is what are now known as fact and dimension tables. A **fact table** is a collection of measurements or metrics in a predefined granularity. A **dimension table** is a collection of entity attributes that support the fact tables. This collection of fact and dimension tables will later be the data warehouse.

Here is an example of a fact table. The fact table has two measurements that measure customers in daily granularity:

Date	Customer ID	Number of clicks	Number of purchases
2021-01-01	1	100	4
2021-01-01	2	10	2
2021-01-02	1	200	10
2021-01-01	2	50	4

Figure 3.42 – Customer fact table in daily granularity

Here is an example of a dimension table with `Customer ID` as the primary key and the attributes:

Customer ID	Name	Age
1	Agnes	34
2	Bony	23
1	Charlie	54
2	Darwin	12

Figure 3.43 – Customer dimension table

As you can see from the examples, the facts and dimension tables are different. So how do they relate together as a data model?

One of the most well-known data models for the Kimball method is the star schema. The star schema follows the fact and dimension table relations. There is a rule of thumb regarding the star schema that a dimension table can't have parent tables, which means the dimension is a denormalized table. Check the following diagram, which provides a high-level illustration of a data warehouse using the Kimball approach. Imagine that all the gray boxes are tables:

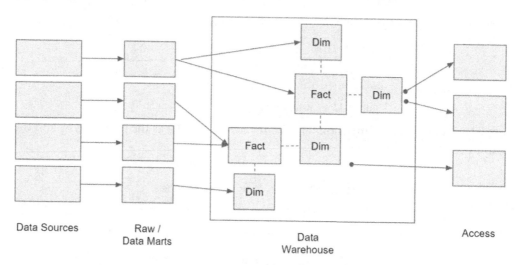

Figure 3.44 – Illustration of the Kimball data model

The pros and cons of both methods are summarized as follows:

	Inmon	Kimball
Date warehouse scope	Enterprise-wide	Business areas
Development time	Longer initial design and implementation time	Shorter time for initial design and implementation
Normalized data model	Highly normalized	Low normalization
Computation performance	Highly computationally expensive; involves many join operations	Lower computation costs; information already denormalized in dimensional tables
Consistency	Highly consistent and highly regulated	Frequently much redundant information and subject to revision

Figure 3.45 – Table comparison; Inmon versus the Kimball method

Use the table comparison as your reference when deciding between the Inmon or Kimball methods. This is usually not a straightforward and quick decision to make. It's a difficult decision because choosing one of them means your entire organization needs to commit to the data model for the long term. An experienced data modeler is usually the best person to decide this. In the next section, we will try to figure out which data model is best in BigQuery.

The best data model for BigQuery

Since both approaches are quite old, the common question is which data model is better for BigQuery. But before answering the question about which data model is best for BigQuery, let's summarize what we've learned so far in terms of which aspects we need to think about when deciding on the data model approach.

A data model needs to do the following:

1. Represent the real-world scenario for the end user
2. Have high data consistency
3. Perform well on the running technology (query speed).
4. Demonstrate efficiency when storing data

The complication we've learned, however, is that the four aspects can't all be perfect at the same time; each point is a trade-off in relation to the other points.

Repeating the example from the previous section, there are cases when we need to sacrifice consistency and efficient storage for better performance and better real-world representation. Or, in the other cases, we may sacrifice performance for high consistency.

Now, let's talk about the technological evolution following the Hadoop era. Modern data technologies are increasingly friendly in terms of storage costs, including BigQuery. Storing data used to be very expensive in days gone by, but it's no longer true in BigQuery (at least compared to non-cloud technologies). For example, in BigQuery, the cost of storing 1 TB of data is $20/month. Compare this to the old days, when companies needed to pay thousands of dollars to store the same amount of data on-premises.

The other aspect that has evolved is computation performance. In the Hadoop technology, data engineers were very cautious of JOIN operations. A JOIN is highly resource-intensive, especially in the original Java MapReduce technology. However, this is no longer true in BigQuery.

Look at my query result in the following screenshot. I did a full table join on 587 GB of data, and the query finished in **23.4** seconds:

Query results   ⬇ SAVE RESULTS

Query complete (23.4 sec elapsed, 587.1 GB processed)

Figure 3.46 – Query time for aggregating 587 GB of data

If you are wondering about the preceding query cost, that query cost is around $3 in BigQuery. (In on-demand, the processing cost is $5 per 1 TB, so a 587 GB query will cost around $3.)

Given the preceding facts about storage and computation, in BigQuery, we may stipulate these two aspects as lower-level priorities. And just to be clear, we are not ignoring these aspects entirely, but if find ourselves in a situation where we need to sacrifice some aspects, then we may choose to sacrifice storage and computation efficiency over data consistency and better representation of the real world (user friendly).

Now let's get back to the main question: Should we use the Inmon method or the Kimball method? My answer is both. You should use either depending on the circumstances.

Let's use a real example. Imagine you are a data engineer. You are working for the finance department of your business user. They have asked for financial statement reports. You might consider using the Inmon method for three reasons:

1. You need high-level consistency for a financial report; you cannot make any mistakes with this kind of report.
2. A financial statement usually requires minimum data source changes.
3. The initial development time is not as critical as highly accurate data.

However, the decision will be different in other cases. In the big data era, we may expect data to arrive more quickly and in greater variety. Organizations tend to store almost all possible data. The main reason is agility in analytics and data science. New data sources, tables, and columns are unavoidable every single day. In this case, if you follow the Inmon method, you may fail to catch up in terms of agility. The Kimball method is a better way to handle such a situation owing to the *user-driven* mindset. If *business users* are happy with the data and able to make business decisions based thereon, then it's good enough even if there are inconsistencies and inefficiencies here and there.

To summarize this long section regarding data models, in the traditional data warehouse era, people chose which data model to use based on technological capabilities and constraints. By using BigQuery as our data warehouse, we are in a situation that has never been seen before. We choose how we want to model the data based on the business use case.

Creating fact and dimension tables

Let's get back to our bike-sharing datasets. Since, in this scenario 2, we already have clear questions from business users, and we don't require high consistency, we will use Kimball's star schema for our data warehouse. Our table schema will look like this:

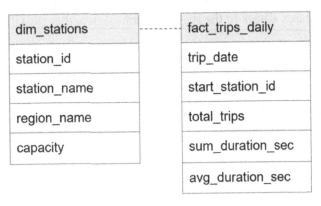

Figure 3.47 – Target table for the fact and dimension tables

These two tables are good examples of fact and dimension tables. The fact table represents measurements for the station ID by date; the granularity is daily. The dimension table represents stations. You can easily imagine a station in the real world given the attributes. A station has a name and it is indicated which region it is in and what the capacity of the station is. This table format will be easier for our user, which, in scenario 2, is an operational business user. Accessing these two tables is a lot easier compared to the raw tables.

Now, let's create our `fact_trips_daily` table by running the Python script in our repository:

```
bigquery_scenario_2_step_3_create_fact_table_daily_trips.py
```

Open the script in Cloud Editor and change the project ID to your project, as we did in the other preceding steps.

After that, check this line in the code:

```
load_date = sys.argv[1] # date format : yyyy-mm-dd
```

This script requires a parameters date in the format `yyyy-mm-dd`. So, you need to provide one when calling the Python command, like this:

```
# python bigquery_scenario_2_step_3_create_fact_table_daily_
trips.py 2018-01-01
```

Run it again to load the next day's data:

```
# python bigquery_scenario_2_step_3_create_fact_table_daily_
trips.py 2018-01-02
```

If successful, the script will create the `fact_trips_daily` table in the `dwh_bikesharing` dataset. Check in the BigQuery console whether the table looks like this:

⊞ fact_trips_daily

SCHEMA	DETAILS	PREVIEW

Row	trip_date	start_station_id	total_trips	sum_duration_sec	avg_duration_sec
401	2018-01-02	109	15	6837	455.8
402	2018-01-02	77	15	13869	924.59999999999991
403	2018-01-02	36	15	7826	521.73333333333335
404	2018-01-02	53	15	60898	4059.8666666666668

Figure 3.48 – The fact_trips_daily table

For the `dim_stations` table, run the Python script in this location:

```
Chapter-3\code\bigquery_scenario_2_step_3_create_dim_table_
stations.py
```

Change the `project_id` variable in the script and run it. If successful, you will see the `dim_stations` table created like this:

⊞ dim_stations

	SCHEMA	DETAILS	PREVIEW		

Row	station_id	station_name	region_name	capacity
1	222	10th Ave at E 15th St	Oakland	3
2	167	College Ave at Harwood Ave	Oakland	7
3	18	Telegraph Ave at Alcatraz Ave	Oakland	11
4	46	San Antonio Park	Oakland	15

Figure 3.49 – The dim_stations table

After successfully generating the two tables, we can continue to the next step. But before that, let's quickly look at an alternative for our tables using one of the features in BigQuery called nested data types.

Alternative data model using nested data types

There is one alternative that we may consider in data modeling with BigQuery, which is nested data types. If we return to the debate regarding normalized versus denormalized tables, one of the reasons why people use normalized tables is for storage efficiency, while one of the advantages of using denormalized tables is ease of use, since we don't need to join tables.

Can we achieve both advantages in a single solution? The answer is yes. You can achieve that in BigQuery using nested data types.

For example, let's look at our bike-sharing region and station tables. In the raw dataset, the original data is denormalized.

Row	region_id	name
1	14	Berkeley
2	5	San Jose
3	12	Oakland
4	13	Emeryville
5	23	8D
6	3	San Francisco

Figure 3.50 – Raw region table

And in our station table, each region has one or more stations.

station_id	name	region_id	capacity
64	5th St at Brannan St	3	0
133	Valencia St at 22nd St	3	0
79	7th St at Brannan St	3	3
102	Irwin St at 8th St	3	4

Figure 3.51 – Raw station table

Looking at our dimension table in the dwh dataset, we decided to denormalize the table to meet the star schema rule. The rule is that you can't have parent tables for a dimension table, or, in other words, you can't join dimension tables to other dimension tables:

station_id	station_name	region_name	capacity
222	10th Ave at E 15th St	Oakland	3
167	College Ave at Harwood Ave	Oakland	7
18	Telegraph Ave at Alcatraz Ave	Oakland	11
46	San Antonio Park	Oakland	15

Figure 3.52 – The dim_stations table

Since one region can have one or many stations, we can store the stations as nested information under regions. This may be hard to imagine, so let's just try to create one by running this query in the BigQuery console. The query will create a region and station as one table:

```
CREATE OR REPLACE TABLE `dwh_bikesharing.dim_stations_nested`
AS
SELECT
    regions.region_id,
    regions.name as region_name,
    ARRAY_AGG(stations) as stations
FROM
`packt-data-eng-on-gcp.raw_bikesharing.regions` regions
JOIN
`packt-data-eng-on-gcp.raw_bikesharing.stations` stations
ON CAST(regions.region_id AS STRING) = stations.region_id
```

```
GROUP BY regions.region_id,
    regions.name;
```

If you look at the `dim_stations_nested` table schema:

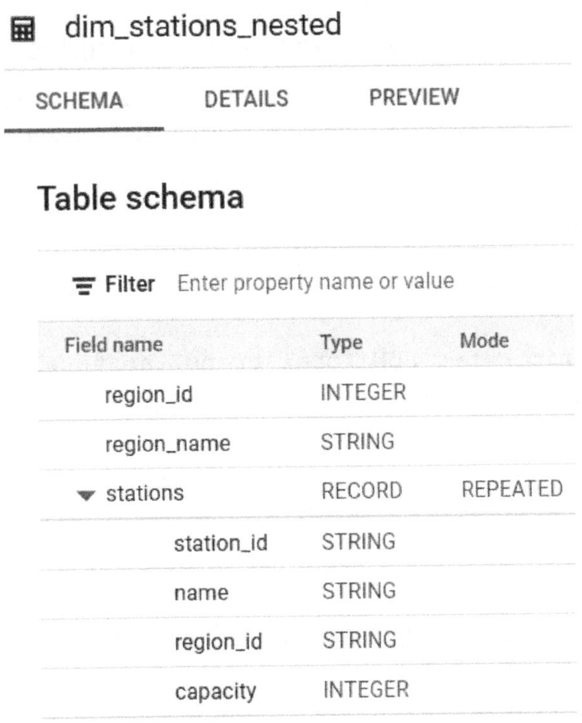

Figure 3.53 – Nested table schema in the SCHEMA tab

You will see that the stations are part of the regions as repeated columns. And if you query the data, you will see that `region_id` and `region_name` are only stored once even though there are multiple station records.

Row	region_id	region_name	stations.station_id	stations.name
1	3	San Francisco	64	5th St at Brannan St
			133	Valencia St at 22nd St
			79	7th St at Brannan St

Figure 3.54 – Nested table content example

The downside of using nested tables is that it's not easy to digest for common SQL users. Business users who are familiar with SQL might get confused with it the first time. But the feature is there, and you can always use it when you need it.

Next, we will move on to the final step to create our reports.

Step 5: Store the business questions result in tables

The final step is to answer the business questions with our fact and dimension tables. This is going to be straightforward. So, let's look at each question and answer with SQL statements:

1. How many bike trips take place daily?

```
CREATE VIEW dm_operational.bike_trips_daily
AS
SELECT trip_date, SUM(total_trips) as total_trips_daily
FROM dwh_bikesharing.fact_trips_daily
GROUP BY trip_date;
```

2. What is the daily average trip duration?

```
CREATE VIEW dm_operational.daily_avg_trip_duration
AS
SELECT trip_date, ROUND(AVG(avg_duration_sec)) as daily_
average_duration_sec
FROM dwh_bikesharing.fact_trips_daily
GROUP BY trip_date;
```

3. What are the top five station names of starting stations with the longest trip duration?

```
CREATE VIEW dm_operational.top_5_station_by_longest_
duration
AS
SELECT trip_date,  station_name, sum_duration_sec
FROM dwh_bikesharing.fact_trips_daily
JOIN dwh_bikesharing.dim_stations
ON start_station_id = station_id
WHERE trip_date = '2018-01-02'
ORDER BY sum_duration_sec desc
LIMIT 5;
```

4. What are the top three region names that have the shortest total trip durations?

```
CREATE VIEW dm_operational.top_3_region_by_shortest_
duration
AS
SELECT trip_date, region_name, SUM(sum_duration_sec) as
total_sum_duration_sec
FROM dwh_bikesharing.fact_trips_daily
JOIN dwh_bikesharing.dim_stations
ON start_station_id = station_id
WHERE trip_date = '2018-01-02'
GROUP BY trip_date, region_name
ORDER BY total_sum_duration_sec asc
LIMIT 3;
```

And that's it. Congratulations on finishing all the steps! Let's summarize what we have covered in this whole chapter.

Summary

In this chapter, we've gone through a lot of practice in terms of how to use BigQuery to build a data warehouse. In general, we've covered the three main aspects of how to use the tools, how to load the data to BigQuery, and the data modeling aspect of a data warehouse.

By following all the steps in this chapter, you will have a better understanding of the data life cycle and you will understand that data moves from place to place. We also practiced the ELT process in this chapter, extracting data from the MySQL database, loading it to BigQuery, and doing some transformations to answer business questions. And on top of that, we did it all on a fully managed service in the cloud, spending zero time worrying about any infrastructure aspects.

By way of a footnote for this chapter, I want to remind you that, even though we have covered the common practice of using BigQuery, we haven't covered all of its features. There are a lot of other features in BigQuery that are worth checking; for example, the partitioned table, the clustered table, the materialized view, the WITH query statement, the streaming insert, machine mearning, and many other cool features besides.

We will cover some of these in later chapters, but not all of them. If you are new to BigQuery, I recommend you focus on the practice, not the features and capabilities.

Why? In my experience, the best way to learn is when you face the issues and find solutions for them. To be able to face the issue, you need to practice more, rather than spend more time knowing all the features without any context.

This chapter is the foundation of data engineering in GCP. GCS and BigQuery are the most important services in GCP. Both products are easy to learn, but understanding how to use them properly by means of extensive practice is very important.

In later chapters, we will almost always use GCS and BigQuery as our underlying storage. For example, in the next chapter, we will start thinking about how to automate our data loading. In this chapter, we used a Python script and manually triggered the script to load the daily data. In the next chapter, we will use Cloud Composer, an Airflow-managed service for automating those processes. But the two are essentially the same, both using GCS and BigQuery as the underlying data storage.

Exercise – Scenario 3

As a final activity in this chapter, you can do a self-assessment exercise to solve an additional business question from business users. Our operational user from scenario 2 wants to ask this additional question:

Show me the top three regions that have the most female riders as of the most recent date (2018-01-02).

Because the gender of members is not yet included in our fact and dimension table, you need to create a different fact and dimension table for this.

Remember that the data model is subjective, especially in the Kimball method. There is no right or wrong answer to the question. As we've discussed in this chapter, everyone can have different data models to represent the real world.

Try to solve it yourself and compare it to the solution in the Git code example:

- `Chapter-3\code\bigquery_self_excercise_create_dim_table_regions.py`

- `Chapter-3\code\bigquery_self_excercise_create_fact_table_daily_by_gender_region.py`

- `chapter-3\code\bigquery_self_excercise_query_answer.sql`

See also

- Kimball data model:

  ```
  https://www.kimballgroup.com/data-warehouse-business-
  intelligence-resources/kimball-techniques/dimensional-
  modeling-techniques/
  ```

- BigQuery features:

  ```
  https://cloud.google.com/bigquery#section-10
  ```

4

Building Orchestration for Batch Data Loading Using Cloud Composer

The definition of *orchestration* is a set of configurations to automate tasks, jobs, and their dependencies. If we are talking about database orchestration, we talk about how to automate the table creation process.

The main objects in any database system are tables, and one of the main differences between an application database and a data warehouse is the creation of tables. Compared to tables in application databases, where tables are mostly static and created to support applications, tables in data warehouses are dynamic. Tables are products, collections of business logic, and data flows.

In this chapter, we will learn how to orchestrate our data warehouse tables from *Chapter 3, Building a Data Warehouse in BigQuery*. We will learn how to automate the table creations using a **Google Cloud Platform** (**GCP**) service called **Cloud Composer**. This will include how to create a new Cloud Composer environment, how it works, and what are the best practices to develop the orchestration using it.

Learning Cloud Composer is relatively easy and you may find out that you can already create an automatic scheduler for our tables in BigQuery in the early pages of this chapter, but the challenge is how we can improve our orchestration jobs to handle common data pipeline issues. Issues that usually happen are data duplication, handling task dependencies, managing connections, handling late data, and many other issues that we will discuss in this chapter.

The approach of this chapter is different from *Chapter 3, Building a Data Warehouse in BigQuery*. Instead of using multiple scenarios, we will do multiple levels of exercises. The goal is for you to understand orchestration maturity step by step. It means that we won't jump to the best orchestration directly from the beginning, because you may find that very confusing. Instead, we will start from the very basics, and little by little improve the code to apply common best practices in Cloud Composer. These are the main topics of this chapter:

- Introduction to Cloud Composer
- Understanding the working of Airflow
- Provisioning Cloud Composer in a GCP project
- Exercise: Build data pipeline orchestration using Cloud Composer

Technical requirements

For this chapter's exercises, we will need the following:

- A Cloud Composer environment
- A Cloud SQL instance
- A **Google Cloud Storage** (**GCS**) bucket
- BigQuery datasets
- Cloud Shell
- A code editor
- Example code and data from `https://github.com/PacktPublishing/Data-Engineering-with-Google-Cloud-Platform/tree/main/chapter-4`

Steps on how to access, create, or configure the technical requirements will be provided later in each exercise.

Introduction to Cloud Composer

Cloud Composer is an Airflow-managed service in GCP. Using Cloud Composer, we don't need to think about the infrastructure, installation, and software management for the Airflow environment. With this, we can focus only on the development and deployment of our data pipeline.

From the perspective of a data engineer, there is almost no difference between Cloud Composer and Airflow. When we learn how to use Cloud Composer, practically we learn how Airflow works.

Now, what is Airflow? Airflow is an open source workflow management tool. What is unique in Airflow is that we use a Python script to manage our workflows.

There are some elements we need to look at from the previous statement. Let's break down the statement into more detail. When talking about workflow management tools, there are three main components here, as follows:

- **Handling task dependencies**
- **Scheduler**
- **System integration**

As a workflow management tool, Airflow will handle the chain of tasks. Let's take a kitchen workflow as an example. If we want to cook pasta, here are the tasks:

1. Prepare the ingredients.
2. Cook the pasta.
3. Serve it on plates.

Each task has a specific output and each task depends on the other, forming a chain of tasks. In Airflow, tasks work the same—each task will have a specific output and may have dependencies on the other tasks that we need to manage.

The second element is the scheduler. If we really love pasta, we might want to cook it every day for breakfast. Then, for example, the order of tasks can be scheduled every day at 5:00 A.M. The same thing in Airflow—each task's dependencies can be scheduled, and Airflow is built for this purpose. Every Airflow feature is made for scheduled tasks rather than a one-time job runner. Back to the kitchen example, it's not about a one-time experimental cooking experience—it's about cooking routines every day.

The third element is system integration. Each task might need integration with tools. Here's an example:

1. Preparing ingredients requires integration with a set of knives.

2. Cooking pasta requires a stove and pans.

3. Serving the pasta requires plates.

In Airflow, each task needs specific tools to run. Tools can be **GCS**, **BigQuery**, **Python**, **Bash scripts**, **an email application programming interface (API)**, and any other services. In the next section, we will learn much more about these tools and how Airflow works.

Understanding the working of Airflow

Airflow handles all three of the preceding elements using Python scripts. As data engineers, what we need to do is to code in Python for handling the task dependencies, schedule our jobs, and integrate with other systems. This is different from traditional **extract, transform, load** (ETL) tools. If you have ever heard of or used tools such as `Control-M`, `Informatica`, `Talend`, or many other ETL tools, Airflow has the same positioning as these tools. The difference is Airflow is not a **user interface** (UI)-based drag and drop tool. Airflow is designed for you to write the workflow using code.

There are a couple of good reasons why managing the workflow using code is a good idea compared to the drag and drop tools. Here's why we should do this:

*   Using code, you can automate a lot of development and deployment processes.

*   Using code, it's easier for you to enable good testing practices.

*   All the configurations can be managed in a `git` repository.

Let's take a look at this example Airflow Python script:

```
dag = DAG('packt_dag', start_date=datetime(2021, 6, 12))
first_task = DummyOperator(task_id='task_1')
second_task = DummyOperator(task_id='task_2')
third_task = DummyOperator(task_id='task_3')


task_1>> task_2>> task_3
```

This is a very simple example of how we will define the three main workflow components.

Every single workflow in Airflow is called a **directed acyclic graph (DAG)**. A DAG is a collection of tasks that are chained together with their dependencies.

In the first line of the preceding code snippet, you can see that we define a DAG in Python code, named `packt_dag`. The `packt_dag` DAG will run starting from June 6, 2021, and this is a part of how we **schedule** the DAG later.

In the second to fourth lines, you can see we define three `DummyOperator` tasks. This is the **system integration** part of our workflow. Airflow uses operators as interfaces to other systems; for example, later, we will use the GCS and BigQuery operators. Not only for GCP-related products, Airflow as an open source product also has operators for other systems such as MySQL, PostgreSQL, Oracle, email **Simple Mail Transfer Protocol (SMTP)**, and many more. This is one of the main advantages of using Airflow: it has a lot of operators available compared to other similar tools.

Now, in the last line, we can see unique Python syntax in Airflow called **bitshift operators**. These are the **jobs** or **tasks dependencies** part of our workflow. The >> syntax indicates the task directions; in the code example, it means `task_1` will start first, followed by `task_2`, and then `task_3`.

The preceding piece of code is the core of what we need to understand in Airflow, and we will learn more about this through practice in the later sections.

Before we continue, I want to quickly introduce you to a glossary of some Airflow terms. We will use the glossary presented here in our later discussions, so it's good to get a glimpse of what those terms are:

- **DAG**: Airflow terminology of a job configuration. A job configuration contains a collection of tasks, scheduling information, and dependencies.

- **DAG Run**: A DAG Run is a term for when a DAG is running. When you trigger or schedule a DAG to run, it is called a DAG Run.

- **Operator**: Operators are collections of connections to different systems. Airflow uses operators to define tasks.

We will repeat these three terms in a later section with a lot of examples, but at this point, it's good to know about them.

Provisioning Cloud Composer in a GCP project

In order to develop our Airflow code, we will need a Cloud Composer environment. In this section, we will create our first Cloud Composer environment using the GCP console.

Follow these steps to create our environment:

1. Go to the **GCP Console** navigation bar.

2. Find and click **Composer** under the **BIG DATA** section, as illustrated in the following screenshot:

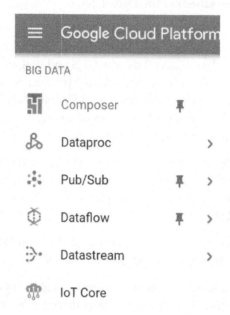

Figure 4.1 – Composer button in the navigation bar

3. After clicking **Composer** from the navigation bar, you may be asked to enable the API (if you have already enabled it, you can ignore this). After enabling the API, you will be on a new web page. We will call this web page **Cloud Composer Console**. Let's continue our steps.

4. Click **CREATE ENVIRONMENT – Composer 1** on the **Cloud Composer Console** webpage.

5. Choose your **Composer Environment** name.

6. Choose us-central1 for the location. You can choose any location, but as the default in this book, we will use the us-central1 region.

> **Important Note**
> You don't need to use Cloud Composer in the same regions as with BigQuery and GCS, but for networking reasons, it's a lot better if you do.

7. Choose 3 for the **Node count** option. Three is the minimum number of nodes for Cloud Composer.

8. Choose the `any` zone.

9. Choose the `n1-standard-1` machine type.

10. Input `20` for the disk size.

11. In the **Service account** field, choose any service account that you see in the option. That is your project default service account.

12. Choose `composer-1.16.6-airflow-1.10.15` for the **Image version** option.

> **Important Note**
>
> The **Image version** option may or may not be there when you read this book. Google might update the version and this version might no longer be there. In that case, `composer-1.x.x-airflow-1.10.X` is generally better to ensure compatibility with examples in this book. When the book was written, Airflow was in progress to be upgraded to the major release, Airflow 2.0.

13. Choose 3 for the Python version.

14. Keep the other options blank or default.

15. Before clicking **CREATE**, let's talk about the expected cost for this environment.

The Cloud Composer cost is based on the cluster hours, which means that if you create an environment for 7 hours for 1 day, you will be billed for those 7 hours. Cloud Composer is not billed based on individual usage—for example, you won't be billed by the number of DAGs or tasks that you have in a day.

So, in our exercise, it depends on how fast you can finish your exercises in this chapter. Let's take an example—if you think that you will finish this chapter in 7 days, then it means the cost is 7 days * cost/24 hours. Cost/24 hours is around **United States dollars (USD)** $2.

So, this means that the total Cloud Composer cost for 7 days is $14. I highly suggest you create a cluster for the exercise in this chapter, and if you are still under the $300 GCP free tier, the total cost is totally reasonable.

Now, back to the GCP console, and let's create our Cloud Composer environment by clicking the **CREATE** button. If successful, your Airflow environment will be ready for you. In the next section, we will learn how to run through the Airflow UI.

Introducing the Airflow web UI

Let's learn about the Airflow web UI. You can access the Airflow web UI from the **Cloud Composer Console** webpage by clicking **Airflow** under the **Airflow webserver** column, as shown in the following screenshot:

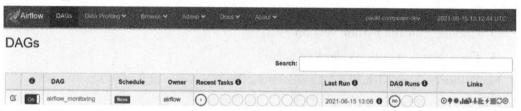

Figure 4.2 – Finding the Airflow button under the Airflow webserver column

Clicking the button will open a new browser tab opening the Airflow web UI. In the UI, you will see a pretty simple and blank web page. The page will list down all of our DAGs on the main page, and as an example, it will come up with one example DAG called `airflow_monitoring`, as follows:

Figure 4.3 – Airflow main UI

As our first step, let's click the `airflow_monitoring` DAG. This will bring up the following **DAG** page:

Figure 4.4 – Airflow DAG page

I have to say that it will be very confusing as a first-time user to see this page. This **DAG** page will show you a lot of useful but scattered information. I have generalized it into three main information categories, as follows:

- Task dependencies
- DAG Runs
- DAG code

For checking task dependencies, you can choose two visualization options, **Tree View** and **Graph View**. Since the `airflow_monitoring` DAG only has one task, it won't show you any dependencies, but later in our exercise, your task dependencies will look like this in **Tree View**:

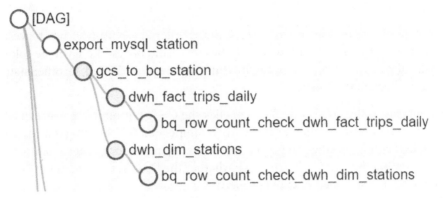

Figure 4.5 – DAG dependencies in Tree View

It shows the task orders from top to bottom as bullet points. This will be very useful for monitoring our DAG Runs. In **Graph View**, you can see better task dependencies. Each box is a task, and each arrow represents the dependencies, like this:

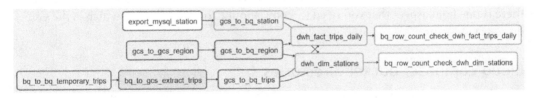

Figure 4.6 – DAG dependencies in Graph View

For me, **Graph View** is better for explaining the task dependencies, but for DAG monitoring purposes, **Tree View** is better.

Now, back to **Tree View**, you will see something like this on the right of your screen. It's a combination of small circles, squares, and times:

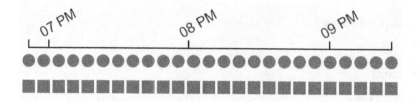

Figure 4.7 – DAG Run indicators

This is unique to Airflow and a very important feature. One circle represents one DAG Run at a specific time, and it will be listed horizontally for the other DAG Runs ordered by the execution time.

At the bottom of the circles, there is a row of boxes ordered vertically. A box represents a single task in a DAG Run. On top of both the circles and boxes, there will be colors. The colors will tell you the status, which can be **Running**, **Success**, **Failed**, or other statuses that you can check in the legend.

Last but not least is the DAG code. You can click the **Code** button. Here, you can see the actual DAG code for this particular DAG. This is important for checking quickly what the DAG is doing without needing to go to the source code repository, and sometimes I use this after updating the DAG code, to check whether the DAG is running the correct code version in case it hasn't been updated properly.

After seeing the task flows, you might be wondering: *Can we create a DAG using the UI?* The answer is no. Airflow is not built as a drag and drop tool. As we've discussed in the previous sections, we will use Python to create a DAG. And for creating a DAG using code, we won't use the UI either. We will need to code in our own environment and submit the DAG to Cloud Composer. We will do that in our exercise, but before that, there is one final aspect that you need to know about Cloud Composer, which is the GCS directory structure.

Cloud Composer bucket directories

Cloud Composer has specific folders in the GCS bucket for airflow management—for example, all of our DAG code is the result of a Python file in the `gs://{composer-bucket}/dags` directory. If you open this directory, you will find the `airflow_monitoring.py` file.

That /dags directory is very important for our development. In practice, you can develop your Airflow DAG in any environment—for example, from your laptop using your favorite **integrated development environment** (**IDE**) or using Cloud Editor. But at the end of the day, the Python file needs to be stored in this directory. By uploading the correct DAG file to this directory, Airflow will automatically schedule and run your DAG based on your configuration, and you can see the DAG in the UI.

To summarize, your Airflow web UI will only be your monitoring dashboard, but the actual code will be in the Cloud Composer GCS bucket. Here is a list of important GCS bucket directories for our development:

GCS directories	Mapped Local Directory	Usage
gs://{composer-bucket}/dags	/home/airflow/gcs/dags	DAGs
gs://{composer-bucket}/plugins	/home/airflow/gcs/plugins	Airflow plugins
gs://{composer-bucket}/data	/home/airflow/gcs/data	Workflow-related data
gs://{composer-bucket}/logs	/home/airflow/gcs/logs	Airflow task logs

Figure 4.8 – Table of GCS directories used by Cloud Composer

Keep all this information in mind for now. You might have missed some of the concepts, terminologies, and ideas at this point, and that is fine. We will learn all of the important aspects when doing the exercises. So, make sure you've created your Cloud Composer environment so that we can start the exercise.

Exercise: Build data pipeline orchestration using Cloud Composer

We will continue our bike-sharing scenario from *Chapter 3, Building a Data Warehouse in BigQuery*.

This exercise will be divided into five different DAG levels. Each DAG level will have specific learning objectives, as follows:

- **Level 1**: Learn how to create a DAG and submit it to Cloud Composer.
- **Level 2**: Learn how to create a BigQuery DAG.

- **Level 3**: Learn how to use variables.

- **Level 4**: Learn how to apply task idempotency.

- **Level 5**: Learn how to handle late data.

It's important for you to understand that learning Airflow is as easy as learning Level 1 DAG, but as we go through each of the levels, you will see the challenges we may have in practicing it.

In reality, you can choose to follow all of the best practices or none of them—Airflow won't forbid you from doing that. Using this leveling approach, you can learn step by step from the simplest to the most complicated way of configuring a DAG. At the end of the chapter, you can choose which level you want to follow for your data engineering journey. And for that, let's start from Level 1.

Level 1 DAG – Creating dummy workflows

The main goal of the Level 1 DAG is for us to understand how to create a DAG using Python, how timing in Airflow works, and how to handle task dependencies.

Please clone or download the example code here:

```
https://github.com/PacktPublishing/Data-Engineering-with-
Google-Cloud-Platform
```

If you haven't cloned the repository from *Chapter 3, Building a Data Warehouse in BigQuery*, please clone the repository from your Cloud Shell and check the code under the `chapter-4` directory.

For the Level 1 DAG example, please check out the code in this file:

```
https://github.com/PacktPublishing/Data-Engineering-with-
Google-Cloud-Platform/blob/main/chapter-4/code/level_1_dag.py
```

As a first step, we want to declare our DAG. The DAG will have information about the following:

1. DAG **identifier (ID)**

2. DAG owner

3. Schedule interval

4. Start date

The DAG code looks like this in Python:

```
args = {
    'owner': ' packt-developer ,
}
with DAG(
    dag_id='hello_world_airflow',
    default_args=args,
    schedule_interval='0 5 * * *',
    start_date=days_ago(1),
) as dag:
```

This is a very common DAG declaration in Airflow. Do remember that a DAG has three important pieces of information: the DAG ID, the time you want to start the DAG, and the interval—in other words, how you want to schedule the DAG. As a note, the DAG ID needs to be unique for the entire Airflow environment.

For `schedule_interval`, it follows the `CronJob` scheduling format. If you are not familiar with the `CronJob` format, it uses five numerical values that represent the following: minute, hour, day(month), month, and day(week).

An asterisk (`*`) means *every*. For example, `* * * * *` means the DAG will run every minute, while `0 1 * * *` means the DAG will run every day at 1:00 A.M.

You don't need to memorize this; you can check this website if you want to generate a `CronJob` format for your scheduled time: `https://crontab.guru/`.

The tricky part of the DAG is `start_date`. It's a little bit counter-intuitive if you're using Airflow for the first time, so here's an illustration of this:

Today is **January 1, 2021**, and I want to create a DAG that runs immediately today.

I want it to be scheduled every day at midnight (`0 0 * * *`).

What should I put as `start_date` in Airflow?

This is not the answer:

```
start_date=datetime(2021, 1, 1)
```

The correct answer is shown here:

```
start_date=datetime(2020, 12, 31)
```

Why? Airflow DAG runtime is a combination of both `start_date` and `schedule_interval`. So, if the start date is **January 1** and scheduled at **midnight**, Airflow will know that **midnight** on **January 1** has already passed, and will start the scheduler tomorrow, on **January 2** at **midnight**.

The same with our illustration—if we want the DAG to start immediately on **January 1**, we need to tell Airflow that the `start_date` value is supposed to be **December 31, 2020** or the day -1.

In the following code example, instead of using the exact date, we will use a `days_ago()` function:

```
days_ago(1)
```

This simply means that if you submit the DAG today for our exercise, the DAG will immediately run.

The other parameters in the DAG declaration are optional—for example, the DAG owner, handling task errors, and other parameters. We will skip these for now but you can find out more about them in the Airflow public documentation.

After learning about DAG, we will learn about **tasks** and **operators**. A DAG consists of one or many tasks. A task is declared using operators. As in our example code, we will use two `BashOperator` instances, and both operators will print words.

The first task will print `Hello` and the second task will print `World`, like this:

```
print_hello = BashOperator(
    task_id='print_hello',
    bash_command='echo Hello',
)


print_world= BashOperator(
    task_id='print_world',
    bash_command='echo World',
)
```

`BashOperator` is one of many operators that are available for Airflow. `BashOperator` is a simple operator for you to run Linux commands.

> **Important Note**
>
> Do not overuse `BashOperator`. If one day you do something too complicated using `BashOperator`, review and check the available native operator if available.

Every operator has a task ID and other parameters, and the parameters are different for each operator. You need to check two things to use operators: first, what are the available parameters; and second: how to import the operator. The Python library directory is not consistent, so you need to check from the public documentation. For example, for `BashOperator`, you need to import this:

```
from airflow.operators.bash_operator import BashOperator
```

Lastly, for the dependency, we will use a bitwise operator. Bitwise operators use `>>` to indicate task dependencies, like this:

```
print_hello >> print_world
```

A task can be dependent on more than one task—for example, if you want `task_three` to run after `task_one` and `task_two` have finished, you can do something like this:

```
[task_one, task_two] >> task_three
```

That's it—we've learned about DAGs, tasks, and dependencies. Check the full code example from the GitHub repository.

Now, let's deploy our DAG file into Cloud Composer.

Deploying the DAG file into Cloud Composer

To deploy our DAG Python file into Cloud Composer, we need to call the `gcloud` command from our Cloud Shell, as follows:

1. Go to Cloud Shell.
2. From Cloud Shell, go to your Python file directory that contains the DAG Python file.
3. Run the following `gcloud` command:

    ```
    gcloud composer environments storage dags import
    --environment [Your Cloud composer environment name]
    --location [Your Cloud composer region] --source [DAG
    Python file].py
    ```

As an example, this is my `gcloud` command:

```
gcloud composer environments storage dags import
--environment packt-composer-dev --location us-central1
--source level_1_dag.py
```

With that, you can check back to the Airflow web UI. A DAG called `hello_world_airflow` will be shown in the UI, as illustrated here:

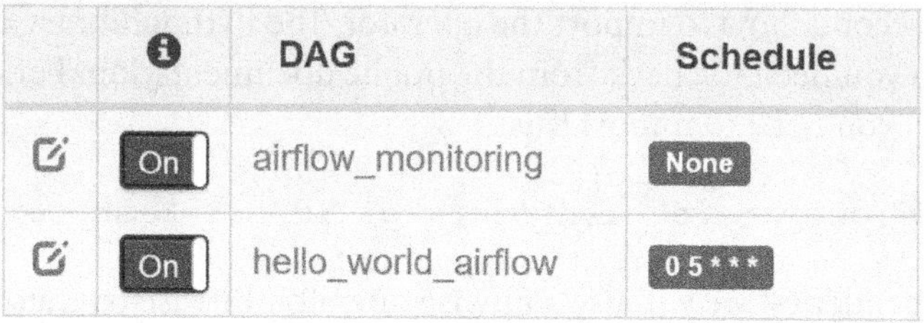

	❶	DAG	Schedule
✍	On	airflow_monitoring	None
✍	On	hello_world_airflow	0 5 * * *

Figure 4.9 – Checking hello_world_airflow DAG

You can also check in your GCS bucket by running the following code:

```
[your cloud composer GCS bucket]/dags/
```

Your DAG Python file is automatically stored in the directory. Every DAG Python file in this bucket directory will be automatically deployed as Airflow DAG and shown in the web UI by Airflow.

Automatically in here means that Airflow has a heartbeat checking for this directory. Airflow will detect any file changes in this directory and will affect the DAG without any additional steps needed.

This also applies to deletion. If you somehow delete a file inside this directory, your DAG will also be deleted, so don't do that. Instead, to delete a DAG properly, we will use the following `gcloud` command:

```
gcloud composer environments storage dags delete
    --environment [Your Cloud composer environment name]
    --location [Your Cloud composer region]
    [DAG Python file].py
```

After learning about deleting DAGs, we now want to learn some of the Airflow important buttons. To do that, let's carry out the following steps:

1. Go back to your Airflow web UI.

2. Click your `hello_world_airflow` DAG.

In our DAG Run indicator buttons, remember that we will have circle and square symbols. Notice that your indicators will be different than what's shown here, and that's fine. They'll be different because your DAG run date will depend on the time you spend running this exercise. For me, the indicators look like this:

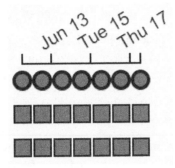

Figure 4.10 – Example DAG Run indicators

Now, let's click one of the circle buttons. One important option here is the **Clear** button. If you click it, you will notice the green color will turn bright green. This simply means your DAG will rerun.

If you click one of the square buttons, you will see many options, like this:

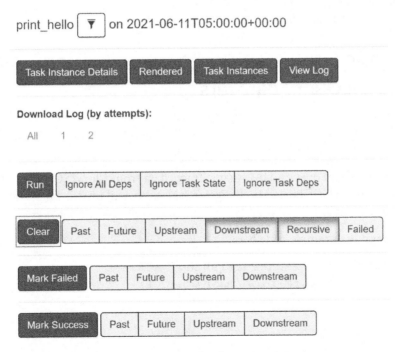

Figure 4.11 – Finding the Clear button on the task page

If you click the **Clear** button from here, your DAG will be retried or rerun at the task level, not the DAG level.

Another important button on this task level page is the **View Log** button. This will show you application-level logs from each independent task. This is very important, and you will need this a lot for the development and debugging of your code.

The log is independent for each task and DAG Run level, which means that if you already have more than one DAG Run and an error occurred on a specific date, you can check a specific log on that date in a particular task to see the error message.

If later you find an error and need to change your DAG Python file, what you need to do is the same as when creating a new one using the `gcloud` command.

And since in Airflow 1.x there is no DAG versioning, the best practice in a production environment is to label the DAG name with versions—for example, `hello_world_dag_v1`. This way, if you need to update your DAG, you will always create a new one labeled with a new version, and then delete the old one after the new version is stable.

Let's summarize what we've learned in this Level 1 exercise. In this exercise, we've learned about the basic features of Airflow. We've learned how to create a DAG with its tasks and dependencies. We deployed the DAG to Cloud Composer, and our `level_1` DAG will run on schedule, starting today. In the next exercise, we will learn how to use GCP native operators to do ELT from Cloud SQL to BigQuery.

Level 2 DAG – Scheduling a pipeline from Cloud SQL to GCS and BigQuery datasets

The main goal of the Level 2 DAG is for us to understand how to create a DAG specifically for doing ELT from the data source to GCS and BigQuery. GCP comes with its own native operators and is pre-installed in Cloud Composer.

In this exercise, we will create a DAG that extracts data from Cloud SQL to our GCS bucket, and from the GCS bucket to BigQuery tables. We will use the bike-sharing tables similar to our exercise in *Chapter 3, Building a Data Warehouse in BigQuery*.

Please check out the example code here:

```
https://github.com/PacktPublishing/Data-Engineering-with-
Google-Cloud-Platform/blob/main/chapter-4/code/level_2_dag.py
```

In this exercise, we will need a Cloud SQL instance to demonstrate extraction using Airflow. The Cloud SQL instance and table that we need are totally the same as what we did in *Chapter 3, Building a Data Warehouse in BigQuery*. So, if you haven't deleted Cloud SQL, you can skip this step. But if you already deleted the instance, please revisit *Chapter 3, Building a Data Warehouse in BigQuery*, and go to the *Creating a MySQL database on Cloud SQL* section.

As a summary, this is what we need to do in the section:

1. Create a Cloud SQL instance.

2. Configure the Cloud SQL service account **identity and access management (IAM)** permission as `GCS Object Admin`.

3. Create a `stations` table from the MySQL console.

4. Import the `stations` table data from a **comma-separated values (CSV)** file.

    To check if you are ready with the instance, run this query from your MySQL console:

    ```
    SELECT * FROM apps_db.stations LIMIT 10;
    ```

    The table should be accessible and contain data, as illustrated in the following screenshot:

```
mysql> SELECT * FROM apps_db.stations LIMIT 10;
+------------+-------------------------------------------------+-----------+----------+
| station_id | name                                            | region_id | capacity |
+------------+-------------------------------------------------+-----------+----------+
| 501        | Balboa Park (San Jose Ave at Sgt. John V. Young Ln |         |        0 |
| 504        | Onondaga Ave at Alemany Blvd                    |           |        0 |
| 505        | Geneva Ave at Moscow St                         |           |        0 |
```

Figure 4.12 – Expected result from MySQL table

If you are already in this state, you are good to go to the next steps. The next steps are given here:

- Using a Cloud SQL operator to extract data to a GCS bucket

- Using GCS storage for a BigQuery operator

- Using `BigQueryOperator` for data transformation

In the next step, we will use an operator to extract data from our Cloud SQL database.

Using a Cloud SQL operator to extract data to a GCS bucket

If in the Level 1 DAG exercise we used `BashOperator`, in this Level 2 DAG, we will use GCP-specific operators. And for extracting data from Cloud SQL, we can use `CloudSqlInstanceExportOperator`.

We can import the operator in Python, like this:

```
from airflow.contrib.operators.gcp_sql_operator import
CloudSqlInstanceExportOperator
```

To declare the task, the code will look like this. The operator has a few parameters that we need to provide—the Cloud SQL project ID, the Cloud SQL instance name, and the body:

```
    sql_export_task = CloudSqlInstanceExportOperator(
project_id=GCP_PROJECT_ID,
body=export_body,
instance=INSTANCE_NAME,
task_id='sql_export_task'
    )
```

The body will contain information about how you want to extract your data. We can define the body using **JavaScript Object Notation (JSON)**. In this exercise, we will export the CSV file to our GCS bucket directory. The code looks like this:

```
EXPORT_URI = 'gs://[your GCS bucket]/mysql_export/from_
composer/stations/stations.csv'


SQL_QUERY = "SELECT * FROM apps_db.stations"


export_body = {
    "exportContext": {
        "fileType": "csv",
        "uri": EXPORT_URI,
        "csvExportOptions":{
            "selectQuery": SQL_QUERY
        }
    }
}
```

The operator parameters are pretty straightforward. If later we run the DAG, this task will export data from your Cloud SQL operator to the GCS bucket. Let's continue to the next step: loading data from GCS to BigQuery.

Using GCS storage for a BigQuery operator

To load data from a GCS bucket to a BigQuery table, we will use `GoogleCloudStorageToBigQueryOperator`. You can import the operator in Python, like this:

```
from airflow.contrib.operators.gcs_to_bq import
GoogleCloudStorageToBigQueryOperator
```

This operator has some parameters that we need to provide, but if you look at it, you will notice that the parameters are actually similar to the BigQuery Python API that we worked with in *Chapter 3*, *Building a Data Warehouse in BigQuery*.

You need to define the source bucket, source objects, the table schema, write disposition, and other parameters that are available in the BigQuery Python API.

So, to load our `stations` table to BigQuery, we can define a task like this:

```
    gcs_to_bq_example = GoogleCloudStorageToBigQueryOperator(
    task_id                            = "gcs_to_bq_example",
    bucket                             = 'packt-data-eng-on-
gcp-data-bucket',
    source_objects                     = ['mysql_export/from_
composer/stations/stations.csv'],
    destination_project_dataset_table  ='raw_bikesharing.
stations',
    schema_fields=[
        {'name': 'station_id', 'type': 'STRING', 'mode':
'NULLABLE'},
        {'name': 'name', 'type': 'STRING', 'mode': 'NULLABLE'},
        {'name': 'region_id', 'type': 'STRING', 'mode':
'NULLABLE'},
        {'name': 'capacity', 'type': 'INTEGER', 'mode':
'NULLABLE'}
    ],
    write_disposition='WRITE_TRUNCATE'
    )
```

The output of this task is that a BigQuery table will be created in the target dataset with the station data in it. With this, we covered the EL part of ELT. Next, we want to do some transformation inside BigQuery using `BigQueryOperator`.

Using BigQueryOperator for data transformation

To transform our table, we will use `BigQueryOperator`. Using `BigQueryOperator`, you can trigger a query and load it to a target table. You can import the operator in Python, like this:

```
from airflow.contrib.operators.bigquery_operator import
BigQueryOperator
```

As an example, do a very simple aggregation to our `stations` table. We will count the number of records in our `stations` table from the `raw_bikesharing` dataset and store it in the `dwh_bikesharing.temporary_stations_count` table. The code will look like this:

```
bq_to_bq  = BigQueryOperator(
    task_id                    = "bq_to_bq",
    sql                        = "SELECT count(*) as count
FROM `raw_bikesharing.stations`",
    destination_dataset_table  = 'dwh_bikesharing.
temporary_stations_count',
    write_disposition          = 'WRITE_TRUNCATE',
    create_disposition         = 'CREATE_IF_NEEDED',
    use_legacy_sql             = False,
    priority                   = 'BATCH'
)
```

I want to highlight three points in this task. The first is the `use_legacy_sql` parameter. The `use_legacy_sql` parameter in default will be set to `True`, so you need to always state `use_legacy_sql = False` to use `BigQueryOperator`. If you are not familiar with BigQuery Legacy SQL, it's literally just a legacy language in BigQuery that you shouldn't use today. What we use today and going forward is called *standard SQL*. So, make sure to set `legacy_sql` to `False` in this operator.

The second point is the priority—the priority default value is `INTERACTIVE`. This is quite risky for our pipeline. If you check in the quota page in the BigQuery public documentation (`https://cloud.google.com/bigquery/quotas`), it states *Concurrent rate limit for interactive queries — 100 concurrent queries*. Interactive queries are also literally meant for interactive queries—or in other words, ad hoc queries by humans from the BigQuery console. Your ETL jobs will face issues when you have more than 100 DAG Runs running BigQuery operators at a time, but it won't happen using `BATCH` priority, so always set the priority value to `BATCH`.

The third point is the `sql` parameter. The `sql` parameter in `BigQueryOperator` widely opens many possibilities. Notice that you can write any **Structured Query Language (SQL)** statement in this operator, such as `CREATE TABLE`, `UPDATE`, `INSERT`, `DELETE`, `CREATE VIEW`, and any other SQL operations. Even if you can, my suggestion is don't. The common usage pattern for this operator is to declare the transformation logic in the `sql` parameter and load the data to the destination table. Using this pattern will handle the table creation and data insertion. If you want to delete the table, there will be a specific operator for that: `bigquery_table_delete_operator`.

After running the preceding task in our DAG, we will have a new `dwh_bikesharing.temporary_stations_count` table.

And with that, we will have a complete ELT process from data source to BigQuery with transformation. To chain the task dependencies, let's use the bitwise operator by writing it in our DAG Python file, as follows:

```
sql_export_task >> gcs_to_bq_example >> bq_to_bq
```

Try to construct the code as a DAG Python file and check with the full example in our GitHub repository:

`https://github.com/PacktPublishing/Data-Engineering-with-Google-Cloud-Platform/blob/main/chapter-4/code/level_2_dag.py`

Deploy the DAG to Cloud Composer and check if the DAG is running successfully. As an example, this is my `gcloud` command that I call from Cloud Shell:

```
gcloud composer environments storage dags import
--environment packt-composer-dev --location us-central1
--source level_2_dag.py
```

If there are any errors, you can check the red indicators and the DAG or task levels, check the logs, and review the steps in this section.

Sometimes, the Cloud SQL extract task will fail because of parallel tasks running at the same time. If you found that issue, try to rerun the failed DAG Run. Remember that you just need to click the red circle indicator, then find the **CLEAR** button. The entire DAG Run will be rerun after that.

Things to be avoided in BigQuery DAG

In this Level 2 DAG exercise, you might already have a good understanding of how to use Airflow for BigQuery. You can use Airflow for loading, transforming, or maybe later to export BigQuery data to other storage.

Even though the code is simple and straightforward, using Python as a configuration file is very risky, in the sense that you can do literally anything in the Airflow DAG using Python.

An extreme case would be to call a **machine learning** (**ML**) library or `matplotlib` in the DAG Python file and run it in the DAG as a Python application. This doesn't make sense since it's an extreme example.

But surprisingly, I found out there are common bad practices that people do when using Python for Airflow DAG. Let's talk about that next.

Avoid using the BigQuery Python library

In the DAG Python file, you can import the BigQuery Python library to load data to BigQuery—for example, like this:

```
from google.cloud import bigquery
client = bigquery.Client()
. . .
query_job = client.query(sql, job_config=job_config)
```

Even if you can, don't. Always use the BigQuery native operators for any BigQuery actions, even though under the hood, both are using operators or using BigQuery Python clients calling the same BigQuery API. There are three main considerations that mean you should only use the operators, outlined as follows:

- Your code will be simpler, standardized, and easy to read as a configuration.

- The operators handle the BigQuery client connections for you.

- The operators will handle the logging for you.

Remember that in Airflow, we use Python for DAG configuration, not to code applications. In this case, standardization and simplicity are very important.

Avoid downloading data to Cloud Composer

Using Python, you can download data from any database or storage. For our example in this exercise, you can download data from a MySQL database, GCS files, and BigQuery. For example, in the DAG Python code, if you ignore the previous recommendation, you can call the GCS client and download files, like this:

```
from google.cloud import storage
storage_client = storage.Client()
. . .
blob.download_to_filename(destination_file_name)
```

The same thing can happen for MySQL and BigQuery. Even if you can, don't.

You don't want to download the files to Cloud Composer workers in general. Cloud Composer and Airflow are not storage systems. What happens if you download files in the DAG Python script is that it will download to the underlying **virtual machine (VM)** hard disks, which are limited, and you don't want that.

Another common example is to load a BigQuery table to a pandas DataFrame in Python. Even though it's not downloading the data to the hard-disk level, loading data to pandas means it will download the table to the workers' memories. In both scenarios, you may have a Cloud Composer issue such as **out-of-memory or hard disk full errors** for all of your DAGs.

Avoid processing data in Python

Airflow is an orchestration tool. The main responsibility of an orchestration tool is to trigger jobs and let other system process the job. This is a special case of using Airflow for orchestrating big data.

What does this mean? Similar to the previous recommendation, one bad practice that might happen is to process big data in Cloud Composer workers. For example, you might be tempted to process data from BigQuery or GCS quickly using pandas for its simplicity, and an Airflow DAG allows you to do that.

But never do that for big data. The Cloud Composer workers won't be powerful enough to process the data volume.

In this exercise, we learned how to do a proper ELT process using GCP native operators. We've learned that every GCP service has native operators in Airflow, and for each service, there are specific operators for each task operation. For example, in BigQuery, you can use GCS to `BigQueryOperator` to load data, `BigQueryOperator` for transforming tables, and `BigQueryDelete` for deleting tables.

Using the native operators will help you simplify your DAG Python code, and on top of that, you will avoid carrying out bad practices that may happen in Airflow.

At this point, you can use the Level 2 DAG code to do any data loading to BigQuery for your needs, but we can improve the code for implementing more best practices for data loading to BigQuery. For that, we will practice Level 3 DAG.

Level 3 DAG – Parameterized variables

The main goal of the Level 3 DAG is for us to load the other tables for our bike-sharing tables. When loading more than one table, we might realize there are variables that we can parameterize to improve our DAG code. Also, in this exercise, we need to start paying more attention to the table time, since we will load trip data that has time information in it.

Please check out the example code here:

```
https://github.com/PacktPublishing/Data-Engineering-with-
Google-Cloud-Platform/blob/main/chapter-4/code/level_3_dag.py
```

In addition, we will also use JSON schema files for our BigQuery tables, which you can obtain from here:

```
https://github.com/PacktPublishing/Data-Engineering-with-
Google-Cloud-Platform/tree/main/chapter-4/code/schema
```

You can check the `level_3_dag.py` code to get familiar with it, but at this point, you don't need to deploy the DAG because before continuing the practice, we will learn some fundamental concepts and Cloud Composer features in the next section.

Understanding types of variables in Cloud Composer

In the Level 2 DAG exercise, we have some variables that are hardcoded in the DAG script—for example, `GCP_PROJECT_ID`, `INSTANCE_NAME`, `EXPORT_URI`, and `SQL_QUERY`.

Imagine in a scenario that you already have a pipeline running in your current Cloud Composer project. Your infrastructure team says that you need to migrate your Cloud Composer cluster to another project for some reason. What do you need to do?

You will need to move all the DAG code from the GCS bucket to the new project. But don't forget that because the variable is hardcoded, you need to change all the `GCP_PROJECT_ID` variables manually one by one for each script.

Are there any better ways to do that? Yes—using variables.

We have three options for declaring variables, as follows:

1. Environment variables
2. Airflow variables
3. DAG variables

DAG variables are variables that we already used, the variables that live in the DAG script, applicable only to the DAG.

The higher-level variables are Airflow variables. You can call Airflow variables from all of your DAG.

Let's create one by following these steps:

1. Go to Airflow web UI.
2. In the top menu bar, find and click **Admin | Variables**, as illustrated in the following screenshot:

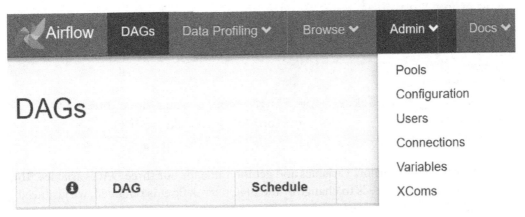

Figure 4.13 – Variables menu under the Admin bar

3. In the Airflow **Variables** page, let's create a new variable by clicking the **Create** button.
4. The variable is a key-value pair. In the key, input `level_3_dag_settings`.

5. In the **Val** value, input the following:

```
{"gcs_source_data_bucket":"packt-data-eng-on-gcp-data-
bucket", "bq_raw_dataset":"raw_bikesharing", "bq_dwh_
dataset":"dwh_bikesharing" }
```

In the example, we want to parameterize the GCS bucket name and BigQuery datasets. These variables might be helpful for other DAGs in the future, so defining these as Airflow variables is a good practice compared to DAG variables.

Notice that the value is defined as a JSON string. This is the recommendation compared to declaring each parameter as individual Airflow variables—for example, key: bq_dwh_dataset; value: dwh_bikesharing. It is not mandatory to follow this pattern, but it's better for Airflow performance. At the backend, Airflow has an internal application database. Every Airflow variable needs an independent database connection when we call it from a DAG. If we have too many variables, then we might open too many database connections for each DAG. If using the JSON, as we do in this example, we will only open one database connection for each DAG.

Now, in your DAG, you can call the variables, like this:

```
from airflow.models import Variable


# Airflow Variables
settings = Variable.get("level_3_dag_settings", deserialize_
json=True)


# DAG Variables
gcs_source_data_bucket = settings['gcs_source_data_bucket']
bq_raw_dataset          = settings['bq_raw_dataset']
bq_dwh_dataset          = settings['bq_dwh_dataset']
```

The code will call the Airflow variables and get the value for our three DAG variables. This way, if the GCS bucket needs to change or the BigQuery dataset is renamed, we just need to change the Airflow variable.

The last and broadest-level variables are environment variables. To set an environment variable, you can set it in the Cloud Composer UI. Follow this step to add one:

1. Go to the **Cloud Composer Console** webpage.

2. Choose your Cloud Composer environment—for example, mine is packt-composer-env.

3. Find the **ENVIRONMENT VARIABLES** button and click it.

4. Click **Edit**.

5. On the **Environment variables** page, click **ADD ENVIRONMENT VARIABLE**.

6. For **Input Name**, insert MYSQL_INSTANCE_NAME (all in uppercase).

7. For **Input Value**, insert mysql-instance (your Cloud SQL instance name).

8. Click **Save**.

Wait a couple of minutes. After finishing, the environment variables will be available for you.

To use it in your DAG, you can load the variables like this:

```
import os
# Environment Variables
gcp_project_id = os.environ.get('GCP_PROJECT')
instance_name  = os.environ.get('MYSQL_INSTANCE_NAME')
```

We use MYSQL_INSTANCE_NAME as a variable, and GCP_PROJECT. You will notice that you never added GCP_PROJECT in the previous step. This is because Cloud Composer already provides some default environment variables, and one of them is GCP_PROJECT. The variable will return the gcp project ID, where the Cloud Composer environment is located.

You will get the benefit of using environment variables when you need to declare the parameter with the DAG deployment. For example, in our gcloud command, you can input an environment variable as one of the arguments, like this:

```
gcloud beta composer environments create --env-
variables=['MYSQL_INSTANCE_NAME'='mysql_instance']
```

This way, you can adjust the variable each time you deploy a DAG.

In the next section, we will add macro variables, which are different from environment variables.

Introducing Airflow macro variables

Airflow macro variables are variables that return information about the DAG Run. For example, you can get the execution date, DAG ID, and task ID. You can see a full list of macros in the Airflow public documentation at the following link:

`https://airflow.apache.org/docs/apache-airflow/stable/macros-ref.html`

One variable that is essential for our data pipeline is the execution date. This is a very important and useful variable that you should use to build your data pipeline. To use the execution date in a DAG, you can use this code:

```
# Macros
execution_date = '{{ ds }}'
```

`{{ ds }}` is an Airflow macro. When you use that format in your DAG, Airflow will render into a value such as `'2021-06-19'`.

Now, let's understand better what the execution date is. In Airflow, remember that in a DAG, you declare two-time information: `start_date` and `schedule_interval`. The start date doesn't always mean the current date; the start date is the time when you expected the DAG to be run the first time. You can choose to use dates in the past, and that means Airflow will run the DAG from past dates.

For example, today is `2021-06-19`.

You define the `start_date` value in the DAG as `2021-06-01`.

Then, there are two different dates that you need to differentiate, as follows:

1. The real human world time at which the DAG runs
2. The expected time when you need the DAG to be run

The first one will be called the DAG start date, and the second one will be called the execution date.

If we set the schedule interval to run daily, starting from today, you will see in your DAG that your DAG start date is `2021-06-19`, but there will be 19 DAG Runs with 19 execution dates from `2021-06-01` to `2021-06-19`.

Back to our topic about the `execution_date` macro, in your DAG, you can use this variable to get your expected date value rather than today's date, which is very helpful for loading data from the past.

In my experience, I found that this concept is hard to digest the first time without really practicing it. So, at this point, just be aware that in the example code we will use Airflow macros such as this: {{ }}, and that means we want to use the DAG Run information for our operator parameters.

Loading bike-sharing tables using Airflow

After learning some new concepts, let's continue our code development. In the previous exercise, we created our tasks for loading the `stations` table. Next, we will create tasks for loading `regions` and `trips` tables.

The `regions` table will be loaded from a GCS bucket, and for the `trips` table, we will extract from the BigQuery public dataset this time. The DAG will look like this:

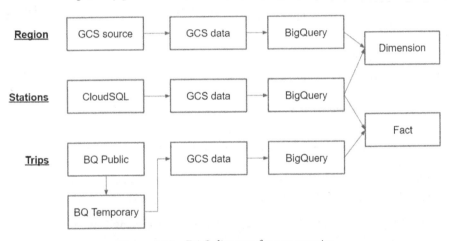

Figure 4.14 – DAG diagram for our exercise

To load regions data from GCS, we will use
`GoogleCloudStorageToGoogleCloudStorageOperator`. The code looks like this:

```
### Load Region Table ###
gcs_to_gcs_region =
GoogleCloudStorageToGoogleCloudStorageOperator(
        task_id              = 'gcs_to_gcs_region',
        source_bucket        = gcs_source_data_bucket,
        source_object        = gcs_regions_source_object,
        destination_bucket   = gcs_source_data_bucket,
        destination_object   = gcs_regions_target_object
)
```

The code will transfer data from one source to the destination object. The rest of the code is the same as for the `stations` table. Check the example code in the repository to review your code.

For the `trips` table, the case will be a little bit non-realistic here. We will load data from GCS to BigQuery, from the public dataset to our `raw_bikesharing` dataset. In reality, we can simply use `BigQueryOperator` to load the data in a single task. But for the purpose of our practice, we will see the BigQuery public dataset as an external database. So, we will extract the table from the public dataset to the GCS bucket and load data from the GCS bucket to our BigQuery dataset. The idea is that you can reuse this pattern if the data source is not BigQuery. You can apply the same pattern to data from different databases such as **Cloud SQL**, **Oracle**, **Hadoop**, or any other data source.

To do that, we will create a temporary BigQuery dataset to store `trips` daily data using the `bq` command. Follow these steps:

1. Open Cloud Shell.

2. Run this command in Cloud Shell:

```
bq --location=us mk \
--dataset \
[your gcp project id]:temporary_staging
```

3. In our DAG, we will add `BigQueryOperator` to extract the table to this temporary dataset, as follows:

```
bq_to_bq_temporary_trips = BigQueryOperator(
    task_id='bq_to_bq_temporary_trips',
    sql=f"""
        SELECT * FROM `bigquery-public-data.san_
francisco_bikeshare.bikeshare_trips`
        WHERE DATE(start_date) = DATE('{execution_date}')
        """,
    use_legacy_sql=False,
    destination_dataset_table=bq_temporary_table_id,
    write_disposition='WRITE_APPEND',
    create_disposition='CREATE_IF_NEEDED')
```

Notice that in the SQL query, we use the `{ execution_date }` variable. That's the variable from this line of code:

```
execution_date = '{{ ds }}'
```

The task will create a table in the `raw_bikesharing` dataset.

4. Lastly, we will store the temporary table in a GCS bucket, as follows:

```
bq_to_gcs_extract_trips = BigQueryToCloudStorageOperator(
task_id='bq_to_gcs_extract_trips',
source_project_dataset_table=bq_temporary_table_id,
destination_cloud_storage_uris=[gcs_trips_source_uri],
print_header=False,
export_format='CSV')
```

After this task, you will have your `trips` data in the GCS bucket, and the rest of the steps are similar to the other tables.

The other improvement that we can do in this Level 3 DAG example is to centralize our BigQuery schema in the GCS bucket. For example, in the Level 2 DAG example, we defined `schema_fields` hardcoded in the DAG code.

In the Level 3 DAG example, the schema is loaded from JSON files. In order to do that, follow these steps:

1. Check the table schema files from this directory:

```
/chapter-4/code/schema/*
```

2. Upload all the files into GCS in this specific bucket:

```
[Cloud Composer Bucket]/data/schema/*
```

For example, you can use the `gsutil` command from Cloud Shell, like this:

```
# gsutil -r cp /chapter-4/code/schema/* [Cloud Composer
Bucket]/data/schema/*
```

The command will copy the schema files from the Cloud Shell environment to the GCS bucket. If there is an error in your environment, check if you called the command in the correct directory. You should call the command from your `git` folder.

3. In the DAG code, we need to read the JSON file—for example, using the self-defined `read_json_schema` function. This function can be found in the `level_3_dag.py` example code.

4. Lastly, the schema in the DAG can be defined like this:

```
bq_trips_table_schema = read_json_schema("/home/airflow/
gcs/data/schema/trips_schema.json")
```

With this improvement, we learned two things. First, we learned that we can store files in the `[Cloud Composer Bucket]/data` directory and we can read the files from our DAG. Second, we can manage the schema better outside of the code, so if we want to change the table schema, we can update the JSON files instead of the DAG files.

Try to continue the code development yourself and check the example code in the GitHub repository to review.

Lastly, try to continue the tasks to the transformation step, by creating `fact_trips_daily` and `dim_stations` tables. The explanation and the SQL queries of both tables can be found in *Chapter 3*, *Building a Data Warehouse in BigQuery*, in the *Creating fact and dimension tables* section. For the DAG, as we've discussed, you can use `BigQueryOperator` to handle these tasks.

There is one more thing that I want to introduce in this Level 3 DAG example, which is `BigQueryCheckOperator`. `BigQueryCheckOperator` is an operator that will check if a condition is met by the query result or not. For example, we want to know if our `fact_trips_daily` table contains any records or not. We can add the operator, like this:

```
bq_row_count_check_dwh_fact_trips_daily =
BigQueryCheckOperator(
task_id='bq_row_count_check_dwh_fact_trips_daily',
sql=f"""
select count(*) from `{bq_fact_trips_daily_table_id}`
""",
use_legacy_sql=False)
```

The operator will trigger a query to BigQuery and check the `count(*)` value to the table. If the result is `0`, the task will fail, and your DAG will be marked as failed. This is a very simple check but is helpful for making sure your ELT process is successful downstream.

In the code, try to do the same thing with the `dim_stations` table. So, at the end of the DAG, we will have two checkers to make sure the table is loaded with records.

Handling dependencies for our bike-sharing tasks

To handle the task dependencies, as usual we will use bitwise operators. But since our tasks are a lot more complicated compared to the Level 2 DAG example, we will review how we should do that. Firstly, take a look at the full task dependency code:

```
export_mysql_station >> gcs_to_bq_station

gcs_to_gcs_region >> gcs_to_bq_region

bq_to_bq_temporary_trips >> bq_to_gcs_extract_trips >> gcs_to_
bq_trips


[gcs_to_bq_station,gcs_to_bq_region,gcs_to_bq_trips] >> dwh_
fact_trips_daily >> bq_row_count_check_dwh_fact_trips_daily


[gcs_to_bq_station,gcs_to_bq_region,gcs_to_bq_trips] >> dwh_
dim_stations >> bq_row_count_check_dwh_dim_stations
```

Our sets of tasks and the preceding bitwise instructions will generate this DAG:

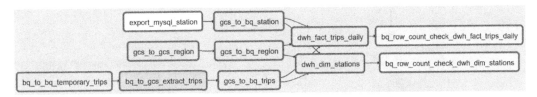

Figure 4.15 – DAG Graph View for trips and stations data

Notice that we introduce multiple task dependencies here. For example, `dwh_fact_trips_daily` and `dwh_dim_stations` will only start when all the `gcs_to_bq` tasks are finished. To do that, we use brackets, like this:

```
[gcs_to_bq_station,gcs_to_bq_region,gcs_to_bq_trips] >> dwh_
fact_trips_daily
```

This bitwise operator means that `dwh_fact_trips_daily` will only run after the three tasks in the bracket are finished.

In this exercise, we improved our DAG by utilizing variables. Variables are a very important element in Airflow. You will find using variables more and more important after creating many DAGs, tasks, and dependencies. Using variables allows you to think about automation. It's a very common practice to create DAG templates and think that you only need to change the variables, so this will be very helpful in speeding up your development time. Before continuing to our Level 4 DAG example, we need to understand the three Airflow features.

Understanding Airflow backfilling, rerun, and catchup

In a data pipeline, we often need to handle data from the past. This is a very common scenario in data engineering. Most of the time, applications as the data sources are created before a data lake or data warehouse, so we need to load data from the past. There are three main terms related to this.

The first one is **backfilling**. Backfilling happens when you need to load data from the past.

For illustration, imagine in a real-life scenario you already run a data pipeline for *7 days* starting from 2021-01-01, without any issue. For some reason, your end user asked you to also load data from 2020-12-01. This is a backfilling scenario. In this case, you need to load the historical data without changing or disturbing your running data pipeline, as illustrated in the following diagram:

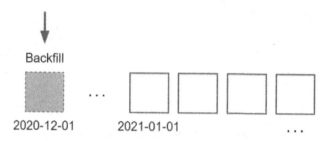

Figure 4.16 – Backfill illustration

In Cloud Composer, you can run backfilling using the gcloud command, like this:

```
gcloud composer environments run \ ${your_composer_environment_
name} \
--location [your composer environment region] \
backfill -- -s [your backfill start date] \
-e [your backfill end date] [your dag id]
```

If you run the preceding command, Airflow will trigger DAG Runs for the given date. Remember our section about using Airflow macros for getting the `execution_date` variable? The `execution_date` variable will return the backfill date.

The second one is a **rerun**. A rerun happens when you need to reload data from the past. The difference between a rerun and a backfill is that a rerun works for a DAG or tasks that have run before. The scenario of using a rerun is when a DAG or tasks have failed, so you need to rerun them, as illustrated in the following diagram:

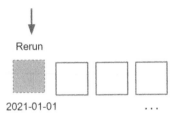

Figure 4.17 – Rerun illustration

You can trigger a rerun from the Airflow web UI. In the web UI, if you click **Clear** in either the DAG or task indicator (in the DAG **Tree View**), the DAG or task will retry, and that's what we call a rerun. A second option is using the `gcloud` command, like this:

```
gcloud composer environments run \
 [your composer environment name] \
   --location [your composer environment region] \
 clear -- [your dag id] -t [your tasks id or regex] -s \
 [your start date] -d [your end date]
```

The command will trigger a rerun of the specific DAG and tasks.

The third one is a **catchup**. A catchup happens when you deploy a DAG for the first time. A catchup is a process when Airflow automatically triggers multiple DAG Runs to load all expected date data. It's similar to a backfill, but the trigger happens automatically as intended, as illustrated in the following diagram:

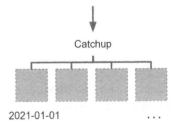

Figure 4.18 – Catchup illustration

For example, today is 2021-01-07.

You declare the start_date value of a DAG is 2021-01-01.

When you deploy the first time, there will be seven DAG Runs automatically running: 2021-01-01 to 2021-01-07.

The preceding scenario is by default how Airflow works for your DAG, but you can disable that behavior. You can set the catchup to False in your DAG declaration—for example, like this:

```
with DAG(
    dag_id='example_dag',
    start_date=datetime(2021, 1, 1),
    catchup=False
) as dag:
```

If you set the catchup parameter to False in your DAG, the catchup won't run.

These three Airflow features are very important and highly relevant to real-world scenarios. Whether you are in the development phase or in production mode, you will use these features.

Back to our Level 3 DAG exercise. If a rerun happens to our DAG, there will be an issue with the current code. Why?

Take a look at our GCS-to-BigQuery task for the trips table:

```
gcs_to_bq_trips = GoogleCloudStorageToBigQueryOperator(
. . .
destination_project_dataset_table   = bq_trips_table_id,
schema_fields                       = bq_trips_table_schema,
write_disposition                   ='WRITE_APPEND'
)
```

See that in our write_disposition parameter, the task will write append the target table with data from the source every time the DAG runs. This is fine only if the DAG runs once for every execution_date parameter. What will happen if we rerun the DAG at any date? The data will be duplicated.

A good task in a DAG is a task that can run and produce the same result every time it runs, and there is a term for this: **task idempotency**.

We will learn how to make sure the task in our DAG code is idempotent for the Level 4 DAG exercise.

Level 4 DAG – Guaranteeing task idempotency in Cloud Composer

The main goal of the Level 4 DAG is to make sure that our tasks are idempotent. More specifically, we will modify our tasks for loading `trips` tables, to make sure there will be no duplication when we rerun the DAG.

Please download the example code from here:

`https://github.com/PacktPublishing/Data-Engineering-with-Google-Cloud-Platform/blob/main/chapter-4/code/level_4_dag.py`

Understanding what task idempotency means

Let's understand more about the task idempotency by way of illustration in the BigQuery table.

Let's say we have a DAG; the DAG will load an `event` table from GCS to BigQuery.

The expected start date is `2021-01-01`.

The current date is `2021-01-03`.

The schedule interval is `daily`.

In this scenario, if we use the `WRITE_APPEND` method, the files from GCS bucket directories will be loaded to BigQuery tables. For an illustration of this, check out the following diagram:

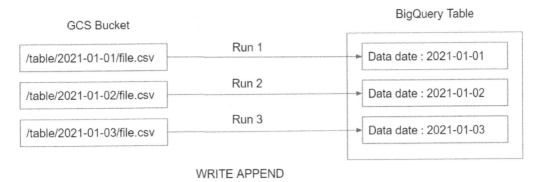

Figure 4.19 – WRITE_APPEND method illustration

Now, if the DAG needs to be rerun for 2021-02-1, then the data loading from the date will run for a second time. The problem is that, because the method is WRITE_APPEND, the data from GCS will be appended to the BigQuery table, and the date will be duplicated on the second run, like this:

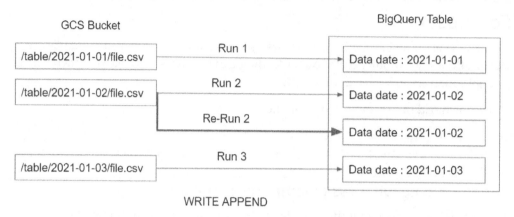

Figure 4.20 – WRITE_APPEND method with rerun illustration

The solution is using WRITE_TRUNCATE instead of WRITE_APPEND for the write disposition parameter. Using WRITE_TRUNCATE and changing the GCS directory source using a wildcard will load every file from the GCS bucket under the /table/ directory to the BigQuery table, and every time there is a new DAG Run, the BigQuery table will be reloaded without duplication.

As an illustration, this diagram shows data loading from the GCS bucket using a wildcard (*) to the BigQuery table:

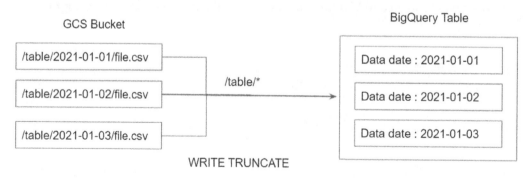

Figure 4.21 – WRITE_TRUNCATE method illustration

If you implement the WRITE TRUNCATE method, your task will be idempotent, which means that every time there is a rerun for any date, the data in BigQuery will always be correct without duplication. The BigQuery table won't have repeated data since the records will be reloaded on each DAG Run. But is this a best practice? The answer is: *not yet*.

This is not yet the best practice. Using this approach, you will notice that the BigQuery table will be rewritten over and over again for the whole table. If you have a table of 1 **terabyte** (**TB**) in size and the DAG already runs for 1 year, Airflow will rewrite 1 TB of data 365 times. And we don't want that—we need the BigQuery partition tables to improve this approach.

Introducing BigQuery partitioning

In this section, before continuing our Cloud Composer exercise, let's take a little step back to BigQuery. There is one essential feature in BigQuery called a BigQuery partitioned table. A BigQuery partitioned table will logically divide the data in the BigQuery table by partitioning it into segments using a key.

There are three partition key options, outlined as follows:

- **Time-unit columns**: Based on a column containing TIMESTAMP, DATE, or DATETIME value

- **Ingestion time**: Based on the timestamp when BigQuery ingests data to the table

- **Integer range**: Based on a column containing the integer value

The most common scenario is using either a time-unit column or ingestion time, and even though you can partition up to an hourly granular level, the most common scenario is still partitioning at a daily level. This feature will benefit mainly cost and performance optimization, but other than those two factors, using BigQuery partitioned tables can help our load jobs.

Take a look at the next example.

We create a table with PARTITION BY (column), as follows:

```
CREATE TABLE example_table
(
val1 INT64,
val2  STRING,
date  DATE,
```

```
)
PARTITION BY (date);
```

Under the hood of BigQuery storage, the `example_table` table will be divided based on the `Date` column, like this:

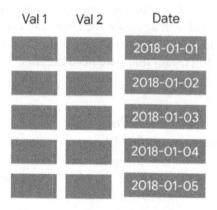

Figure 4.22 – BigQuery rows and columns example

Every table record will be stored in a separate storage location. With this, it's theoretically the same as having multiple tables with the same schemas. But you don't need to worry about this, as BigQuery will handle this seamlessly. What you can do as a user is to access the table, and filter the table using the `partition` column, like this:

```
SELECT val1
FROM example_table
WHERE date = '2018-01-03';
```

The query will only access a partial amount of data from the table, which is the `val1` column at `2021-01-03`.

This is the idea of partitioned tables in BigQuery. The other main reason why people use partitioned tables in BigQuery is for cost optimization. We will discuss more on this subject from a cost strategy point of view later in *Chapter 10, Cost Strategy in GCP*, when we focus on the subject of GCP costs.

Back to our exercise—at this point, we will use the BigQuery partitioned table to help us to optimize the WRITE_TRUNCATE issue. We will still use WRITE_TRUNCATE rather than the WRITE_APPEND disposition. but we will only write and truncate the table for a specific partition. This way, we don't need to rewrite the entire table every time the DAG runs.

In the next section, we will use what we've learned about BigQuery partitioned tables and the WRITE_TRUNCATE method in our DAG.

Airflow jobs that follow task idempotency for incremental load

Please take a look at our example code and check the difference between the `level_3_dag.py` and `level_4_dag.py` files.

First, we want to use the Airflow macro that returns the execution date but with no dash, like this: 20210101. The macro is ds_nodash, as illustrated here:

```
extracted_date_nodash  = '{{ ds_nodash }}'
```

Now, in the trips table, notice that bq_trips_table_id has a postfix in the `level_4_dag.py` file:

```
destination_project_dataset_table  = bq_trips_table_id +
f"${extracted_date_nodash}",
```

With this, the destination table ID will look like this:

```
project.raw_bikesharing.trips$20210101
```

The $ postfix followed by the date means that you are targeting a specific table partitioned to load your data. In the preceding example, you will load data to the trips table at the 2021-01-01 partition.

In the gcs source object, we also want to use this extracted date information to get the daily data from a specific GCS directory, like this:

```
gcs_trips_source_object = f"chapter-4/trips/{extracted_date_
nodash}/*.csv"
```

Finally, in GoogleCloudStorageToBigQueryOperator, we will modify the parameters a little bit. We add the time_partitioning parameter by DAY on the start_date field, as follows:

```
time_partitioning                        = {'time_partitioning_
type':'DAY','field': 'start_date'}
```

This means that our trips table will be partitioned using a time-unit column, which is the start_date column, and the granularity of the partition is by DAY.

Now this is our full task code, we will keep `write_disposition` set to `WRITE_TRUNCATE`, as follows:

```
gcs_to_bq_trips = GoogleCloudStorageToBigQueryOperator(
task_id                              = "gcs_to_bq_trips",
bucket                               = gcs_source_data_bucket,
source_objects                       = [gcs_trips_source_
object],
destination_project_dataset_table    = bq_trips_table_id,
schema_fields                        = bq_trips_table_schema,
time_partitioning                    = {'time_partitioning_
type':'DAY','field': 'start_date'},
write_disposition                    ='WRITE_TRUNCATE'
)
```

With this, every time there is a rerun on a particular date, the table partition will be rewritten, but again, only on a specific partition date, as illustrated in the following diagram:

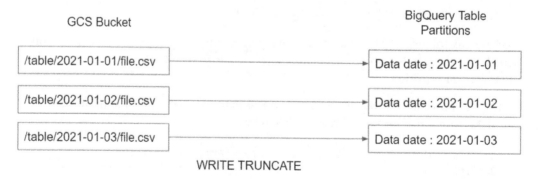

Figure 4.23 – WRITE_TRUNCATE method with BigQuery partitioned table illustration

With this, your DAG and all tasks are idempotent. Imagine that you want to retry any tasks on any expected day—in that case, you do not need to worry. The tasks are safe to rerun and there will be no data duplication, thanks to the `WRITE_TRUNCATE` method. And also, for the `partitioned_by` date, the table will only rewrite the records on the rerun execution day.

Level 5 DAG – Handling late data using a sensor

The main goal of the Level 5 DAG is for us to understand how to handle late data. Handling late data means being able to create a flexible DAG runtime depending on the upstream data arrival.

In this exercise, we will use an Airflow sensor to handle the condition and learn about the **poke** mechanism in the sensor.

First, let's understand what late data is and why it's an issue for scheduling.

Imagine you have two DAGs. The first DAG loads data from GCS to a BigQuery raw table, as follows:

```
GCS → BigQuery raw table → BigQuery DWH tables
```

The second DAG will load data from the BigQuery raw table to a data mart table, as follows:

```
BigQuery DWH tables → BigQuery data mart
```

Here are the two scenarios:

- The data sources from GCS are ready at 5:00 A.M.
- The requirement is to have a data mart table ready by 6:00 A.M.

What can go wrong in this scenario? To answer that, let's do some pseudocode to handle the requirements, as follows:

1. The data is ready by 5:00 A.M. For a time buffer, let's add 10 minutes, which means that we can create a scheduler that runs at 5:10 A.M. every day for the first DAG. In our DAG, we can define the following:

   ```
   schedule_interval = 10 5 * * *
   ```

2. The second DAG is dependent on the first DAG. Let's assume the first DAG will be finished after 30 minutes or at 5:40 A.M. For a time buffer, let's add 5 minutes on top of that. Then, we can create a scheduler that runs at 5:45 A.M. every day for the second DAG. In our second DAG, we can define the following:

   ```
   schedule_interval = 45 5 * * *
   ```

Sounds good? Yes—it will be good for most cases, assuming that the first DAG will be finished in less than 35 minutes.

Now, imagine what will happen if the first DAG is 10 minutes late, or—in other words—the first DAG finished in 45 minutes rather than 30 minutes.

If the first DAG finished late, then the second DAG will start blindly. *Blindly* means that the DAG will run without knowing that the upstream data is not actually there yet, and that is very bad.

In a real-world scenario, DAG dependencies are everywhere—there can be tens to hundreds (or even more) DAG dependencies in a day. If one DAG is late, imagine the implications on all the downstream DAGs. All your daily data will be corrupted just because some DAGs are late by a couple of minutes. How should we avoid that? The answer is by using Airflow sensors.

Introducing Airflow sensors

Airflow came up with a feature called a sensor. A sensor is a mechanism to check some conditions before starting a DAG Run.

The question now is: *What are the conditions?* There are many conditions that we can set. One of the most common in the GCP pipeline is using an operator called GoogleCloudStorageObjectSensor.

Let's see the operator code first. Pay attention to the parameters here:

```
data_input_sensor = GoogleCloudStorageObjectSensor(
object=f'dir/{execution_date_nodash}/_SUCCESS',
poke_interval=60
)
```

There are two important parameters here: object and poke_interval. When you have GoogleCloudStorageObjectSensor in your DAG, this operator will watch over the GCS object in the given directory. The operator will check the existence of the file in that specific directory.

If the object doesn't exist in the directory, the operator will wait. It will wait and keep checking every 60 seconds, and that's what you set in the poke_interval parameter. If you think about it, it will be very useful for our DAG dependencies, in that the downstream DAG can wait before it runs the other tasks.

Let's get back to our scenario and improve our pseudocode, as follows:

1. The data is ready by 5:00 A.M. We can create a scheduler that runs at 5:00 A.M. every day for the first DAG without any time buffer. In our DAG, we can define the following:

```
schedule_interval = 0 5 * * *
```

Our first task will start with the sensor, like this:

```
data_source_sensor = GoogleCloudStorageObjectSensor(
. . .
object=f'data_source/{{ ds }}/data.csv',
poke_interval=60
)
```

As an additional step, at the end of the task, we will write a file to GCS as a signal. Here's an example of this:

```
success = GoogleCloudStorageToGoogleCloudStorageOperator(
    . . .
    destination_object=f'dag_success/first_dag/{{ ds }}/_
SUCCESS'
)
```

2. For the second DAG, let's no longer assume anything from the first DAG. We don't assume how long the first DAG will take to finish. The first DAG can finish in 1 minute, 5 minutes, or 1 hour—we don't need to assume. Rather, we will start the schedule at the same time as the first DAG, which is 5:00 A.M., and what we will do is to put a sensor on the signal directory from the first DAG. So, the logic will look like this:

```
schedule_interval = 0 5 * * *
```

And as the first task in our DAG, we will use the sensor, like this:

```
upstream_sensor = GoogleCloudStorageObjectSensor(
. . .
object=f'dag_success/first_dag/{{ ds }}/_SUCCESS'
poke_interval=60
)
```

And that's it—with the new logic, the first DAG will send a signal file into a directory in the GCS bucket, and later, the downstream DAGs can use this signal to automatically start or wait for the DAG to run.

In summary, you will need Airflow sensors for better DAG dependencies compared to relying on a fixed schedule time. The Airflow sensor has a poking mechanism that checks the availability of some conditions—for example, checking the existence of a GCS file.

Now, as the final exercise in this chapter, let's add a signal and sensor to our DAG code. The idea is that we want to create a new DAG. The new DAG will write BigQuery data mart tables using data from our bike-sharing fact table. We want this DAG to run only after the fact table is successfully loaded.

Please download the example code for the Level 5 DAG and Level 5 DAG downstream from here:

```
https://github.com/PacktPublishing/Data-Engineering-with-
Google-Cloud-Platform/blob/main/chapter-4/code/level_5_dag.py
```

```
https://github.com/PacktPublishing/Data-Engineering-with-
Google-Cloud-Platform/blob/main/chapter-4/code/level_5_
downstream_dag.py
```

Let's create a new DAG called `level_5_downstream_dag.py` for our downstream DAG. These are the steps:

1. We need an empty file for our signal—for example, this `_SUCCESS` file. This static file will be useful for later steps. So, let's copy the file from our code example to your GCS bucket. You can use the GCP console or run `gsutil` command from Cloud Shell, like this:

    ```
    gsutil cp [your local git directory]/chapter-4/code/_
    SUCCESS gs://packt-data-eng-on-gcp-data-bucket/chapter-4/
    data/signal/_SUCCESS
    ```

2. First, we want to add a new task to `level_5_dag`. The task will put the `_SUCCESS` file in a specific directory. The task will only run if all other tasks are successfully run. So, let's add this task to `level_5_dag`, as follows:

    ```
    send_dag_success_signal =
    GoogleCloudStorageToGoogleCloudStorageOperator(
            task_id='send_dag_success_signal',
            source_bucket=gcs_source_data_bucket,
            source_object=f'chapter-4/data/signal/_SUCCESS',
            destination_bucket=gcs_source_data_bucket,
    ```

```
        destination_object=f'chapter-4/data/signal/
    staging/level_5_dag_sensor/{extracted_date_nodash}/_
    SUCCESS')
```

Notice that the task is actually only copying our _SUCCESS file from the first step, but the key is the destination_object parameter. The destination object directory is specifically put under /dag name/DAG run date (extracted_date).

This way, we can use the directory for our sensor in our next DAG.

3. Create a new Python file for our new downstream DAG. The task in the DAG will simply create a new BigQuery table from the fact table, like this:

```
    data_mart_sum_total_trips  = BigQueryOperator(
    task_id = "data_mart_sum_total_trips",
        sql                        = f"""SELECT
    DATE(start_date) as trip_date,
                                        SUM(total_trips)
    sum_total_trips
                                        FROM `{bq_fact_
    trips_daily_table_id}`
                                        WHERE trip_date =
    DATE('{execution_date}')""",
        destination_dataset_table  = sum_total_trips_
    table_id,
        write_disposition          = 'WRITE_TRUNCATE',
        time_partitioning          = {'time_
    partitioning_type':'DAY','field': 'trip_date'},
        create_disposition         = 'CREATE_IF_NEEDED',
        use_legacy_sql             = False,
        priority                   = 'BATCH'
    )
```

Besides the preceding main task, there are two tasks that we should add to this DAG. We will follow best practice in this section, with a sensor and a signal. The sensor operator will look like this:

```
    input_sensor = GoogleCloudStorageObjectSensor(
        task_id='sensor_task',
        bucket=gcs_source_data_bucket,        object=f'data/
    signal/{parent_dag}/{execution_date_nodash}/_SUCCESS',
```

```
        mode='poke'
        poke_interval=60,
        timeout=60 * 60 * 24 * 7
    )
```

This is identical to our example before; we define the object to our directory. The directory is constructed by the parent DAG's name and the execution date.

For our signal in this DAG, let's add this code:

```
    send_dag_success_signal =
GoogleCloudStorageToGoogleCloudStorageOperator(
        task_id='send_dag_success_signal',
        source_bucket=gcs_source_data_bucket,
        source_object=f'chapter-4/data/signal/_SUCCESS',
        destination_bucket=GCS_BUCKET_JOB_CONFIG,
        destination_object='data/signal/staging/{{ dag }}/{{ ds
}}/_SUCCESS'
    )
```

The signal file from this task won't be used by any other DAG in this exercise, but that's the point of this Level 5 exercise. As a data engineer who develops with Airflow, it's a best practice to keep this as a standard. In doing this, you will always have DAGs that provide a signal for any other downstream data pipelines.

That's it—with these setups, your second DAG will start only if `level_5_dag` successfully runs. Please check the full code in the example code. Try to build a solution yourself first and compare it with the example code.

Before we summarize the chapter, don't forget to delete both the Cloud Composer and Cloud SQL instances. Both services are billed by the number of hours running, so make sure you deleted both of the instances after you've finished with the exercises. You can delete them from the GCP console with the **Delete** button, or you can run `gcloud` commands.

For Cloud SQL, delete the instance by running the following command:

```
# gcloud sql instances delete [CLOUDSQL INSTANCE NAME]
```

For Cloud Composer, delete the environment by running the following command:

```
# gcloud composer environments delete [CLOUD COMPOSER
ENVIRONMENT_NAME] --location [LOCATION]
```

Let's close this chapter with a summary.

Summary

In this chapter, we learned about Cloud Composer. Having learned about Cloud Composer, we then needed to know how to work with Airflow. We realized that as an open source tool, Airflow has a wide range of features. We focused on how to use Airflow to help us build a data pipeline for our BigQuery data warehouse. There are a lot more features and capabilities in Airflow that are not covered in this book. You can always expand your skills in this area, but you will already have a good foundation after finishing this chapter.

As a tool, Airflow is fairly simple. You just need to know how to write a Python script to define DAGs. We've learned in the *Level 1 DAG* exercise that you just need to write simple code to build your first DAG, but a complication arises when it comes to best practices, as there are a lot of best practices that you can follow. At the same time, there are also a lot of potential bad practices that Airflow developers can make.

By learning the examples in different code levels in this chapter, you learned that DAG code decisions can lead to potential data issues, and as data engineers, it's our job to make sure we know which best practice we should apply. Every organization may have different conditions, and every condition may lead to different use cases. Understanding the potential risk and understanding Airflow's best practices are key to building the best orchestrator for your data pipelines.

In the next chapter, we will go back to storage and processing components, but we will use **Dataproc** as an alternative approach to BigQuery. Just as we compared Cloud Composer and Airflow, in Dataproc you will learn about Hadoop because both are correlated tightly together. We will learn about both Dataproc and Hadoop to build our data lake.

5

Building a Data Lake Using Dataproc

A data lake is a concept similar to a data warehouse, but the key difference is what you store in it. A data lake's role is to store as much raw data as possible without knowing first what the value or end goal of the data is. Given this key differentiation, how to store and access data in a data lake is different compared to what we learned in *Chapter 3*, *Building a Data Warehouse in BigQuery*.

This chapter helps you understand how to build a data lake using Dataproc, which is a managed Hadoop cluster in Google Cloud Platform (GCP) But, more importantly, it helps you understand the key benefit of using a data lake in the cloud, which is allowing the use of ephemeral clusters.

Here is the high-level outline of this chapter:

- Introduction to Dataproc
- Building a data lake on a Dataproc cluster
- Creating and running jobs on a Dataproc cluster
- Understanding the concept of the ephemeral cluster
- Building an ephemeral cluster using Dataproc and Cloud Composer

Technical requirements

Before we begin the chapter, make sure you have the following prerequisites ready.

In this chapter's exercises, we will use these GCP services: Dataproc, GCS, BigQuery, and Cloud Composer. If you never open any of these services in your GCP console, open it and enable the API.

Make sure you have your GCP console, Cloud Shell, and Cloud Shell Editor ready.

Download the example code and the dataset here: `https://github.com/PacktPublishing/Data-Engineering-with-Google-Cloud-Platform/tree/main/chapter-5`.

Be aware of the cost that might occur from Dataproc and the Cloud Composer cluster. Make sure you delete all the environments after the exercises to prevent any unexpected costs.

Introduction to Dataproc

Dataproc is a Google-managed service for Hadoop environments. It manages the underlying virtual machines, operating systems, and Hadoop software installations. Using Dataproc, Hadoop developers can focus on developing jobs and submitting them to Dataproc.

From a data engineering perspective, understanding Dataproc is equal to understanding Hadoop and the data lake concept. If you are not familiar with Hadoop, let's learn about it in the next section.

A brief history of the data lake and Hadoop ecosystem

The popularity of the data lake rose in the 2010s. Companies started to talk about this concept a lot more, compared to the data warehouse, which is similar but different in principle. The concept of storing data as files in a centralized system makes a lot of sense in the modern era, compared to the old days when companies stored and processed data typically for regular reporting. In the modern era, people use data for exploration from many data sources. Exploration can mean anything, including answering hypothetical questions about customer behavior, finding potential fraud, A/B testing, and doing machine learning.

The concept of storing and processing huge amounts of data is actually nothing new. Google was the pioneer of this in the early 2000s. Their ambitious goal of storing all the web page information in the world on their server was where the story began. In their use case, there were no other options; they couldn't store the web pages in common database tables. They needed to store their data as unstructured data and distribute it across multiple machines for scalability.

The great success of the technology behind it and how the world saw Google becoming a very successful data-driven company made a lot of companies want to do the same thing. Unfortunately, not all companies were able to do it at the time. The storage costs didn't make sense and no technology was popular enough to support it – not until 2003, when Google published how their technology works with **Google File System (GFS)** and MapReduce. In 2006, the open source Hadoop was published, inspired by the two technologies. As a result, companies all around the world started to adopt it, and the rest is history.

A deeper look into Hadoop components

In my experience, understanding Hadoop is not only good for adding our knowledge to the ETL landscape. Understanding Hadoop can help you understand the principle of parallel processing in big data and why it's different from common database technologies.

Essentially, Hadoop consists of three main components:

- A **Distributed File System (DFS)**, or as it is called in the Hadoop environment, the **Hadoop Distributed File System (HDFS)**: This is the concept that a system will automatically split your files into multiple parts. The goal is for you to be able to store terabytes to petabytes of data on multiple physical hard disks.

- **MapReduce**: This is the concept that defines how to process data in parallel. The goal is for you to be able to process data using multiple CPUs, hard disks, and memory at the same time. In recent years, Spark has become a more popular framework for doing parallel processing, but as a concept, Spark still uses the MapReduce concept.

- **Yarn**: This is a resource management tool in Hadoop. Yarn is an important part of Hadoop for allocating resources, in terms of how much CPU and memory are available in the cluster and how much it should allocate to each individual job.

These are the three main components of Hadoop. But nowadays, you can see Hadoop as an ecosystem rather than just these three main components. Hadoop is well known because of how active and how big the community is; for example, you might have heard the following:

- Hadoop can do real-time streaming.

- Hadoop can do machine learning.

- In Hadoop, you can create a data warehouse.

All of these statements are correct, but it needs more than just the three core components. For example, for streaming, you might need Kafka, Flume, and Spark Streaming. To creatie a data warehouse, you might need Hive or Impala. In summary, Hadoop is an ecosystem; it's a collection of many open source projects that are compatible with each other.

Let's take a quick look at the simplified Hadoop components in this figure, where the starting point is the servers:

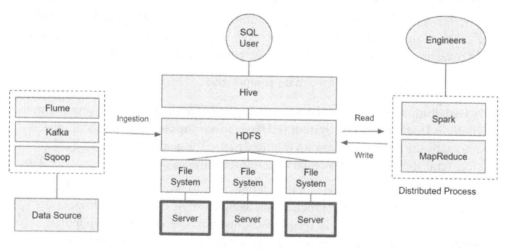

Figure 5.1 – Hadoop high-level architecture

Hadoop has one too many working servers or, in Hadoop terms, **worker nodes**. The worker nodes are simply computers with a filesystem where you can store files. HDFS sits on top of these multiple filesystems; when you store data in HDFS, Hadoop seamlessly distributes the files to these filesystems. You can create a table structure on top of the files using Hive, so SQL users can access the data using the SQL language. The other option is to process it using distributed processing frameworks such as Spark or MapReduce. These frameworks can read and write directly to HDFS.

There are tools that are usually used to ingest data to HDFS, for example, Flume, Kafka, and Sqoop. *Figure 5.1* is just a very simplified summary of the Hadoop ecosystem; in the marketplace, there are a lot of other alternatives for each component. If this is the first time you have learned about Hadoop, don't fall into a trap where you think you need to understand all of the products and their alternatives. Instead, focus on understanding how HDFS works and how Spark or MapReduce can process data in HDFS. The other components will come naturally with time when you understand HDFS and the processing framework.

At this point, you may already have a high-level understanding of what Hadoop is. To continue our learning about data engineering on GCP, we need to also think about how much Hadoop knowledge you need if you are working in a GCP environment.

The answer depends on how new Hadoop is for you and what your organizational direction is in using Hadoop. But assume that you are new to both Hadoop and GCP, and your organization has no strong opinion on Hadoop. It's best to focus your Hadoop understanding on it being a data processing framework.

How much Hadoop-related knowledge do you need on GCP?

Since most functionalities of open source products have native alternatives in GCP, it's recommended to avoid using unmanaged open source products and to use managed services. For example, Hive is an open source product for creating tables on top of HDFS. On GCP, we will avoid using it because BigQuery is a much better alternative to create table structures. As another example, HDFS as a storage system for a data lake is also not really relevant in GCP since it's replaceable by a serverless service, **Google Cloud Storage (GCS)**. Even though they are not identical, they serve the same purpose.

The most common Hadoop use case in GCP is for a data processing framework such as MapReduce or Spark. A lot of data engineers really love Spark because of its simplicity, and it has a big community following. Because of this and many other reasons, data engineers prefer processing big data using Spark. And if we want to compare it to MapReduce, Spark is a much more popular and robust framework. Let's take a deeper look at what Spark is and some of its key terms.

Introducing the Spark RDD and the DataFrame concept

Spark is a framework for distributed processing. With Spark, we can create programs or applications to extract, transform, and load data in a distributed manner. Note that Spark is a framework that was built using Scala, and by default, Scala is the preferred language to develop Spark programs. But there is an alternative you can use – a Spark Python API called PySpark. We will use PySpark consistently with the Python programming language throughout the exercises in the book.

Spark is a framework on its own; there are many features and concepts in Spark. In this book, we will focus only on the core concepts. With Spark, you can process ETL in a distributed manner, all thanks to the **Resilient Distributed Dataset (RDD)** concept. The RDD is a unique concept in Spark. It distributes your data between multiple machines. And as for the word *resilient*, it means the dataset is fault-tolerant. For example, imagine you run a Spark job where the RDD stores data on multiple machines, but then one machine turns off for some reason. The resiliency in Spark will ensure your job is still running and smart enough to get a replacement from other machines.

You can think of an RDD as arrays or lists in Python. For example, in Python you can define a list like this:

```
this_is_a_list = [1,2,3,4,5]
```

In Spark, you can define an RDD using the Python list like this:

```
this_is_RDD = spark_context.parallelize(this_is_a_list)
```

Using the previous code, the `this_is_RDD` variable is an RDD. As an illustration of how it differs from other variables, you can't print an RDD like this:

```
print(this_is_RDD)
```

You can't print an RDD as you would print list variables. Later, we will try it, in the *Exercise – Building a data lake on a Dataproc cluster* section.

An RDD is an abstract dataset. When you define an RDD from a list, the list becomes distributed. The previous example won't really make sense because it only contains five data units (1–5). But if you have a list that contains millions of pieces of data, the RDD will distribute the data between multiple memories, such as **Random Access Memory (RAM)** across different machines (servers). We will practice using RDD later, in the *Exercise – Building a data lake on a Dataproc cluster* section; for now, let's just keep RDDs in mind.

On top of an RDD, there is another abstraction layer called a **Spark DataFrame**. You can think of a Spark DataFrame like pandas in Python. Like the relationship between a Python list and a Spark RDD, a Spark DataFrame is similar to pandas but distributed. With a Spark DataFrame, we can give a schema to our files on the fly. On top of that, we can use SQL to transform the data in an RDD. As a best practice, always transform all RDDs into a Spark DataFrame when possible. A Spark DataFrame is better than using an RDD because it provides more optimization in the process. Use an RDD only when you don't have a clear schema or delimiter. We will learn how to use both in the exercise, but to summarize, in Spark there are two important concepts – an RDD and a Spark DataFrame.

Introducing the data lake concept

When talking about Hadoop, it's inevitable that we talk about data lakes. Hadoop and data lakes are inseparable. The popularity of Hadoop made the world invent the term data lake

To refresh your learning about what the difference is between a data lake and a data warehouse, please review *Chapter 1*, *Fundamentals of Data Engineering*, in the *What makes a data lake different from a data warehouse?* section.

There are three main factors that make a data lake unique as a system. Let's look at each of them in detail.

The ability to store any kind of data

A data lake system needs to be able to store any kind of data. To clarify the word *any*, people like to break it down into three different categories:

- Structured (table)
- Semi-structured (CSV, JSON, or XML)
- Unstructured data (image, audio, or logs)

But in my experience, these three categorizations won't really help you other than as an introduction. It's a great way to introduce the capabilities of a data lake to new people, but at the end of the day, what you see as a data engineer are files. If the technology you use is meant for data lake storage (such as GCS), you don't actually need to do anything. There is no additional configuration that you need to do to prepare structured, semi-structured, or unstructured data; they're all the same – files.

So, the keyword here is *any*. It means that in a data lake, the system should be able to store data in a file format rather than in a database table. For me, it's a lot simpler to think in this way.

The ability to process files in a distributed manner

A data lake should be able to handle files regardless of the format and size. We've talked about the format previously; the key is that the system needs to be able to read files.

But size is another key differentiator here. A data lake needs to be able to distribute data processes. A distributed process means that the system is able to break down data processes into smaller chunks and run them in parallel on more than one machine (computer).

The other terminology for this is being able to *scale out*. If data in the data lake keeps getting bigger and bigger, the solution is not to *scale up* the machine but to *scale out*. Scaling up means upgrading the server specification and scaling out means adding more servers. Scaling up is limited and scaling out is limitless.

As an example, to read data from a file, you can actually use any programming language, such as Python. You can read data from files in Python and then load the file content into variables or a pandas DataFrame, and process the data. But Python by itself won't distribute the process between multiple machines; it needs different frameworks to do that. The most well-known distributed processing frameworks are MapReduce and Spark. But there are others, such as Flink, Dataflow, and Dremel. So, the key here is that a data lake needs to be able to process data in a distributed manner.

The ability to focus on loading the data first

The third factor is a development mindset. A data engineer who builds a data lake needs to know that the focus of building it is to store data first; the business logic and structure come later. This means that the mindset is to store as many files as possible from multiple different data sources in the data lake and let the other teams or departments figure out the value of the data. The other teams could be data scientists, data analysts, or business analysts.

There are cases when organizations try to adopt a data lake by purchasing data lake technology, but the mindset is not adjusted in terms of data being costly, not clean, useless, or unstructured. In this case, the organization will have endless debates about what the difference is between a data lake and a data warehouse. So, the key here is to **focus on loading the data first**.

> **Important Note**
>
> A new term arose in the late 2020s, the **data lakehouse**. This started when companies started to realize that the majority of their data was structured. In this case, it's a lot simpler to just store data in a database table compared to a file system. As long as the database system is able to distribute the data and processing, it's a lot more convenient to store data as a table. The data lake mindset doesn't change when loading the data first, but instead, people use the term *data lakehouse*. For the purpose of learning, we can ignore this since there are no fundamental changes in the underlying technology.

If we take a look back at what Hadoop is, all three data lake factors fit into the Hadoop ecosystem:

- Hadoop stores data in HDFS as files.

- Hadoop processes data in a distributed manner using MapReduce or Spark.

- Hadoop engineers know that the majority of their job is to develop, maintain, and manage data loading jobs from data sources to HDFS.

Now, how does Hadoop fit in the GCP ecosystem? Since there are a lot of overlapping components from open source Hadoop to GCP components, we need to better understand the Hadoop positioning on GCP.

Hadoop and Dataproc positioning on GCP

Based on my experience working with organizations that use Dataproc on GCP, one of the common reasons they are using Dataproc is because they were already using the Hadoop ecosystem before moving to GCP. This means that the organization has already invested a lot of time and effort in scripting ETL code and has a lot of developers that are very familiar with Hadoop. In this case, it's best to move everything as is from GCP to Dataproc without many changes.

In this case, Dataproc will save the organization a lot of time and infrastructure effort to provision a Hadoop cluster. Creating a Hadoop cluster using Dataproc will take around 5 minutes. Compare this to the efforts needed to create a Hadoop cluster ourselves, including installing the operating system, installing Hadoop, and configuring the Hadoop configurations, which might take days to finish.

The biggest user experience change is the storage layer. Although HDFS and GCS are very similar in nature, (both can store files and are accessible by Dataproc seamlessly), the best practice is to use GCS compared to HDFS because it's serverless. And for further implementation, it's a lot better; compared to HDFS, data in GCS is compatible with almost all other GCP services, such as BigQuery, AI Platform, and Cloud SQL. We will talk more about this in the *Using Cloud Storage as an underlying Dataproc file system* section and try both storing and accessing data in HDFS and GCS.

There are a lot of concepts and key terms that we've learned so far in this chapter. Before learning about the other Dataproc features and concepts, let's start our exercise in this chapter.

Exercise – Building a data lake on a Dataproc cluster

In this exercise, we will use Dataproc to store and process log data. Log data is a good representation of unstructured data. Organizations often need to analyze log data to understand their users' behavior.

In the exercise, we will learn how to use HDFS and PySpark using different methods. In the beginning, we will use Cloud Shell to get a basic understanding of the technologies. In the later sections, we will use Cloud Shell Code Editor and submit the jobs to Dataproc. But for the first step, let's create our Dataproc cluster.

Creating a Dataproc cluster on GCP

To create a Dataproc cluster, access your navigation menu and find **Dataproc**. You will find the **CREATE CLUSTER** button, which leads to this **Create a cluster** page:

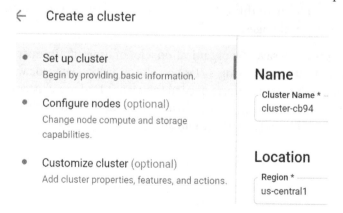

Figure 5.2 – Create a cluster page

There are many configurations in Dataproc. We don't need to set everything. Most of them are optional. For your first cluster, follow this setup:

- **Cluster Name**: Choose your cluster name.

- **Location**: `us-central1`

- **Cluster type**: `Standard (1 Master, N workers)`

- **Versioning**: The versioning options can be different from time to time since Google updates versions. Choose any version, for example, in my case the latest is 2.0 (Debian 10, Hadoop 3.2, Spark 3.1).

- **Component Gateway**: Enable Component Gateway.

Move to the **Configure nodes** section. We will set the minimum specifications for our machines:

- **Machine type**: `n1-standard-2`

- **Primary disk size**: `30 GB`

Now, move to the **Worker nodes** section.

- Machine type : **n1-standard-2**

- **Primary disk size**: `30 GB`

If all set, find and click the **CREATE** button. If you are lost, the equivalent `gcloud` command is like this:

```
gcloud beta dataproc clusters create packt-dataproc-cluster
--enable-component-gateway --region us-central1 --zone us-
central1-a --master-machine-type n1-standard-2 --master-
boot-disk-size 30 --num-workers 2 --worker-machine-type
n1-standard-2 --worker-boot-disk-size 30 --image-version
2.0-debian10 --optional-components JUPYTER
```

If all steps are correct, it will start provisioning the Dataproc cluster. It will take around 2–5 minutes until it is finished. While waiting, let's familiarize ourselves with some of the options that we skipped during configuration. These options are very useful features in Dataproc, mostly for optimization. All of these are optional, so they're good to know at this point:

- **Autoscaling**: Autoscaling is a feature in Dataproc to automatically scale up and scale down the number of worker nodes. The scaling is based on the resource availability in YARN.

- **Initialization actions**: This feature is for when you need to run any actions after Hadoop is installed on machines. A common example is to install some dependency libraries.

- **Custom Image**: You can choose the base image for your underlying Hadoop cluster. This will be useful, for example, when you have specific requirements for the OS version.

- **Component Gateway**: In the Hadoop ecosystem, there are many open source projects that have a web UI. For example, the Jupyter Notebook and Zeppelin. Enabling Component Gateway will give you access to those web UIs seamlessly. Google will manage the web proxies. Without this enabled, you'll need to configure the access to the web UI yourself.

- **Secondary worker nodes**: Dataproc allows secondary workers in a Hadoop cluster. Secondary workers are sets of machines that will be dedicated to processing only, not storing data. The most common use case is to use secondary workers in preemptible mode. With this, overall, jobs are faster and cheaper compared to having fewer workers or using non-secondary workers. But the trade-off is stability. Preemptible secondary worker nodes have a higher chance of being dropped internally by GCP. The best practice is to use preemptible secondary workers for less than 50% of the total number of workers.

As these configurations are optional, use them only when you need them. In other words, only consider using them when you find potential optimization in your Hadoop workloads. As always, focus on implementation first and optimization later.

Check that your Dataproc cluster has been created successfully. In the next section, we will use it to try storing data in HDFS and process it using Spark.

Using Cloud Storage as an underlying Dataproc file system

Now our Hadoop cluster is ready, we can start using the core Hadoop components. The first component that we will try using is the HDFS.

These are the steps we will perform in this section:

1. Accessing HDFS from Hadoop node shell
2. Loading data from GCS to HDFS
3. Creating a Hive table on top of HDFS
4. Accessing an HDFS file from PySpark
5. Accessing a GCS file from PySpark

Let's look at each of these steps in detail.

Accessing HDFS from Hadoop node shell

One way to access HDFS in our Hadoop cluster is by accessing the Linux command line from the master node. To do that, follow these steps:

1. Go to the Dataproc console and select your cluster name.
2. On the **Cluster details** page, find the **VM INSTANCES** tab.
3. You will see three VM instances there, and one of them will have the **Master** role.
4. Click on the **SSH** button, which you will find on the right of the **Master** node VM:

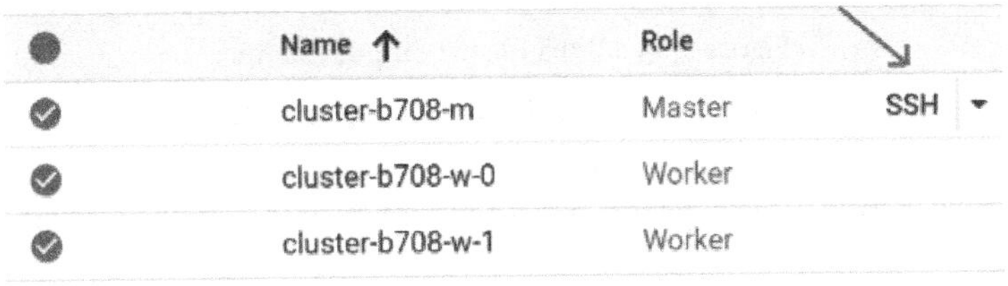

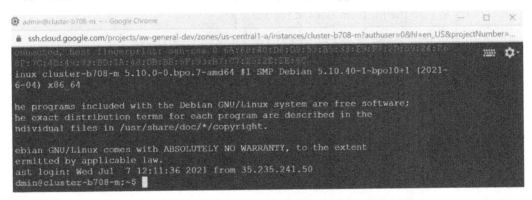

Figure 5.3 – The SSH button on the right of the screen

5. Wait for around 1 minute until the command line appears as follows:

Figure 5.4 – Command line for the Hadoop Master node instance

Note that this is not Cloud Shell; this is the Hadoop master node Linux. We can access HDFS from here using the command line. Let's try that by typing the following:

```
# hdfs dfs -ls ../
```

The command will give you the list of folders inside HDFS like this:

```
admin@cluster-b708-m:~$ hdfs dfs -ls ../
Found 10 items
drwxr-xr-x   - admin hadoop          0 2021-07-05 09:52 ../admin
drwxrwxrwt   - hdfs  hadoop          0 2021-07-05 09:32 ../hbase
drwxrwxrwt   - hdfs  hadoop          0 2021-07-05 09:32 ../hdfs
drwxrwxrwt   - hdfs  hadoop          0 2021-07-05 09:32 ../hive
drwxrwxrwt   - hdfs  hadoop          0 2021-07-05 09:32 ../mapred
drwxrwxrwt   - hdfs  hadoop          0 2021-07-05 09:32 ../pig
drwxr-xr-x   - root  hadoop          0 2021-07-07 08:43 ../root
drwxrwxrwt   - hdfs  hadoop          0 2021-07-05 09:32 ../spark
drwxrwxrwt   - hdfs  hadoop          0 2021-07-05 09:32 ../yarn
drwxrwxrwt   - hdfs  hadoop          0 2021-07-05 09:32 ../zookeeper
```

Figure 5.5 – HDFS file list output example

The 10 folders are not stored in the OS-level file system; they're in HDFS. To verify that, you can run `ls` in the shell and you won't see those 10 folders in the Linux file system. This might sound abstract at this point, but it will get clearer and clearer after some practice.

Loading data from GCS to HDFS

In this step, we want to load data from a file in the master node to HDFS. To illustrate that, let's try to load the file from our Git repository.

```
https://github.com/PacktPublishing/Data-Engineering-with-
Google-Cloud-Platform
```

Copy all the folders from `chapter-5` to your GCS bucket if you haven't done so in the previous chapters. For example, you can use the `gsutil` command like this from Cloud Shell:

```
# cd Data-Engineering-with-Google-Cloud-Platform
# gsutil cp -r chapter-5 gs://[BUCKET NAME]/from-git
```

If the data is already in GCS, we now can load it to our master node. Go to the **DataProc master node shell** and use the `gsutil` command like this:

```
# gsutil cp gs://[BUCKET NAME]/from-git/chapter-5/dataset/
simple_file.csv ./
```

Try to run the `ls` command and you can see `simple_file.csv` is now in your master node.

To explain more about what we were doing, we just prepared our exercise to load data to HDFS. It can be done as long as the data is in the master node, for example, you can transfer data to the master node using FTP or download any data from the internet. The key is that we want to have a file in the master node.

Any data in the master node can be loaded to HDFS using the command line like this:

```
# hdfs dfs -mkdir ../../data
# hdfs dfs -mkdir ../../data/simple_file
# hdfs dfs -put simple_file.csv ../../data/simple_file/
```

The command will load data from the Linux file system to HDFS. With that, you can see the file in HDFS using the command like this:

```
# hdfs dfs -ls ../../data/simple_file/
```

You will see `simple_file.csv` shown in HDFS under the `data` folder.

Creating a Hive table on top of HDFS

One alternative to access the file is using Hive. Hive is a tool to give a schema to your file. To do that, let's access Hive Shell from our command line by typing `hive` in our master node shell, like this:

```
admin@cluster-b708-m:~$ hive
Hive Session ID = e51ac435-a5ba-4afe-8ddd-84bd12c30e9a

Logging initialized using configuration in file:/etc/hive/conf.dist/hiv
nc: true
Hive Session ID = 78ed5adb-6505-4d7b-a0a1-f332256d6a2b
hive> □
```

Figure 5.6 – Accessing Hive Shell from the command line

Now you are in Hive Shell. You can run SQL syntaxes in this shell. As an example, try to run the following:

```
SELECT 1;
```

You will see it's running as a job. Now let's create our first table in Hive using our data in HDFS like this:

```
CREATE EXTERNAL TABLE simple_table(
    col_1 STRING,
    col_2 STRING,
```

```
    col_3 STRING)
ROW FORMAT DELIMITED FIELDS TERMINATED BY ','
STORED AS TEXTFILE
location '/data/simple_file'
TBLPROPERTIES ("skip.header.line.count"="1")
;
```

The CREATE EXTERNAL TABLE statement will create a table called simple_table using data from the file directory in HDFS. If the table is successfully created, you can access it using the following:

```
SELECT * FROM simple_table;
```

The table results will show like this:

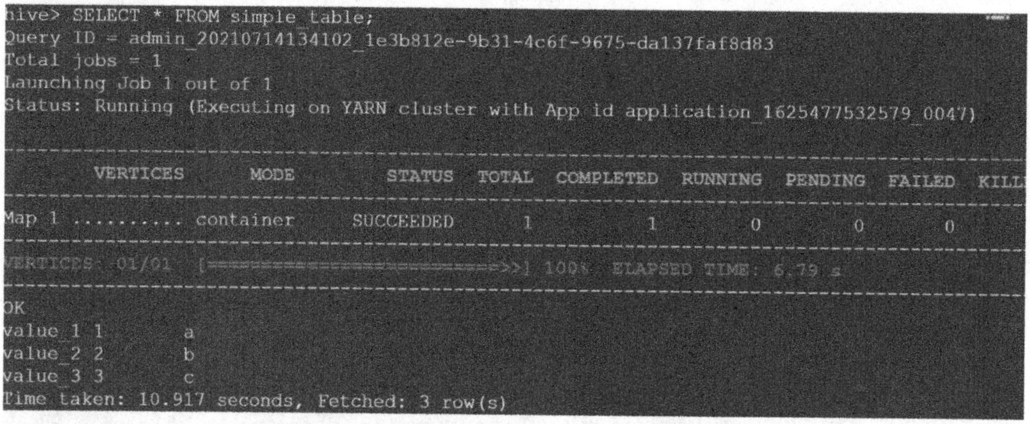

```
hive> SELECT * FROM simple_table;
Query ID = admin_20210714134102_1e3b812e-9b31-4c6f-9675-da137faf8d83
Total jobs = 1
Launching Job 1 out of 1
Status: Running (Executing on YARN cluster with App id application_1625477532579_0047)

        VERTICES      MODE      STATUS    TOTAL  COMPLETED  RUNNING  PENDING  FAILED  KILL

Map 1 .......... container   SUCCEEDED    1         1         0        0        0

VERTICES: 01/01  [==========================>>] 100%  ELAPSED TIME: 6.79 s

OK
value_1 1      a
value_2 2      b
value_3 3      c
Time taken: 10.917 seconds, Fetched: 3 row(s)
```

Figure 5.7 – Example Hive table result

To exit, in Hive Shell, type the following:

```
exit;
```

You will be back at the master node. As you can see, with Hive, you can access CSV files using SQL. This fundamental concept of processing data directly from a file is the key differentiator between data lake technology compared to databases.

Accessing an HDFS file from PySpark

The second alternative to process data in HDFS is using PySpark. You can access PySpark using the Spark shell. To do that, type pyspark; in the master node like this:

```
hive> exit;
admin@cluster-b708-m:~$ pyspark
```

Figure 5.8 – Accessing pyspark from the command line

With that command, you will be directed to the Spark shell, as shown in the following figure:

```
      / __/__  ___ _____/ /__
     _\ \/ _ \/ _ `/ __/  '_/
    /__ / .__/\_,_/_/ /_/\_\   version 3.1.1
       /_/

Using Python version 3.8.10 (default, May 11 2021 07:01:05)
Spark context Web UI available at http://cluster-b708-m.us-central1-a.c.aw-general-dev
:44009
Spark context available as 'sc' (master = yarn, app id = application_1625477532579_004
SparkSession available as 'spark'.
>>>
```

Figure 5.9 – Spark shell example

The Spark shell is a good tool for practice and doing simple tests. In reality, we will develop Spark applications in our IDE or Cloud Editor. We will do that later, in the next exercise, but as a starter, let's use the Spark shell.

The Spark shell actually works as a Python shell, and you can use any Python code in here. For example, you can use this common Python syntax:

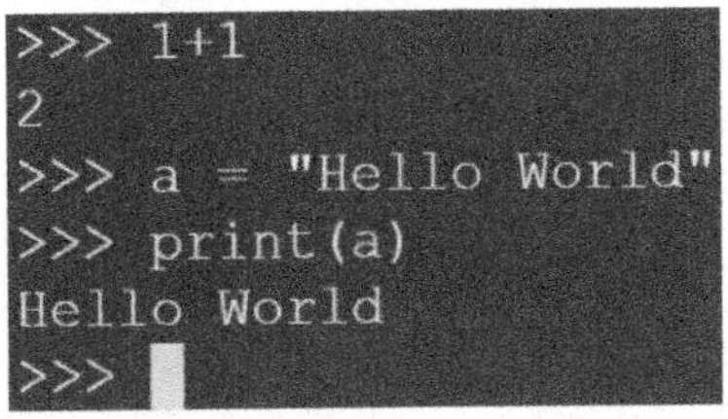

```
>>> 1+1
2
>>> a = "Hello World"
>>> print(a)
Hello World
>>>
```

Figure 5.10 – Example Spark shell similar to Python

But the difference is, in the Spark shell, you can use the Spark Context. Let's use Spark Context to load our data from HDFS. We will access the file in HDFS from the master node, which is named packt-dataproc-cluster-m.

To do that, use this node and don't forget to change the master node name to yours:

```
simple_file = sc.textFile('hdfs://packt-dataproc-cluster-m/
data/simple_file/simple_file.csv')
simple_file.collect()
```

The code will print out the file contents as an array:

```
['col_1,col_2,col3', 'value_1,1,a', 'value_2,2,b',
 'value_3,3,c']
```

If this is the first time you have used Spark, congratulations! You just experienced using one of the most popular big data processing frameworks in the world. Spark is a very widely used framework for processing big data. I have found that a lot of companies include Spark as a job requirement and in the interview process for data engineer roles. So, knowing about the Spark concept will be very beneficial on your data engineering journey.

So, what really happens? What actually is the `simple_file` variable?

When we call `sc.textFile` to the `simple_file` variable, the `simple_file` variable will become an RDD. Try typing `type(simple_file)`, like this:

```
>>> type(simple_file)
<class 'pyspark.rdd.RDD'>
>>> 
```

Figure 5.11 – Check the RDD file type

You will see the variable type is RDD. To refresh our memory about RDDs, you can review the *Introducing Spark RDD and DataFrame concept* section.

Note that we accessed the HDFS files by pointing to the master node instead of the data nodes. That is the default mechanism in Hadoop. Even though the master node doesn't store the real files, the master node has the index to all the files in the data nodes. This means, even if you have many data nodes in your Hadoop cluster, you don't need to know where files are actually stored in the data nodes; you just need to access the files from the master node. It will automatically read the required files from the data nodes.

Understanding RDDs in PySpark

An interesting feature about RDDs is the concept of lazy computation. Lazy computation processes instructions only when they're needed. For example, let's define this in Python code:

```
variable_a = 10
variable_b = variable_a * 10
variable_c = variable_b * variable_a
print(variable_c)
```

If you run the previous code in Python, it will execute each variable and store the results in memory for each variable. So, if we print variable_c, what actually happens in Python is it stores three different pieces of data in memory for each variable.

The same principle cannot be applied to big data. It's wasteful to store data in variable_a and variable_b since both variables are essentially just formulas. In the lazy computation concept, we will only process all the formulas when we call print(variable_c).

Back to our exercise. Let's sum up the number in col_2. We use this RDD:

```
['col_1,col_2,col3', 'value_1,1,a', 'value_2,2,b',
'value_3,3,c']
```

We expect the result to be 6:

```
6 = 1 + 2 + 3
```

Let's use the following PySpark syntax and understand it step by step:

1. Since the value still contains the CSV headers, we want to filter out any value that contains 'col':

    ```
    rdd_without_header = simple_file.filter(lambda row: 'col'
    not in row)
    ```

2. The values are delimited by commas, so we need to split them using the Python split method. But instead of using a for loop, we will use the map function. Using the map function in Spark will distribute the process:

    ```
    split = rdd_without_header.map(lambda row:  row.
    split(','))
    ```

3. We will get the col_2 value and convert it into an integer:

    ```
    rdd_col_2 = split.map(lambda row: int(row[1]))
    ```

4. Finally, we will sum the values and print them:

    ```
    sum = rdd_col_2.sum()
    ```
    ```
    print(sum)
    ```

If all is correct, the code will print 6. To try lazy computation, try printing any variable other than the variable sum. You won't see any data from other variables. rdd_without_header, split, and rdd_col_2 are variables that store the formula (logic). They won't compute or store any data before we call the sum() method. Imagine you have 1 billion records in your .csv file. You will save all the unnecessary memory stores to all the variables that only contain formulas.

Accessing GCS files from PySpark

In the previous section, we stored and accessed data in HDFS. This time, we want to see how easy it is to change the file storage from HDFS to GCS.

To do that, check that simple_file.csv is already in your GCS bucket. We did this in the previous section, using the gsutil cp command. For example, in my environment, it's located here:

```
gs://[BUCKET NAME]/chapter-5/dataset/simple_file.csv
```

Now, back to the PySpark shell, type this:

```
simple_file = sc.textFile('gs://[BUCKET NAME]/from-git/
chapter-5/dataset/simple_file.csv')
```

The code is exactly the same as when we accessed data from HDFS. To compare, remember this line from the previous section:

```
simple_file = sc.textFile('hdfs://packt-dataproc-cluster-m/
user/admin/data/simple_file/simple_file.csv')
```

The difference is only in the file location. Spark can access data in GCS seamlessly even though the file is not stored in the Hadoop cluster. And with that, you can continue the rest of the code exactly the same. For example, you can use this same syntax:

```
rdd_without_header = simple_file.filter(lambda row: 'col' not
in row)
```

To quit the PySpark shell, use quit().

As a summary of this section, we've seen that there is no difference in the development effort using HDFS or GCS. The trade-off of using HDFS or GCS is in the I/O latency versus compatibility and maintenance. You can optimize the I/O latency by using SSD in HDFS on Hadoop cluster VMs. That's the fastest possible option. But for compatibility with other GCP services and less maintenance effort, GCS is the clear winner. In the next section, we will start the hands-on practice. We will try different approaches to using Dataproc. As a starter, let's begin the exercise by creating a Dataproc cluster.

Exercise: Creating and running jobs on a Dataproc cluster

In this exercise, we will try two different methods to submit a Dataproc job. In the previous exercise, we used the Spark shell to run our Spark syntax, which is common when practicing but not common in real development. Usually, we would only use the Spark shell for initial checking or testing simple things. In this exercise, we will code Spark jobs in editors and submit them as jobs.

Here are the scenarios that we want to try:

- Preparing log data in GCS and HDFS

- Developing Spark ETL from HDFS to HDFS

- Developing Spark ETL from GCS to GCS

- Developing Spark ETL from GCS to BigQuery

Let's look at each of these scenarios in detail.

Preparing log data in GCS and HDFS

The log data is in our GitHub repository, located here:

```
https://github.com/PacktPublishing/Data-Engineering-with-
Google-Cloud-Platform/tree/main/chapter-5/dataset/logs_example
```

If you haven't cloned the repository, clone it to your Cloud Shell environment.

Clone the syntax from Cloud Shell and copy the log file folders into `gcs`:

```
gsutil cp -r log_examples/*  gs://[BUCKET NAME]/chapter-5/
dataset/log_examples/
```

Now, go to the Hadoop master node shell, copy our folder there, and use the HDFS put command to load the files into HDFS, like this:

```
gsutil cp -r gs://[BUCKET NAME]/from-git/chapter-5/dataset/
logs_example.
```

```
hdfs dfs -copyFromLocal logs_example ../../data
```

With that command, the logs will be ready in HDFS.

Developing Spark ETL from HDFS to HDFS

If we look at the logs file, the records are like this:

```
97.116.185.190 - - [17/May/2015:11:05:59 +0000] "GET /
articles/dynamic-dns-with-dhcp/ HTTP/1.1" 200 18848 "http://
ubuntuforums.org/showthread.php?t=2003644" "Mozilla/5.0
(Windows NT 5.2; WOW64) AppleWebKit/537.36 (KHTML, like Gecko)
Chrome/32.0.1700.107 Safari/537.36"
```

This is common Apache web log data. The data contains some information: the user IP that accesses the website, the access time, the HTTP GET access information, and all the other information.

For our exercise, we want to use the HTTP GET access information to provide two metrics.

We want to calculate how many user requests each article has. Take these three records as an example:

```
/articles/dynamic-dns-with-dhcp
```

```
/articles/ssh-security
```

```
/articles/ssh-security
```

We expect an output file that contains this information:

```
dynamic-dns-with-dhcp,1
```

```
ssh-security,2
```

The challenge is that the records are not structured data. You can't load the files to the BigQuery table to run a SQL query. This is an unstructured data condition, which is the best case for PySpark. So, let's create a PySpark application to handle this. Our first application will read data from HDFS and store the output back in HDFS.

To do that, open Cloud Shell Editor and create a new working folder and a file named pyspark_job.py.

In the code, let's import SparkSession:

```
from pyspark.sql import SparkSession
```

Declare the Spark session like this:

```
spark = SparkSession.builder \
.appName('spark_hdfs_to_hdfs') \
.getOrCreate()

sc = spark.sparkContext
sc.setLogLevel("WARN")
```

SparkSession is what makes a Python file have a Spark connection to the Hadoop cluster. We will use the Spark session to declare an RDD, run map, run reduce, and create a Spark DataFrame.

First, let's load our data from HDFS:

```
MASTER_NODE_INSTANCE_NAME="[Your Master Node instance name]"
log_files_rdd = sc.textFile('hdfs://{}/data/logs_example/*'.
format(MASTER_NODE_INSTANCE_NAME))
```

This is similar to the exercise using the Spark shell when we declared an RDD that connected data to an HDFS directory. This time, we specify the file location in our logs directory.

The next step is to split the logs with the " " delimiter space; this code line will split each record so that we can access the records like an array:

```
splitted_rdd = log_files_rdd.map(lambda x: x.split(" "))
```

We can access the array like this:

```
selected_col_rdd = splitted_rdd.map(lambda x: (x[0], x[3],
x[5], x[6]))
```

The previous code snippet highlights the following:

- x[0] will give you the 97.116.185.190 IP.

- x[3] will give you the [17/May/2015:11:05:59 access time.

- X[5] will give you the GET method.

- X[6] will give you the /articles/dynamic-dns-with-dhcp/ URL.

At this point, our data is already structured; we can create a Spark DataFrame using the RDD, like this:

```
columns = ["ip","date","method","url"]
logs_df = selected_col_rdd.toDF(columns)
logs_df.createOrReplaceTempView('logs_df')
```

We can tell Spark to structure the RDD into a DataFrame with .toDF(columns). And so that we can access the DataFrame later in an SQL statement, we should use the logs_df.createOrReplaceTempView('logs_df') syntax.

When we declare a Spark DataFrame, we can access the DataFrame using SQL in Spark, like this:

```
sql = f"""
  SELECT
  url,
  count(*) as count
  FROM logs_df
  WHERE url LIKE '%/article%'
  GROUP BY url
  «»»
article_count_df = spark.sql(sql)
print(" ### Get only articles and blogs records ### ")
article_count_df.show(5)
```

In the previous code, notice that you use SQL to access a table named logs_df. Remember that that is not a table anywhere in any database. Instead, that is our Spark DataFrame that we declared in the previous statement. The SQL is answering our question about which article the user accesses.

The last step is to store the result back in HDFS. To do that, use this code:

```
article_count_df.write.save('hdfs://{}/data/article_count_
df'.format(MASTER_NODE_INSTANCE_NAME), format='csv',
mode='overwrite')
```

That will write the result from our SQL to HDFS as CSV files. And that's it – you have your Spark application ready to run in Dataproc. To make sure your code is correct, check it against the complete code in the code repository:

```
https://github.com/PacktPublishing/Data-Engineering-with-
Google-Cloud-Platform/blob/main/chapter-5/code/pyspark_hdfs_
to_hdfs.py
```

As an example, here is my Cloud Shell Editor with the pyspark code (ignore the error warning):

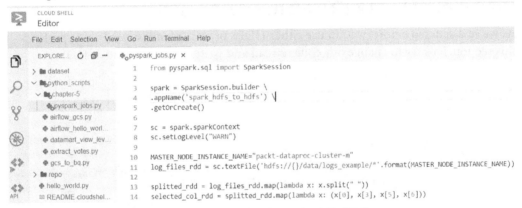

Figure 5.12 – Pyspark code in Cloud Shell Editor

To run it in your Dataproc cluster, you need to upload the code to GCS. You can do that from GCS or by using gsutil, like this:

```
gsutil cp  pyspark_job.py gs://[BUCKET NAME]/chapter-5/code/
```

Finally, you can submit it as a job to Dataproc using the Dataproc console in the job section or by using the gcloud command from Cloud Shell, like this:

```
gcloud dataproc jobs submit pyspark --cluster=[YOUR CLUSTER
NAME] --region=us-central1 gs://[BUCKET NAME]/chapter-5/code/
pyspark_job.py
```

If all is correct, then the job will start, and you can check it in the console. As an example, here are my jobs, showing the **Failed** and **Succeeded** jobs:

Figure 5.13 – Example Spark jobs on Dataproc

To check whether the output file is already in HDFS, use the HDFS `dfs -ls` command or, as an alternative, access it using Hive or the PySpark shell.

Developing Spark ETL from GCS to GCS

As we've discussed before, we can use either HDFS or GCS seamlessly from PySpark. In this section, let's try to change our code to read and write to GCS instead of HDFS.

To do that, we just need to make a simple modification to our code. More specifically, check your PySpark code when it's reading data from an RDD. Change it to access GCS, like this:

```
BUCKET_NAME="[Your GCS Bucket name]"
log_files_rdd = sc.textFile('gs://{}/from-git/chapter-5/
dataset/logs_example/*'.format(BUCKET_NAME))
```

And finally, the line where we write back to HDFS:

```
article_count_df.write.save('gs://{}/chapter-5/job-result/
article_count_df'.format(BUCKET_NAME), format='csv',
mode='overwrite')
```

To submit the job, we can perform the exact same step as in the previous section by copying the Python file into GCS and running it using the `gcloud` command. Try it yourself, and if you have any issues, revisit the previous section; all the steps should be the same.

The commands are as follows:

```
gsutil cp  pyspark_job.py gs://[BUCKET NAME]/chapter-5/code/
```

```
gcloud dataproc jobs submit pyspark --cluster=[Your Cluster
```

```
name] --region=us-central1 gs://[BUCKET NAME]/chapter-5/code/
pyspark_job.py
```

If successful, check your GCS bucket directory; your output file should be in GCS now. Here is an example from my bucket. You will notice that there are multiple file parts in the output folder, like this:

Buckets ❯ packt-data-eng-on-gcp-data-bucket ❯ chapter-5 ❯ job-result ❯ article_count_df ⎙

| UPLOAD FILES | UPLOAD FOLDER | CREATE FOLDER | MANAGE HOLDS | DOWNLOAD |

Filter by name prefix only ▼   ≡ Filter | Filter objects and folders

☐	Name	Size	Typ
☐	▤ _SUCCESS	0 B	app
☐	▤ part-00000-60fa753a-9c9c-4ab9-a785-f7fe229761ab-c000.csv	159 B	app
☐	▤ part-00001-60fa753a-9c9c-4ab9-a785-f7fe229761ab-c000.csv	259 B	app
☐	▤ part-00002-60fa753a-9c9c-4ab9-a785-f7fe229761ab-c000.csv	268 B	app
☐	▤ part-00003-60fa753a-9c9c-4ab9-a785-f7fe229761ab-c000.csv	133 B	app
☐	▤ part-00004-60fa753a-9c9c-4ab9-a785-f7fe229761ab-c000.csv	250 B	app

Figure 5.14 – Check the multiple file partitions from the job's output

If you open those files, each file contains partial records from the output. This is another good perspective on what's called a distributed file system and processing. In this case, there are five file parts (**part-00000** to **part-00004**); you may find yours are different. In the background of our Spark job, it parallelizes the execution into five streams, and each stream produces individual output files. And for downstream usage, it doesn't matter how many file parts are there. All you need to do is access the /article_count_df/*.csv directory.

As another possible extension to your exercise – remember that you can also create a BigQuery external table to access the output files. With this, you will get a clear picture of how a data lake works to process unstructured data to produce output for downstream users.

At the end of the day, as data engineers, we would like to process unstructured data into structured data so that more users can gain information from the data. From our example case, not many people in an organization know how to process log data to gain information. It is a data engineer's responsibility to be able to process unstructured information into more meaningful information for other users.

Developing Spark ETL from GCS to BigQuery

The last alternative that we have is to read and write data directly from BigQuery using PySpark. In the previous exercise, you may have used the BigQuery external table to access data from the GCS output file. Another option is to store the output directly to BigQuery as a native table.

To do that, let's jump to the section where we stored our output to GCS and change it to BigQuery, like this:

```
article_count_df.write.format('bigquery') \
.option('temporaryGcsBucket', BUCKET_NAME) \
.option('table', 'dwh_bikesharing.article_count_df') \
.mode('overwrite') \
.save()
```

And for the job submission, after copying the code to your GCS bucket, you need to add the BigQuery jars connector, like this:

```
gcloud dataproc jobs submit pyspark --cluster=packt-dataproc-
cluster --region=us-central1 gs://packt-data-eng-on-gcp-data-
bucket/chapter-5/code/pyspark_jobs.py  --jars gs://spark-lib/
bigquery/spark-bigquery-latest_2.12.jar
```

The preceding code will make our PySpark job write the Spark DataFrame into a BigQuery table. As an example, I put the table into the dwh_bikesharing dataset with a table named article_count_df.

All the other lines of code are the same. As you can see from these three I/O alternatives, you have the flexibility to read and write data from HDFS, GCS, or BigQuery from the Dataproc cluster. You may choose to store the data directly in a native BigQuery table if you are working with structured data that has a clear table schema. In general, accessing data from HDFS is faster than GCS, and GCS is faster than BigQuery. But this is a general rule of thumb; how much faster still depends on the data volume. A lot of times, the time difference is not significant compared to the ease of using the slower storage connection. With that in mind, focus on the use case; if your use case uses all structured data, then use BigQuery as your underlying storage. If you need more flexibility to store all of your data in files, use GCS. And if the processing time is critical, use HDFS on the SSD.

Understanding the concept of the ephemeral cluster

After running the previous exercises, you may notice that Spark is very useful to process data, but it has little to no dependence on Hadoop storage (HDFS). It's very convenient to use data as is from GCS or BigQuery compared to using HDFS.

What does this mean? It means that we may choose not to store any data in the Hadoop cluster (more specifically, in HDFS) and only use the cluster to run jobs. For cost efficiency, we can smartly turn on and turn off the cluster only when a job is running. Furthermore, we can destroy the entire Hadoop cluster when the job is finished and create a new one when we submit a new job. This concept is what's called an ephemeral cluster.

An **ephemeral cluster** means the cluster is not permanent. A cluster will only exist when it's running jobs. There are two main advantages to using this approach:

- **Highly efficient infrastructure cost**: With this approach, you don't need to have a giant Hadoop cluster with hundreds of workers hanging and waiting for jobs. It's typical for organizations that adopt Hadoop on-premises to have this giant cluster model. But since we have this flexibility to destroy and create clusters easily in the cloud, we can reduce all the unnecessary costs from idle clusters and worker machines.

- **Dedicated resource for isolated jobs**: With this approach, every set of jobs can run in a dedicated cluster. A dedicated cluster means you can specify the following:

  - The OS version

  - Hadoop versions

  - Dependency libraries

  - Cluster specs

  This will remove all the common issues in Spark about resource allocation and dependency conflicts. When jobs are isolated, you know exactly the expected job completion time given a specific cluster spec.

An ephemeral cluster is the recommended Hadoop cluster model on GCP. But there are times when you can't use the ephemeral model. You shouldn't use an ephemeral cluster in the following instances:

- You need to use HDFS and Hive as your underlying data storage for the data lake.

- You need to use the user interface on the Hadoop cluster, for example, Hue, the Jupyter Notebook, or Zeppelin.

Remember that in the ephemeral model, your cluster literally will be deleted. The data in the cluster machines will also be gone after each job. In the preceding case, using a permanent Dataproc approach is the only option.

If we decide to use the ephemeral cluster approach, then a question may come up – how do we sync the cluster creation and deletion with a job?

There are many ways; you can do it manually and automatically. One automatic option is using the Dataproc workflow template. Let's practice using it to understand the next section.

Practicing using a workflow template on Dataproc

A workflow template is a feature in Dataproc that can help you manage simple job dependencies. Using a workflow template, you can also define an ephemeral cluster as a part of jobs. This means that if you run jobs using a workflow template, it will automatically create a new Dataproc cluster, run the jobs, and drop the cluster after it finishes.

To create a workflow template, go to the Dataproc console. In the left sidebar, find **Workflows**, like this:

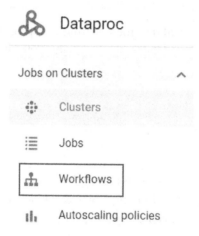

Figure 5.15 – The Workflows menu in the Dataproc console

Find and click the **CREATE WORKFLOW TEMPLATE** button and configure some important options:

- **Template ID**: `run_pyspark_job`
- **TTL**: `30 minutes`

Click **Next**.

On the next page, click **CONFIGURE MANAGED CLUSTER**, which will be similar to the options that we have when creating a Dataproc cluster. This time, we can use the **Single Node** cluster type:

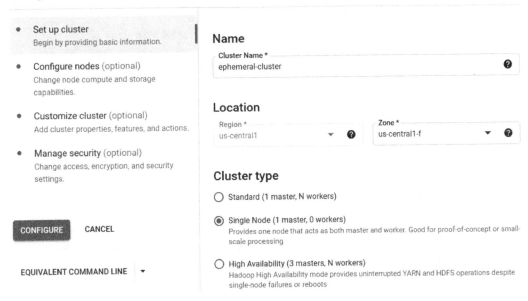

Figure 5.16 – Choose a Single Node cluster

Don't forget to configure the node to use `n1-standard-2` machines with 30 GB storage. This will save a little bit on costs.

If finished, click **Next**. You will be on the **Job config** page; find and click the **ADD JOB** button. This is to add our PySpark job; we need to provide the code location in GCS and the required JAR files. In our case, we need the BigQuery connector library.

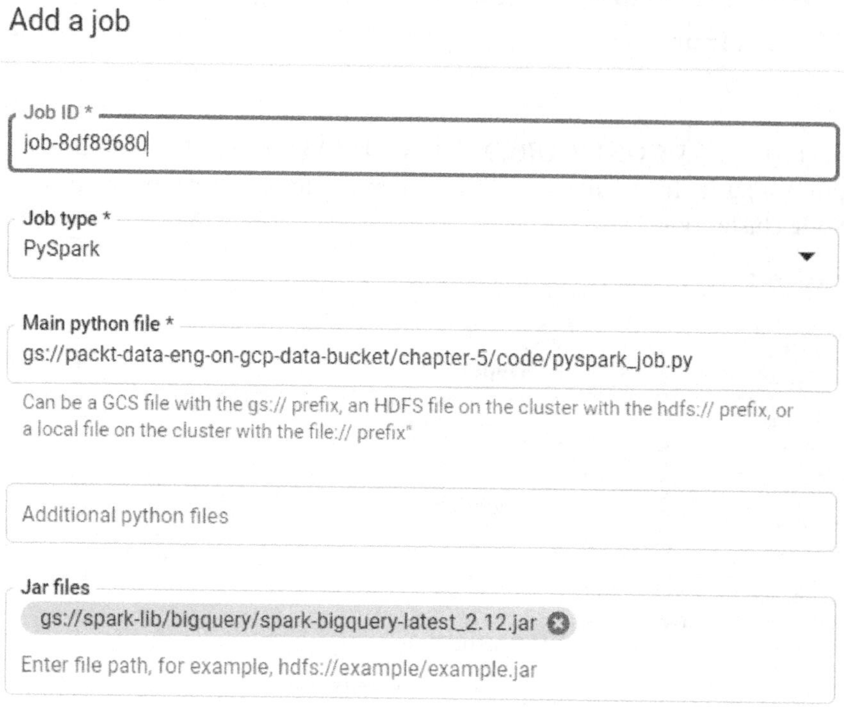

Add a job

Job ID *

job-8df89680

Job type *

PySpark

Main python file *

gs://packt-data-eng-on-gcp-data-bucket/chapter-5/code/pyspark_job.py

Can be a GCS file with the gs:// prefix, an HDFS file on the cluster with the hdfs:// prefix, or a local file on the cluster with the file:// prefix"

Additional python files

Jar files

gs://spark-lib/bigquery/spark-bigquery-latest_2.12.jar

Enter file path, for example, hdfs://example/example.jar

Figure 5.17 – Example job configuration

If finished, find the **CREATE** button at the bottom of the screen. You should see your workflow template is there. Click **RUN** to try it:

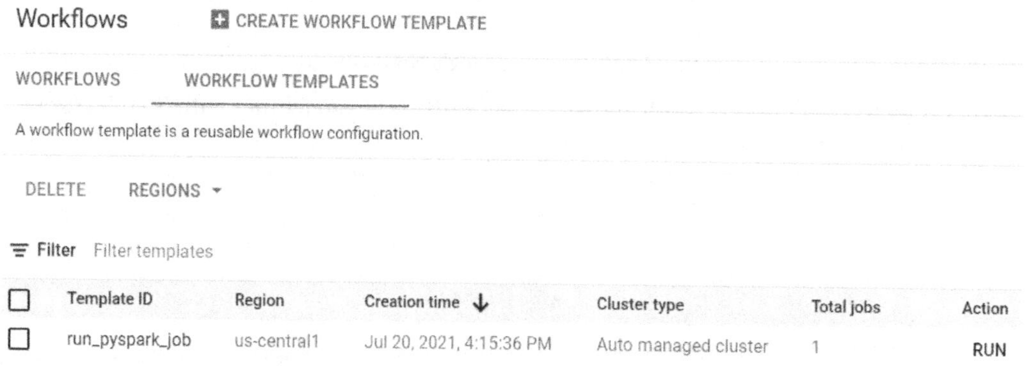

Workflows   CREATE WORKFLOW TEMPLATE

WORKFLOWS   WORKFLOW TEMPLATES

A workflow template is a reusable workflow configuration.

DELETE   REGIONS ▾

Filter   Filter templates

Template ID	Region	Creation time ↓	Cluster type	Total jobs	Action
run_pyspark_job	us-central1	Jul 20, 2021, 4:15:36 PM	Auto managed cluster	1	RUN

Figure 5.18 – A Dataproc workflow template

While running, we can check three different menus to see what really happens:

1. In the **WORKFLOWS** tab, you can see the workflow template is running:

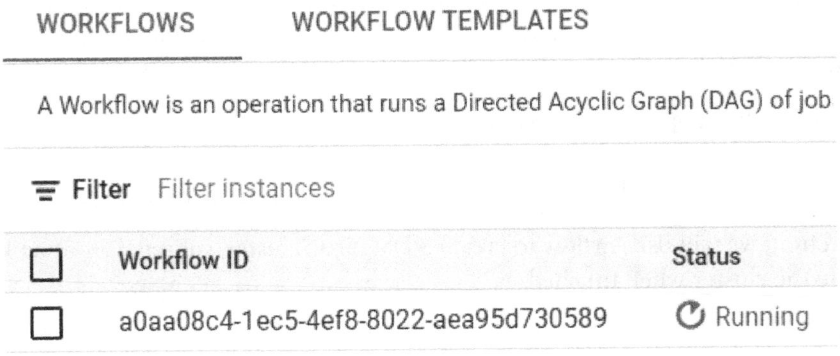

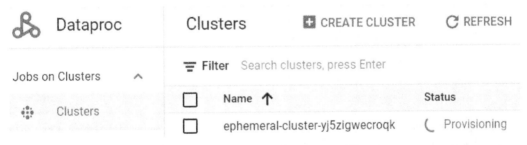

Figure 5.19 – A workflow template is running

2. In the Dataproc **Clusters** menu, you can see a newly created cluster:

Figure 5.20 – A Dataproc cluster is provisioned

3. After the cluster is successfully provisioned, you can see the job is running in the **Jobs** menu.

4. Wait for around 5 minutes after the job has finished; you should then see that the cluster has gone.

What we've looked at here is a Dataproc ephemeral cluster to run a PySpark job. As you can see, the cluster lives only when running a job; after that, it will automatically be destroyed. If you want to rerun the job, you can go back to the **WORKFLOW TEMPLATES** menu and run it again.

In this exercise, we only run one job in the template. The workflow template can also run multiple jobs as a **Directed Acyclic Graph** (**DAG**), with job dependencies that you can configure while creating the template.

Building an ephemeral cluster using Dataproc and Cloud Composer

Another option to manage ephemeral clusters is using Cloud Composer. We learned about Airflow in the previous chapter to orchestrate BigQuery data loading. But as we've already learned, Airflow has many operators and one of them is of course Dataproc.

You should use this approach compared to a workflow template if your jobs are complex, in terms of developing a pipeline that contains many branches, backfilling logic, and dependencies to other services, since workflow templates can't handle these complexities.

In this section, we will use Airflow to create a Dataproc cluster, submit a `pyspark` job, and delete the cluster when finished.

Check the full code in the GitHub repository:

```
Link to be updated
```

To use the Dataproc operators in Airflow, we need to import the operators, like this:

```python
from airflow.providers.google.cloud.operators.dataproc import (
    DataprocCreateClusterOperator,
    DataprocDeleteClusterOperator,
    DataprocSubmitJobOperator,
)
```

After importing the three Dataproc operators, we can create a cluster, delete a cluster, and submit a job using Airflow DAG. If you don't remember how to create and submit a DAG to Cloud Composer, please revisit the *Level 1 DAG - Creating dummy workflows* section in *Chapter 4, Building Orchestration for Batch Data Loading Using Cloud Composer*.

The first up is `DataprocCreateClusterOperator`; this operator will create a Dataproc cluster. You can specify the cluster configuration using a `json` string, like this:

```python
CLUSTER_NAME = 'ephemeral-spark-cluster-{{ ds_nodash }}'
cluster_config_json = {
    «worker_config": {
      «num_instances": 2
    }
}
create_cluster = DataprocCreateClusterOperator(
    task_id="create_cluster",
    project_id=PROJECT_ID,
```

```
    cluster_config=cluster_config_json,
    region=REGION,
    cluster_name=CLUSTER_NAME,
    idle_delete_ttl=600
)
```

In the previous example, we configured the number of workers to be two. There are many other configurations that we can specify; the full list can be found in this public documentation:

```
https://cloud.google.com/dataproc/docs/reference/rest/v1/
ClusterConfig
```

The other thing that we specify is the `idle_delete_ttl` value to be `600 seconds`. This means that if the DAG fails for any reason, the cluster will automatically be deleted after 600 seconds. Lastly, another trick is to add a postfix to our cluster name; for this example, we use the date from the Airflow macro variable. Using this date as the cluster name will prevent a collision between jobs with different execution dates. This will be useful if the DAG is running multiple backfills.

Next, we want to add a task for submitting a `pyspark` job. To do that, we need the job's code URI, and in our example, because we need to use the BigQuery connector, we can specify the `jar` file in the PySpark job configuration, like this:

```
PYSPARK_URI = 'gs://[BUCKET NAME]/chapter-5/code/pyspark_gcs_
to_bq.py'
PYSPARK_JOB = {
    «reference»: {«project_id": PROJECT_ID},
    «placement»: {«cluster_name": CLUSTER_NAME},
    «pyspark_job": {"main_python_file_uri": PYSPARK_URI,
    «jar_file_uris":["gs://spark-lib/bigquery/spark-bigquery-
latest_2.12.jar"]
    }
}
pyspark_task = DataprocSubmitJobOperator(
    task_id="pyspark_task", job=PYSPARK_JOB, location=REGION,
project_id=PROJECT_ID
)
```

In the previous example, we only have one job. Remember that you can add as many `PySpark job` tasks as needed. And lastly, after the jobs are finished, we want the cluster to be deleted. It's a simple task, like this:

```
delete_cluster = DataprocDeleteClusterOperator(
    task_id="delete_cluster", project_id=PROJECT_ID, cluster_
name=CLUSTER_NAME, region=REGION
)
```

The DAG dependency is very simple, like this:

```
create_cluster >> pyspark_task >> delete_cluster
```

For this exercise, you are free to try running it if you still have the Cloud Composer environment running. But if you don't, just remember that if you want to develop Spark jobs using an ephemeral cluster, you have two options, as follows:

- A workflow template
- Cloud Composer

Use the first option if jobs are simple, but it's very common for data engineers to choose Cloud Composer so that they can combine all the best practices from Cloud Composer with Dataproc, BigQuery, and GCS.

Summary

This chapter covered one component of GCP that allows you to build a data lake, called Dataproc. As we've learned in this chapter, learning about Dataproc means learning about Hadoop. We learned about and practiced the core and most popular Hadoop components, HDFS and Spark.

By combining the nature of Hadoop with all the benefits of using the cloud, we also learned about new concepts. The Hadoop ephemeral cluster is relatively new and is only possible because of cloud technology. In a traditional on-premises Hadoop cluster, this highly efficient concept is never an option.

From the perspective of a data engineer working on GCP, using Hadoop or Dataproc is optional. Similar functionality is doable using full serverless components on GCP; for example, use GCS and BigQuery as storage rather than HDFS and use Dataflow for processing unstructured data rather than Spark. But the popularity of Spark is one of the main reasons for people using Dataproc. Spark is powerful, easy to understand, and very popular across organizations globally. As a data engineer, being able to develop Spark will be of huge benefit to finding data engineering roles in your career. And as a company, using Spark as the main system will make recruitment easier since the talent pool is big compared to other data processing frameworks.

In this book, we focused on the core concepts in Spark. We've learned about using RDDs and Spark DataFrames. These two concepts are the first entry point before learning about other features such as Spark ML and Spark Streaming. As you get more and more experienced, you will need to start to think about optimization – for example, how to manage parallelism, how to fasten-join, and how to maximize resource allocation.

In the next chapter, we will learn about another data processing framework, **Dataflow**. Dataflow is a serverless service that processes structured and unstructured data, but we will focus on using Dataflow for streaming a data pipeline.

6

Processing Streaming Data with Pub/Sub and Dataflow

Processing streaming data is becoming increasingly popular, as streaming enables businesses to get real-time metrics on business operations. This chapter describes which paradigm should be used—and when—for streaming data. The chapter will also cover how to apply transformations to streaming data using Cloud Dataflow, and how to store processed records in BigQuery for analysis.

Learning about streaming data is easier when we really do it, so we will exercise creating a streaming data pipeline on **Google Cloud Platform (GCP)**. We will use two GCP services, **Pub/Sub** and **Dataflow**. Both of the services are essential in creating a streaming data pipeline. We will use the same dataset as we used for practicing a batch data pipeline. With that, you can compare how similar and different the approaches are.

As a summary, here are the topics that we will discuss in this chapter:

- Processing streaming data
- Exercise—Publishing event streams to Cloud Pub/Sub
- Exercise—Using Cloud Dataflow to stream data from Pub/Sub to BigQuery

Let's get started!

Technical requirements

Before we begin the chapter, make sure you have the following prerequisites ready.

In this chapter's exercises, we will use these GCP services: **Dataflow**, **Pub/Sub**, **Google Cloud Storage (GCS)**, and **BigQuery**. If you have never opened any of these services in your GCP console, open them and enable the **application programming interface (API)**.

Make sure you have your **GCP console**, **Cloud Shell**, and **Cloud Shell Editor** ready.

Download the example code and the dataset from here:

```
https://github.com/PacktPublishing/Data-Engineering-with-
Google-Cloud-Platform/tree/main/chapter-6
```

Be aware of the cost that might occur from **dataflow streaming**. Make sure you delete all the environment after the exercises to prevent unexpected costs.

This chapter will use the same data from *Chapter 5*, *Building a Data Lake Using Dataproc*. You can choose to use the same data or prepare new data from the GitHub repository.

Processing streaming data

In the big data era, people like to correlate big data with real-time data. Some people say that if the data is not real-time, then it's not big data. This statement is partially true. In practice, the majority of data pipelines in the world use the batch approach, and that's why it's still very important for data engineers to understand the batch data pipeline. From *Chapter 3*, *Building a Data Warehouse in BigQuery*, to *Chapter 5*, *Building a Data Lake Using Dataproc*, we focused on handling batch data pipelines.

However, real-time capabilities in the big data era are something that many data engineers need to start to rethink in terms of data architecture. To understand more about architecture, we first need to have a clear definition of what real-time data is.

From the end-user perspective, real-time data can mean anything—anything from faster access to data, more frequent data refreshes, and detecting events as soon as they happen. From a data engineer perspective, what we need to know is *how* to make it happen. For example, if you search any keyword in Google Search, you will get an immediate result in real time. Or, in another example, if you open any social media page, you can find your account statistics and the number of friends, visitors, and other information in real time.

But if you think about it, you may notice that there is nothing new in both of the examples. As an end user, you can get fast access to the data because of the backend database, and this is a common practice dating from the 1990s. In big data, what's new is the real time in terms of incoming data and processing. This specific real-time aspect is called **streaming data**. For example, you need to detect fraud as soon as an event happens. In most cases, detecting fraud needs many parameters from multiple data sources, which are impossible to be handled in the application database. If fraud has no relevance to your company, you can think of other use cases such as real-time marketing campaigns and real-time dashboards for sales reporting. Both use cases may require a large volume of data from multiple data sources. In these kinds of cases, being able to handle data in streams may come in handy.

Streaming data for data engineers

Streaming data in data engineering means a data pipeline that flows data from the upstream to the downstream as soon as the data is created. In nature, all data is created in real time, so processing data in batches is a way to simplify the process.

What does this mean?

If you think about how every piece of data is created, it's always in real time—for example, a user registered to a mobile application. The moment the user registered, data was created in the database. Another example is of data being input into a spreadsheet. The moment the data entry is written in the spreadsheet, data is created in the sheet. Looking at the examples, you can see that data always has a value and the time when it's created. Processing streaming data means we process the data as soon as the data is inputted into a system.

Take a look at the following diagram. Here, there are two databases: the source database and the target database. For streaming data, every time a new record is inserted into the source database (illustrated as boxes with numbers), the record is immediately processed as an event and inserted into the target database. These events happen continuously, which makes the data in the target database real-time compared to the source database:

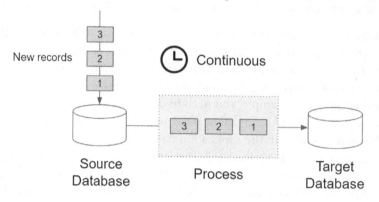

Figure 6.1 – Streaming data illustration

In data engineering, the antonym for *stream* is *batch*. Batching is a very common approach for data engineers to process data. Even though we know data is real-time in nature, it's a lot easier to process data in a set time. For example, if your **chief executive officer (CEO)** wants to know about the company's revenue, it's a lot easier to populate the purchase history in a month and calculate the revenue, rather than build a system then continuously calculate the purchase transactions. Or, in a more granular level, a batch is commonly done on a weekly, daily, or hourly basis. The batch approach is a widely used practice in the data engineering world; I can say 90% of the data pipeline is a batch.

Take a look at the following diagram. Here, the two databases are the same as in *Figure 6.1*. The nature of how data is inserted into the source database is also the same—it's always real-time from the source database perspective. The difference is in the processing step, where the records are grouped into batches. Every batch is scheduled individually to be loaded to the target database:

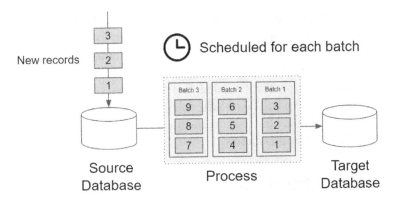

Figure 6.2 – Batch data illustration

There are two major reasons why processing data in batches is more popular compared to streams. The first is because of the data user's needs. The data user, who is usually called a decision maker, naturally asks for information over a period of time. As we've discussed in the previous example, common questions are *How much X in a day?* or *How many X in a month?*. It's very rare to have a question such as *How much X occurred this second compared to the last second?*.

The second reason is the complexity of technology. Batching is easier than streaming because you can control a lot of things in a batch—for example, you can control how you want to schedule data pipeline jobs. This doesn't apply to stream processing. A streaming process is one job; once it runs, it will process all the incoming data and it never ends. To handle all the complexities, we need specific sets of technologies.

In GCP, the common technology stack uses Pub/Sub and Dataflow. The following diagram shows the most common pattern for processing streaming data from data sources to BigQuery tables:

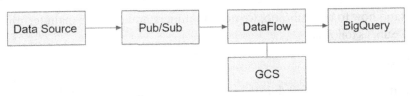

Figure 6.3 – High-level data streaming pattern

We will need Pub/Sub to control the incoming and outgoing data streams as messages. The next step is to set Dataflow jobs that accept the messages to process the data as a streaming process. Dataflow will process the data in a distributed manner, and since Dataflow is a serverless service, we don't need to think about the servers. Dataflow will need GCS to store data temporarily if needed, and as the final process, it will stream the data to BigQuery tables. There will be no scheduler in the picture; all processes are long-running jobs and we will learn how to schedule them in the exercise later. For now, let's learn the basics of Pub/Sub and Dataflow.

Introduction to Pub/Sub

Pub/Sub is a messaging system. What messaging systems do is receive messages from multiple systems and distribute them to multiple systems. The key here is *multiple systems*. A messaging system needs to be able to act as a bridge or middleware to many different systems.

Check out this diagram to get a high-level picture of Pub/Sub:

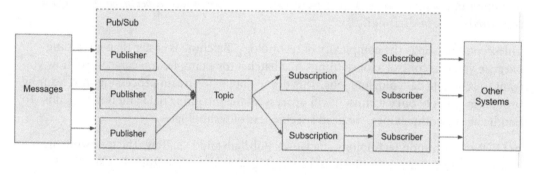

Figure 6.4 – Pub/Sub terminologies and flows

To understand how to use Pub/Sub, we need to understand the four main terminologies inside Pub/Sub, as follows:

- **Publisher**

  The entry point of Pub/Sub is the publisher. Pub/Sub uses the publisher to control incoming messages. Users can write code to publish messages from their applications using programming languages such as Java, Python, Go, C++, C#, **PHP: Hypertext Preprocessor (PHP)**, and Ruby. Pub/Sub will store the messages in topics.

- **Topic**

    The central point of Pub/Sub is a topic. Pub/Sub stores messages in its internal storage. The sets of messages that are stored in Pub/Sub are called topics. As an analogy, Pub/Sub topics are similar to tables in a database—and using that analogy, Pub/Sub messages are similar, with rows or records in the tables.

- **Subscription**

    At the other end, each topic can have one or many subscriptions. Subscriptions are entities that have an interest in receiving messages from the topic. For example, for one topic that has two subscriptions, the two subscriptions will get identical messages from the topic.

- **Subscriber**

    A subscriber is different from a subscription. Each subscription can have one or many subscribers. The idea of having multiple subscribers in a subscription is to split the loads. For example, for one subscription that has two subscribers, the two subscribers will get partial messages from the subscription.

As an addition to those four main terminologies, there is one more important term, which is **acknowledge (ack)**. Ack is not a component or object in Pub/Sub, which is why I didn't include it in the preceding terminologies.

Back to our last point about subscribers—after messages are delivered by the subscriber, the subscriber will acknowledge them. In Pub/Sub, this is called **ack**. When a message is *ack-ed*, the topic will stop sending the message to the subscriber. In scenarios when the publisher can't *ack* the message for any reason—for example, a code error, a server overload, or any other reason—the Pub/Sub topic will retry sending the message up until it's either successfully ack-ed or expired.

This bunch of terminologies might sound abstract to you at this point, but it's a good start to be familiar with common terms. The easiest way to understand Pub/Sub is by using it. We will practice Pub/Sub in the next section, but before that, let's get familiar with Dataflow.

Introduction to Dataflow

Dataflow is a data processing engine that can handle both batch and streaming data pipelines. If we want to compare with technologies that we already learned about in this book, Dataflow is comparable with Spark—comparable in terms of positioning, both technologies can process big data. Both technologies process data in parallel and can handle almost any kind of data or file.

But in terms of underlying technologies, they are different. From the user perspective, the main difference is the serverless nature of Dataflow. Using Dataflow, we don't need to set up any cluster. We just submit jobs to Dataflow, and the data pipeline will run automatically on the cloud. How we write the data pipeline is by using Apache Beam.

Apache Beam is an open source tool to define data pipelines, but instead of executing them, Apache Beam will send the data pipelines to an execution engine such as Dataflow. Not only Dataflow—Apache Beam can run data pipelines on Direct Runner, Apache Flink, Nemo, Samza, and other engines. But the key here is the relationship between Apache Beam and Dataflow—we write code using the Apache Beam **software development kit** (**SDK**), and Apache Beam will run the data pipeline using Dataflow. Later in the exercise, we will learn about Apache Beam and run it using Direct Runner and Dataflow. In the next section, we will start the exercises in this chapter by creating our first Pub/Sub topic.

Exercise – Publishing event streams to cloud Pub/Sub

In this exercise, we will try to stream data from Pub/Sub publishers. The goal is to create a data pipeline that can stream the data to a BigQuery table, but instead of using a scheduler (as we did in *Chapter 4, Building Orchestration for Batch Data Loading Using Cloud Composer*), we will submit a Dataflow job that will run as an application to flow data from Pub/Sub to a BigQuery table. In the exercise, we will use the bike-sharing dataset we used in *Chapter 3, Building a Data Warehouse in BigQuery*. Here are the overall steps in this Pub/Sub section:

1.   Creating a Pub/Sub topic
2.   Creating and running a Pub/Sub publisher using Python
3.   Creating a Pub/Sub subscription

Let's start by creating a Pub/Sub topic in the next section.

Creating a Pub/Sub topic

We can create Pub/Sub topics using many approaches—for example, using the GCP console, the `gcloud` command, or through code. As a starter, let's use the GCP console. Proceed as follows:

1. Open the console and find **Pub/Sub** in the navigation bar, as illustrated in the following screenshot:

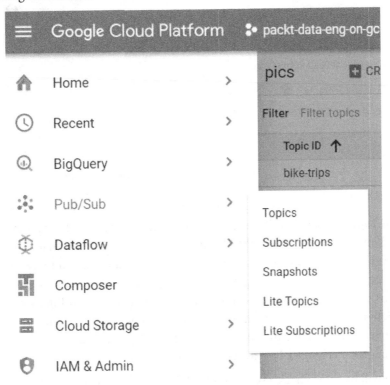

Figure 6.5 – Pub/Sub menu from the navigation bar

If this is the first time you have accessed Pub/Sub, you will be asked to enable the API. Do that by clicking the **ENABLE Pub/Sub API** button.

2. On the **Topics** page, find the **CREATE TOPIC** button. It looks like this:

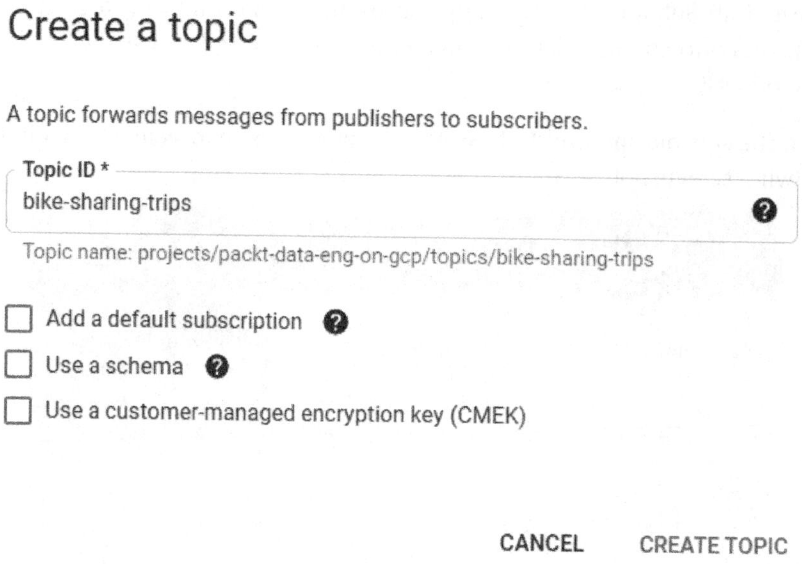

Create a topic

A topic forwards messages from publishers to subscribers.

Topic ID *

bike-sharing-trips   ❷

Topic name: projects/packt-data-eng-on-gcp/topics/bike-sharing-trips

☐ Add a default subscription ❷

☐ Use a schema ❷

☐ Use a customer-managed encryption key (CMEK)

CANCEL   CREATE TOPIC

Figure 6.6 – Example of topic creation in Pub/Sub

In the **Topic ID** field, I will use `bike-sharing-trips` as the topic name or **identifier** (**ID**) to store our bike-sharing messages. Remember that a topic name is similar to a table name in BigQuery—it needs to be unique and representative of the message later. But also remember that in databases, we have higher-level groups such as `dataset`, where you can group tables in a dataset. In Pub/Sub, there is no higher-level object, so be mindful when naming your topic—it needs to be as informative as possible. In this exercise, I use `bike-sharing` to describe what the dataset group is and `trips` to represent the content.

There will be three checkboxes—uncheck all of them. We will create our subscription manually later to understand Pub/Sub subscription better. Once done, finish the process by clicking **CREATE TOPIC**.

3. Check your topic by clicking it on the page. You will see an empty topic without messages. We will start sending messages using a publisher in the next section.

Creating and running a Pub/Sub publisher using Python

For sending messages using a publisher, we should write code. As a standard in this book, we will use Python, but there are many other programming languages you can use that you can check in the *Pub/Sub public documentation*.

Let's start by opening our Cloud Shell environment. The example code is accessible from the repository: `https://github.com/PacktPublishing/Data-Engineering-with-Google-Cloud-Platform`.

If you already cloned the repository from previous chapters, open the `chapter-6/code/pubsub_publisher.py` file. Then, proceed as follows:

1. First, we need a Python function. The Python function will return a **JavaScript Object Notation (JSON)** record containing bike-sharing trip data. To simplify the example, we will generate five columns—`trip_id`, `start_date`, `start_station_id`, `bike_number`, and `duration_sec`. The Python function code looks like this:

```python
def create_random_message():
    trip_id = randint(10000,99999)
    start_date = str(datetime.utcnow())
    start_station_id = randint(200,205)
    bike_number = randint(100,999)
    duration_sec = randint(1000,9999)

    message_json = {'trip_id': trip_id,
            'start_date': start_date,
            'start_station_id': start_station_id,
            'bike_number':bike_number,
            'duration_sec':duration_sec
            }
    return message_json
```

As you can see from the preceding code, this is a simple function that randomizes some integers for our example message. Messages in Pub/Sub can be anything—they can be free text—but in this example, we will send messages in JSON format.

2. For the Pub/Sub publisher, we will call `PublisherClient` from the Python package, like this:

```python
project_id = "packt-data-eng-on-gcp"
topic_id = "bike-sharing-trips"

publisher = pubsub_v1.PublisherClient()
topic_path = publisher.topic_path(project_id, topic_id)
```

This is straightforward Python code to call the client. Do remember to change the `project_id` value to your GCP project ID.

3. What we now need to do is to send the message—we will simply loop 10 times to send exactly 10 messages. You can change the number as you like. Here is the code:

```
for i in range(10):
    message_json = create_random_message()
    data = json.dumps(message_json)
    publish_future = publisher.publish(topic_path, data.
encode("utf-8"))
    publish_future.add_done_callback \
    (get_callback(publish_future, data))
    publish_futures.append(publish_future)
```

These lines of code will call the `create_random_message` function to get a JSON value and convert it into a string using `json.dumps()`. The message will be published using the `publisher.publish()` method.

4. Then, to make sure the message is successfully published and can handle errors when we fail to send it, we define it in the callback function. The callback function looks like this:

```
def get_callback(publish_future, data):
    def callback(publish_future):
        try:
            # Wait 60 seconds for the publish call to
succeed.
            print(publish_future.result(timeout=60))
        except futures.TimeoutError:
            print(f"Publishing {data} timed out.")

    return callback
```

The callback will wait for 60 seconds before it returns an exception.

5. And lastly, insert this code:

```
futures.wait(publish_futures, return_when=futures.ALL_
COMPLETED)


print(f"Published messages with error handler to {topic_
path}.")
```

The line will instruct our application to wait until all records are done and will print out all the message IDs.

Go back to Cloud Shell, and try to run the Python code using the following Python command:

```
#python3 pubsub_publisher.py
```

If successful, it will look like this:

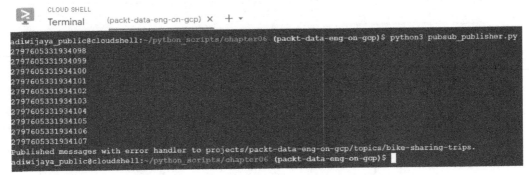

Figure 6.7 – Example pubsub_publisher application's output

Now, go back to your Pub/Sub console, and you will see the graphs show some activity in the topics, as illustrated here:

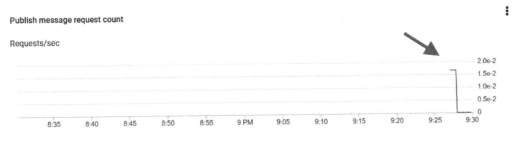

Figure 6.8 – Monitoring topic activity from a graph

If you can't see the line in the graph, don't worry—it takes around 5 minutes before the graph refreshes. To read the messages, we need a subscription. We will create one in the next section.

Creating a Pub/Sub subscription

In this section, we will create a Pub/Sub subscription. We will try creating one using the console. To do that, follow these steps:

1. From the **Pub/Sub topic** page, find and click the **CREATE SUBSCRIPTION** button at the bottom of the page. The button is under the **SUBSCRIPTIONS** tab—check out this screenshot for an example of this:

Figure 6.9 – Finding the CREATE SUBSCRIPTION button

   On the **CREATE SUBSCRIPTIONS** page, there are some options that you can choose. If you remember, there was a checkbox for adding a default subscription when creating a topic—this is one of the reasons we didn't check on that. We want to create one manually so that we can learn about the options and some of its concepts.

2. Define a **Subscription ID** value—feel free to choose any name. For example, I use `bike-sharing-trips-subs-1`.

3. The second option is **Delivery Type**; we have two options here: `pull` and `push`. In general, the `pull` option is recommended for the data pipeline use case. In the data pipeline, the subscriber can call the Pub/Sub client to pull the data from the subscription topic—for example, Dataflow can pull from a subscription topic. In that case, we use the `pull` method. The `push` method is used if the subscriber can't use the Pub/Sub client. The `push` method will provide a **HyperText Transfer Protocol (HTTP)** endpoint to deliver the message continuously. Neither method really affects the throughput, both can provide high throughput, but the `push` method has a smaller throughput quota. As a comparison, the pull to push throughput difference is around 30:1, you can check the exact quota in the public documentation at `https://cloud.google.com/pubsub/quotas#quotas`.

4. The third option is the **Message Retention Duration**. This is to set up how long we want to keep unacknowledged (unacked) messages. The consideration is cost versus risk. If we keep unacked messages longer, the risk of losing the messages is lower but means we need to pay for stored messages.

5. The **Expiration period** field is straightforward. If there is no subscriber activity in the **Subscription** field, the subscription will be deleted automatically after the expiration period.

6. The last option that we will talk about is the **Acknowledgement deadline** option. This is to set up how many seconds you expect it will take for the subscription to resend the message if the message is not acked. This is related to how much the subscriber can handle the message. If the process in the subscriber is light and the throughput is low, you can set the deadline lower. If the process is heavy, set the deadline longer so that the subscriber won't get overwhelmed by messages.

As for this exercise, I will set the message retention duration to **10 minutes** and the expiration period to **1 day**.

There are other options in the form but we will ignore these for now; you can always revisit this later. After finishing with all the configurations, click **CREATE**.

Now, we want to check our messages. You can see the **MESSAGES** tab beside the **SUBSCRIPTIONS** tab—go there and click the **VIEW MESSAGES** button.

This is a way for us to check the messages in a topic. We use this menu only in the development phase. In reality, the publishers are applications. We can imagine this process as a subscriber—to do that, find and click the **PULL** button. You will not see any message yet, as in the following screenshot:

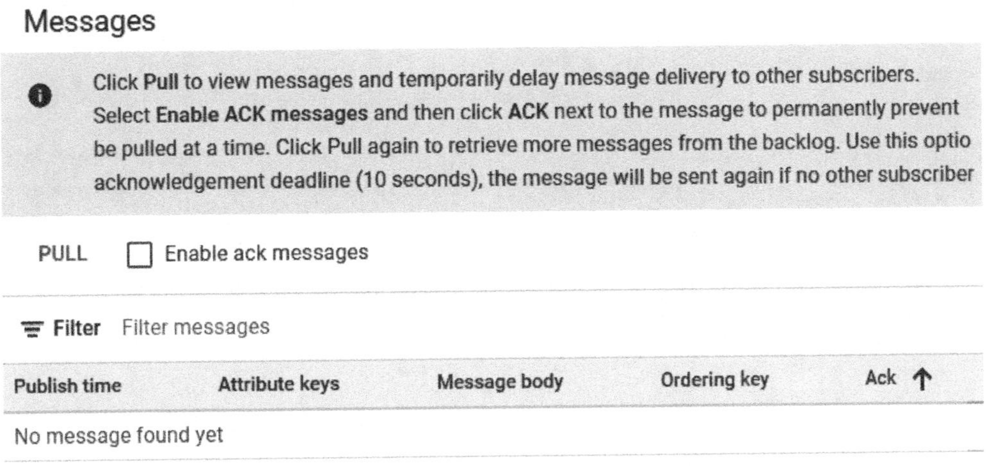

Messages

> ℹ Click **Pull** to view messages and temporarily delay message delivery to other subscribers. Select **Enable ACK messages** and then click **ACK** next to the message to permanently prevent be pulled at a time. Click Pull again to retrieve more messages from the backlog. Use this optio acknowledgement deadline (10 seconds), the message will be sent again if no other subscriber

PULL   ☐ Enable ack messages

≡ Filter   Filter messages

Publish time	Attribute keys	Message body	Ordering key	Ack ↑

No message found yet

Figure 6.10 – Example blank messages screen

Now, we want to publish some messages to our topic using Python code. Please follow these steps:

1. Back to Cloud Shell, and let's run our `pubsub_publisher.py` Python code again. You can run it more than one time to publish more than 10 messages. For example, I will run it twice in Cloud Shell, like this:

```
adiwijaya_public@cloudshell:~/python_scripts/chapter06 (packt-data-eng-on-gcp)$ python3 pubsub_publisher.py
2798900147080360
2798900147080361
2798900147080362
2798900147080363
2798900147080364
2798900147080365
2798900147080366
2798900147080367
2798900147080368
2798900147080369
Published messages with error handler to projects/packt-data-eng-on-gcp/topics/bike-sharing-trips.
adiwijaya_public@cloudshell:~/python_scripts/chapter06 (packt-data-eng-on-gcp)$ python3 pubsub_publisher.py
2798899773594891
2798899773594892
2798899773594893
2798899773594894
2798899773594895
2798899773594896
2798899773594897
2798899773594898
2798899773594899
2798899773594900
Published messages with error handler to projects/packt-data-eng-on-gcp/topics/bike-sharing-trips.
adiwijaya_public@cloudshell:~/python_scripts/chapter06 (packt-data-eng-on-gcp)$
```

Figure 6.11 – Running the pubsub_publisher apps twice

2. Go back to the **Pub/Sub View Message** page and click the **PULL** button again— you will see exactly 20 messages with the publish time and the message body, as illustrated in the following screenshot:

PULL   ☐ Enable ack messages

≡ Filter   Filter messages   ?

Publish time	Attribute keys	Message body	Ack ↑
Aug 3, 2021, 9:37:18 PM	–	{"trip_id": 64569, "start_date": "2021-08-03 13:37:18.339846", "start_station_id": 2	Deadline exceeded
Aug 3, 2021, 9:37:18 PM	–	{"trip_id": 10769, "start_date": "2021-08-03 13:37:18.340442", "start_station_id": 2	Deadline exceeded
Aug 3, 2021, 9:37:18 PM	–	{"trip_id": 94581, "start_date": "2021-08-03 13:37:18.340581", "start_station_id": 2	Deadline exceeded

Figure 6.12 – The messages are shown after being pulled

Another option is to check the **Enable ack messages** option, and the **ACK** button will appear on the right side—if you click it, the message will be gone.

Figure 6.13 – Finding the ACK button on the screen

That's the nature of Pub/Sub. A Pub/Sub publisher is an application that sends a message to a topic. A topic can have multiple subscriptions, and when a subscriber successfully processes the topic's message, it will be acked. When a message is acked, then the message will be deleted because it's successfully delivered. The process from publisher to subscriber happens in milliseconds, and Pub/Sub can handle multiple publishers and subscribers without scalability issues, which is why Pub/Sub is essential when creating a streaming process. In the next section, we will use Dataflow as the subscriber. Dataflow will subscribe to our topic, transform the data, and store the data in BigQuery.

Exercise – Using Cloud Dataflow to stream data from Pub/Sub to GCS

In this exercise, we will learn how to develop Beam code in Python to create data pipelines. Learning Beam will be challenging at first as you will need to get used to the specific coding pattern, so in this exercise, we will start with a `HelloWorld`-level code. But the benefit of using Beam is it's a general framework. Generally, you can create a batch or streaming pipeline with similar code. You can also run using different runners. In this exercise, we will use Direct Runner and Dataflow. As a summary, here are the steps:

- Creating a `HelloWorld` application using Apache Beam
- Creating a Dataflow streaming job without aggregation
- Creating a Dataflow streaming job with aggregation

To start, you can check the code for this exercise here: `https://github.com/PacktPublishing/Data-Engineering-with-Google-Cloud-Platform/blob/main/chapter-6/code/beam_helloworld.py`

Creating a HelloWorld application using Apache Beam

The application that we want to create will read the `logs_example.txt` file from GCS, do some transformation, and store the output back in GCS. We will run this application as a batch data pipeline. If you haven't stored the `logs_example.txt` file in GCS, store it anywhere in your bucket. Let's start our code—you can create code in Cloud Editor and later run the application using Cloud Shell. Proceed as follows:

1. First, let's import the libraries, like this:

```
import apache_beam as beam
import argparse
import logging

from apache_beam.transforms.combiners import Sample
from apache_beam.options.pipeline_options import
PipelineOptions
```

2. We're going to read data from a GCS file and write the output back to GCS, so let's create variables to store the path. Here is an example, but change the bucket and path based on where you store your file:

```
INPUT_FILE = 'gs://[YOUR BUCKET]/from-git/chapter-6/
dataset/logs_example.txt'
OUTPUT_PATH = 'gs://[YOUR BUCKET]/chapter-6/dataflow/
output/output_file'
```

3. We'll now define our data pipeline—this is the basic code for Beam. First, the main Python application runs the `run` function. In the `run` function, we declare the Beam pipeline. In the pipeline, we can declare the steps. The code pattern is unique to Beam. A step is formatted like this:

```
| 'step name' >> Beam step
```

Every step can be declared using the pipe. We can define names for each step—this is optional, but it's recommended to always put the step name. Later, when we use Dataflow, the step name will be useful for monitoring. And the last part is anything after `>>`—that is, the Beam steps. This can be anything from declaring **input and output (I/O)**, a `Map` function, a `print` value, and many other possibilities.

4. In our `HelloWorld` application, let's start with three steps, as follows:

A. Reading the file from GCS

B. Sampling 10 records

C. Printing the records as logs

Here is a code example to declare the pipeline and the steps:

```
def run():
    with beam.Pipeline(options=beam_options) as p:(
        p
        |   'Read' >> beam.io.textio.ReadFromText(INPUT_
FILE)
        |   'Sample' >> Sample.FixedSizeGlobally(10)
        |   'Print' >> beam.Map(print)
    )


if __name__ == '__main__':
    logging.getLogger().setLevel(logging.INFO)
    run()
```

There are a couple of things that you need to be aware of from this short code example. Notice that at the end of our pipeline, we print the records using `beam.Map(print)`. This is a very useful function to know what's happening to our data at each step, but this is not something you should do in the real data pipeline—this is only for development and debugging purposes. Second, data from the `'Read'` step might be very big, so don't forget to sample the data before printing to avoid your application printing too many rows, which can break your terminal.

Now, to run the data pipeline, follow these steps:

1. Open Cloud Shell and install the Apache Beam package.

We need to set up Cloud Shell so that it can run the Beam application. Installing the Beam package is actually simple using the `pip install` command, but if you install it in Cloud Shell, you may get an installation error. Therefore, we need a **virtual environment (venv)**. If you are not familiar with venv in Python, you can check in the Python public documentation about it: `https://docs.python.org/3/tutorial/venv.html`.

2. Install the Python venv.

   In any of your Cloud Shell folders, let's create a new folder called `venv`, install the venv package, and activate it. Here's the code you'll need for this:

   ```
   mkdir venv
   cd venv
   python3 -m venv beam-env
   source beam-env/bin/activate
   ```

   After running the commands, Python will use the dedicated environment for our Beam program.

3. Install the `apache-beam` package.

   To install the `apache-beam` package in the environment, run these commands:

   ```
   pip install --upgrade pip
   pip install wheel
   pip install 'apache-beam[gcp]==2.34.0'
   cd [your hello world python code directory]
   ```

   After running the preceding commands, you will be able to import the package from your Python code.

Make sure to activate the venv (`beam-env`) for running Beam applications. For example, if you close Cloud Shell or your browser, when you go back to Cloud Shell, your environment will no longer use the `beam-env` environment. In that case, you need to restart your terminal.

In case you need to exit from the venv, call `deactivate` from the command line, like this:

```
# deactivate
```

If you deactivate the environment, you will not be able to call `apache-beam` from the Python code.

After creating the required code and installing the package, we will learn how to run it. Follow these steps to run the Beam application:

1. Still in Cloud Shell, declare two environment variables, `project_id` and `region`, as follows:

   ```
   export PROJECT_ID=[YOUR PROJECT ID]
   export REGION=us-central1
   ```

2. Run the Beam application as a typical Python function in the command line. Check this out as an example:

```
python3 beam_helloworld.py \
    --project=$PROJECT_ID \
    --region=$REGION \
    --runner=DirectRunner \
    --temp_location=gs://$BUCKET_NAME/chapter-6/dataflow/
temp
```

Notice in the preceding command that we declare `runner` and `temp_location` parameters. You can choose any GCS path in your bucket for the `temp_location` parameter. For the runner, we will choose Direct Runner for now. Direct Runner means the application will run on your local machine. In this case, Beam will run the code on the Cloud Shell environment—or, in other words, this is not yet a Dataflow application. Later, we will just need to change the runner to run Dataflow jobs.

If successful, the application will look like this:

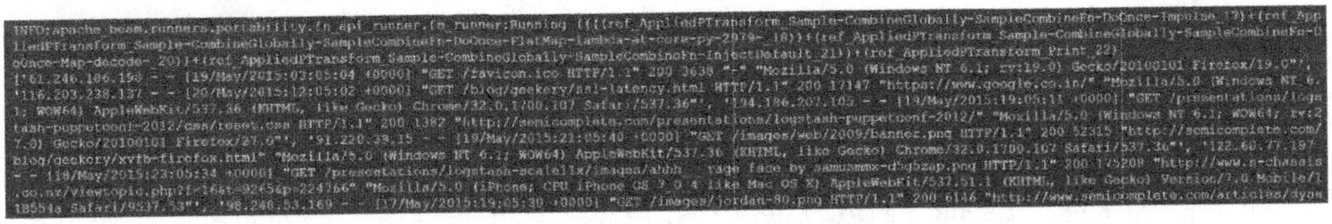

Figure 6.14 – Example output after running Dataflow using Direct Runner

The application will print out the records from the example logs. In the next steps, we will transform and store the records in a GCS bucket. But before that, I'll summarize what you've done so far in this section, as follows:

1. You created a very simple Beam code in Python for printing out the records from a file that is stored in a GCS bucket.

2. You activated a Python venv and installed the `apache-beam[gcp]` package in that environment.

3. You ran the Beam application using Direct Runner from the command line in Cloud Shell. If successful, the program will print out the records in Cloud Shell.

As the last steps in this section, we will go back to our Beam code and change the code a little bit to perform data transformation. After the data transformation, we will load the result to GCS instead of printing it to Cloud Shell. Follow these final steps:

1. Now, back to our code, and let's try to split the records by space. The idea is to get the **Internet Protocol (IP)** address, date, HTTP method, and the **Uniform Resource Locator (URL)**. We will do this using the Map function. To do that, let's prepare a new Python function that will process each input, and the output is an object with four pieces of information. The code is illustrated here:

```python
def split_map(records):
    rows = records.split(" ")
    return {
                'ip': str(rows[0]),
                'date': str(rows[3]),
                'method': str(rows[5]),
                'url': str(rows[6]),
            }
```

2. Declare the split_map function in our pipeline using the Map function, like this:

```python
def run():
    with beam.Pipeline() as p:(
        p
        |   'Read' >> beam.io.textio.ReadFromText(INPUT_
FILE)
        |  'Split' >> beam.Map(split_map)
        |  'Sample' >> Sample.FixedSizeGlobally(10)
        |  'Print' >> beam.Map(print)
    )
```

Notice that it is actually similar to Spark code, which we learned about in *Chapter 5, Building a Data Lake Using Dataproc*. But as you can see, the Map function comes from the Beam package (beam.Map). When you read data from the text file, it will be stored in a parallel data structure called a PCollection. The PCollection can be processed in the next step using the Map function, and the process will result in another PCollection. As another comparison to Spark code, a PCollection is comparable to a **Resilient Distributed Dataset (RDD)**.

PCollections are unique to Beam. Another feature in Beam is **Parallel Do** (ParDo). You use ParDo to transform a PCollection. Back to our previous example, as an alternative, we can also use ParDo to split our data, instead of using the Map function. The key difference between ParDo and the Map function in Beam is that Map always returns one row at a time, while ParDo is more flexible—it can return one to many rows per process. For splitting records, both approaches can work.

3. As a practice exercise, let's try using ParDo. For ParDo, we need to follow the format by declaring the Split function as a Python class. In the Split class, we need a process function that accepts elements. Notice that the function returns an array instead of a single object. Check out these lines of code to see the standard Python format that will be used by ParDo in Beam:

```python
class Split(beam.DoFn):
    def process(self, element):
        rows = element.split(" ")
        return [{
            'ip': str(rows[0]),
            'date': str(rows[3]),
            'method': str(rows[5]),
            'url': str(rows[6]),
        }]
```

4. Back to the Beam pipeline step, and change the Map line to ParDo.

    Change this line:

```python
| 'Split' >> beam.Map(split_map)
```

    The line should now look like this:

```python
| 'Split' >> beam.ParDo(Split())
```

5. Let's try to aggregate the URL by counting it and writing it into GCS to the output path. Our final Beam pipeline code will look like this:

```python
def run():
    with beam.Pipeline() as p:(
        p
            | 'Read' >> beam.io.textio.ReadFromText(INPUT_
FILE)
        #| 'Split' >> beam.Map(split_map)
            | 'Split' >> beam.ParDo(Split())
```

```
          | 'Get URL' >> beam.Map(lambda s: (s['url'], 1))
          | 'Count per Key' >> beam.combiners.Count.
    PerKey()
        #| 'Sample' >> Sample.FixedSizeGlobally(10)
        #| 'Print' >> beam.Map(print)
          | 'Write' >> beam.io.textio.WriteToText(OUTPUT_
    PATH)
```

6. Back to Cloud Shell, and run the new pipeline using Direct Runner as we learned before. If successful, the application will write the output to your GCS output path that you defined in the OUTPUT_PATH variable.

7. Check the output in the GCS bucket. The file should contain values in this array string format:

```
[('/blog/geekery/field-extraction-tool-fex-release.html',
 1)]
```

The values might be different in your file, but the format should be the same.

Since we are now sure that the application is working perfectly, let's run it as a Dataflow job. To do that, follow these simple steps:

8. In the command line when running the Beam application, change the runner from DirectRunner to DataflowRunner.

Change this line:

```
    --runner=DirectRunner \
```

The line should now look like this:

```
    --runner=DataflowRunner \
```

9. Run the Beam application from your Cloud Shell environment.

10. After running it from Cloud Shell, go to the **Dataflow** page in your GCP console. Check that your job is running and the status is showing as **Succeeded**, as illustrated in the following screenshot:

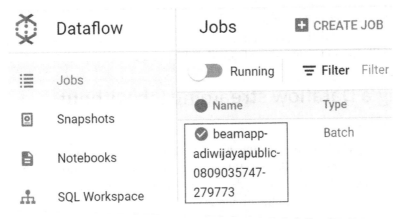

Figure 6.15 – Example of a successful job in the Dataflow console

And when you open the job, you can see our steps are there as a graph, as illustrated in the following screenshot:

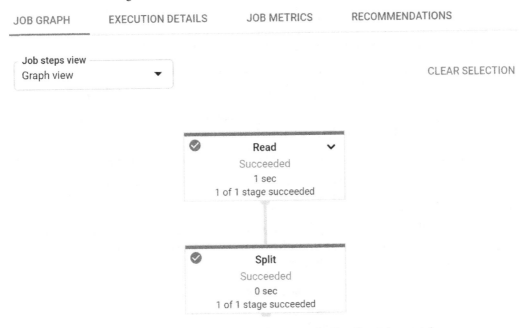

Figure 6.16 – Example of successful steps in the Dataflow Jobs console

With this, you have successfully created your first Dataflow job. The job was created using Beam in batch mode. Remember that you develop a Dataflow job using Apache Beam. In the development phase, you should use DirectRunner instead of DataflowRunner. Compared to DataflowRunner, the DirectRunner deployment time is faster because it runs in the local machine. But in terms of scalability, monitoring, and production standards, DataflowRunner is the right option.

In the next section, we will learn how to deploy a streaming job in Dataflow. We will use the Pub/Sub topic that we created from previous sections. The Dataflow streaming application will stream the messages from Pub/Sub to a BigQuery table.

Creating a Dataflow streaming job without aggregation

In this section, you will see how simple it is to change a batch application to a streaming application in Beam and Dataflow. In this section, we will use the Pub/Sub topic that we created before. To start our code, you can create a new Python file or use the `HelloWorld` application from the previous section.

You can also check the code from the GitHub repository at this link: https://github.com/PacktPublishing/Data-Engineering-with-Google-Cloud-Platform/blob/main/chapter-6/code/beam_stream_bikesharing.py.

Follow these steps to start the exercise:

1. Open the Beam code in your Cloud Editor environment.

2. Compared to the batch example, in this example, the variables are the Pub/Sub subscription ID and the BigQuery `table_id` output:

```
INPUT_SUBSCRIPTION= 'projects/packt-data-eng-on-gcp/
subscriptions/bike-sharing-trips-subs-1'
```

And here is the BigQuery table ID in the `output_table` variable:

```
OUTPUT_TABLE = 'packt-data-eng-on-gcp:raw_bikesharing.
bike_trips_streaming'
```

3. Don't forget to adjust the project name, Pub/Sub topic, and the BigQuery table ID based on your environment. In the Beam pipeline, we read from the Pub/Sub subscription. The code looks like this:

```
parser = argparse.ArgumentParser()
args, beam_args = parser.parse_known_args()
beam_options = PipelineOptions(beam_args, streaming=True)
def run():        with beam.Pipeline(options=beam_options)
as p:(
        p | "Read from Pub/Sub" >> beam.
io.ReadFromPubSub(subscription=input_subscription)
```

4. There are two options—**From Topic/From Subscription**. If using a topic, a subscription will be created automatically, but since we know there are many options in a subscription, it's better to manually create a subscription to make sure we know what's happening. Also, notice that we define the streaming parameter as `True` in the `PipelineOptions`. `Message` output from Pub/Sub. As this is in byte format, we need to convert it, as follows:

```
    | 'Decode' >> beam.Map(lambda x:
x.decode('utf-8'))
            | "Parse JSON" >> beam.Map(json.loads)
```

5. The message from Pub/Sub is in the form of JSON strings, so we need to decode this to `utf-8` format and parse the JSON. The last step is to write to the BigQuery table, as follows:

```
 | 'Write to Table' >> beam.io.WriteToBigQuery( OUTPUT_
TABLE,
 schema='trip_id:STRING,start_date:TIMESTAMP,start_
station_id:STRING,bike_number:STRING,duration_
sec:INTEGER',
   write_disposition=beam.io.BigQueryDisposition.WRITE_
APPEND)
     )
```

In the preceding code, we defined a table schema and wrote a disposition parameter. That's it—with this code, you can now start streaming data to your Pub/Sub topic, and the data will be loaded to BigQuery in real time.

To test if the streaming application works, it's going to be a bit tricky. To do that, we need some setups. We need to open three environments, as follows:

- One Cloud Shell tab to run the `beam_stream_bikesharing` code
- The BigQuery console to check if the records are loaded
- One Cloud Shell tab to run Pub/Sub publisher code

The first environment is a tab in Cloud Shell to run this command. Don't forget to adjust the `temp_location` parameter based on your own path if necessary. The code is illustrated in the following snippet:

```
python3 beam_stream_bikesharing.py \
  --project=$PROJECT_ID \
  --region=$REGION \
```

```
--runner=DirectRunner \
--temp_location=gs://$BUCKET_NAME/chapter-6/dataflow/temp
```

When you run the `beam_stream_bikesharing` code from the command line, your Beam code will start and wait for incoming data streams. As an example, here is the first environment in Cloud Shell that you will have:

Figure 6.17 – The first environment is running the Dataflow application

For the second environment, we need a BigQuery console, but we need to do that in a different browser tab.

Open a new browser tab and go to the BigQuery console. In the BigQuery editor, write a **Structured Query Language** (**SQL**) query to read data from our streaming table. You can see an example query here:

```
SELECT * FROM `raw_bikesharing.bike_trips_streaming` ORDER BY
start_date DESC:
```

In summary, in the first environment, you have the Beam streaming application running. The application waits for new data streams from the upstream environment. In the second environment, you have the BigQuery editor. You will use the query to check the incoming data. As an example, here is our second environment:

⊕ *UNSAVE... 2 ▾   ✕

▶ RUN   ⬇ SAVE ▾   ⊕ SCHEDULE ▾   ⚙ MORE ▾

```
1   SELECT * FROM `packt-data-eng-on-gcp.raw_bikesharing.bike_trips_streaming
2   ORDER BY start_date desc;
```

Figure 6.18 – The second environment in accessing BigQuery

In the third environment, you will need a new Cloud Shell tab. We will need this terminal to run our `pubsub_publisher` Python code.

To do that, you can add a new tab by clicking the plus (+) icon in the Cloud Shell terminal. In this new tab, go to the Pub/Sub publisher Python code. As an example, here is your third environment:

Figure 6.19 – The third environment is running the pubsub_publisher

After you are ready with the three environments, follow these steps:

1. Make sure you've run the first environment, which is the Beam streaming code.

2. Go to the third environment and run the `pubsub_publisher.py` code in Python. The code will send 10 messages to the Pub/Sub topic.

3. Finally, go to the BigQuery console, run the query, and check if the table is there and new records are coming. You can run the publisher code as many times as you like, and check if the BigQuery has new records immediately after you run the publisher.

If successful, when you query the BigQuery table, you can see there will be new records immediately after you publish messages to Pub/Sub. To end this exercise, close the Beam streaming application from the first environment using this command:

```
# ctrl+c
```

If you find any errors, try to recheck everything. If everything is successful, we can continue to run the streaming apps on Dataflow now. Do that by changing the runner to `DataflowRunner`, as we've done before.

Now, we need to be aware of what's happening at this point. When we run the Beam streaming pipeline using Dataflow, the job won't be finished unless we cancel the job. To check that, go to the **Dataflow** page in the GCP console. You can see in the following screenshot that your streaming application is on, with a job type of **Streaming**:

● Name	Type	End time	Elapsed time
⟳ beamapp-adiwijayapublic-0809061506-043357	Streaming		2 min 3 sec

Figure 6.20 – Example of Dataflow streaming job running

Open the job, and in your other environment, try to run the Pub/Sub publisher code again. In the Dataflow job, on the right panel, you can see some statistics—for example, the number of elements added. In my case, I ran the publisher three times so that the **Elements added** field displays 30 messages, as illustrated in the following screenshot:

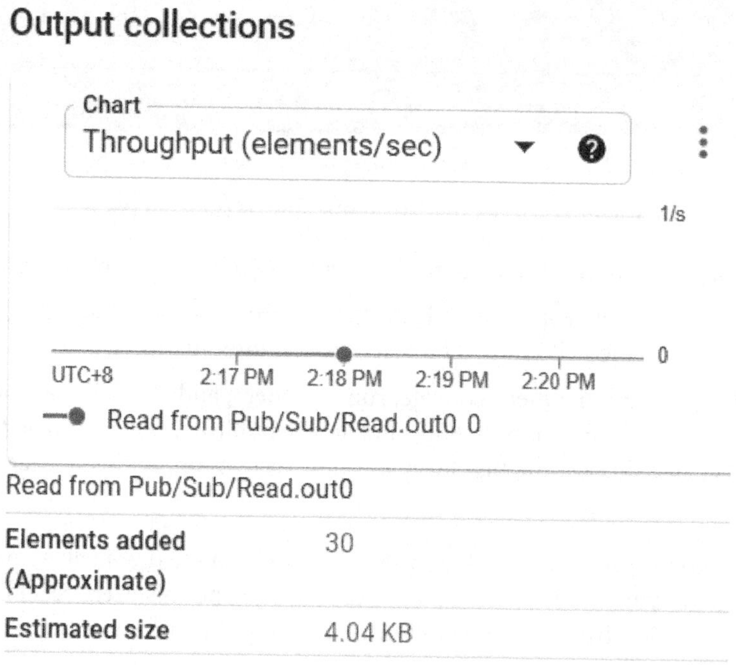

Output collections

Figure 6.21 – Checking streaming output metrics

With that, you've made it. You've successfully created a streaming data pipeline on Dataflow that is serverless and requires less maintenance.

In terms of the cost, Dataflow is billed by the number of worker hours. For example, in Dataflow, the minimum number of workers is one. One worker means one **virtual machine (VM)** is created; if the streaming runs for 24 hours, then the cost is *1 x 24 x the VM cost* (depends on the size). The number of workers can expand automatically when the data volume increases, but we can also set the maximum number of workers to prevent surprising costs. For now, take your time to understand the Dataflow job console, logs, and graphs. After that, you should stop the Dataflow job. You can do that by clicking the **STOP** button. There are two options—you can read a description about the difference between **Cancel** and **Drain** in the documentation, as it's pretty well described there. For now, let's choose the **Cancel** option and make sure the job is canceled.

In this section, we streamed data from raw messages to raw records in BigQuery, which is an ELT approach. We loaded data to BigQuery and let any downstream transformation happen in BigQuery. In the next and last exercise in this chapter, we will try to transform the data by aggregating the PCollection before storing it in BigQuery.

Creating a streaming job with aggregation

In this final section, we want to aggregate the streaming data. For example, let's sum up the duration seconds from the bike-trip data for each starting station ID. Looking back to the exercise in *Chapter 4*, *Building Orchestration for Batch Data Loading Using Cloud Composer*, we created a data mart that calculates the same metric, but daily. See this screenshot for a reminder of our data mart table:

▦ facts_trips_daily

ℹ This is a partitioned table. Learn more

SCHEMA   DETAILS   **PREVIEW**

Row	trip_date	start_station_id	total_trips	sum_duration_sec	avg_duration_sec
1	2018-01-01	277	1	1224	1224.0
2	2018-01-01	178	1	179	179.0
3	2018-01-01	270	1	424	424.0

Figure 6.22 – Preview of the facts_trips_daily table in BigQuery

In this section, we will create a table that has `start_station_id` and `sum_duration_sec` information but will be appended in near real time.

Why near real time? Because if you think about aggregation in streaming data, you need to think about time windows. For example, even if the data is streamed in real time, we want to sum up the duration in seconds for each time window. Let's see an example while doing it.

You can check out a code example from the following GitHub link: `https://github.com/PacktPublishing/Data-Engineering-with-Google-Cloud-Platform/blob/main/chapter-6/code/beam_stream_aggr.py`.

You can use the beam_stream_aggr.py code example to check the final code. For our practice, continue by trying to do it yourself. To do that, go back to your Beam streaming pipeline code. Go to the Parse JSON step. This time, we want to define a fixed time window of 60 seconds. In the later steps, we will sum up the duration_sec value. Given the 60-second window, it means the result will calculate the value every 60 seconds. You can change the window's duration—for example, to 1 second or 1 hour. See the following UseFixedWindow step:

```
| "Parse JSON" >> beam.Map(json.loads)
| "UseFixedWindow" >> beam.WindowInto(beam.window.
FixedWindows(60))
```

The next step is to group the message for each start_station_id parameter. We will use Map and a lambda function to create a key-value pair. The key is start_station_id and the value is duration_sec. The step is followed by the sum operation per key. The code is illustrated here:

```
| 'Group By User ID' >> beam.Map(lambda elem: (elem['start_
station_id'], elem['duration_sec']))
| 'Sum' >> beam.CombinePerKey(sum)
```

At this point, the Pcollection from the Sum step will result in the sum from each start_station_id parameter. Imagine each new result appended to the BigQuery table—you will lose information about the time. Since the data will keep being appended, you need the time information, so we will add an AddWindowEndTimestamp step. This time, we will create a BuildRecordFn ParDo function that will add the window time to our records, as follows:

```
| 'AddWindowEndTimestamp' >> (beam.ParDo(BuildRecordFn()))
```

Here is the BuildRecordFn class:

```
class BuildRecordFn(beam.DoFn):
    def process(self, element,  window=beam.DoFn.WindowParam):
        window_start = window.start.to_utc_datetime().
isoformat()
        return [element + (window_start,)]
```

That's all for the aggregation part. Remember that aggregating data in streams compared to batches is a little bit different as you need to be aware of times. Data is always coming in streams, so the concept of using scheduling times, as we usually do in batch pipelines, is no longer relevant in streaming pipelines.

The final step is to add the schema and write the result to BigQuery. To load data to BigQuery, one of the options is to use the JSON format. We can do that using Map and a lambda function, as follows:

```
| 'Parse to JSON' >> beam.Map(lambda x : {'start_station_id':
x[0],'sum_duration_sec':x[1],'window_timestamp':x[2]})
```

When writing to the BigQuery table, you can change the OUTPUT_TABLE table to a new target table. Here's an example of this:

```
OUTPUT_TABLE = 'packt-data-eng-on-gcp:dwh_bikesharing.bike_
trips_streaming_sum_aggr'
```

And here's how you do this:

```
| 'Write to Table' >> beam.io.WriteToBigQuery(OUTPUT_
TABLE,                          schema='start_station_
id:STRING,sum_duration_sec:INTEGER,window_timestamp:TIMESTAMP',
                    create_disposition=beam.
io.BigQueryDisposition.CREATE_IF_NEEDED,
                       write_disposition=beam.
io.BigQueryDisposition.WRITE_APPEND)
```

That's all for the code. You can check your code with the code provided in the GitHub repository examples. Similar to the previous exercise, run the code using both DirectRunner and DataflowRunner. Publish some messages using the Pub/Sub publisher code. If all goes successfully, you will see a BigQuery result like this:

⊞ bike_trips_streaming_sum_aggr

SCHEMA	DETAILS	PREVIEW

Row	start_station_id	sum_duration_sec	window_timestamp
1	202	61668	2021-08-01 08:57:00 UTC
2	205	43271	2021-08-01 08:58:00 UTC
3	205	7195	2021-08-01 08:54:00 UTC

Figure 6.23 – BigQuery table containing data from the stream job

You can see each `start_station_id` value will have the `sum_duration_sec` value for every 60 seconds. If needed, you can create a view on top of the table to sum up the `sum_duration_sec` value for each `start_station_id` value, like this:

```
CREATE VIEW bike_trips_realtime
AS
SELECT start_station_id, SUM(sum_duration_sec) as sum_duration_
sec
FROM bike_trips_straming_sum_aggr
GROUP BY start_station_id;
```

If all is complete, don't forget to cancel the Dataflow job by clicking the **STOP** button in the Dataflow job console.

Summary

In this chapter, we've learned about streaming data and we learned how to handle incoming data as soon as data is created. Data is created using the Pub/Sub publisher client. In practice, you can use this approach by requesting the application developer to send messages to Pub/Sub as the data source, or a second option is to use a **change data capture (CDC)** tool. In GCP, you can use a Google provided tool for CDC called Datastream. CDC tools can be attached to the backend database like CloudSQL to publish data changes such as insert, update, and delete operations. We as data engineers are responsible for using Pub/Sub, as we've learned in this chapter.

The second part of streaming data is how to process the data. In this chapter, we've learned how to use Dataflow to handle continuously incoming data from Pub/Sub to aggregate it on the fly and store it in BigQuery tables. Do keep in mind that you can also handle data from Pub/Sub using Dataflow in batch manner.

With experience in creating streaming data pipelines on GCP, you will realize how easy it is to start creating one from an infrastructure aspect. You don't need to think about any VM, software installation, capacities, and other infrastructure stuff. You can just focus on the code and configurations.

The majority of the code is in Beam. As you've experienced from the exercise in this chapter, learning about Beam needs time. There are many concepts and features that are unique to Beam and streaming, but this is simply because Beam is very powerful and flexible, and it can run on top of different runners. Beam can handle batch and streaming data pipelines with very few modifications. Take time to learn how to use it, and as always, focus on your use case. Learning all syntaxes and features of Beam at once is not practical—expand your skills and knowledge of this tool with what you need from your use case.

Finishing this chapter will give you a strong foundation in data engineering. I can say that the concepts and skills that you've learned from the first chapter to the sixth already cover 70% of data engineering practice. The last 30% is to expand your knowledge to other areas in data, development practice, and GCP foundations.

In the next chapter, we will expand our knowledge of data to data visualization. Most of the time, data visualization is the best way to show other people how valuable the data is. It's the end of data downstreaming that many people and businesses can appreciate the most. We will learn how to visualize data using a free GCP tool called Google Data Studio. With Google Data Studio, you can visualize data from BigQuery with a drag and drop experience.

7

Visualizing Data for Making Data-Driven Decisions with Data Studio

Visualizing data helps stakeholders to concentrate on important KPIs and empowers them to make data-driven decisions. Data engineers need to analyze the underlying structure of the data and also curate custom reporting layers on top to enable the development of dashboards and reports.

This chapter will discuss in detail the dashboarding product **Google Data Studio**, which can be leveraged to visualize data coming from different sources, including **BigQuery**, to build compelling reports. And on top of that, we will learn what a data engineer should see from a **data visualization** point of view.

At a high level, here is a list of content that will be covered in this chapter:

- Unlocking the power of your data with Data Studio

- From data to metrics in minutes with an illustrative use case

- Understanding how Data Studio can impact the cost of BigQuery

- How to create a materialized view and understanding how BI Engine works

After finishing this chapter, you will understand the positioning of Google Data Studio and how to use it to create a visualization dashboard using data from BigQuery. Let's get started!

Technical requirements

Before we begin this chapter, make sure you have the following prerequisites ready. In this chapter's exercises, we will use these **Google Cloud Services (GCP)** services – **Data Studio** and **BigQuery**.

We will use the data output from exercises in *Chapter 3, Building a Data Warehouse in BigQuery*, or *Chapter 4, Building Orchestration for Batch Data Loading Using Cloud Composer*. In both chapters, we produced a BigQuery dataset called `dwh_bikesharing`. Make sure you've finished the exercises from those chapters.

Unlocking the power of your data with Data Studio

Data Studio is a tool for you to visualize your data fully on the cloud. There are two main reasons why we need data visualization; the first is exploration and the second is reporting:

- **Data visualization for exploration**

  As a data engineer, even though visualizing data is not your main responsibility, there are times when visualizing data may help in your job. For example, at times when you need to optimize your data pipeline, you may need to analyze a job's performance. Visualizing the job's data will help you get more information. If you have a data science background, you may be familiar with tools such as Jupyter Notebook. It is a fully fledged tool for data analytics, including visualization for exploration. But in our case, we may only need to quickly visualize a bar chart from a BigQuery table, for example. And in that case, Data Studio is the best option due to its simplicity and seamless connectivity to BigQuery.

- **Data visualization for reporting**

  The second reason for visualization is reporting. The department that is in charge of this is usually a team called the **Business Intelligence** (**BI**) team, comprising business users, data analysts, or business analysts. Each organization has its own preferences as to how they name their divisions. Data engineers don't usually need to be responsible for reports, but understanding the nature of reports is important for us since this is the last downstream of our whole work as data engineers. And the success of data engineering teams a lot of the time can be measured by looking at how satisfied these end users are.

Before we begin our exercise, let's understand the positioning of Data Studio in the data visualization space. As mentioned before, Data Studio is a fully managed tool on the cloud. This means that you can literally start developing your report, visualizing charts, sharing the report, and more without leaving your browser. Another advantage of using Data Studio is its simplicity as a tool. For example, later on in the *Exercise – Exploring the BigQuery INFORMATION_SCHEMA table using Data Studio* section, you will experience visualizing your data in less than 10 clicks from a BigQuery table.

But Data Studio is not positioned to be a replacement for fully fledged BI tools such as **Tableau**, **Looker**, and **Power BI**. These tools have much wider functionalities. I will take Looker as an example since it's comparable directly with Data Studio as a Google product, but the other BI tools are similar in nature.

> **Important Note**
>
> *Looker* is a fully fledged modern BI tool. The tool can serve up real-time dashboards for in-depth, consistent analysis. It enforces multiple-user collaboration; for example, there are power users, analysts, and business users. For more information, please check their public website: `https://looker.com/`.

Using Looker as an example, users can have a permission hierarchy to both manage dashboards and access them. Another thing in Looker is that you can have version control, which manages your dashboards. Data Studio doesn't have those capabilities; it is a lot simpler and very straightforward to use.

From data to metrics in minutes with an illustrative use case

Now let's start our exercise; we will try to use data visualization for exploration and reporting. You will only need Data Studio and BigQuery for the exercise in this chapter. Note that using Data Studio is *free*.

There will be two main things that we will be doing in this section:

- Exploring the BigQuery INFORMATION_SCHEMA table using Data Studio
- Creating a Data Studio report using data from a bike-sharing data warehouse

Before trying Data Studio, let's get familiar with **INFORMATION_SCHEMA** in BigQuery.

Understanding what BigQuery INFORMATION_SCHEMA is

INFORMATION_SCHEMA is a collection of tables in BigQuery that stores your BigQuery metadata. For example, if you want to know how many tables you have in your project, you can use the table INFORMATION_SCHEMA view. The other common example is that you might be wondering how much a query costs per job, day, or month. To do that, you can access the jobs INFORMATION_SCHEMA view. You can find the full list of available INFORMATION_SCHEMA views here: https://cloud.google.com/bigquery/docs/information-schema-intro.

Let's try the jobs INFORMATION_SCHEMA as our example. We will access it and use it for quick exploration in the *Exercise – Exploring the BigQuery INFORMATION_SCHEMA table using Data Studio* section.

To access INFORMATION_SCHEMA, follow these steps:

1. Go to the BigQuery page in the Cloud console.
2. In the **Editor** tab, write this query:

```
SELECT *
FROM
    `region-us`.INFORMATION_SCHEMA.JOBS_BY_PROJECT;
```

3. Run the query and check the result. The result of the query should be as follows:

creation_time	project_id	project_number
2021-05-29 07:49:18.377 UTC	packt-data-eng-on-gcp	320986546290

Figure 7.1 – Example result from INFORMATION_SCHEMA

There will be many other columns that you can check. Scan through all the columns and try to get familiar with them. The information is very helpful for debugging and monitoring purposes. For example, I found out that one of the most interesting columns for users is `total_bytes_billed`. This column gives an estimation of how many bytes were read from the query. With this number, you can calculate the cost for each query for on-demand pricing users.

For example, in one of my job queries, the `total_bytes_billed` value is `10485760`. Remember that it is in bytes; if we convert it to terabytes, it will be 0.00001 TB. If we use the US region, the on-demand cost is $5 per TB. So the cost for this query is as follows:

```
Query cost = $5 * 0.00001 TB
Query cost = $0.00005
```

With this knowledge, you can explore many things about your BigQuery costs, for example, how much you spend on BigQuery every day. Let's do that in Data Studio in the next section.

In the next section, we will begin our exercise. Make sure your GCP console is opened in your browser and let's get started.

> **Important Note**
> You can check the pricing for other regions in this documentation:
> `https://cloud.google.com/bigquery/pricing`.

Exercise – Exploring the BigQuery INFORMATION_ SCHEMA table using Data Studio

In this exercise, we will use BigQuery query results to be shown in Data Studio. We will explore the basic functionalities in Data Studio using the INFORMATION_SCHEMA table as an example use case.

Here are the high-level steps:

1. Run a query in the BigQuery editor.

2. Explore the result using Data Studio.

3. Show the time-series chart for visualizing daily billed bytes.

Let's start with the first step:

1. Run a query in the BigQuery editor. Open your BigQuery editor and run the following query:

```
SELECT
EXTRACT(DATE FROM creation_time) as creation_date,
SUM(total_bytes_billed) as sum_total_bytes_billed
FROM
 `region-us`.INFORMATION_SCHEMA.JOBS_BY_PROJECT
 GROUP BY EXTRACT(DATE FROM creation_time);
```

The query accesses the same INFORMATION_SCHEMA table as in the previous section. But this time, we aggregate it using the creation_date column to sum up the total_bytes_billed value.

2. Explore the result using Data Studio.

After the results are shown, click the **EXPLORE DATA** button. The button is in the middle of your screen, as shown in the following figure:

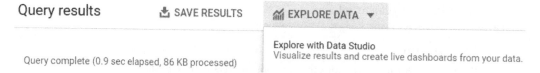

Figure 7.2 – Finding Explore with Data Studio

You will be redirected to a new browser tab, opening the **Data Studio Explorer** page. An authorization popup will be shown if this is the first time you have opened Data Studio. The page shows your data and some inputs, as in the following figure:

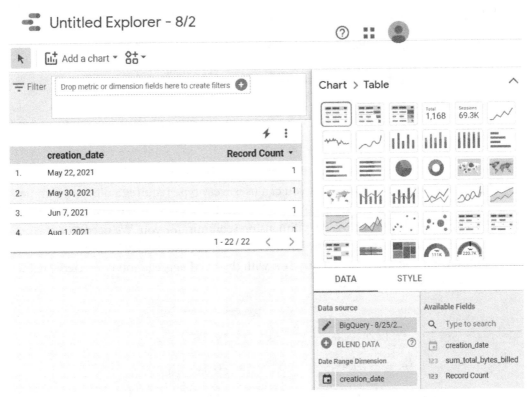

Figure 7.3 – Example of the Data Studio main page

Remember that this is the **Data Studio Explorer** page. Later on in the *Exercise – Creating a Data Studio report using data from a bike-sharing data warehouse* section, we will see another similar page called the **Report** page. In the **Explorer** page, you can see that the user experience is very user-friendly. Most of the exploration can be done using clicks.

For the first step in the **Explorer** page, let's change the **Explorer** title to Explore - BigQuery Information Schema.

You can do that by clicking the title, as in the following:

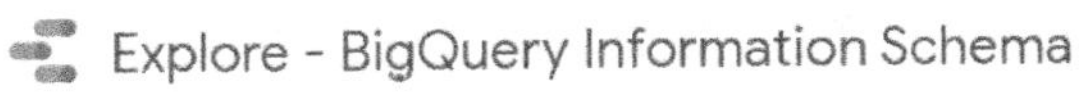

Explore - BigQuery Information Schema

Figure 7.4 – Data Studio title bar

3.   Show a time-series chart for visualizing daily billed bytes.

Next, on the right panel, choose the **Time series** chart:

Figure 7.5 – Finding the time series icon

There are many chart types that you can use; every type requires a different number of dimensions and metric data. As you can see, Data Studio is not smart enough to automatically pick the correct dimension (column) for you. We need to set the correct input for our charts. For our use case, choose creation_date as **Dimension** and sum_total_bytes with the **SUM** aggregation type. Here are the inputs that you can follow:

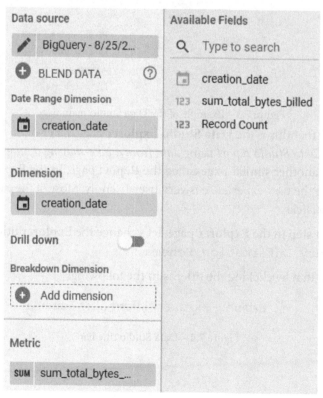

Figure 7.6 – A configuration example for our chart

After choosing the correct input, you can see your time-series chart is shown properly. Note that your result will be different from my example. The chart in your Data Studio is showing your real `total_bytes_billed` value from your historical queries in BigQuery. As an example, here is what it looks like in my chart:

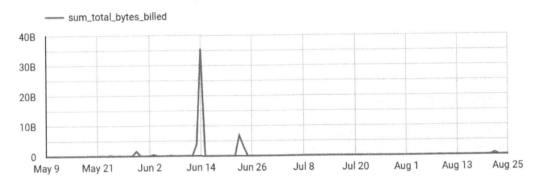

Figure 7.7 – Output from the time-series chart

One thing that we can do next is filter the data; the input is at the top of the screen. It's pretty straightforward; for example, I chose to only show the records from **Aug 1, 2021**:

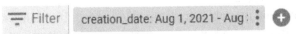

Figure 7.8 – Filtering the graph by date

Try it on your **Explorer** page to get familiar with the feature.

As you have seen in this section, showing BigQuery results in exploration charts is only a few clicks away. This is one of the reasons Data Studio is one of the best tools for exploring BigQuery data. The connection is seamless and there are almost no prerequisites to start using Data Studio. In the next section, we will try to create a report in Data Studio using our *bike-sharing* data.

Exercise – Creating a Data Studio report using data from a bike-sharing data warehouse

In this exercise, we will create a report. From the definition, the difference between a report and exploration is clear. Exploration is a phase or activity that you do on an ad hoc basis to find answers from your data. A report is a collection of information that is created from data for other people's benefit. When creating reports, people should think about how the end users use the information and how they access it. In Data Studio, creating exploration and creating reports have very similar steps. There are two additional steps when creating reports:

1. Managing the report layout

2. Sharing with other users

We will do both of the steps in this exercise, and as an additional step, we want to practice *loading data sources from a BigQuery table*. Remember that in the previous exercise, we used the BigQuery query's *result*, not the table.

For the data and use case, we will use the bike-sharing data from our data warehouse dataset created in *Chapter 3, Building a Data Warehouse in BigQuery*, from the *Creating a fact and dimension table* section. To refresh our memory, in that section we created two tables in the `dwh_bikesharing` dataset, `facts_trips_daily` and `dim_stations`. If you haven't done that, you can revisit the chapter or use any other table. If you want to use other tables, you could use tables from the BigQuery public dataset. If you do that, focus only on Data Studio capability in this exercise without worrying about the use case.

At a high level, here are the steps that we will do in this exercise:

1. Add the `fact_trips_daily` data source to the report.

2. Add and blend the `dim_stations` data source.

3. Answer the questions using charts.

4. Manage the report's layout.

5. Share the report.

Let's start with the first step:

1. Add the `fact_trips_daily` data source to the report.

    From your Data Studio page, click the Data Studio icon in the top left of your screen. The icon looks like this:

Figure 7.9 – Data Studio icon

That will redirect you to the Data Studio main page. On the main page, find the **Create** button in the top left and click **Report**.

You will be redirected to add data to a report form. In this form, take a moment to see what the options are that you can choose. You can see that Data Studio is not only able to use data from BigQuery; there are also hundreds of other connectivity options that you can use. For our exercise, let's choose BigQuery, under the **Google Connectors** section.

The next step is to select the table; for that, choose your project, dataset, and, finally, the table name. To check your steps, here is the screen at this step:

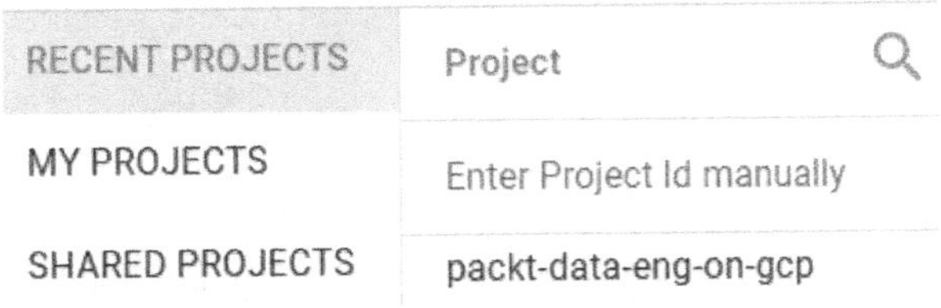

Figure 7.10 – Find and choose your GCP project

After finding your facts_trips_daily table, click **ADD TO REPORT**. You will be redirected again to the report editor page, as shown in the following figure:

Figure 7.11 – An example of the output after adding new data

Note that **Data source** under the **DATA** tab on the right panel shows your table name. If you compare this to our previous exercise, the last exercise didn't point to any table in the data source.

2. Add and blend the `dim_stations` data source.

The next step is to add another table, which is our `dim_stations` dimension table. To do that, in the menu bar, click **Resource | Manage added data source**. You can find the button where shown in the following screenshot:

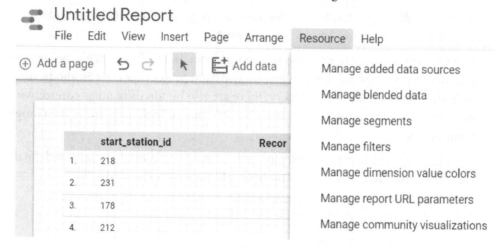

Figure 7.12 – Finding the Manage added data sources button under Resource

After clicking the button, you will be on the **SELECT DATASOURCE** page, similar to our previous steps. Find the `dim_stations` table and click **Add**.

Back on the report editor page, find the **BLEND DATA** button. It's located in the **Data | Data source** section.

Just in case your right panel shows **Theme** and **Layout** instead of **DATA** and **STYLE**, click the table in the editor pane. Click this table:

	start_station_id	Record Count ▾
1.	33	4
2.	295	4
3.	311	4

Figure 7.13 – Make sure the table is selected

Your right panel should show **DATA** and **STYLE** options. Under **DATA**, you can find the **BLEND DATA** button, which you then click.

On the **Blend Data** page, you will see `fact_trips_daily` shown as your data source, and you can click **ADD A TABLE**. You will see that `dim_stations` will be available for you to choose, as in the following screenshot:

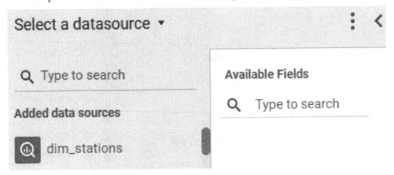

Figure 7.14 – Selecting a data source page

After clicking it, you will see that we need to input some information in the panel using drag and drop. Under the `dim_stations` panel, find the **Join Keys** section. In **JOIN KEYS**, drag `station_id` to the missing box. An alternative option is clicking the **Missing** box and then selecting `station_id` from the dropdown.

After that, we need to correctly define **Dimensions** and **Metrics** for both `fact_trips_daily` and `dim_stations`.

For `fact_trips_daily`, here are the configurations:

- **Dimensions**: No dimensions
- **Metrics**:
- **SUM** | `sum_duration_sec`
- **AVG** | `avg_duration_sec`

For `dim_stations`, here are the configurations:

- **Dimensions**: `station_name`
- **Metrics**:
- **SUM** | `capacity`

Check whether your input looks like this screenshot:

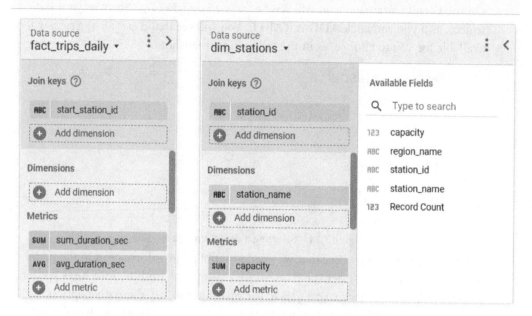

Figure 7.15 – A configuration example for the data sources

After choosing all the correct inputs, click **SAVE**.

3. Answer the questions using charts. For the first chart, let's use the **Bar** chart to show the *top 5 stations by total duration*. To do that, click the table on the editor pane so that you can choose the chart type. To open the chart options, click the top-right panel that reads **Chart** > **Table**. After clicking the panel, the chart option will be shown. Choose the **Bar** chart:

Figure 7.16 – Finding the column chart icon

After changing to a **Bar** chart, in the data panel, choose the station name for the dimension. In both the **Metric** and **Sort** sections, choose `sum_duration_sec` using **SUM** aggregation:

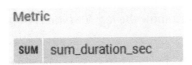

Figure 7.17 – Choosing sum_duration_sec in the Metric section

If successful, your column chart will look like this:

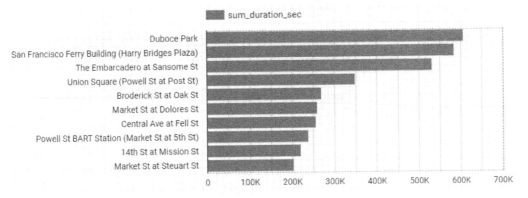

Figure 7.18 – Column chart result

To only show the top five, go to the **STYLE** panel and input 5 in the **Bars** option:

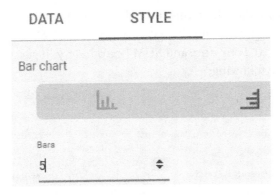

Figure 7.19 – Finding the Bars option under the STYLE section

To add the second chart, click **Add a chart** on the top of your screen, as in the following screenshot:

Figure 7.20 – Find the Add a chart button

For the second chart, let's show the *top 10 stations by average duration*. For this, we'll choose the tree map.

For **Metrics**, choose **AVG** | avg_duration_sec. And lastly, we want to limit the number of boxes in the tree map to only 10 boxes. To do that, still in the **DATA** tab, find a section called **Total rows**. The default is **500** rows; change it to **10**.

If successful, the chart will look like this:

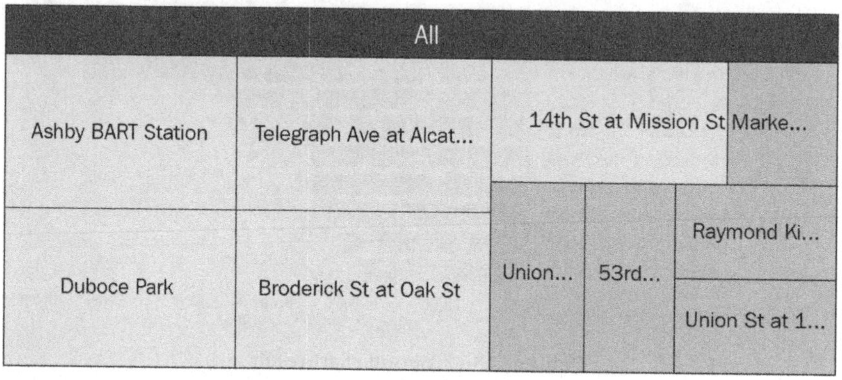

Figure 7.21 – A tree chart output example

And lastly, add another chart; this time, choose the table chart. For the dimension, choose station_name, and change the metrics to **SUM** | sum_duration_sec, **AVG** | avg_duration_sec, and **SUM** | capacity. If successful, the table chart will look like the following:

	station_name	sum_duration_sec ▾	avg_dura...	capacity
1.	Duboce Park	606,292	11,734.23	19
2.	San Francisco Ferry Building (Harry Bridges Plaza)	583,050	2,381.09	38
3.	The Embarcadero at Sansome St	531,122	2,328.99	23
4.	Union Square (Powell St at Post St)	347,934	3,590.34	27
5.	Broderick St at Oak St	268,348	9,583.86	27
6.	Market St at Dolores St	258,630	3,078.93	19
7.	Central Ave at Fell St	256,576	2,547.41	31
8.	Powell St BART Station (Market St at 5th St)	236,968	3,075.72	35

1 - 100 / 248   < >

Figure 7.22 – A table chart output example

4. Manage the report's layout.

At this point, I'm sure you are already comfortable creating your own report. Play around with other buttons and functionalities. For example, you can add static text, a changing layout, and many other options. Remember that in report creation, you are creating the report for someone else, so be mindful of how to lay out the charts. If you are done, you can click the **VIEW** button in the top right of your screen and see your report there. For example, here is mine; you don't need to follow every single detail here:

Bike Sharing Report

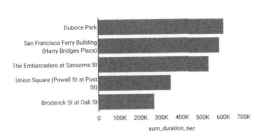

Top 5 Station by Total Duration

Top 10 Station by Average Duration

Table Detail

	station_name	sum_duration_sec ▾	avg_duration_sec	capacity
1.	Duboce Park	606,292	11,734.23	19
2.	San Francisco Ferry Building (Harry Bridges Plaza)	583,050	2,381.09	38
3.	The Embarcadero at Sansome St	531,122	2,328.99	23
4.	Union Square (Powell St at Post St)	347,934	3,590.34	27
5.	Broderick St at Oak St	268,348	9,583.86	27
6.	Market St at Dolores St	258,630	3,078.93	19
7.	Central Ave at Fell St	256,576	2,547.41	31

1 - 100 / 248   〈 〉

Figure 7.23 – A full-screen example of the bike-sharing report

5. Share the report. As a final step, let's share the report with other people by email. You can do that by clicking the **SHARE** button. The form looks like the following:

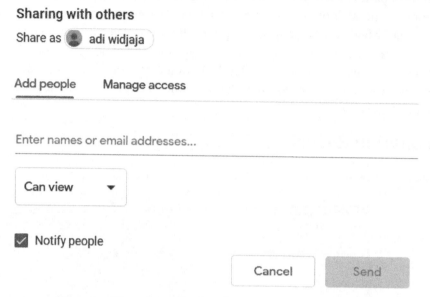

Figure 7.24 – Finding the SHARE button

When sharing a report with other users, the user can access the report without needing BigQuery viewer permission to the underlying table. The permission to the BigQuery table is dependent on your email as the data source owner.

To summarize our two exercises, we've practiced showing both the BigQuery table and the BigQuery query's results in Data Studio. As you can see, Data Studio is an easy tool for both exploration and creating reports. On top of that, Data Studio is totally free to use. But as a data engineer, you need to be aware of how it impacts the cost of BigQuery. When you share your report with other users, the usage of the underlying BigQuery table will increase. It will increase either linearly or exponentially with the number of users. We will discuss this in our next section.

Understanding how Data Studio can impact the cost of BigQuery

At a very high level, the total BigQuery cost is driven by *how big your data is* and *the amount of usage*. Both factors work as multipliers. For example, if you have a table that's 1 TB in size and you access the table 10,000 times in a month, it means the BigQuery cost will be *1 TB x 10,000 x \$5 = \$50,000 / month*.

Whether $50,000 is expensive or not depends on your organization. But we will ignore the context and focus on the cost driver aspects, so let's say $50,000 is expensive. Now the questions are *what kind of table could be 1 TB in size?* and *how can a table be accessed 10,000 times in a month?* Let's discuss these questions in the following sections.

What kind of table could be 1 TB in size?

To answer that, let's take a look at our data warehouse diagram from *Chapter 3, Building a Data Warehouse in BigQuery*, in the following figure:

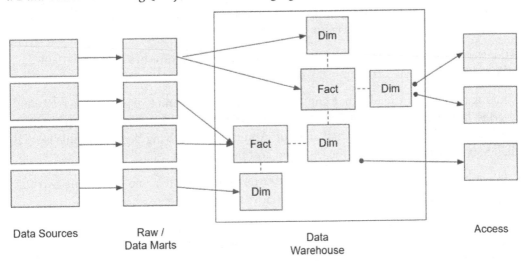

Figure 7.25 – High-level data layers

When looking at the diagram, remember that most data in the **Access** layer is already specifically created for reports. This means that it's already been filtered and aggregated, so the data in the **Access** layer is less likely to be big. Big tables more commonly come from a *transactional table in the* **Raw** *layer* and *fact tables are in the data warehouse*. But the *fact table* in the data warehouse can also be shrunk down in size if it is aggregated at a lower time granularity. For example, in our exercise, we created `fact_daily_trips`, which only had daily-level granularity.

How can a table be accessed 10,000 times in a month?

There are two main factors that can drive the numbers:

- Number of users using the table per month (`#user`)
- How many times each user accesses the table per month (`#user access`)

For example, say a table is very popular and is accessed by 10 unique users in a month. And each day, every user needs to schedule a report based on the table for every half an hour; or, in other words, there will be 48 queries per user per day, which is 1,440 queries per user per month. Then, the total queries will be as follows:

10 unique users x 1,440 user / month = 14,400 queries / month

Now, what does this have to do with Data Studio? First, Data Studio is a very good way for data engineers to share data adoption with non-data people across organizations. But at the same time, it means more users will be accessing BigQuery data. As previously mentioned, when a user accesses data from a Data Studio report or Explorer, the queries are triggered to BigQuery. This factor drives #user up.

And every time a user changes the data filter or chart order, refreshes data, and many other actions, that will drive up #user access.

Looking back at our calculation example, at first, it might sound like a lot to have 10,000 queries. But looking at the number, it is pretty normal to have 10 users where each user needs to refresh the data every half an hour. And if the underlying BigQuery table is 1 TB, then $50,000 would indeed be the expected cost per month.

Can we avoid that number? Yes. The general rule of thumb is to avoid having the two big multiplier numbers at the same time. What does that mean?

Avoid scenarios where big tables are accessed to the reporting tool such as Data Studio. Even if it's a thing to be avoided, it's a very common practice that happens in the real world. For simplicity, organizations sometimes don't spend much time thinking about data architecture and use any raw data to be used by Data Studio. This leads to the *two big multiplier numbers at the same time* scenario, when large tables are queried many times by tens or hundreds of end users.

But all scenarios other than that are fine; for example, if you have large tables that are accessed by only a few users in a month, that's totally fine. In other cases, a lot of users accessing several small tables in a given month is also totally fine. Try to calculate things yourself with the given formula.

So, the key here is trying to be mindful of both of the multipliers. Since Data Studio is a very easy-to-use tool and BigQuery is a very powerful query engine, both of the combinations sometimes make organizations forget to design a proper data architecture. A proper data model, as we discussed previously, is when data is divided into a raw layer, a data warehouse, and an access layer. This practice will improve your cost optimization for BigQuery.

Another thing that we can do is think about cache. There are two unique cache features in BigQuery called **Materialized Views** and **BI Engine**; both features are there to improve BigQuery caching. We will learn about the features in the next section.

How to create materialized views and understanding how BI Engine works

BigQuery has a feature called materialized views. It's not a table, nor a view; it's a materialized view. To understand it, let's go back to what a table is compared to a view. One of the reasons you create tables is that you want to store transformation results to be used for downstream usage. The reason you create a view instead of a table is that you need the data in real time, but with a view, you always pre-compute all the processes. A materialized view is somewhere in between. With materialized views, you can have real-time access, but the processes aren't pre-computed.

It's easier to understand is by trying it in practice, so let's set up a scenario. Let's use our `facts_trip_daily` table and run this query from the BigQuery console:

```
SELECT trip_date, sum(sum_duration_sec) as sum_duration_sec
FROM `packt-data-eng-on-gcp.dwh_bikesharing.facts_trips_daily`
GROUP BY trip_date
;
```

The query will output the sum of the duration by the trip date. To continue the experiment, we need to disable the BigQuery default cache. To do that, click **MORE | Query Settings**. The button is shown in the following screenshot:

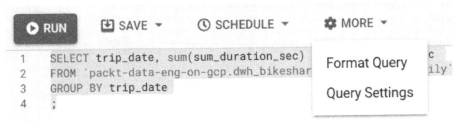

Figure 7.26 – Find the Query Settings button under the MORE button

The **Query Settings** page will open; find the **Use cached results** checkbox under **Resource Management**. Uncheck the box and click **Save**.

Now, run the query and check the bytes processed at the top of the **Results** query:

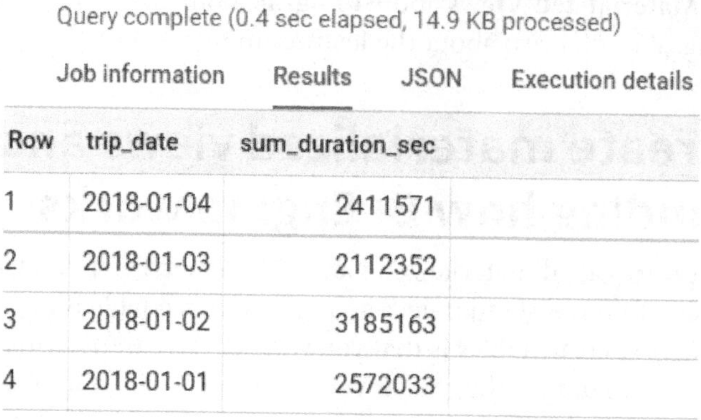

Query complete (0.4 sec elapsed, 14.9 KB processed)

| | Job information | Results | JSON | Execution details |

Row	trip_date	sum_duration_sec
1	2018-01-04	2411571
2	2018-01-03	2112352
3	2018-01-02	3185163
4	2018-01-01	2572033

Figure 7.27 – Example query result in BigQuery

For example, my experiment shows that 14.9 KB was processed. Now, if you rerun the query, BigQuery will process the same amount of bytes.

If you create a view on top of that query, you can get the real-time result, but the bytes processed will still be the same. Remember that in on-demand BigQuery pricing, the total bytes processed determines the cost.

Now, try to create a materialized view by running this query:

```
CREATE MATERIALIZED VIEW `dwh_bikesharing.facts_trips_daily_
sum_duration_sec`
AS
SELECT trip_date, sum(sum_duration_sec) as sum_duration_sec
FROM `dwh_bikesharing.facts_trips_daily`
GROUP BY trip_date
;
```

After running the query, you can see your materialized view is created in your dataset:

Figure 7.28 – A materialized view example from the table list

After successfully creating it, try to rerun the query:

```
SELECT trip_date, sum(sum_duration_sec) as sum_duration_sec
FROM `packt-data-eng-on-gcp.dwh_bikesharing.facts_trips_daily`
GROUP BY trip_date
;
```

After running twice, the bytes processed will be reduced significantly. In my case, it is 64 B compared to 14 KB from the previous run:

Query complete (0.6 sec elapsed, 64 B processed)

Job information	Results	JSON	Execution details

Row	trip_date	sum_duration_sec
1	2018-01-03	2112352
2	2018-01-02	3185163
3	2018-01-04	2411571
4	2018-01-01	2572033

Figure 7.29 – Example query result

This can significantly reduce your BigQuery costs, especially if the underlying table is often used in a Data Studio report and the aggregation occurs often. And notice that you don't need to call the materialized view using a query such as this:

```
SELECT * FROM `dwh_bikesharing.facts_trips_daily_sum_duration_
sec`
```

Materialized Views works as a cache in BigQuery; the goal is to provide real-time tables and, at the same time, reduce processing. But to use it, you need to know all the capabilities and limitations. At the time that this book was written in 2021, Materialized Views was a relatively new feature; check out the list of its limitations in the public documentation:

```
https://cloud.google.com/bigquery/docs/materialized-views-
intro#limitations
```

It's recommended to use Materialized Views whenever possible. Having Materialized Views in your BigQuery dataset will automatically reduce background processing and costs. Your Data Studio end users don't need to change anything from their side.

Another caching mechanism that is available in BigQuery and is exclusively for BI tools such as Data Studio is BI Engine; we will talk about that in the next section.

Understanding BI Engine

Unlike Materialized Views, BI Engine is a feature that only needs to be enabled. BI Engine is a caching mechanism in BigQuery for use by BI tools such as Data Studio. Another difference between BI Engine and Materialized Views is that BI Engine caches almost every query result, whereas Materialized Views only caches aggregated, filtered, or inner-join results. The only limitation in BI Engine is that the cache size is small. So, as long as the total query result size per project is under 100 GB in memory, your query with Data Studio is free.

To enable BI Engine, you just need to go to the menu from the **BigQuery** navigation menu, as shown in the following screenshot:

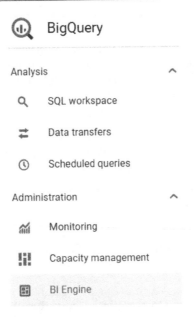

Figure 7.30 – Finding the BI Engine button under the BigQuery Administration menu

After enabling the **Reservation API**, you will be directed to the **Reservation** page. The first option is **Configure**:

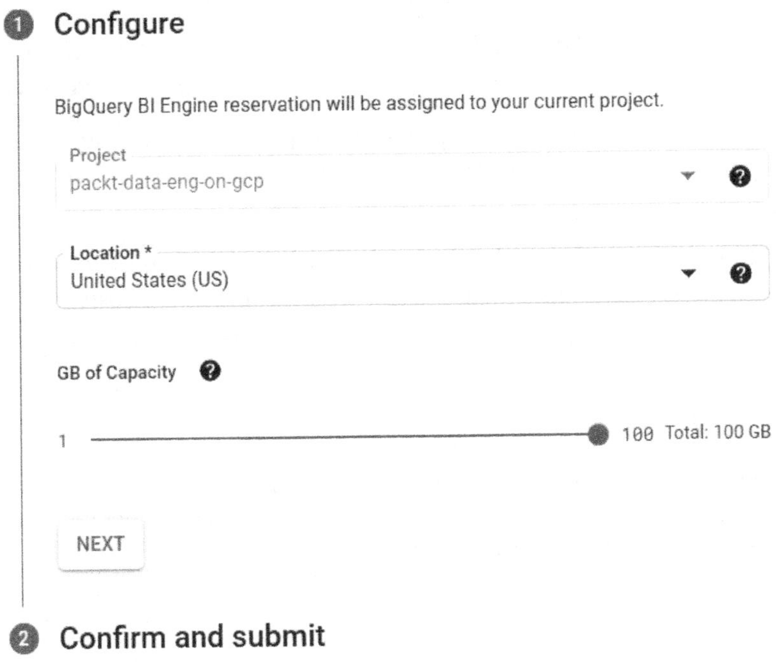

1 Configure

BigQuery BI Engine reservation will be assigned to your current project.

Project
packt-data-eng-on-gcp

Location *
United States (US)

GB of Capacity

1 ———————————————————————————— 100 Total: 100 GB

NEXT

2 Confirm and submit

Figure 7.31 – An example of the BI Engine configuration menu

> **Warning**
>
> For this exercise, *don't* create the BI Engine reservation! For this practice you don't need create the BI Engine reservation! There are no other steps that required BI Engine in this book. Use BI Engine when you use BigQuery and DataStudio for production.

What you need to do to activate BI Engine is just fill in the **Location** field and its capacity. What you need to understand at this point is that BI Engine works according to memory capacity. As long as your query fits your memory capacity, you can optimize your BigQuery costs in general. If you are in the **BI Engine** page, you can close it now. Don't confirm or create the reservation here because it's very expensive, if only for practice.

Lastly, if you want to check whether your Data Studio chart utilizes BI Engine, you may notice there is a lightning icon at the top right of every chart, as shown here:

trip_date ▾	start_statio...	avg_durati...	sum_durati...
1... Jan 2, 2018	324	2,731.33	196,656
2... Jan 2, 2018	71	1,174.57	16,444

Figure 7.32 – The top-right lightning icon

If the lightning icon appears like that, it means the Data Studio chart uses BI Engine; if the icon has a cross through it, the table's size means it doesn't fit within BI Engine's limitations.

And with that, you now know the two optimization approaches that you can use to optimize BigQuery costs that might occur from Data Studio usage. The key point is to be mindful.

As a data engineer, you always need to be aware of the implications of your end users' data usage. It doesn't mean that Data Studio will always affect BigQuery costs significantly. Knowing how to optimize is the key message in these last sections.

Summary

In this chapter, we learned how to use Data Studio using BigQuery as the data source. We learned how to connect the data, create charts in Explorer, and create reports for sharing the charts and information with other users.

Through the exercises in this chapter, you have learned about not only how to create charts but also the point of view of your end users. In the exercises, you realized how important it is to create a proper data model in your datasets. Imagine if your tables didn't have proper naming conventions, weren't aggregated properly, or followed any other bad practices that can happen in a data warehouse. Since we already learned all the good data engineering practices and code from the previous chapters, it's now very easy for us to use our example tables to visualize things in Data Studio.

And lastly, as data engineers, we need to be the ones who understand and are aware of the cost implications in our data ecosystem. In this chapter, we learned about BigQuery `INFORMATION_SCHEMA`, Materialized Views, and BI Engine. Knowledge of these three is not only applicable to Data Studio but to BigQuery as a whole.

In the next chapter, we will again visit an area that is not core to the data engineer's role. We will learn about **machine learning**; even though machine learning is more related to the role of data scientist, understanding it is important for data engineers. Nowadays, since most people and organizations are already aware that machine learning involves not only math and statistics but also engineering and operations, it's not rare to find that data engineers are the ones who manage and maintain the machine learning pipeline. In the next chapter, we will learn about machine learning terminology and how to build a machine learning pipeline in GCP.

8
Building Machine Learning Solutions on Google Cloud Platform

The first **machine learning (ML)** solution came from the 1950s era. And I believe most of you know that in recent years, it's become very popular. It's undeniable that the discussion of **artificial intelligence (AI)** and ML is one of the hottest topics in the 21st century. There are two main drivers of this. One is the advancement in the infrastructure, while the second is data. This second driver brings us, as data engineers, into the ML area.

In my experience discussing ML with data engineers, there are two different reactions – either very excited or totally against it. Before you lose interest in finishing this chapter, I want to be clear about what we are going to cover.

We are not going to learn about ML from any historical stories nor the mathematical aspects of it. Instead, I am going to prepare you, as data engineers, for potential ML involvement in your GCP environment.

As we learn about the full picture of ML in this chapter, you will realize how close this subject is to data engineering roles. In any organization, it is very likely for us data engineers to be involved in ML discussions or projects. And on top of that, GCP has a lot of unique services that we can utilize to create end-to-end ML projects.

The following high-level topics will be covered in this chapter:

- A quick look at ML
- Exercise – practicing ML code using Python
- The MLOps landscape in GCP
- Exercise – leveraging pre-built GCP models as a service
- Deploying ML pipelines with Vertex AI

After reading and completing the exercises in this chapter, you will be able to do the following:

- Understand the different stages of the ML pipeline and how it varies from generic ETL pipelines.
- Get hands-on experience setting up different GCP products and services to build ML pipelines.
- Derive insights using pre-trained models with services such as Vision API, Cloud Natural Language, and more.

Next, let's look at the prerequisites for this chapter.

Technical requirements

For this chapter's exercises, we will use the following GCP services:

- BigQuery
- GCS
- Vertex AI Pipelines
- Vertex AI AutoML
- Google Cloud Vision AI
- Google Cloud Translate

If you have never opened any of these services in your GCP console, try to open them and enable the respective API if required.

Make sure you have your GCP console, Cloud Shell, and Cloud Editor ready.

Download the example code and the dataset from `https://github.com/PacktPublishing/Data-Engineering-with-Google-Cloud-Platform/tree/main/chapter-8`

Now, let's get started!

A quick look at machine learning

First, let's understand what ML is from a Data engineering perspective. ML is a data process that uses data as input. The output of the process is a generalized formula for one specific objective.

For better illustration, let's imagine some of the real-world use cases that use ML. The first example is a recommendation system from an e-commerce platform. This eCommerce platform may use ML to use the customer's purchase history as input data. This data can be processed to calculate how likely each customer will purchase other items in the future. Another example is a cancer predictor that uses X-ray images from the health industry. A collection of X-ray images with cancer and without cancer can be used as input data and be used to predict unidentified X-ray images.

I believe you've heard about those kinds of ML use cases and many other real-world use cases. For data engineers, it's important to notice that ML is not that different compared to data processes – it needs data as input and output. One of the key differences is the *generalized formula*, which is the key point in ML. The *generalized formula* is where some mathematical formulas come in. For example, you might have heard of regression, decision trees, neural networks, and k-means, which are called **ML models**.

We will use one ML model later called **Random Forest**. With the Random Forest model, you can create an application that learns from historical data and predicts new data. But we won't talk about this any further – our focus will be to use it as a Python package and understand its position in an end-to-end ML pipeline.

Another big aspect of ML is the terminology. Interestingly, some terms are specifically used in ML (usually by data scientists), which are used by data engineers for referring to similar things. Let's learn about some of the important ones:

- **Dataset**: This is data that will be used for ML input. It can be in any data format, but typically, it's stored in a database table or files. Compared to what data engineers expect from raw data, a *dataset* in the ML space usually expects a cleaner version of data.

For example, a dataset in table format has three columns:

- **Rain/No Rain**
- **Humidity**
- **Temperature**

- **Features**: Features are a set of information in the dataset that will be used for the ML training process. If a dataset is in a table format, features are columns in the dataset. For example, the features from the previous example are **Humidity** and **Temperature**.

- **Target**: Target is the information that we want to predict in the future. For example, the target from the previous example is **Rain/No Rain**.

- **Accuracy/Model performance**: Metrics or measurements that are used to calculate how good the ML model is. For example, 90% of the predictions correctly predict rain.

- **Hyperparameter**: When you're creating an ML model, there are certain parameters that you can provide as input. Many of them need trial and error to find the best input parameter, such as the number of trees in Random Forest.

- **Batch prediction**: This is used for predicting the future using new data in bulk. For example, you can predict the next week's **Rain/No Rain** forecast from Monday to Sunday based on this week's **Humidity** and **Temperature** values.

- **Online prediction**: For predicting the future using new data in real time. The most common practice is using an API – for example, an API that accepts input for two values – **Humidity** and **Temperature**. The output is either **Rain** or **No Rain**.

Knowing the terminology will help us communicate better with Data scientists. We'll get some real experience of using it in the next section.

Exercise – practicing ML code using Python

In this section, we will use some of the terminologies we provided in the previous section. We will practice creating a very simple ML solution using Python. The focus for us is to understand the steps and start using the correct terminologies.

For this exercise, we will be using Cloud Editor and Cloud Shell. I believe you either know or have heard that the most common tool for creating ML models for Data scientists is Jupyter Notebook. There are two reasons I choose to use the editor style. One, not many Data engineers are used to the notebook coding style. Second, using the editor will make it easier to port the files to pipelines.

For the example use case, we will predict if a credit card customer will fail to pay their credit card bill next month. I will name the use case **credit card default**. The dataset is available in the BigQuery public dataset. Let's get started.

Here are the steps that you will complete in this exercise:

1. Preparing the ML dataset by using a table from the BigQuery public dataset
2. Training the ML model using Random Forest in Python
3. Creating Batch prediction using the training dataset's output

As a simple first step, go to your **BigQuery** console and create a new dataset called `ml_dataset` in the US multi-region.

Preparing the ML dataset by using a table from the BigQuery public dataset

We want to copy the table from the BigQuery public data to our newly created dataset. To do that, find the `credit_card_default` table in the `bigquery-public-data` project, under the `ml_datasets` dataset. If you haven't pinned the `bigquery-public-data` project to your project, please revisit *Chapter 3, Building a Data Warehouse in BigQuery*.

After finding the `credit_card_default` table, click it. You will see, the **COPY** button, as shown here:

Figure 8.1 – The Copy button in the BigQuery console

Set the destination to your project and dataset. Name it `credit_card_default`, as shown in the following screenshot:

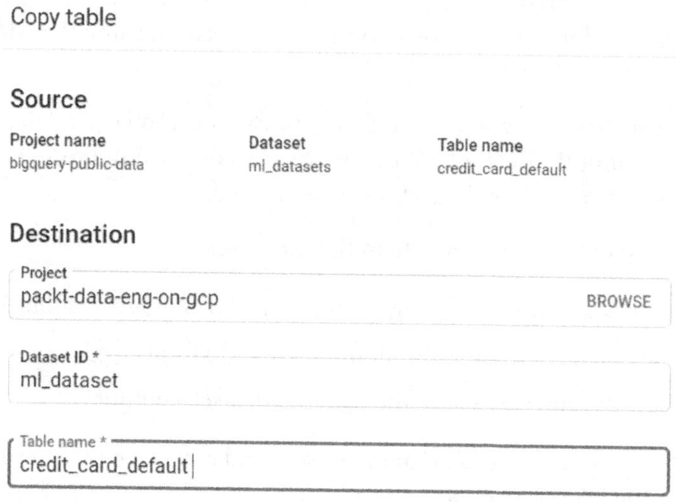

Copy table

Source

Project name	Dataset	Table name
bigquery-public-data	ml_datasets	credit_card_default

Destination

Project
packt-data-eng-on-gcp   BROWSE

Dataset ID *
ml_dataset

Table name *
credit_card_default|

Figure 8.2 – Copy table configuration

After clicking **COPY**, the table will appear in your dataset.

> **Note**
> We will use this table for this chapter and the rest of the exercises in this book. So, make sure that you complete this setup correctly.

Back to our terminologies, we can call this table the ML dataset. There are a lot of ML features here, such as `limit_balance`, `sex`, `education_level`, and many more. The target column should be `default_payment_next_month`. As usual, you can check the table's content by clicking **PREVIEW** on the BigQuery table:

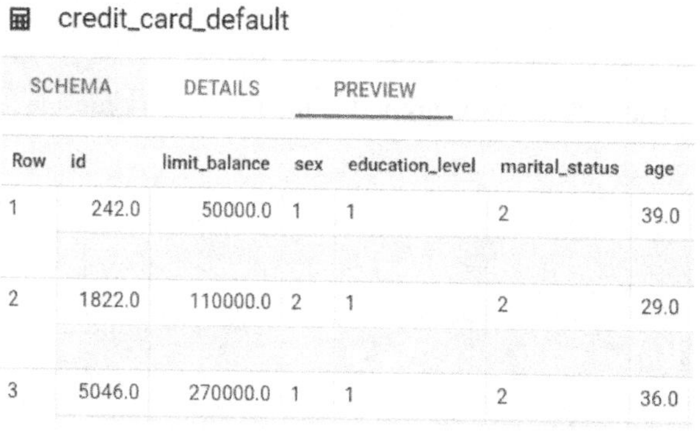

▦ credit_card_default

| SCHEMA | DETAILS | PREVIEW |

Row	id	limit_balance	sex	education_level	marital_status	age
1	242.0	50000.0	1	1	2	39.0
2	1822.0	110000.0	2	1	2	29.0
3	5046.0	270000.0	1	1	2	36.0

Figure 8.3 – credit_card_default table preview

At this point, feel free to take your time. You might need some time to understand the table's content. Once you're done, we can start coding our ML code. You can check the full example code at `https://github.com/PacktPublishing/Data-Engineering-with-Google-Cloud-Platform/blob/main/chapter-8/code/credit-card-default-ml.py`.

In the next section, we will use some Python code to train the ML model using data from the BigQuery table.

Training the ML model using Random Forest in Python

To train the ML model, there are six main steps, as follows:

1. Import the necessary library and defining variables.

    First, we need to import the ML package. In our example, we will use `RandomForestClassifier` from `sklearn`:

    ```
    from sklearn.ensemble import RandomForestClassifier
    # TODO : Change to your project id
    project_id = "packt-data-eng-on-gcp"
    ```

    Don't forget to change `project_id` to your project's ID.

2. Load the data from BigQuery into a pandas DataFrame and select the necessary features.

    The second step is to load our dataset into pandas. A pandas DataFrame is acceptable input for the `RandomForestClassifier` package. To do that, we must call the BigQuery client and convert init to a pandas DataFrame:

    ```
    client = bigquery.Client()


    sql = f"""
    SELECT limit_balance, education_level, age, default_
    payment_next_month FROM '{dataset_table_id}';
    """


    dataframe = (client.query(sql).result().to_dataframe())
    ```

    For simplicity, we will only use three features – `limit_balance`, `education_level`, and `age`. The target will be `default_payment_next_month`.

3. Split the data into train and test datasets.

The third step is to split the pandas DataFrame into four train and test datasets:

```
X_train, X_test, y_train, y_test = train_test_
split(features, target, test_size=0.3)
```

The `train` and `test` step is a very common step when it comes to creating an ML model. The goal of this step is to have different datasets for checking the accuracy later. `test_size` is `0.3`, which means that 70% of the data will be used for training and that the rest of it (30%) can be used for checking its accuracy.

4. Perform the ML training using `RandomForestClassifier`.

    The next step is to train the model. First, we need to define `RandomForestClassifier`. Later, we will call the `fit` method to train the model:

    ```
    random_forest_classifier = RandomForestClassifier(n_
    estimators=100)
    ```

    ```
    random_forest_classifier.fit(X_train,y_train)
    ```

    The training process happens when we trigger the `fit` method. Notice that there is a variable there called `n_estimators = 100`. This is one example of a hyperparameter. `n_estimators` defines how many trees will be used in the Random Forest model. No one knows what the best number we should put here is, and that's part of the hyperparameter.

5. Predict the test data and calculate the model's accuracy.

    The next step is to calculate the model's accuracy. We will use the `random_forest_classifier` variable to predict the testing data.:

    ```
    y_pred=random_forest_classifier.predict(X_test)
    print("Accuracy:",metrics.accuracy_score(y_test, y_pred))
    ```

    In this step, this is not what's called Batch or online prediction. Even though we are using the `predict` method in this step, the goal of this step is only to calculate the accuracy score. At the end of this step, you will know the accuracy of the model.

6. Save the model as a file.

    Finally, our model should be stored as a file. Do this by calling the `joblib.dump` function:

    ```
    joblib.dump(random_forest_classifier, model_name)
    ```

    This step will write a `.joblib` file in your local filesystem.

7. At the end of these steps, you will get an ML file that you can use to predict future credit card default datasets.

Creating Batch Prediction using the training dataset's output

In the same Python file, let's look at the `predict_batch` function:

1. Load the new dataset for batch prediction.

    Similar to the training model step, we must load the data from the BigQuery table, as follows:

    ```
    client = bigquery.Client()
    sql = f"""SELECT limit_balance, education_level, age FROM
    '{dataset_table_id}' LIMIT 10;"""
    dataframe = (client.query(sql).result().to_dataframe())
    ```

    For simplicity, we will use the same table but select only the feature columns and limit it to only 10 rows. In reality, the table for prediction should be taken from a different table. The table should contain sets of data that have no target column.

2. Use the ML model to predict the batch dataset.

    The next step is simply predicting the data. To do that, we need to load the model from our previous step:

    ```
    loaded_model = joblib.load(model_name)
    prediction=loaded_model.predict(dataframe)
    ```

    The function will print its prediction for the 10 unlabeled records. That can result in a correct or incorrect prediction. And that's the nature of ML – it can give both right and wrong answers.

3. Use the ML model to predict online data.

    For online prediction, you can use the `predict_online` function. The following is a very simplified example of online prediction:

    ```
    limit_balance = 1000
    education_level = 1
    age = 25
    feature_json = json.dumps([[limit_balance, education_
    level, age]])
    predict_online(feature_json)
    ```

As you can see, the nature of online prediction is giving a single input so that a function will return the result in real time. In reality, this simplified function needs to be served as a web API. The `limit_balance`, `education_level`, and `age` features will be the API parameters that are used as inputs for prediction. This part is typically done by web developers, so we will not cover this topic in this book.

To close this exercise, let's summarize it. Even though the given example is a very simple use case, we learned about the steps that are required in ML and its terminologies. At this point, we realize that we have an ML pipeline. Here are the steps we followed:

1. Load the required ML libraries.
2. Data loading.
3. Feature selection.
4. Data splitting.
5. Model training.
6. Model evaluation.
7. Model deployment.
8. Batch prediction.
9. Simulate an online prediction.

We will learn how to manage an ML pipeline in GCP later in the *Deploying a dummy workflow with Vertex AI Pipeline* section. But before we use the GCP service, we need to understand better what services in GCP are related to ML. And to learn about service positioning, we need to understand what MLOps is. We will discuss this in the next section.

The MLOps landscape in GCP

In this section, let's learn what are GCP services related to MLOps. But before that, let's first understand what MLOps is.

Understanding the basic principles of MLOps

When we created the ML model in the previous section, we created some ML code. I found that most ML content and its discussion on the public internet is about creating and improving that part of ML. Some examples of typical topics include how to create a Random Forest model, ML regression versus classification, boosting ML accuracy with hyperparameters, and many more.

All of the example topics mentioned previously are part of creating ML code. In reality, ML in a real production system needs a lot more than that. Take a look at the following diagram for the other aspects:

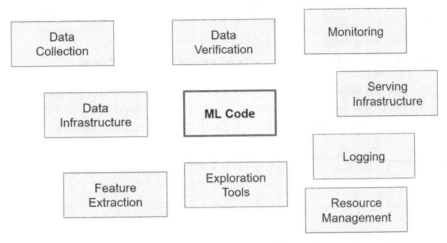

Figure 8.4 – Various ML aspects that ML code is only a small part of

As you can see, it's logical to have the other aspects in an ML environment. For example, in our previous exercise, the credit card data has already been formed, was clean, and was ready for our training step. As a Data engineer, you can imagine the effort needed before that, so it's logical to have data collection, data verification, and feature extraction processes.

So, where should the training process happen? In our local machine (laptop), or a **virtual machine (VM)**? How about the dependencies? Combined with all the other aspects, this usually takes 90% of the effort compared to the ML code.

The practice of building and maintaining all of these aspects in ML is what's called MLOps. Understanding all the aspects of MLOps requires us to understand several different areas of expertise, including ML models, data, orchestration, containerization (Docker), web services, monitoring, and much more. This is why ML is a very broad topic and, most of the time, requires more than one team or expert to handle the entirety of MLOps.

If you start everything from scratch, it will probably take months, if not years, to complete all the stacks. Are there any ways to simplify this? Yes. In GCP, most of the stacks are available as managed services.

Is it going to be that easy? No – not in terms of the learning journey. Understanding and creating MLOps won't be as easy as creating a table and querying it in BigQuery. MLOps has many components and the topics are very broad. But managed services help reduce the development time a lot. In the next section, we'll look at the landscape of MLOps in GCP.

Introducing GCP services related to MLOps

In GCP, you can find almost all you need for MLOps. First, let's start by looking at what is available in our GCP console. In your GCP console, open Vertex AI in the **GCP** navigation menu, under **Vertex AI**. You will see that there are many services:

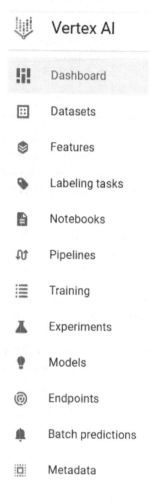

Figure 8.5 – List of Vertex AI services in the GCP navigation menu

You can open each service and read the description to find out about its positioning. I'll quickly highlight the flow of each service using a scenario where you would want to build an ML model. You have the raw data in BigQuery. So, what services should you use and when?

First, you must create a Vertex AI **Notebooks** instance and play around with the BigQuery data to create experimental ML models. The ML models can also be called ML code. Once you're satisfied with the ML code, to automate the code, you must automate the process using the Vertex AI's **Pipelines service**, which will automate all the steps. These steps may include creating a Vertex AI **Datasets service**, a Vertex AI **Features service**, a Vertex AI **Labeling tasks service**, and a Vertex AI **Training service**. The **Training** step will store an ML model in the Vertex AI's **Models service**. Later, the model can be used for the Vertex AI **Batch predictions service** and to start a Vertex AI **Endpoints service** for online prediction. Finally, you can store any metadata from any steps to the Vertex AI's **Metadata service**, such as the model's accuracy.

As you can see from the previous scenario, every service under Vertex AI can be used for an end-to-end ML scenario. There are two things to note here. First, you still need other GCP services outside Vertex AI, such as GCS, BigQuery, IAM, and others. Vertex AI services are specifically used to handle ML operations, but the other GCP services are still needed. Second, all Vertex AI services are optional. For example, you can decide to only use Vertex AI Pipelines for orchestration, but store the models as files in GCS and not use Vertex AI Models. Or, as another example, you could just use the Training service to use the AutoML feature; none of the others would be required. There are many things you must consider when you're deciding to use all or some of these services, such as cost, regional availability, and the learning curve.

Later in this chapter, we will learn how to use almost all these services, but before that, I want to highlight two other things about the ML services in GCP – the evolution of these ML services in GCP and the ML model training approaches.

ML services on GCP evolve rapidly. This may lead to some confusion when you start looking for examples and tutorials on the public internet. For example, at the time of writing, there are three options in GCP for creating an ML pipeline. One is the marketplace, where you can find a service called Kubeflow Pipelines. The second option is to use AI Platform, while the third option is to use Vertex AI. This is because some services are older than others. If this is still the case when you are reading this book, hopefully, this explanation will clear up any confusion. If it is no longer the case, you will still see some old yet valuable articles on the public internet that mention different service names.

Historically speaking, all the ML services on GCP were separated into individual services. The services were only grouped in the **Navigation** menu, under **Artificial Intelligence**. The second generation was the AI Platform. The following screenshot shows that there are two menus under the **ARTIFICIAL INTELLIGENCE** category – **Vertex AI** and **AI Platform**:

Figure 8.6 – In the Navigation menu, there are two options – Vertex AI and AI Platform

AI Platform's vision was to combine all the MLOps-related services under one umbrella. This way, you, as a GCP user, can get a better experience by performing end-to-end ML scenarios on a single platform. The latest generation is Vertex AI. There are many new features and advancements in terms of ML services, but at the same time, AI Platform is still relatively new and users are still adopting it, hence the umbrella has been separated into two – Vertex AI and AI Platform. In short, AI Platform is a legacy umbrella for the MLOps services, while Vertex AI is the latest and the future. We will use various Vertex AI services later in this chapter, but if you want to research the ML topics on GCP, you may still find the AI Platform topics on the public internet very useful.

For the ML model training process, there are four main approaches that you can utilize on GCP:

- Pre-built models
- AutoML
- BigQuery ML
- A custom model in a custom environment

These approaches are there as options for three-dimensional decision points: development time, the amount of expertise, and the cost. What does this mean?

An ideal condition for a data science team in a company when building ML is having a lot of *experienced* Data scientists. In terms of time, the Data Scientists have *a lot of time* to experiment and find the best model for each use case and ensure that the infrastructure *costs as little as possible*. In this ideal case, creating a custom model in a custom environment is the best approach. But not every condition is ideal – some companies don't have Data Scientists, some need to model as soon as possible, and some have very limited budgets. In these situations, we need to make decisions from the other options available.

A pre-built model is a group of trained ML models provided by Google Cloud. The lists of models are continuing to grow, but as an example, at the time of writing, there are models for detecting image to text, translating languages, eCommerce item recommendations, and others that you can check in your GCP console under the **Artificial Intelligence** section via the **Navigation** menu. This approach requires almost zero ML experts and experiment time. As a user, you just need to call the API using the client library and you can make the predictions immediately. The downside is that the model is limited to what's been provided, so you can't handle edge cases. And the cost is relatively more expensive for heavy users because it's charged by the number of API calls.

AutoML is a term in ML where you, as an ML code developer, no longer need to decide what ML algorithm is the best for your model. AutoML will automatically try many possibilities and parameters. The number of trials is based on time. As a developer, you just need to tell AutoML how much time you want to give, and AutoML will return the best possible model in that given time. This approach can handle your edge cases, needs a small amount of Data Scientists, and needs almost zero experiment time. The downside is the cost of the infrastructure. It's relatively more expensive compared to building a custom model. The upside, besides the development time, is the accuracy, since AutoML has proven to be more accurate than self-built custom models.

The last option is BigQuery ML. BigQuery ML is an approach for training ML models using SQL queries. This approach allows you to create custom ML models with any available algorithm provided by BigQuery. This approach is suitable when you want to train ML models but you are more comfortable using SQL compared to programming languages such as Python or R, plus with libraries such as TensorFlow and scikit-learn.

Different scenarios need different approaches. In general, if we only consider the development and experimentation time, then here is a list in order from the least to the most time-consuming:

1. Pre-built model
2. AutoML
3. BigQuery ML
4. A custom model in a custom environment

In the next section, we will start our exercise. There, we will start by using a pre-built model while using the Python API to detect text in images, using AutoML from the GCP console, and building a custom model using scikit-learn using a Vertex AI pipeline.

> **Note**
>
> We will not be using BigQuery ML here. The steps are straightforward and relatively easy if you already know how to use BigQuery. Go back to *Chapter 3, Building a Data Warehouse in BigQuery*, and *Chapter 4, Building Orchestration for Batch Data Loading Using Cloud Composer*, for the steps on creating an ML pipeline; they are similar to those for creating a data pipeline.

Exercise – leveraging pre-built GCP models as a service

In this exercise, we want to use a GCP service called Google Cloud Vision. Google Cloud Vision is one of many pre-built models in GCP. In pre-built models, we only need to call the API from our application. This means that we don't need to create an ML model.

In this exercise, we will create a Python application that can read an image with handwritten text and convert it into a Python string.

The following are the steps for this exercise:

1. Upload the image to a GCS bucket.
2. Install the required Python packages.
3. Create a detect text function in Python.

Let's start by uploading the image.

Uploading the image to a GCS bucket

In the GCS console, go to the bucket that you created in the previous chapters. For example, my bucket is `packt-data-eng-on-gcp-data-bucket`.

Inside the bucket, create a new folder called `chapter-8`. This is an example from my console:

packt-data-eng-on-gcp-data-bucket

OBJECTS	CONFIGURATION	PERMISSIONS	RETENTION	LIFECYCLE

Buckets > packt-data-eng-on-gcp-data-bucket > chapter-8

Figure 8.7 – Example GCS bucket folder for storing the image file

We want to upload the image file into this folder. You can upload any image that contains text, or you can use the example provided at https://github.com/ PacktPublishing/Data-Engineering-with-Google-Cloud-Platform/ blob/main/chapter-8/dataset/chapter-8-example-text.jpg.

The image that we want to upload looks like this:

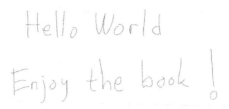

Figure 8.8 – The image that we will process using Google Cloud Vision AI

This image is of handwritten text with no format. I have intentionally used my handwritten text as an example to show that Google Cloud Vision can convert any text – it's not limited to computer-generated fonts. After downloading the file to your local computer, upload it to GCS in your newly created folder.

Next, we want to install the necessary packages. Go to your Cloud Shell and install the following two Python packages:

```
pip install google-cloud-vision
pip install google-cloud-translate
```

Google Cloud Vision and Google Cloud Translate will be installed. We will use the Translate package to detect what language is used in the text and to illustrate how to use two pre-built models in one application.

Creating a detect text function in Python

Now, go to your Cloud Shell and Cloud Editor. Here, we will start writing the code for our application. You can find the full code example at https://github.com/ PacktPublishing/Data-Engineering-with-Google-Cloud-Platform/ blob/main/chapter-8/code/pre-built-vision-ai.py.

Please make sure that you use python3 for this code example, which is available in Cloud Shell by default. To run the example code, run the following command:

```
# python3 pre-build-vision-ai.py
```

Upon running it for the first time, you may get an error message from the Vision API, like so:

Your application has been authenticated using end user credentials from the Google Cloud SDK or Google Cloud Shell, which are not supported by vision.googleapis.com.

This error message means that Google Cloud highly recommends that you use a service account instead of a user account to call the Vision API. But for development purposes, you can log in as a service account using the following `gcloud` command:

```
# gcloud auth application-default login
```

Try this out in your Cloud Shell – run the command and follow the instructions. The instructions are pretty straightforward, so I won't go through them here. As a summary, here are the steps:

1.   After running the command, you will be asked a yes or no confirmation question. Choose *yes*.

2.   After confirming, a URL link will be shown in Cloud Shell. Open the link in any browser.

3.   In your browser, log in with your Google account.

4.   At this point, you will get a verification code. Copy and paste this code into Cloud Shell. The following is an example:

```
Enter verification code: 4/xxxxxxxxxx
```

After completing all these steps, you will get a message saying that the credential can be used for any library:

These credentials will be used by any library that requests Application Default Credentials (ADC).

Make sure that you've got that message before continuing or running the Vision API example code. Now, let's start looking at the code.

First, we need to import the Vision and Translate APIs from the `google.cloud` package:

```
from google.cloud import vision
from google.cloud import translate_v2 as translate
```

Make sure that you change the project ID, bucket name, and folders according to your environment:

```
# TODO: Change to your project id and your gcs file uri
project_id = "packt-data-eng-on-gcp"
gcs_uri = "gs://packt-data-eng-on-gcp-data-bucket/chapter-8/
chapter-8-example-text.jpg"
```

You need to define the clients to call both APIs:

```
vision_client = vision.ImageAnnotatorClient()
translate_client = translate.Client()
```

The following is the main function for our `detect_text`:

```
def detect_text(gcs_uri: str):
    print("Looking for text from image in GCS: {}".format(gcs_
uri))

    image = vision.Image(
        source=vision.ImageSource(gcs_image_uri=gcs_uri)
    )

    text_detection_response = vision_client.text_
detection(image=image)
    annotations = text_detection_response.text_annotations
    if len(annotations) > 0:
        text = annotations[0].description
    else:
        text = ""
    print("Extracted text : \n{}".format(text))

    detect_language_response = translate_client.detect_
language(text)
    src_lang = detect_language_response["language"]
    print("Detected language {}".format(src_lang))


detect_text(gcs_uri)
```

The function uses the `text_detection` method from `vision_client` to read the image and output the text. The output is stored in a text variable that will be used in the Translate API. The Translate API uses the `detect_language` method and will detect what language is in the image. For further usage, you can use the Translate API to translate the text into other languages.

To finish the exercise, run the python code from Cloud Shell, for example: `python3 pre-built-vision-ai.py`

The code will print the extracted text *Hello World Enjoy the book!*

And that's it – that is how easy it is to implement ML using pre-built models in GCP! What is good about pre-built models is that you can immediately predict new datasets without thinking about training the machine learning model. So long as the API is suitable for your needs, you can use it immediately. But there are very common cases where we need to create an ML model. One way to do this with minimal effort is by using AutoML. In the next section, we will learn how to use AutoML in GCP.

Exercise – using GCP in AutoML to train an ML model

As we learned earlier in this chapter, AutoML is an automated way for you to build an ML model. It will handle the model selection, hyperparameter tuning, and various data preparation steps. Specifically for the data preparation part, it will not be smart enough to transform data from very raw tables and automatically create clean features. What AutoML will do, however, is perform simple data preparation tasks, such as detecting numeric, binary, categorical, and text features, and then apply the required transformation to be used in the ML training process. Let's learn how to do this. Here are the steps that you will complete in this exercise:

- Create Vertex AI datasets.
- Set up the AutoML training.

For the use case and dataset, we will use the credit card default dataset from our previous exercise. First, go to your GCP console and find and click **Vertex AI**. If you haven't enabled the API, there will be a button to enable **Vertex API**, so click it to enable it.

Under the **Vertex AI** console, go to the **Datasets** menu:

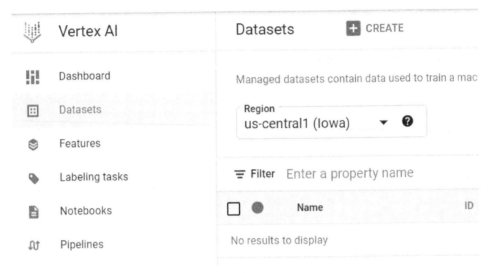

Figure 8.9 – Finding the Vertex AI Datasets menu from the GCP navigation menu

Datasets under Vertex AI are not the same as the BigQuery datasets. You can load data from a BigQuery table, but this is a different feature than the one in BigQuery. Let's try this out:

1. Create a Vertex AI dataset.

    Find the **CREATE** button at the top of the page and click it.

    Set the dataset's name to credit_card_default.

In the **Select a data type and objective** section, choose **TABULAR Regression/
classification**. This is a very important selection that will be used by AutoML:

Select a data type and objective

First select the type of data your dataset will contain. Then select an objective, which is the outcome
model types

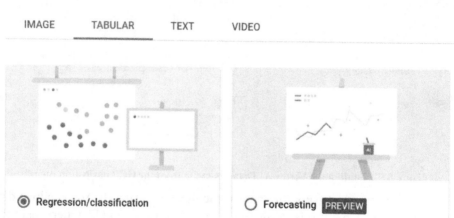

Figure 8.10 – Choosing the Regression/classification option

After choosing this option, click the **CREATE** button. It will take around 5 seconds
to complete, at which point you will be redirected to the data source selection page.

Under **Select a data source**, choose **Select a table or view from BigQuery**.

Find your `credit_card_default` table from your project. Then, click
CONTINUE. Here is the example BigQuery path from my project; you need
to find yours:

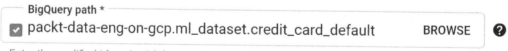

Figure 8.11 – Example BigQuery path format

At this point, you will be directed to a page where you can see some useful
information about your datasets. In the next step, we will train an ML model using
the dataset that we created in this step.

2. Train the ML model using AutoML.

    Still on the same page, at the top right, you will see the **TRAIN NEW MODEL** button – click it.

    For **Training method**, set the objective to **Classification** and use **AutoML**.

    Then, click **Continue**.

    Under **Model details**, you need to specify a **Target column**; choose `default_payment_next_month`.

    Under **Training options**, you can choose to set each column as either **Categorical** or **Numerical** under **Transformation** or set everything to **Automatic**. The important thing now is to exclude the unwanted features. We can do that by clicking the delete icon to the right of each column. The icon looks like this:

    Figure 8.12 – Delete icon

    Make sure that you only include `age`, `education_level`, and `limit_balance`. The other columns should be excluded. It will look like this:

	Column name ↑	Transformation	BigQuery type	BigQuery mode	Missing % (count)	Distinct values	Correlation w/ target	
☐	age	Automatic ▾	FLOAT	NULLABLE	-	·		⊖
☐	bill_amt_1	Automatic ▾	FLOAT	NULLABLE	-	·		⊕
☐	bill_amt_2	Automatic ▾	FLOAT	NULLABLE	-	·		⊕
☐	bill_amt_3	Automatic ▾	FLOAT	NULLABLE	-	·		⊕
☐	bill_amt_4	Automatic ▾	FLOAT	NULLABLE	-	·		⊕
☐	bill_amt_5	Automatic ▾	FLOAT	NULLABLE	-	·		⊕
☐	bill_amt_6	Automatic ▾	FLOAT	NULLABLE	-	·		⊕
☐	default_payment_next_month `Target`		STRING	NULLABLE	-	·		
☐	education_level	Automatic ▾	STRING	NULLABLE	-	·		⊖
☐	id	Automatic ▾	FLOAT	NULLABLE	-	·		⊕
☐	limit_balance	Automatic ▾	FLOAT	NULLABLE	-	·		⊖

Figure 8.13 – Choosing columns

Once you're satisfied with the features you've selected, click **CONTINUE**.

3. Choose the compute and pricing for AutoML.

    After clicking **CONTINUE** in the previous step, you will see the **Compute and Pricing** option. This is an option that you need to pay attention to. With this option, you can choose how much time you want AutoML to try to find the best model. At this point, don't continue to the next step before reading through these pricing considerations.

The link to the pricing guide is provided on that page, under **Pricing guide**. Check this guide to decide if you want to continue with the process or not. The minimum cost is around $20 for 1 training hour. If you don't have much of your free trial budget left ($300) you can stop the AutoML exercise here. If you want to try running it and don't have issues with the cost, click **START TRAINING**.

This step will trigger a training job that you can monitor in Vertex AI's **Training** menu. The `credit_card_default` job will be shown there:

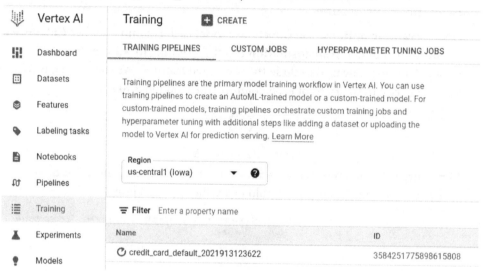

Figure 8.14 – The training job is running

This process will take a maximum of 1 hour, but it can be faster if AutoML can no longer improve its accuracy.

Once you're done, you can check the Vertex AI **Models** menu. You will see a lot of interesting model metrics here, such as **F1 score**, **Precision**, **Recall**, and **ROC AUC**:

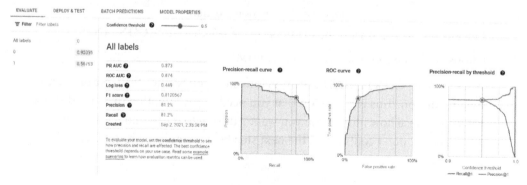

Figure 8.15 – Model labels and metrics under the EVALUATE tab

If you are not familiar with all of these metrics, don't worry – we won't be using them. These metrics are important information that is usually used by Data Scientists to determine if it's a good model or not. In very simple terms, all of these numbers show ML model accuracy.

Once you're satisfied with the model, there are two common next steps. First, you can deploy the model as an API for online prediction. In Vertex AI, you can click the **DEPLOY & TEST** menu and get the API up and running. The second option is performing batch prediction; for example, by using another table in BigQuery to predict the user's defaults. To do this, you can click **BATCH PREDICTIONS**. Both options are very straightforward, so we won't look at them in this exercise.

To summarize, at the end of this exercise, you will have an ML model that you can use to predict credit card defaults. The model was built using AutoML from Vertex AI. As you have experienced, there are three things that you don't need to do when using AutoML:

- You don't need to code.

- You don't need to know about any ML algorithms.

- You don't need to worry about the infrastructure.

The whole process typically takes less than 1 hour, which can reduce a lot of time and effort when you're building an ML model. But there are scenarios where we will want to create an ML model, which is possible. On top of that, if you want to automate the steps and process, we can use Vertex AI Pipeline.

In the next exercise, we will learn about Vertex AI Pipeline. We will use Vertex AI Pipeline to create a custom ML model using the same code from the *Exercise – practicing ML code using Python* section.

Exercise – deploying a dummy workflow with Vertex AI Pipeline

Before we continue with the hands-on exercise, let's understand what Vertex AI Pipeline is. Vertex AI Pipeline is a tool for orchestrating ML workflows. Under the hood, it uses an open source tool called Kubeflow Pipeline. Similar to the relationship between Airflow and Cloud Composer or Hadoop and DataProc, to understand Vertex AI Pipeline, we need to be familiar with Kubeflow Pipelines.

Kubeflow Pipeline is a platform for building and deploying portable, scalable ML workflows based on Docker containers. Using containers for ML workflows is very important compared to data workflows. For example, in data workflows, it's typical to load BigQuery, GCS, and pandas libraries for all the steps. Those libraries will be used in both the upstream and downstream steps. In ML, the upstream is data loading; the other step is building models that need specific libraries such as TensorFlow or scikit-learn, while the final step is to calculate the accuracy. And on top of that, each process needs different machine specifications. Implementing each step on containers is very helpful for ML workloads.

This idea is great, but in reality, it is very difficult to achieve without tools such as Kubeflow. Imagine that you need to understand the principles of Docker, Kubernetes, data engineering, and ML models at the same time. The Docker and Kubernetes part is usually not something that Data Scientists are familiar with. And that's where Kubeflow Pipeline fills in the gap. With Kubeflow Pipeline, Data Scientists can simplify the containerization code, yet all the pipelines will be running in containers. With Vertex AI Pipeline, you're not only simplifying the code but also the infrastructure. Using it, you don't need to think about Kubernetes clusters, networking, or installing Kubeflow. You just need to understand how to use the SDKs (`kfp` and `google-cloud-pipeline-components`). We will learn how to use these SDKs in the next section.

In this exercise, we will create a dummy workload. This dummy workload has nothing to do with ML – we will just print text. What we are going to focus on is becoming familiar with the code and how to run it on Vertex AI Pipeline.

The following are the high-level steps:

1. Install the SDKs.
2. Create a dedicated regional GCS bucket.
3. Develop the pipeline on Python.
4. Monitor the pipeline on the Vertex AI Pipeline console.

To start, let's install the required libraries in Python. To do that, go to your Cloud Shell and use the following commands to install the necessary libraries:

```
# pip3 install kfp --upgrade
# pip3 install -U google-cloud-pipeline-components
```

Note that there will be an error message about compatibility issues when you run the `kfp` installation. This issue is not a blocker, so we can ignore it and continue to the next section. But if it is a blocker in the future, please check the public Kubeflow documentation on how to install the Kubeflow Pipelines SDK, which you can find at `https://www.kubeflow.org/docs/components/pipelines/sdk/install-sdk/#install-the-kubeflow-pipelines-sdk`.

Now, let's create a GCS bucket.

Creating a dedicated regional GCS bucket

We need to create a GCS bucket for this exercise. The bucket will be used by Vertex AI Pipeline to store temporary files, the steps, and the output. The GCS bucket's location should be the same as where Vertex AI Pipeline is located. And for that reason, we need to create a new GCS bucket instead of using our existing GCS bucket from the previous chapters. To refresh our memory, our previous bucket was located in a multi-region US location, which is different from regional `us-central1`, for example.

Let's create a new GCS bucket. Go to the GCS console and create a new bucket using any name. For example, my new bucket name is `packt-data-eng-on-gcp-vertex-ai-pipeline`.

As we mentioned previously, the important option that you need to be aware of is **Location type**. Choose **Region** here and set **Location** to **us-central1**:

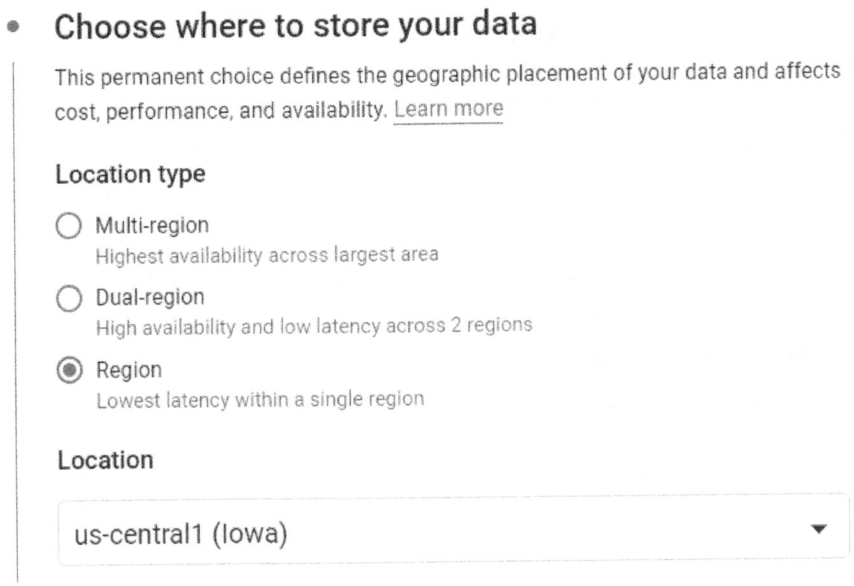

Figure 8.16 – Choosing a Location type and Region

Now that we've created the GCS bucket, we can look at the example code. In the next section, we will go through the example code for defining Vertex AI Pipeline.

Developing the pipeline on Python

In this section, we will go through the Python code that calls Kubeflow SDK to build Vertex AI Pipeline. The code example for this chapter can be found at the following link:

```
https://github.com/PacktPublishing/Data-Engineering-with-
Google-Cloud-Platform/blob/main/chapter-8/code/practice-
vertex-ai-pipeline.py
```

In this example, we will start by understanding how the SDK works and how to run the code in Vertex AI. We will not be completing any ML steps in this section. I suggest that you focus on the code part when you're defining the steps, dependencies, and deployment to Vertex AI.

Let's start with the first simple step:

1. The first step is to import the required libraries:

    ```
    from kfp.dsl import pipeline
    from kfp.v2 import compiler
    from kfp.v2.dsl import component
    from kfp.v2.google.client import AIPlatformClient
    ```

    As you can see, we are using the `kfp` library, which is the open source Kubeflow Pipeline library that you can also use without Vertex AI. But since we will be using Vertex AI, we will need to import `AIPlatformClient`. Don't be confused about AI Platform versus Vertex AI. Since AIPlatform is the predecessor of Vertex AI, the client library is still named `AIPlatformClient` instead of `VertexAIClient`.

2. Define the Vertex AI Pipeline steps.

    Next, we want to declare the steps in our pipeline. Each step is declared using Python functions. For example, our first step will be named `step_one`. This function will print the input text and return the text's value:

    ```
    @component(output_component_file="step_one.yml")
    def step_one(text: str) -> str:
        print(text)
        return text
    ```

Notice that we put @component in the function, which is an important step. This is the step where we can configure the container. For example, take a look at the step_two and step_three functions:

```
@component(output_component_file="step_two.yml", base_
image="python:3.9")
```

We can declare the base image that we want to load for this function. The default value is Python 3.7. This means that, in the step_one function, it will run on top of different Python versions compared to step_two and step_three. Another option is to have the packages installed. Take a look at the step_four function. This time, we specified packages_to_install with the google-cloud-storage package:

```
@component(packages_to_install=["google-cloud-storage"])
def step_four(text1: str, text2: str, gcs_bucket: str):
    from google.cloud import storage

    output_string = f"text1: {text1}; text2: {text2};"

    storage_client = storage.Client()
    bucket = storage_client.get_bucket(gcs_bucket)
    blob = bucket.blob(f"practice-vertex-ai-pipeline/
artefact/output.txt")
    blob.upload_from_string(output_string)
    print(output_string)
```

By defining packages_to_install in the component, the container will install the packages before running the code. If you are not familiar with the container concepts, then this is a good example of the benefits. Here, you can see that each step can use different images and packages. Another possibility is that you can build a Docker image and import it directly as a step instead of defining the code as functions, which will give you the benefit of portability. But we will not practice that in this book.

3. Define the Vertex AI Pipeline step's dependencies.

The next step is to declare the pipeline and the step's dependencies. Take a look at the following code:

```
@pipeline(
    name="practice-vertex-ai-pipeline",
    description="Example of Vertex AI Pipeline",
    pipeline_root=pipeline_root_path,
)
def pipeline(text: str = "Hello"):
    step_one_task = step_one(text)
    step_two_task = step_two(step_one_task.output)
    step_three_task = step_three(step_one_task.output)
    step_four_task = step_four(step_two_task.output,
step_three_task.output)
```

The step's dependencies – or in other words, task chaining – are not declared explicitly. The chains are declared when the task's input is taken from other tasks' output. For example, step_two uses the output from step_one as its input. step_three also uses the output from step_one, while step_four uses the outputs of step_two and step_three. The following diagram shows the expected dependencies:

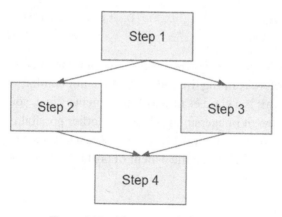

Figure 8.17 – The expected steps flow

After defining the dependencies, we expect the same pipeline when we run it in Vertex AI Pipeline.

1. Compile and submit the Vertex AI Pipeline job.

    Next, we need to export all of our code into a JSON file. The JSON file needs to be in a very specific format so that Vertex AI can understand the information. To do that, use the following code:

    ```
    compiler.Compiler().compile(
        pipeline_func=pipeline, package_path=f"{pipeline_
    name}.json"
    )
    ```

    The compiler code will export the pipeline code into a JSON file in your local system. The next step is to submit the JSON file to Vertex AI Pipeline:

    ```
    api_client = AIPlatformClient(project_id=project_id,
    region=region)
    response = api_client.create_run_from_job_spec(
        job_spec_path=f"{pipeline_name}.json", pipeline_
    root=pipeline_root_path
    )
    ```

    And that's all that we need in our Python code. Run it as a normal Python application, like so:

    ```
    # python practice-vertex-ai-pipeline.py
    ```

    Running the code will trigger the pipeline submission to Vertex AI Pipeline.

Before checking this in the GCP console, let's recap what we've done in this section. In this section, we learned how to code Vertex AI Pipeline tasks. Tasks can be written as Python functions. These Python functions won't be run as a normal Python application in your Cloud Shell. The functions are going to be wrapped as containers with all the configurations that we declared in @component. The Python code that you ran did two things. First, it compiled the task functions and dependencies into a json file. Second, it submitted the JSON file to Vertex AI Pipeline. And just to repeat, the step_one to step_four Python functions won't be run on Cloud Shell or your local machine; instead, they will be run on a Vertex AI Pipeline cluster as containers. In the next section, we will check our pipeline in the console.

Monitoring the pipeline on the Vertex AI Pipeline console

To check if our pipeline has been submitted, go to **Vertex AI Pipelines** in your GCP console. If there is no issue with your code, you will see that the pipeline is running under the **Run** list:

Figure 8.18 – Vertex AI Pipeline is running

If you click your pipeline name, you will see its details, as well as its steps, as expected:

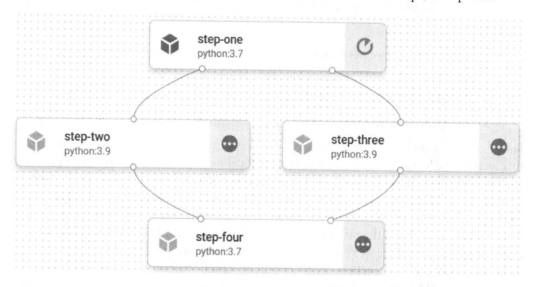

Figure 8.19 – Detailed steps under the running pipeline

step-two and **step-three** depend on **step-one**, while **step-four** depends on **step-two** and **step-three**. It will run for about 3 minutes for all the steps. If there are any errors, you can click the **VIEW LOGS** button to check the error logs in any of the steps:

VIEW LOGS

Figure 8.20 – The VIEW LOGS button

If all steps are successful, **step-four** will create a file in the GCS bucket:

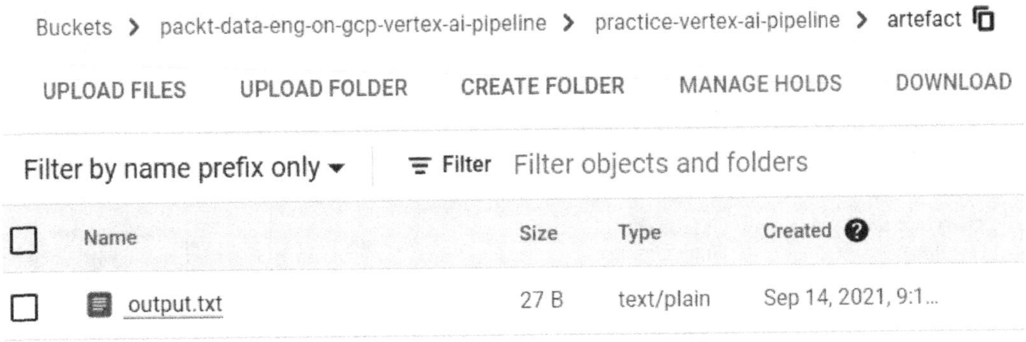

Buckets ❯ packt-data-eng-on-gcp-vertex-ai-pipeline ❯ practice-vertex-ai-pipeline ❯ artefact

UPLOAD FILES   UPLOAD FOLDER   CREATE FOLDER   MANAGE HOLDS   DOWNLOAD

Filter by name prefix only ▾   ≡ Filter   Filter objects and folders

	Name	Size	Type	Created ❷
☐	🗐 output.txt	27 B	text/plain	Sep 14, 2021, 9:1...

Figure 8.21 – Checking the GCS bucket to find the output file

You can check and open the output.txt file. The output should look like this:

```
text1: Hello; text2: Hello;
```

And with that, you now have the fundamental knowledge to create a pipeline in Vertex AI Pipeline. In the next and last exercise for this chapter, we will create a pipeline that creates an ML model and a pipeline for predicting new datasets using the model.

Exercise – deploying a scikit-learn model pipeline with Vertex AI

In this exercise, we will simulate creating a pipeline for an ML model. There will be two pipelines – one to train the ML model and another to predict new data using the model from the first pipeline. We will continue using the Credit Card Default dataset. The two pipelines will look like this:

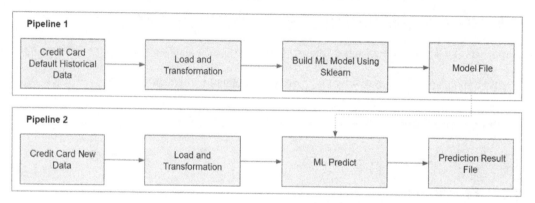

Figure 8.22 – Steps in the two pipelines

Later in this section, we will load data from BigQuery. But instead of storing the data in pandas, we will write the output to a GCS bucket. We will be doing this as we don't want to return an in-memory Python object from the function. What I mean by an in-memory Python object, in this case, is a pandas DataFrame. This also applies to other data structures, such as arrays or lists. Remember that every step in Vertex AI Pipeline will be executed in a different container – that is, in a different machine. You can't pass the pandas DataFrame from one machine to the others. What you can do, however, is store the output data in storage such as GCS. We can pass the GCS location to the other machine to continue the downstream steps.

The following are the high-level steps for this exercise:

1. Create the first pipeline, which will result in an ML model file in GCS.

2. Run the first pipeline in Vertex AI Pipeline.

3. Create the second pipeline, which will use the model file from the prediction results as a CSV file in GCS.

4. Run the second pipeline in Vertex AI Pipeline.

In general, what you need to do is check the code example for the first and second pipelines. Make sure that you've changed all the variables as per your environment (GCP project ID, GCS bucket) and deploy the pipelines to Vertex AI ones by running the Python code from your Cloud Shell environment. Let's start with the first step.

Creating the first pipeline, which will result in an ML model file in GCS

Before I start explaining the code parts, please check the code example. You can find the full code at `https://github.com/PacktPublishing/Data-Engineering-with-Google-Cloud-Platform/blob/main/chapter-8/code/ai-pipeline-credit-default-train.py`.

As usual, you can use Cloud Editor and Cloud Shell to edit the code and run it. Let's go through the code. I'll explain it by breaking it down into three parts:

1. First, we must define the first pipeline's step by loading the BigQuery table into a GCS bucket.

    First, let's take a look at the `load_data_from_bigquery` function:

    ```
    @component(packages_to_install=["google-cloud-
    bigquery","google-cloud-storage","pandas","pyarrow"])
    def load_data_from_bigquery(bigquery_table_id: str,
    output_gcs_bucket: str) -> str:
        from google.cloud import bigquery
        from google.cloud import storage


        project_id = "packt-data-eng-on-gcp"
        output_file = "ai-pipeline-credit-default-train/
    artefacts/train.csv"


        bq_client = bigquery.Client(project=project_id)
        sql = f"""SELECT limit_balance, education_level, age,
    default_payment_next_month FROM '{bigquery_table_id}';"""
        dataframe = (bq_client.query(sql).result().to_
    dataframe())


        gcs_client = storage.Client(project=project_id)
        bucket = gcs_client.get_bucket(output_gcs_bucket)
        bucket.blob(output_file).upload_from_
    ```

```
      string(dataframe.to_csv(index=False), 'text/csv')


      return output_file
```

First, you will notice that there are packages that we need to install in this step. We declared the list in `packages_to_install`. This function will call a BigQuery table. Note that in this example, the query is a very simple `SELECT` statement. You can define any transformation process in the query. The more you can aggregate and limit the data in BigQuery, the better. Processing the data in BigQuery is a lot more scalable compared to processing the data in a pandas DataFrame. At the end of this step, we will export the pandas DataFrame to the GCS bucket. As you can see, we will only return the file location at the `return` statement.

2. Define the train model function step.

    For the next step, we want to train the model using the file that's been stored in GCS. Take a look at the following `train_model` function – specifically, in this particular row:

    ```
    dataframe = pd.read_csv(f'gs://{gcs_bucket}/{train_file_
    path}')
    ```

    We load the data from the GCS bucket, not directly from BigQuery or local files. This is a common practice in ML model pipelines as it keeps each step as a stateless operation. You might be wondering why we shouldn't directly access the BigQuery table and combine both the data load step and modeling step as one function. As I mentioned previously, this approach will give you flexibility regarding which packages you want to install for each step. This way, you can have high consistency for each step.

    The other line of code that you might want to check is when we store the Random Forest classifier model as a file in GCS:

    ```
    random_forest_classifier = RandomForestClassifier(n_
    estimators=n_estimators)
        random_forest_classifier.fit(x_train,y_train)


    joblib.dump(random_forest_classifier, model_name)


    bucket = storage.Client().bucket(gcs_bucket)
    blob = bucket.blob(output_file)
    ```

```
blob.upload_from_filename(model_name)

print(f"Model saved in : {output_file}")
```

Similar to the first step, we need to store the result in GCS. This way, the output can be used by any other container or steps. In this case, we stored the `.joblib` file in the GCS bucket.

3. Compile and deploy the training pipeline to Vertex AI.

    As the final step in our train pipeline example, we just need to trigger a run to Vertex AI Pipeline. Take a look at the following lines:

```
@pipeline(
    name=pipeline_name,
    description="An ML pipeline to train credit card
default",
    pipeline_root=pipeline_root_path,
)
def pipeline():
    load_data_from_bigquery_task = load_data_from_
bigquery(bigquery_table_id, gcs_bucket)
    train_model(gcs_bucket, load_data_from_bigquery_task.
output, target_column, 100, model_name)
```

This code is similar to the code that we looked at when we learned about the dummy pipeline. What is important is the task dependencies. Remember that the task's order is determined by the tasks' input and output. In this case, the first task's output is a string that contains a GCS file called `uri`. The `train_model` function uses the output as input. This way, the pipeline will know the task's order.

The important lesson that we learned in this example code is how to implement the ML training steps in Vertex AI Pipeline format. As a reminder, double-check the variables and make sure that you've changed the `project_id` and `gcs_bucket` variables. Once you're done, run the file as Python code, as we learned in the previous exercise.

For example, run the following command from Cloud Shell:

```
# python ai-pipeline-credit-default-train.py
```

The preceding code will submit the pipeline job to Vertex AI. Now, let's continue to the next step.

Running the first pipeline in Vertex AI Pipeline

After compiling and running the code, go back to the GCP console to check Vertex AI Pipeline. The training model steps will run. Make sure that both steps are running successfully:

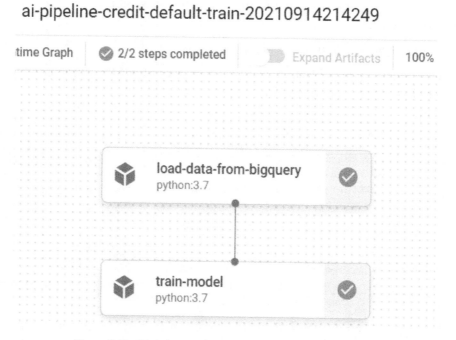

Figure 8.23 – Training pipeline steps in the Vertex AI console

If you see any errors in any of the steps, always check the logs. If the steps were successful, they will produce the model in the GCS file. Now, you can check if the file is already in your expected GCS path:

Figure 8.24 – Checking the model file in the GCS bucket

We will use the `cc_default_rf_model.joblib` file for our second pipeline. For future consideration, you can add a model version to the model's filename. This is a common practice; the goal is for you to be able to choose which model version you want to use for prediction. In the ML world, the newest model doesn't always mean the best. Data scientists usually have some metrics for consideration when deciding which model version is the best. This is one of the reasons why the model training pipeline needs to be separate from the prediction pipeline. With this separation, the pipeline's run frequency can be different. For example, the model can refresh once every month and the prediction can run once every day.

Creating the second pipeline, which will use the model file from the prediction results as a CSV file in GCS

Now, let's continue with the second pipeline. You can find the full code in the `ai-pipeline-credit-default-predict.py` file.

Similar to the first pipeline, what you need to do is change `project_id` and `gcs_bucket` to yours. Besides changing the variables, make sure you've read the example code carefully and try to understand each step.

If you see the code, you must already be familiar with it. There is nothing new here – we are just combining what we've learned from the previous exercises. Let's jump to the line where we define the pipeline:

```
def pipeline():
    load_data_from_bigquery_task = load_data_from_
bigquery(bigquery_table_id, gcs_bucket)
    predict_batch(gcs_bucket,
    load_data_from_bigquery_task.output,
  "ai-pipeline-credit-default-train/artefacts/cc_default_rf_
model.joblib",
    "ai-pipeline-credit-default-predict/artefacts/prediction.
csv" )
```

This pipeline will have two tasks – loading data from BigQuery and using both the data and the `cc_default_rf_model.joblib` file to make predictions. The output will be stored as a CSV file called `prediction.csv`.

Once you've finished looking at the example code for the second pipeline for batch prediction, run the Python code.

For example, run the following command from your Cloud Shell:

```
# python ai-pipeline-credit-default-predict.py
```

The code will submit the pipeline job to Vertex AI. Now, let's continue to the last step.

Running the second pipeline in Vertex AI Pipeline

Finally, let's check if your pipeline is running successfully. Check that the pipeline runs on Vertex AI Pipeline; it should show the following two steps:

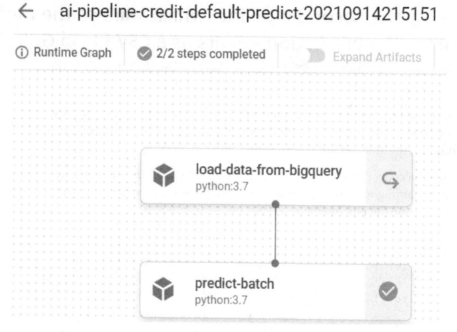

Figure 8.25 – Batch prediction pipeline steps in the Vertex AI console

If you find the icon in any of the steps is a green arrow instead of a checked icon, this means that the step was running using a cache. If you've run a successful step more than once, then the step will run using a cache to perform faster. You can disable the cache by changing the following line of code:

```
response = api_client.create_run_from_job_spec(
    job_spec_path="{pipeline_name}.json",
    pipeline_root=pipeline_root_path,
    enable_caching=False
)
```

Enabling or disabling the cache will not change the result. And with that, you've completed all the exercises in this chapter. Before summarizing this chapter, let's summarize what we've done in this exercise.

In this exercise, you learned how to create ML pipelines using Vertex AI Pipeline and define each ML step as Python functions. The steps that you've defined won't be run in your local machine or Cloud Shell. The code and the logic inside the steps will be used as instructions and will be run on containers in the Vertex AI cluster on the cloud. At the end of our first pipeline, we have the ML model file, while at the end of the second pipeline, the result is the prediction file.

Summary

In this chapter, we learned how to create an ML model. We learned that creating ML code is not that difficult and that the surrounding aspects are what make it complex. On top of that, we also learned about some basic terminologies such as AutoML, pre-built models, and MLOps.

As I mentioned in the introduction, ML is not a core skill that a Data engineer needs to have. But understanding this topic will give a data engineer a bigger picture of the whole data architecture. This way, you can imagine and make better decisions when designing your core data pipelines.

This chapter is the end of our big section on *Building Data Solutions with GCP Components*. Starting from *Chapter 3, Building a Data Warehouse in BigQuery,* to *Chapter 8, Building Machine Learning Solutions on Google Cloud Platform*, we've learned about all the fundamental principles of Data Engineering and how to use GCP services. At this point, you are more than ready to build a data solution in GCP.

Starting from the next chapter, which is the final part of this book, we cover how to use the products we've mentioned so far. A good data engineer not only knows how to develop a solution but also decides on important aspects outside the solution itself. For example, creating a GCP project is easy, but how many projects should you create? What is the purpose of the projects? Should I assign one or many users to the project? These are a few of the many important questions to be considered when building top-notch solutions for an organization.

We will also cover the thinking process for deciding on user and project structures, how to estimate the cost for solutions, and how to make sure the development process can be tested and deployed automatically using CI/CD concepts. After completing these remaining chapters, you will have gained far more technical knowledge. In the final chapter, we will review and summarize how to use all this new knowledge and help boost your confidence so that you can accelerate your personal goals.

Section 3: Key Strategies for Architecting Top-Notch Data Pipelines

The final part of this book will talk about anything on top of how to use the products. A good data engineer not only knows how to develop a solution, but also decides important aspects outside the solution itself; for example, creating a GCP project is easy, but how many projects should you create? What is the purpose of the projects? Should I assign one or multiple users to the project? Those are just a few of the many important questions to be considered and decided in order to build top-notch solutions for an organization.

This will include the thought process behind how to decide user and project structures, how to estimate the cost of the solutions, and how to make sure the development can be tested and deployed automatically using the CI/CD concept. Finally, if you have followed all the learning chapters, you should have acquired a lot of in-depth technical knowledge, and in the final chapter, we will review and summarize how to use all this new-found knowledge to boost confidence so that you can accelerate your personal goals after finishing the book.

This section comprises the following chapters:

- *Chapter 9, User and Project Management in GCP*
- *Chapter 10, Cost Strategy in GCP*
- *Chapter 11, CI/CD on Google Cloud Platform for Data Engineers*
- *Chapter 12, Boost Your Confidence as a Data Engineer*

9

User and Project Management in GCP

This chapter will cover how to design and structure users and projects in **Google Cloud Platform** (**GCP**). At this point, this is one of the key differentiators of whether your solution will only stay as a development solution or become a production-ready solution. A production-ready solution should consider user and project governance properly based on the organization's needs. And on top of that, this chapter will also include an example approach to provision the project automatically using an infrastructure-building tool, Terraform.

Specifically, in this chapter we will cover the following topics:

- Understanding **Identity and Access Management** (**IAM**) in GCP
- Planning a GCP project structure
- Controlling user access to our data warehouse
- Practicing the concept of **Infrastructure as Code** (**IaC**) using Terraform

Let's check out the technical requirements of this chapter.

Technical requirements

In this chapter's exercises, we will use the following GCP services:

- **IAM**
- **BigQuery**
- **Google Cloud Storage (GCS)**
- **Data Catalog**

If you've never opened any of these services in your GCP console before, open them and enable the **Application Programming Interface (API)**. We will also use an open source software called **Terraform**. It's downloadable from their public website at `https://www.terraform.io/downloads.html`. The step-by-step installation will be discussed in the *Exercise – creating and running basic Terraform scripts* section.

Make sure you have your **GCP console**, **Cloud Shell**, and **Cloud Shell Editor** ready.

Download the example code and the dataset here: `https://github.com/PacktPublishing/Data-Engineering-with-Google-Cloud-Platform/tree/main/chapter-9/code`.

Understanding IAM in GCP

IAM is a central manager that manages who can access what—in other words, authorization. IAM manages all authorization within GCP. The concept is simple—you grant roles to accounts so that the accounts have the required permission to access specific GCP services. Here is a diagram for an account that needs to query a table in BigQuery:

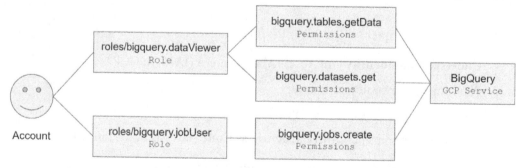

Figure 9.1 – IAM roles, permissions, and GCP service correlation

In the example shown in the previous diagram, in order to access a BigQuery table, an account needs, at a minimum, two roles: *data viewer* and *job user*. These roles contain multiple permissions to specifically perform an operation in BigQuery.

Let's go through each of the important terms that we use in the IAM space, as follows:

- **Account**—An account in GCP can be divided into two—a user account and a service account:

  - **User account**—Your personal email is a user account.

  - **Service account**—A service account is a special kind of account used by an application or a **virtual machine (VM)** instance, not a person. We've experienced using service accounts in some of our exercises from the previous chapters—for example, the service account for Cloud SQL, Cloud Composer, Dataproc, and other GCP services.

We have service accounts for running Cloud Composer, Dataflow, and Dataproc. Remember from those exercises in earlier chapters that these GCP services can access BigQuery tables. These services use service accounts for accessing tables instead of user accounts. If you want to check which service account you have used, follow these steps:

1. Open your GCP console.

2. Go to the **IAM & Admin** page from the navigation menu.

3. Click **Service Accounts**.

   Check out this screenshot if you can't find the button:

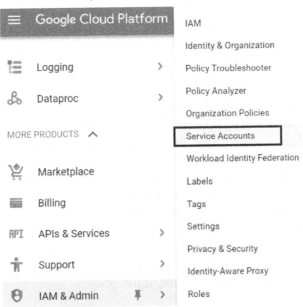

Figure 9.2 – Finding the Service Accounts button from the navigation menu

Depending on how many exercises you have followed, at a minimum, you will see a service account with the *[random number]-compute@developer.gserviceaccount.com* domain. That is a default service account that is automatically created when a project is created.

- **Permission**—A permission is the most specific level of requirement to access a GCP service. For example, to query a table in BigQuery, you need at least two permissions, `bigquery.jobs.create` and `bigquery.tables.getData`.

  How can you know which permissions are required for each service? You need to check the public documentation for each service. Let's take BigQuery again as an example—a list of permissions is documented here: `https://cloud.google.com/bigquery/docs/access-control#bq-permissions`.

  One thing to note is that you can't give permission to accounts. What you can give to accounts are roles. Permission lists are contained in the roles.

- **Role**—A role contains a set of permissions that allows you to perform specific actions on Google cloud resources. There are three categories of roles: *basic*, *predefined*, and *custom* roles. You can read a full explanation from the public documentation here: `https://cloud.google.com/iam/docs/understanding-roles`.

  I will not re-explain those three categories; instead, I will give context and outline which categories should be used.

For context, what you've used in this entire book is the basic role. Your user account has the **roles/owner** role in your project. The **roles/owner** role is a superuser—it has all permissions to all resources in the project. It's for this reason you don't need to add any additional roles to your user account in our exercises.

The most commonly used role by many users in GCP is the predefined role, and I suggest you focus on using the predefined role compared to the other two. The reason that using basic roles is not a best practice is that these roles are too permissive. As these roles are applied to all resources, this is very risky in terms of security. For example, imagine you give the **roles/editor** role to a data engineer who wants to develop a data pipeline in BigQuery. The user can access BigQuery, but at the same time that user can access and edit all other resources such as **Google Kubernetes Engine (GKE)**, **Google App Engine (GAE)**, and any other services to which a data engineer shouldn't have access. The better kinds of roles are predefined roles in BigQuery. You can check out predefined roles in BigQuery in the public documentation at `https://cloud.google.com/bigquery/docs/access-control#bigquery`.

And lastly, let's look at the **custom** role. The custom role is there in case the set of permissions in the predefined roles does not fit with your organization's needs. In that case, you can use a custom role, but remember there is an operational overhead when creating a custom role. In summary, use the predefined role if possible and only use a custom role if needed. Only use basic roles for projects that are used for practice, training, or demonstrations.

In more general terms, giving only the required access to the right person is the best practice, and there is a term for that: the **principle of least privilege**.

> **Note**
> The principle of least privilege is not only known in GCP, but it's a common principle that is used in computer science. The *principle* means giving a user account or process only those permissions that are essential to perform its intended function.

Let's summarize this section. In this section, we revisited common terms that we've used throughout the book. We took a deeper look at each of the terms to understand better how IAM works in GCP. There are three key things to note, as follows:

- The difference between a user account and a service account
- The relation between account, permission, and role
- The principle of least privilege

These three points are very important to understand to be a good data engineer in GCP. Make sure you understand them well. In the next section, we will learn how to plan a GCP project structure.

Planning a GCP project structure

After practicing a lot of exercises from the previous chapters, I believe you will be more familiar with GCP. From the exercises, you've learned about GCP services, their positioning, and how to use them. In this section, we will take a step back. We will look at those GCP services from a higher-level point of view.

In all the previous exercises throughout the book, we used only one project. All the GCP services such as BigQuery, GCS buckets, Cloud Composer, and the other services that we used are enabled and provisioned in one project. For me, I have a project called `packt-data-eng-on-gcp`. The same from your side—you must have your own project, either using the default project or a new one that we created in *Chapter 2, Big Data Capabilities on GCP*. That's a good enough starting point for learning and development, but in reality, an organization usually has more than one project. There are many scenarios and variations on how to structure projects in an organization.

Just one simple example as an illustration. An organization uses GCP for hosting its e-commerce website, and on top of that, they have a data warehouse for reporting and **machine learning (ML)** applications. In that case, one possible project structure is to use one dedicated project for hosting the core application and database, one project for storing data in BigQuery and GCS for the data warehouse, and one other project for training the ML model using Vertex AI. Check out the following diagram for an illustration of this:

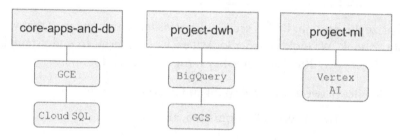

Figure 9.3 – Project structure alternative 1 illustration

The project structure is good enough, and it makes sense to differentiate each separate workload. But if you think again, why not put it all in one project? That's doable too, as illustrated here:

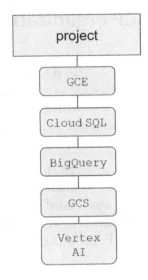

Figure 9.4 – Project structure alternative 2 illustration

In other alternatives, you can separate each service into one specific project. That's doable too, as illustrated here:

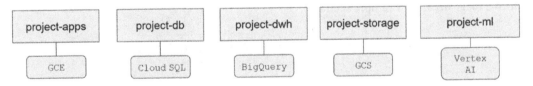

Figure 9.5 – Project structure alternative 3 illustration

There is no right or wrong answer to choose between these three alternatives. In my experience working with many companies, there is no single company project structure that is the same as the others. Typically, a new company will start with the second alternative, which uses one project for everything, but gradually grows along with time and complexity. What is important is to understand what the considerations are.

Before continuing with the considerations, let's familiarize ourselves with the other abstraction on top of GCP projects—folders and organization.

Understanding the GCP organization, folder, and project hierarchy

A GCP project organizes all your Google cloud resources. Resources in GCP can be services, billing, accounts, authentications, logs, and monitoring. Resources from one project can be used and accessed by other resources from other projects. As long as the permissions to resources are correctly set, there is no restriction on accessing them between projects.

For example, take a look at *Figure 9.3* (approach 1). The Cloud SQL database from the application's project can be accessed by Cloud Composer in the data project. Another example—a user account that was created in an app project can access data from BigQuery in the data project. Remember that, as mentioned before, accounts and authentications are also resources. The key point here is that resources in GCP projects are not isolated.

Now, let's talk about the GCP folder. One GCP folder can contain one to many GCP projects. GCP folders can also contain one to many other GCP folders—or, in other words, it is possible to have multiple GCP folder levels. Using GCP folders will give you the benefit of IAM permissions inheritance. The key word here is *inheritance*. Take a look at this diagram as an example scenario:

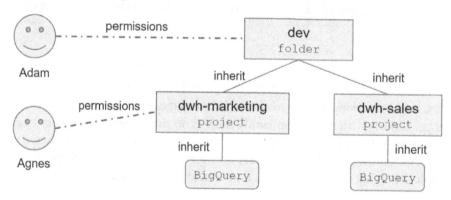

Figure 9.6 – GCP folder, project, and service inheritance illustration

We have a GCP folder called dev. The dev folder contains two GCP projects that have BigQuery resources. There are two users. The first user, **Adam**, needs viewer access to all BigQuery datasets under the dev folder. The second user is **Agnes**—she is only allowed to access all the datasets in the marketing project. In that case, you can grant the BigQuery viewer role in the dev project to **Adam**, and the BigQuery viewer role in the marketing project to **Agnes**. **Adam** will automatically get access to all projects under the dev folder—or, in other words, he can access all child projects under the dev folder. The dev folder is the parent of the product and marketing projects.

If we are talking about the folder concept in general (not within any GCP context), it's natural to think about folders as a way to tidy up objects. For example, on your personal computer, you create a folder to tidy up your documents, images, or any other files. I found a lot of the time that people use this intuition to decide on a folder and project hierarchy in GCP. Even though it's not entirely wrong, having folders without the benefit of IAM permissions inheritance is not really useful. For example, you have a very tall folder hierarchy such as this, but all the permissions are set individually at a project level:

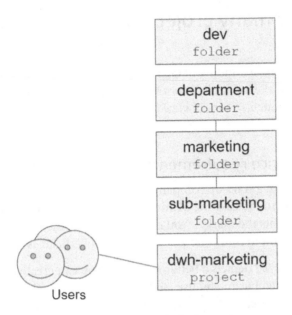

Figure 9.7 – Tall GCP folder hierarchy

The hierarchy in the previous diagram is using a top-bottom mindset. A top-bottom mindset thinks about which parent folders should be created on top and which child folders should be added at the bottom. In this case, the folders will give you almost no benefit in GCP—they will only give you more operation overhead.

Rather than doing that, it's better to think and plan from the bottom-up approach. Think about which permissions can be grouped and inherited together from the individual projects. If you can find any user, user group, or service account that by default always needs access to a set of projects, that's a good reason to create a parent folder. With that mindset, you will have a better GCP folder hierarchy.

The key point is that using a GCP folder allows you to inherit IAM permissions to child folders and projects. Decide the hierarchy from the bottom up instead of adopting a top-bottom approach.

The last part of a hierarchy is the GCP organization. Compared to folders and projects, deciding on how many organizations to have is simple. There is typically only one GCP organization in a company. In other words, the GCP organization is the single root to all folders and projects in GCP.

With this deeper understanding of the concepts, we can decide better about the key question that we will discuss in the next section.

Deciding how many projects we should have in a GCP organization

After getting a better understanding of GCP organizations, folders, and projects, we now know that deciding on the hierarchy is not based on a *tidying-up* mindset. Deciding on the hierarchy from a benefits point of view is better. I summarized these into three main benefits.

IAM and GCP service requirements

Imagine you are starting a start-up company with a small team. Your team wants to start the development and release the **Minimum Viable Product** (**MVP**) quickly to test whether your product fits the market. You don't have any dedicated people yet to manage operations, and you want to minimize any operational overhead as much as possible.

In that scenario, *Figure 9.4* depicts a better approach. You can create one GCP project that is developed by your small team and use all the GCP services in that one GCP project. Splitting GCP projects based on IAM and GCP services doesn't really help when you have a small development team.

In the other scenario, imagine you are starting to use GCP for a corporation. The corporation has more than one team that uses GCP for specific use cases. That's a good indication that you need different sets of IAM and GCP services or API requirements for each team. Usually, each team has different workloads, access levels, or purposes on GCP. In that case, it's a good practice to separate projects based on teams when the IAM and GCP service required for each team is totally different.

Our previous example from *Figure 9.3* is a good example. You can see that the application team, data team, and ML team have different GCP service needs. They must also have different roles and permissions. In that case, the approach depicted in *Figure 9.3* is in general better than the one shown in *Figure 9.4*.

If we compare *Figure 9.3* to *Figure 9.5*, the question you should ask again is: *Are there any IAM and GCP service benefits?*

If your company has a specific team to manage each individual GCP service, then you can consider the approach in *Figure 9.5*. But talking about which are more common practices, it's more common that one team manages multiple GCP services. For example, the data engineering team that uses the data project typically needs a set of BigQuery, Cloud Composer, and GCS permissions. Separating the IAM permissions into three different projects for the same team gives no benefit at all. So, in general, the approach shown in *Figure 9.3* is better.

Project limits and quota

Each service in GCP has limits and quotas. It's a good practice to split projects to avoid hitting those limits and quotas. For example, a company uses only BigQuery on GCP. For the IAM requirements, each team requires the same sets of permission for accessing BigQuery. But the teams are using BigQuery heavily and have more than 1,000 active users.

In the given example, if we refer back to point number one about IAM permissions' benefits, it's fine to use only one GCP project. But from a quota factor, this is a potential issue. If you check in the BigQuery public documentation about quotas (`https://cloud.google.com/bigquery/quotas#query_jobs`), you can see one of the quotas is *Concurrent rate limit for interactive queries: 100.*

Remember that quotas are on a per-project basis, which means that one project can only handle 100 interactive queries. If the company has 1,000 active users, then there will be potential issues. In this case, it's good to split the projects.

Each service has its own limits and quotas—you need to read the public documentation to be aware of them and plan the number of projects based on this factor.

Cost tracking

Another benefit of splitting projects is to track the cost distribution within an organization. You can check your billing dashboard from the GCP console. If you have never opened the billing dashboard, I suggest you try it. Go to your GCP console and go to **Billing** from the navigation menu. From the dashboard, you can see the current month and trends, and one of the metrics is the cost per project. If your organization needs clear cost tracking for each different team or different initiative, you can do that by splitting the project. Note that this is only for tracking purposes—the billing will still be billed to one billing account.

As a summary of this section, you've learned that using GCP in an organization or company usually needs more than one GCP project. The difficult question is: *How many projects does your organization need?* There is no right or wrong answer to this architectural question—we can use the three approaches discussed previously to decide on this. The key is to balance between operational overhead and the benefits that you aim for when splitting projects.

Controlling user access to our data warehouse

After learning about user access on an organization, folder, and project level, we will take a look specifically at the **Access Control List** (**ACL**) in BigQuery. An ACL is actually the same concept as IAM, but the ACL terminology is more commonly used when talking about data space. Planning an ACL in BigQuery means planning who can access what in BigQuery.

At a very high level, there are two main types of GCP permission in BigQuery, as follows:

- **Job permissions**—BigQuery has job-level permissions. For example, for a user to be able to run a query inside the project, they need `bigquery.jobs.create`.

  Note that being able to run a query job doesn't mean having access to the data. Access to the data is managed by the other permissions, which will be explained next.

- **Access permissions**—This one is a little bit more complicated compared to job permissions. If we talk about data access, we first need to understand that the main goal of planning ACLs is to secure the data as granularly as possible. Similar to what we discussed in the previous sections, we need to think about *the principle of least privilege*, meaning that you only give the right access to the right users.

  In BigQuery, you can grant data access to BigQuery users on many levels. Here is a list in order from the highest to the least granular level:

  I.   Project

  II.   Dataset

  III. Table

  IV.   Column- and row-level security

Inheritance is also applied here. If you grant a BigQuery viewer role to a user at a project level, the user will be able to access all the datasets, tables, columns, and rows under the project. At a minimum, a user needs BigQuery table-level viewer permissions to run a query on a table, and if needed, you can prevent the user from accessing certain columns and rows.

Granting access to a user in BigQuery is straightforward. I believe at this level, you can already find the **Menu** button or at least the public documentation for checking the steps.

Check the public documentation for controlling access to a BigQuery dataset: `https://cloud.google.com/bigquery/docs/dataset-access-controls`.

What I will do is use an example scenario to explain the thinking process for planning the ACL.

Use-case scenario – planninga BigQuery ACL on an e-commerce organization

Imagine you work for an e-commerce company. The company has four user groups, as follows:

- **Data Engineer**
- **Marketing**
- **Sales**
- **Head of Analysts**

From the data source side, the company has six tables, as follows:

- `user_profile`
- `user_address`
- `customer_checkouts`
- `customer_carts`
- `event_campaigns`
- `campaign_metrics`

After interviewing a user from each user group, these are their access requirements for the table:

- The **Data Engineers** group can create and view all tables.

- The **Head of Analysts** group can view all tables except user_profile and user_address.

- **Sales** can view data in customer_checkouts and customer_carts.

- **Marketing** can view data in event_campaigns, campaign_metrics, and user_profile.

- **Marketing** cannot access credit card number columns that are stored in the user_profile table. This will be discussed in the next section, *Column-level security in BigQuery*.

From the given scenario, take a look at this diagram to see a list of our puzzle pieces:

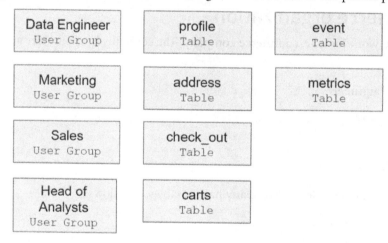

Figure 9.8 – User groups and tables

What we need to plan and decide is this: *How would you grant data access to the user groups?* Try to think of your own solution and check with this solution.

To answer this question, we need to map the user groups to the tables based on the access requirements. As an illustration, it looks like this:

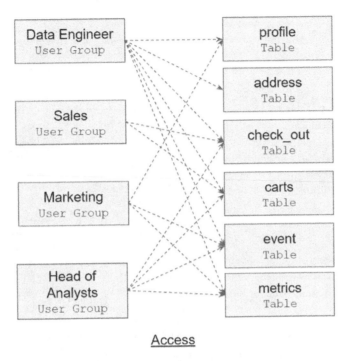

Access

Figure 9.9 – User group-to-table mapping

Remember that you can grant data access to a project, a dataset, or a table level. One alternative is to grant table-level access individually based on the requirements. But that is not scalable—for example, if you already know that a data engineer will always have access to all tables, in the future there will be new upcoming tables, and you don't want to grant access manually one by one to all tables. We need to utilize the power of inheritance by thinking about grouping.

We can group some of the tables into datasets. For example, take a look at the following diagram:

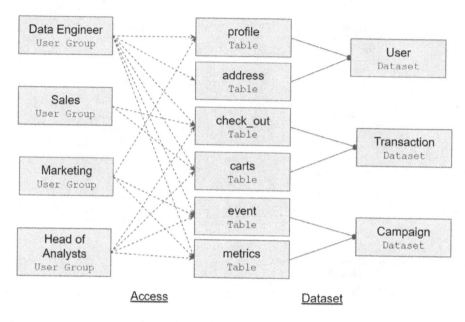

Figure 9.10 – User group, table, and dataset mapping

The idea is to create datasets based on the data access requirements. For example, since the **Sales** team needs access to two tables, `check_out` and `carts`, we can create a dataset named **Transaction**. This way, we can give the BigQuery viewer role in the **Transaction** dataset to the **Sales** team.

As a final solution, here are possible BigQuery roles for the user groups:

User Group	Role	Resource
Data Engineer	BigQuery Data Editor `roles/bigquery.dataEditor`	Project level
Head of Analytics	BigQuery Data Viewer `roles/bigquery.dataViewer`	Transaction dataset Campaign dataset
Sales	BigQuery Data Viewer `roles/bigquery.dataViewer`	Transaction dataset
Marketing	BigQuery Data Viewer `roles/bigquery.dataViewer`	Campaign dataset user_profile table

Figure 9.11 – User group, IAM roles, and GCP resources table

We used predefined roles for the user group. With the given role, each user group will have the required permissions to each resource, at either a project, dataset, or table level.

There is one requirement that we haven't met with the solution, which is that the **Marketing** team can't access one specific column in the user_profile table. We need to apply column-level security in BigQuery to handle that requirement, which will be covered in the next section.

Column-level security in BigQuery

Setting up column-level security in BigQuery is a little bit tricky compared to granting project-, dataset-, or table-level access. There are a couple of terminologies that you need to understand. We need to know what **taxonomy** and **policy tags** are and their relation to Data Catalog and BigQuery, but once you understand the concept, it will be easy and will totally make sense.

> **Note**
>
> This is not an exercise section—I will explain the concepts while giving an example of what it will look like on the GCP console. Feel free to follow the example or just try to understand the flow.

In BigQuery, preventing a user from accessing certain columns in tables is not as straightforward as clicking a button and putting the username in a form. Instead, we need to think first about why we want to prevent those users. A common reason for example is to prevent users from accessing **Personally Identifiable Information** (**PII**) columns.

For example, you have a **users** table in BigQuery. The **users** table has three columns: cc_number, last_activity_date, and status. To get more relevancy to a real-life scenario, imagine the **users** table has 100 columns instead of 3 columns, but in this example, we will just use these three columns for simplicity. Take a look at this BigQuery table schema for our **users** table:

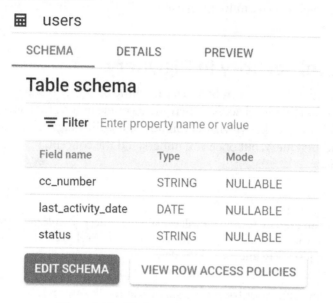

Figure 9.12 – BigQuery users table schema

Your business users need access to the table, but you don't want them to access the credit card number column. How do you do that?

One approach is to create an **Extract, Transform, Load** (ETL) pipeline and transform the table into two tables. One table contains only the credit card number, while the other table is without the credit card number. Another approach is to create a view on top of the table, but one reason you want to do column-level security in BigQuery is that you want to minimize creating new objects and data transformation.

At this point, we know that we want to prevent users from accessing a column because it contains a credit card number. The credit card number can be classified as PII data. PII data can contain many other classes—for example, name, address, phone number, and any other PII data. All of those rules are the taxonomy. The taxonomy contains those data policy classifications, and in GCP, we can define that under the **Data Catalog** menu.

Data Catalog is a fully managed and highly scalable data discovery and metadata management service, and one of the features under **Data Catalog** is defining the taxonomy. Take a look at this example of what it looks like in the **Data Catalog** menu:

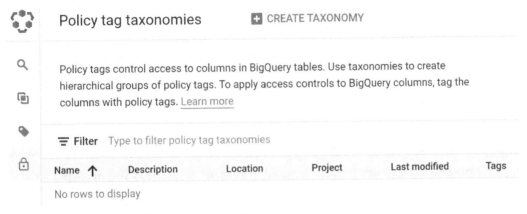

Figure 9.13 – Policy tag taxonomies page

There are three steps in order to apply policy tags to the BigQuery column:

1. Creating a new taxonomy
2. Defining policy tags
3. Adding policy tags to a BigQuery schema

Let's go through each of the steps, as follows:

1. **Creating a new taxonomy**

    You can create a new taxonomy from the **Policy tag taxonomies** sub-menu under the **Data Catalog** console.

    On the taxonomy page, you will find the **Policy tags** form. In this form, you can define policy tags. One taxonomy can have one to many policy tags. As explained before, you can define your data classification in the policy tags, such as a list of PII, or other classifications—for example, departments, sensitivity level, or any other classification, depending on your organization's needs.

2. **Defining policy tags**

Back to our example, in our taxonomy, we will set the `pii` tag as the parent and the credit card number as the child of `pii.`, as illustrated in the following screenshot:

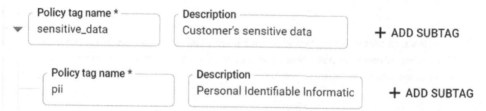

Figure 9.14 – Policy tags page

Note that these policy tags can be used in as many columns as you need, not strictly only in our **users** table.

After creating policy tags and a taxonomy, make sure to enable the **Enforce access control** toggle, as illustrated in the following screenshot. This will activate our column-level security in BigQuery when a table is using these policy tags:

Enforce access control

Access to BigQuery columns tagged with the policy tags below will be restricted to users with the Fine-Grained Reader role.

Figure 9.15 – Enforce access control toggle

That's all that we need to do in the **Data Catalog** console.

3. **Adding policy tags to a BigQuery schema**

Next, in our BigQuery table, we need to add a policy tag to our table.

Back in our **users** table, go to the **SCHEMA** tab. You can edit the schema and click the **ADD POLICY TAG** button on each column, as follows:

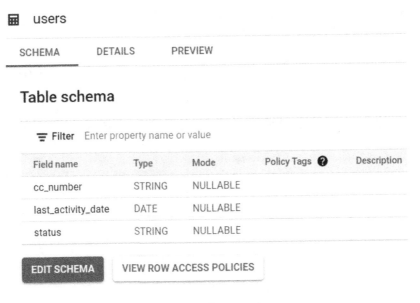

Figure 9.16 – Editing a schema

In our case, we want to add the credit card number policy tag to the `cc_number` column, as illustrated in the following screenshot:

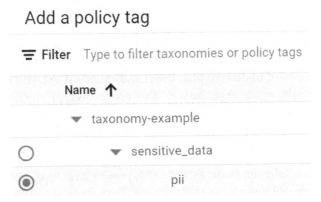

Figure 9.17 – Adding a policy tag to the credit card number taxonomy

That's the last step to enable column-level security.

If a user doesn't have access to the credit card number policy tag, they will get this error when selecting the column:

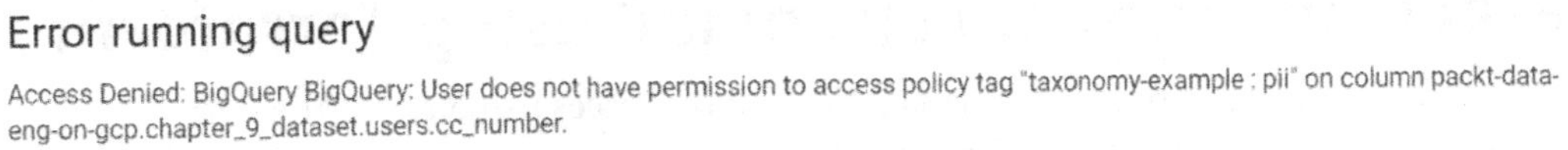

Error running query

Access Denied: BigQuery BigQuery: User does not have permission to access policy tag "taxonomy-example : pii" on column packt-data-eng-on-gcp.chapter_9_dataset.users.cc_number.

Figure 9.18 – Example error message

But since the user has table-level access to the table, they can use `EXCEPT (cc_number)` to access the table, like this:

```
1   SELECT * EXCEPT(cc_number) FROM `packt-data-eng-on-gcp.chapter_9_dataset.users`
```

Processing location: US

Query results   SAVE RESULTS   EXPLORE DATA ▼

Query complete (0.3 sec elapsed, 68 B processed)

Job information   Results   JSON   Execution details

Row	last_activity_date	status
	2021-01-01	ACTIVE
	2021-01-01	ACTIVE
	2021-01-02	ACTIVE
	2021-01-03	NOT ACTIVE

Figure 9.19 – Using EXCEPT Structured Query Language (SQL) syntax in BigQuery

To grant access to the user, the permission needs to be granted to the policy tags under the taxonomy, not to the BigQuery column.

With this concept, it becomes very clear to the whole organization about data access control. Instead of thinking about the permission from users to table columns individually one by one, what you need to do is to plan the classifications. First, you need a grand plan for the taxonomy for the whole organization. This process is typically done once through a collaboration of data engineers, data governors, and the legal team. The rest of the process is about tagging each column in BigQuery using policy tags. All column-level security will be automatically applied to all users.

After learning about all the fundamentals of IAM, project structure, and BigQuery ACLs, in the last section, we will jump a little bit to the infrastructure space. We will learn about the concept called *IaC*. The concept is rarely a data engineer's responsibility, but understanding it and the benefits of using it will have a big impact on how we plan and design our data resources.

Practicing the concept of IaC using Terraform

IaC is a concept and approach to managing GCP resources using code. The term *infrastructure* here means all GCP resources such as BigQuery datasets, GCS buckets, IAM, and all other resources that we've learned about throughout the book.

When we practice all the exercises, we create resources using the GCP console **user interface (UI)** or the `gcloud` command. After learning how projects and resources can be very much within an organization, imagine someone needs to do that manually one by one using the UI. With an IaC approach, we will use code to provision the resources. There are many software options for doing this, and one of the most commonly used is Terraform.

Terraform is an open source IaC software tool. You, as the developer, declare which resources your organization needs in the Terraform scripts. The scripts can be run on any machine, from your local laptop, Cloud Shell, or VM. Note that you don't need to install Terraform as an application—what you need to do is just download it from the internet. Let's learn how to do this by way of a practical example.

Exercise – creating and running basic Terraform scripts

In this exercise, we will practice running the Terraform scripts using Cloud Shell. The scripts will create a BigQuery dataset in your existing project. These are the steps:

1. Downloading Terraform to Cloud Shell
2. Configuring the Terraform backend to a GCS bucket
3. Using variables in Terraform
4. Running a Terraform script using Cloud Shell
5. Configuring a BigQuery dataset using Terraform

Let's start by opening the Cloud Shell environment to download Terraform.

Downloading Terraform to Cloud Shell

You can find the download link for the latest version from the Terraform public website: `https://www.terraform.io/downloads.html`.

For example, in your Cloud Shell environment, run the following command to download the file to your terminal:

```
#wget https://releases.hashicorp.com/terraform/1.0.8/
terraform_1.0.8_linux_amd64.zip
```

After downloading, you will have a `.zip` file in your terminal. Unzip the file using the `unzip` command from the command line, as follows:

```
#unzip terraform_1.0.8_linux_amd64.zip
```

And lastly, let's move the Terraform file to the `/usr/local/bin/` path so that we can call the file an application, as follows:

```
#sudo mv terraform /usr/local/bin/
```

If all is complete, let's try to call the Terraform command to check the version, as follows:

```
# terraform --version
```

The command should run like this:

```
adiwijaya_public@cloudshell:~ (packt-data-eng-on-gcp)$ terraform --version
Terraform v1.0.8
on linux_amd64
```

Figure 9.20 – Checking Terraform version from the command line

You will see the Terraform version installed on your machine. Make sure you are successfully doing this before continuing to the next step.

Configuring the Terraform backend to a GCS bucket

In this step, we will start scripting the Terraform configurations. Open your Cloud Editor environment and create a new folder called `terraform-basic`. In the folder, create a file named `backend.tf`. The `.tf` format is a special file format used by Terraform. All files with this format will be written as configurations when we run the `terraform` command.

In the `backend.tf` file, write the following script in Cloud Editor, and don't forget to change the bucket name to your own GCS bucket:

```
terraform {
  backend «gcs» {
    bucket = «packt-data-eng-on-gcp-data-bucket»
    prefix = «terraform-backend-basic»
  }
}
```

This script will configure Terraform to use a GCS bucket to store the configuration files in the GCS bucket, in a folder that's stated in the *prefix*, which in this example is `terraform-backend-basic`.

Using variables in Terraform

Next, we need to create a file called `main.tf`. In the file, add this script:

```
provider "google" {
  project = var.project_id
}
```

The `provider` script tells Terraform to load all `google` (GCP) libraries. Remember that Terraform is an open source software, and it can manage many other environments outside of GCP.

Inside the `provider` configuration, we also declare the `project_id` variable, but I use a variable here instead of a static value. By calling `var.`, it means the value should be declared as a variable. Using variables is optional, but they are an important feature in Terraform, so let's start using them as early as possible.

To declare the variable, let's create another file named `variables.tf`. Use the following script inside the file:

```
variable "project_id" {
  type = string
}
```

The `variable` script doesn't set the `project_id` value yet—it just says that a variable named `project_id` exists. There are some options to set the variable; in this exercise, we will use a file to set the variable. To do that, create a file named `terraform.tfvars`.

In the file, set the `project_id` variable, like this. Don't forget to change the project ID from the `packt` example to your project ID:

```
project_id  = "packt-data-eng-on-gcp"
```

With that, that's all you need to run Terraform. Check this screenshot to see whether you have the same files:

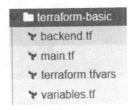

Figure 9.21 – terraform-basic folder in Cloud Editor

If this is the first time you have practiced using Terraform, you might be wondering what you've been doing up until this point. I experienced this the first time I scripted Terraform code. That's common, and you will get the idea after running it.

As a summary, what you've created are the minimum required files and configurations to run Terraform scripts for managing GCP resources. Terraform needs the backend configuration to GCS, the provider, and—optionally—variables.

Running Terraform scripts using Cloud Shell

To run the Terraform scripts, go back to Cloud Shell. We will run Terraform init, plan, and apply commands. Remember these commands in order:

1. terraform init
2. terraform plan
3. terraform apply

That's an important order for running Terraform properly. First, let's run the terraform init command, inside the terraform-basic folder. Make sure you are inside the folder, not outside. Run this command:

```
# terraform init
```

You will have this program running:

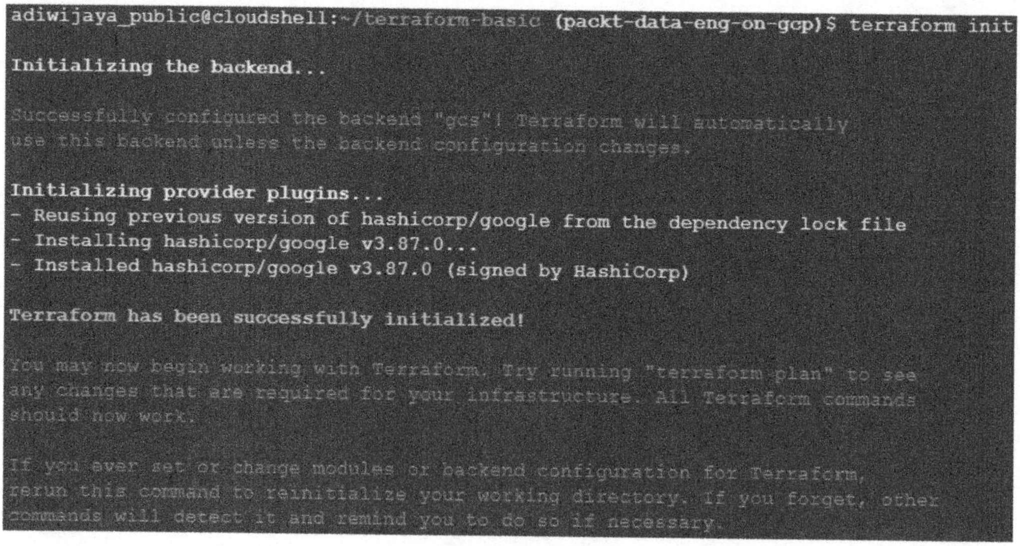

Figure 9.22 – Output from the terraform init command

The `terraform init` command will install the required library into the folder. By *install*, this means creating a hidden folder named `.terraform`.

Next, run the `terraform plan` command, as follows:

```
# terraform plan
```

The command will say that there will be no changes, as illustrated in the following screenshot:

```
adiwijaya_public@cloudshell:~/terraform-basic (packt-data-eng-on-gcp)$ terraform plan

No changes. Your infrastructure matches the configuration.
```

Figure 9.23 – Output from the terraform plan command

The `terraform plan` command is a way for you to check what Terraform will do to your GCP resources. Terraform can add, change, or destroy any resources in your project. This is a step for you to make sure the list of actions is expected. As an example in our case, this is expected to have no changes because we haven't configured any resources in the Terraform scripts.

Lastly, let's run the `terraform apply` command, as follows:

```
# terraform apply
```

It will say `Apply complete! With 0 added, 0 changed, destroyed`. Again, this is expected, and we will add a resource in the next step.

Configuring a BigQuery dataset using Terraform

Back in Cloud Editor, go to the `main.tf` file. Under the `provider` section, add the following `google_bigquery_dataset` resource script:

```
    provider "google" {
  project = var.project_id
}
resource "google_bigquery_dataset" "new_dataset" {
  project     = var.project_id
  dataset_id = "dataset_from_terraform"
}
```

This configuration will tell Terraform to create a BigQuery dataset called `dataset_from_terraform`.

To run it, go back to Cloud Editor and run the `terraform plan` command, as follows:

```
# terraform plan
```

Terraform will tell you, *If you run the terraform apply command later, I will create a dataset with this configuration:*

```
Terraform will perform the following actions:

  # google_bigquery_dataset.new_dataset will be created
  + resource "google_bigquery_dataset" "new_dataset" {
      + creation_time               = (known after apply)
      + dataset_id                  = "new_dataset"
      + delete_contents_on_destroy  = false
      + etag                        = (known after apply)
      + id                          = (known after apply)
      + last_modified_time          = (known after apply)
      + location                    = "US"
      + project                     = "packt-data-eng-on-gcp"
      + self_link                   = (known after apply)

      + access {
          + domain          = (known after apply)
          + group_by_email  = (known after apply)
          + role            = (known after apply)
          + special_group   = (known after apply)
          + user_by_email   = (known after apply)

          + view {
              + dataset_id = (known after apply)
              + project_id = (known after apply)
              + table_id   = (known after apply)
            }
        }
    }

Plan: 1 to add, 0 to change, 0 to destroy.
```

Figure 9.24 – Output from terraform plan command with actions list

Since the output is as expected, let's continue by running the `terraform apply` command, as follows:

```
# terraform apply
```

The command will ask you to type `yes`—do that and click *Enter*. Once done, you can check your BigQuery console, and you will find the dataset is already created for you.

Adding a BigQuery dataset using Terraform is just one very small example of what you can do. Almost all GCP resources can be managed by Terraform, and you can check the full list in their public documentation: `https://registry.terraform.io/providers/hashicorp/google/latest/docs`.

Understanding IaC will give you an idea of how GCP resources are managed in a big organization. The teams that usually handle this are **Development Operations** (**DevOps**) or the infrastructure team, but it's not uncommon for data engineers to contribute to the code, especially to manage the resources that are related to data engineering.

Self-exercise – managing a GCP project and resources using Terraform

In case you need more examples and experience in using Terraform for handling more complex resources, you can continue the exercise to create other resources. This self-exercise will be a good practice for you to summarize all the knowledge from this chapter.

In this self-exercise, try to create Terraform scripts that meet these requirements:

- A new project with any name of your choice
- Enable the BigQuery API
- Three BigQuery datasets named `stg_dataset`, `dwh_dataset`, and `datamart_dataset`
- A service account for handling any BigQuery workloads within the project (data owner)

If finished, try to run it from your Cloud Shell environment. Check the result if all the resources are created. If you want to see the full code, you can check the solution in the repository, at `https://github.com/PacktPublishing/Data-Engineering-with-Google-Cloud-Platform/tree/main/chapter-9/code/terraform-complete-project`.

If you can finish the self-exercise, congratulations! You've experienced how to manage a GCP project with resources using code. If you can't finish it, that's fine too. You've learned a lot about all the important topics for planning GCP projects in a big organization.

Summary

Let's summarize this chapter. In this chapter, we covered three important topics in GCP—namely, IAM, project structure, and BigQuery ACLs. And as an addition, we've learned about the IaC practice.

Understanding these four topics lifts your knowledge from being a data engineer to becoming a cloud data architect. People with these skills can think not only about the data pipeline but also the higher-level architecture, which is a very important role in any organization.

Always remember the principle of least privilege, which is the foundation for architecting all the topics of IAM, project structure, and BigQuery ACLs. Always make sure only to give the right access to the right user.

In the next chapter, we will learn about costs. We want to understand how we should strategize costs in GCP. Strategizing doesn't only mean calculating the cost but also managing and optimizing it.

10
Cost Strategy in GCP

This chapter will cover one of the most frequently asked questions from stakeholders – the solution's cost. Each GCP service has different pricing mechanisms. In this chapter, we will look at what valuable information you will need for calculating cost.

On top of that, we will have a section dedicated to BigQuery. We will discuss the difference between two options for the BigQuery pricing models – on-demand and flat-rate. Finally, we will revisit the BigQuery features for partitioned and clustered tables. Understanding these features can optimize a lot of your future costs in BigQuery.

The following topics will be covered in this chapter:

- Estimating the cost of your end-to-end data solution in GCP
- Tips for optimizing BigQuery using partitioned and clustered tables

Technical requirements

For this chapter's exercises, we will be using BigQuery and GCP pricing calculators from the internet that you can open using any browser.

Estimating the cost of your end-to-end data solution in GCP

While trying out the exercises in this book, we've briefly discussed the cost that might be incurred when using various GCP services. You may have already been billed by some of the resources, so you may be wondering, "*How much will it cost in a full production system*?" This question is important and is often asked by stakeholders.

As a data engineer, it will be great if you can estimate the end-to-end data solution cost upfront. To estimate the cost in GCP, first, we need to understand that not all GCP services use the same pricing calculation.

> **Note**
> The pricing model that's described in this book is based on the latest information at the time of writing. Google Cloud can change the pricing model for any service at any time.

There are three types of pricing models:

- **Machine (VM)-based**: There are GCP resources that are billed with the machines. The bills that are generated by the machines have three factors:

  - Number of machines

  - Machine size

  - Total hours

  For example, we used Cloud Composer in *Chapter 4, Building Orchestration for Batch Data Loading Using Cloud Composer*. Cloud Composer uses this pricing model. We choose the number of workers, the worker size, and how long to use Cloud Composer for, from creating it to deleting it. The term **worker** in Cloud Composer refers to machines or **Google Cloud Engine** (**GCE**) instances. The actual usage is not a factor in this model. So long as Cloud Composer is active, even if you never use it, it will still count toward the bills.

  As a summary, the formula is as follows:

  Cost = Number of workers x Worker size x Total hours

Here is the list of data-related GCP services that use this pricing calculation:

- Cloud Composer
- Dataflow
- Dataproc

- **Usage-based**: Another pricing model is the usage-based model. The factor that affects the bills is based on the usage of the given service. The definition of usage is different from one service to another. For example, for **Google Cloud Storage** (**GCS**), the definition of usage in GCS is the total amount of storage that's used.

  Here is the list of data-related GCP services that use this pricing calculation:

  - GCS
  - Pub/Sub
  - BigQuery on-demand
  - BigQuery Storage

- **Flat rate**: Lastly, some services use a flat rate model. Flat rate means that you commit to purchasing a fixed amount of resources for a fixed amount of time.

  For example, we learned about BI Engine in *Chapter 7, Visualizing Data for Making Data-Driven Decisions with Data Studio*. We can configure the reservation based on the total capacity per hour. Other time range options include daily, monthly, and annually.

  Here is the list of data-related GCP services that use this pricing calculation:

  - BI Engine flat rate
  - BigQuery flat rate

Understanding these three pricing models will give you an idea of what should be considered when estimating each of the GCP services.

Out of all these GCP services, BigQuery is unique in that you, as a user, can choose the pricing model. We will discuss this in the next section.

Comparing BigQuery on-demand and flat-rate

BigQuery's pricing is more complicated compared to most of the other GCP services. BigQuery has three pricing areas: analysis, storage, and ingestion. Each of these areas has different terms and conditions. You can check out the full details by looking at the public documentation: `https://cloud.google.com/bigquery/pricing`.

I will use the next section to talk specifically about analysis pricing. Compared to the other areas, analysis pricing is the one that needs a decision from you or your organization. There are two options: on-demand and flat-rate. Let's understand these two options.

BigQuery on-demand

The on-demand model is based on the number of bytes that are processed for each query. For example, let's say you have a table named `transaction` and that the transaction table's size is 10 GB. Now, let's say that a user runs the following query:

```
SELECT * FROM transaction;
```

This query will cost 10 GB multiplied by the BigQuery cost per TB. The BigQuery cost per TB is different for each region. For example, in the US, it costs $5.00 per TB. You can check the public documentation for the cost in other locations: `https://cloud.google.com/bigquery/pricing#on_demand_pricing`.

Back to the example, if there are 100 users where each of the users runs the same query and each of the users runs the query once a day, in a month, the cost will be as follows:

cost = (10GB / 1000)TB X 100 users X 30 days X $5.00

The monthly cost for BigQuery on-demand, based on its usage, will be **$150**.

BigQuery flat-rate

The flat-rate model is based on how slots you purchase for a certain period. This period can be hourly (flex slots), monthly, or annually.

As an example, let's use the same scenario from the BigQuery on-demand example. But this time, let's use the flat-rate model by purchasing 200 slots a month.

Using the US region as an example, the cost will be as follows:

Cost = 200 slots x $20 (monthly cost per 1 slot)

The monthly cost for the BigQuery flat-rate pricing, based on the total slots purchased, will be $4,000.

> **Note**
>
> A BigQuery slot is the smallest processing unit in BigQuery. It represents virtual CPUs and memory. Every query in BigQuery needs slots. The number of slots that are required for each query depends on the data's size and the query's complexity. Check out the public documentation if you want to learn more about how BigQuery slots work: `https://cloud.google.com/bigquery/docs/slots`.

At this point, you understand that these two pricing models can result in a vastly different cost for your organization. The flat rate looks a lot more expensive in this scenario. But imagine an organization that has more than 100 tables that are 10 GB in size. Here, your monthly cost will be around $15,000 ($150 x 100), while in the flat-rate model, it remains at $4,000.

There are many factors that you can use to decide on which of these two options to use, such as the number of workloads, users, usage per day, or any other metrics that are relevant to your organization. One option is not better than the other – it depends on the situation. But as a very general practice, the on-demand pricing model should be your first choice when you start using BigQuery. It's suitable for early users or organizations that have BigQuery costs that are less than $2,000 per month because the minimum slot purchase is $2,000 for 100 slots per month. If the monthly cost is already more than $2,000, start evaluating your usage and consider using the flat rate.

Now, who should think about and decide on this pricing model in an organization? The answer depends on the organization, but it's quite common for data engineers to decide or at least give input on this matter.

In the next section, we will try to use the GCP cost calculator tool to estimate the cost of each GCP service.

Using the GCP cost calculator tool

Google Cloud has a pricing calculator tool that you can access from their public page: `https://cloud.google.com/products/calculator`.

This calculator can help you estimate the cost based on your estimated requirements. If you open the page, you will see that there are lists of GCP services. Each GCP service has input. Let's use BigQuery again as an example:

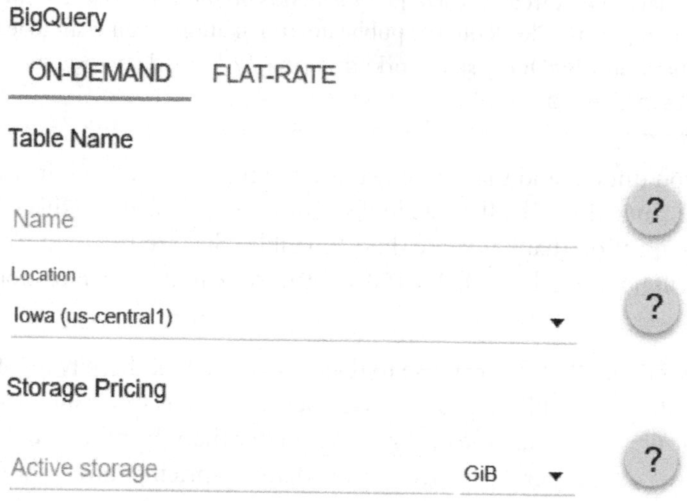

BigQuery

ON-DEMAND   FLAT-RATE

Table Name

Name   ?

Location
Iowa (us-central1)   ▼   ?

Storage Pricing

Active storage   GiB   ▼   ?

Figure 10.1 – BigQuery ON-DEMAND cost calculator

As you can see, the calculator allows us to choose on-demand or flat-rate pricing and all the required inputs. As another example, let's check out the other services, such as Dataproc:

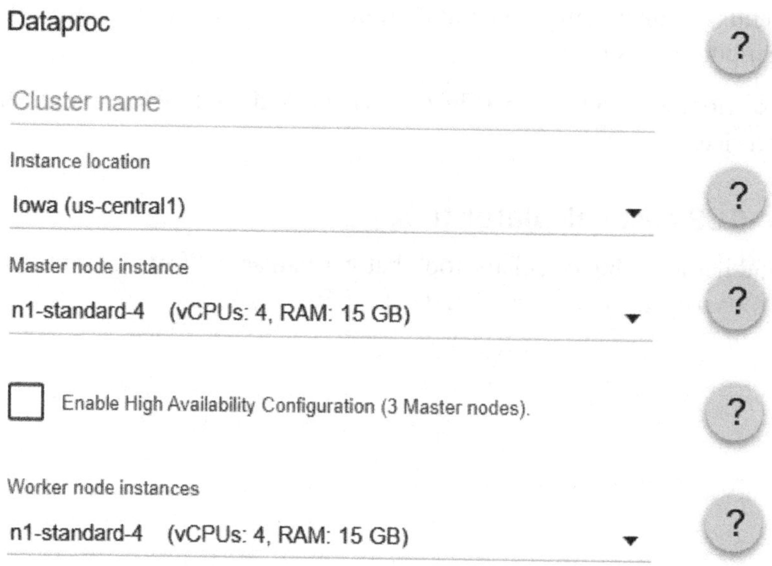

Dataproc   ?

Cluster name

Instance location
Iowa (us-central1)   ▼   ?

Master node instance
n1-standard-4   (vCPUs: 4, RAM: 15 GB)   ▼   ?

☐ Enable High Availability Configuration (3 Master nodes).   ?

Worker node instances
n1-standard-4   (vCPUs: 4, RAM: 15 GB)   ▼   ?

Figure 10.2 – Dataproc cost calculator

In the calculator's input, you can see that the inputs are the machine's sizes, the number of workers, and the estimated hours. This is what we discussed previously regarding the pricing model types. With this knowledge, you can fill in the inputs in the pricing calculator and get the estimated cost for your GCP services.

Example – estimating data engineering use case

Let's try to simulate what we've learned so far by looking at an example use case. Imagine that you are a data engineer. Your organization plans to use GCP for data analytics. Your **Chief Data Officer** (**CDO**) has asked you to estimate the monthly cost, given these requirements:

- The source data will be stored as uncompressed CSV files in a GCS bucket. The file size is 100 GB daily.

- Some data engineers are experienced in developing ETL on Hadoop. They need a permanent Hadoop cluster with the following specification: three master nodes and 10 worker nodes, where each node must have at least has four vCPUs and 15 GB memory with 200 GB SSD storage per node.

- The data warehouse should be in BigQuery. There will be 20 end users that will access the BigQuery tables. They are active users that will access the tables 5 days a week.

- To orchestrate the Dataproc jobs and BigQuery ELT process, Cloud Composer is needed. The specification is three workers with the default machine size.

- There will be streaming data. The data will be ingested from one Pub/Sub topic to one subscription. The subscription's output should be processed using Dataflow. The data stream size is 2 GB per hour and doesn't need any snapshot or data retention in Pub/Sub. You should set Dataflow's maximum workers to three using the `n1-standard-1` machine type.

- All data should be stored and processed in the US location.

- There will be only one environment for development and production. This means that you only need to calculate the estimation once, assuming you only have one environment.

How much is the monthly cost for your organization based on the given requirements?

You can use this example as an exercise. With this exercise, you can learn how to imagine an end-to-end architecture based on the requirements. Then, you can use the pricing calculator to calculate the cost of each component.

If you are done or just want to see the example solution, here is one solution from my calculations. First, here is the high-level architecture diagram for the data analytics environment for the organization:

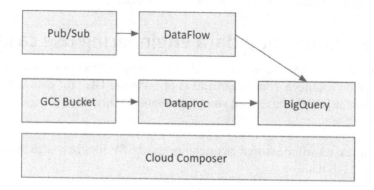

Figure 10.3 – High-level architecture diagram

We've discussed all these components throughout this book, starting from handling streaming data using Pub/Sub, processing it using Dataflow, and storing the data in BigQuery. For the batch data, we can use the GCS bucket, process the data using Dataproc, and store the data to BigQuery. Finally, all the orchestration and scheduling processes will use Cloud Composer.

Now, let's look at the available GCP services, their cost components, their requirements, and the cost from the calculator's output. Note that there is a possibility that the cost components and the estimated cost stated here will be different compared to your calculator's output. This is because Google Cloud may update its calculator and pricing at any time. You don't need to worry much about that because what we want to focus on is exercising how to convert requirements into cost estimation. You don't need to compare the literal cost to my example output.

The cost components can be broken down into six GCP services. Let's look at each one in detail.

Pub/Sub

For Pub/Sub, we can use the following two statements from the requirements:

- The data will be ingested from one Pub/Sub topic to one subscription.

- The data stream size is 2 GB per hour and doesn't need any snapshot or data retention in Pub/Sub.

In the calculator, you can use this information to calculate the volume of bytes that's published daily and set the number of subscriptions to one. You can keep the other inputs blank since we don't need any snapshot and data retention to be performed. Take a look at the following Pub/Sub cost components table:

GCP Service	Cost Component	Requirements	Cost
Pub/Sub	The volume of bytes published daily	48 GB (2 GB x 24 hours)	$112.11
	Number of subscriptions	1	

Table 10.1 – Pub/Sub cost components table

The Pub/Sub monthly cost is estimated to be $112.11.

Dataflow

For Dataflow, we can use the following three statements from the requirements:

- There will be streaming data
- The data stream size is 2 GB per hour
- The Dataflow maximum workers will be three using the n1-standard-1 machine type.

In the calculator, you can use these requirements as input for the job type, the data that's been processed, the hours the job runs per month, the number of worker nodes that are used by the job, and the worker node instance type. Take a look at the following Dataflow cost components table:

GCP Service	Cost Component	Requirements	Cost
Dataflow	Job type	Streaming	$189.55
	Data processed	2 GB	
	Hours the job runs per month	720 hours (24 hours x 30 days)	
	Number of worker nodes used by the job	3	
	Worker node instance type	n1-standard-1	

Table 10.2 – Dataflow cost components table

The Dataflow monthly cost is estimated to be $189.55.

Cloud Storage

For Cloud Storage, we can use the following statement from the requirements:

- The source data will be stored as uncompressed CSV files in a GCS bucket. The file size is 100 GB daily.

In the calculator, you can use this requirement as input for the total amount of storage. Assuming that the data is stored every day for 1 month, we can assume that, in 1 month, the data size will be 3,000 GB. Take a look at the following Cloud Storage cost components table:

GCP Service	Cost Component	Requirements	Cost
Cloud Storage	Total amount of storage	3,000 GB (100 GB x 30 days)	$60

Table 10.3 – Cloud Storage cost components table

The Cloud Storage monthly cost is estimated to be $60.

Dataproc

For Dataproc, we can use the following two statements from the requirements:

- They need a permanent Hadoop cluster with the following specification: 3 master nodes + 10 worker nodes.

- Each node must have at least four vCPUs and 15 GB memory with 200 GB SSD storage per node.

In the calculator, you can check the **Enable High Availability Configuration (3 Master nodes)** check box to calculate the three master nodes and use the n1-standard-4 machine type to meet the node's specifications. Take a look at the following Dataproc cost components table:

GCP Service	Cost Component	Requirements	Cost
Dataproc	Master node instance	n1-standard-4	$2,062.63
	Enable High Availability Configuration (three master nodes)	Yes	
	Worker node instance	n1-standard-4	
	Number of normal worker nodes	10	
	Hours the cluster runs per month	720 hours (24 hours x 30 days)	
	Storage (per node)	PD SSD – 200 GiB	

Table 10.4 – Dataproc cost components table

If you see the preceding output in the calculator, then there will be more than one cost table. Compute Engine and storage disk costs will also be shown. You need to use the total estimated cost instead of the Dataproc cost. The total estimated cost is the result of adding Dataproc, Compute Engine, and the storage disk cost.

Looking at the total estimated cost, the Dataproc monthly cost is estimated to be $2,062.63.

Cloud Composer

For Cloud Composer, we can use the following statement from the requirements:

- To orchestrate the Dataproc jobs and BigQuery ELT process, Cloud Composer is needed. The specification is three workers with the default machine size.

In the calculator, Cloud Composer is pretty simple. You just need to define the number of workers, which will be three in our case. Take a look at the following Cloud Composer cost components table:

GCP Service	Cost Component	Requirements	Cost
Cloud Composer	Number of workers	3	$298.73
	Average hours per day each server is running	24	
	Average days per week each server is running	7	

Table 10.5 – Cloud Composer cost components table

The Cloud Composer monthly cost is estimated to be $298.73.

BigQuery

For BigQuery, we need to make some assumptions. The assumption won't be 100% accurate, but this is good enough for estimation purposes.

For storage calculation, let's assume that the data warehouse and data mart layers will store the same size as the data source. This means that we will have the raw data from the data source – that is, 100 GB – the data warehouse that has already transformed using data model 100 GB, and the data mart for the end user, which will be 100 GB. Thus, the total storage that's needed is 300 GB every day:

Queries = 20 end users x 5 days x 4 weeks x 100 GB

Assuming all 20 users access the tables in the data mart once a day, the active storage becomes as follows:

Active storage = 300 GB x 30 days

With these assumptions, we can make the following calculations:

GCP Service	Cost Component	Requirements	Cost
BigQuery	Queries	20 end users x 5 days x 4 weeks x 100 GB (40,000 GB)	$397.08
	Active storage	300 GB x 30 days (9,000 GB)	

Table 10.6 – BigQuery cost component table

After calculating all the services in the Google Cloud cost calculator, we will get the following monthly cost estimation summary:

Service	Cost Monthly
Pub/Sub	$112.11
Dataflow	$189.55
Cloud Storage	$60
Dataproc	$2,062.63
Cloud Composer	$298.73
BigQuery	$397.08
Total	$3,120.1

Table 10.7 – GCP services monthly cost summary table

To conclude our simulation, remember that to estimate the end-to-end solution cost in GCP, you need to prepare three things:

- A list of GCP services
- The cost components
- How to use the cost components as input in the Google Cloud cost calculator

Of course, there must be a gap between the estimation and reality. The reality can be more or less expensive – it depends on the real usage and how much our assumptions are close to reality. But having the cost estimation table can help you and your organization make important decisions, as well as whether you want to go with the proposed solutions or make any adjustments. For example, in our results, Dataproc seems expensive compared to the other services. This can lead to a discussion with the team about whether you should substitute the component or go with the plan.

In the next section, we will revisit the two important BigQuery features: partitioned and clustered tables. In my experience, these two features play a significant role in the total cost of the entire end-to-end data solution. Understanding the implication that using these two features has on the cost is especially important.

Tips for optimizing BigQuery using partitioned and clustered tables

BigQuery tables can store data from zero bytes to petabytes of data. There will be no difference between creating a small-sized table or a large-sized table. To simplify the context and for illustration purposes only, let's say a small-sized table ranges from KBs to 100 GB. The large-sized tables range from 100 GB to PBs of data. Technically, both tables are the same, but if you think about optimizing performance and cost, we can configure the tables using two features called **BigQuery partitioned table** and **BigQuery clustered table**.

These features are helpful for both on-demand and flat-rate pricing. In the on-demand pricing, the features will cut the billed bytes and will reduce the overall cost that is calculated from the billed bytes. With flat-rate pricing, it doesn't affect it directly. Remember that the cost of flat-rate pricing is flat per period. But when you're using features, it will reduce the number of slots needed for the queries. If we need fewer slots, this means we can reduce the number of purchased slots.

In this section, I will use the on-demand scenario as an example. Since BigQuery on-demand can affect the cost directly, it's easier to imagine and calculate the impact. Now, let's understand both features.

Partitioned tables

We discussed and completed an exercise using partitioned tables in *Chapter 4, Building Orchestration for Batch Data Loading Using Cloud Composer*, in the *Introduction to BigQuery partitioning* section.

Let's quickly refresh on the important points that we should execute in this chapter.

BigQuery partitioned tables will divide the data in BigQuery tables using partitions into segments using a key. This key can be a time-unit column, the ingestion time, or an integer column. The most common practice is using either the time-unit column or the ingestion time daily.

For an illustration, please see *Figure 10.4*. This figure shows a BigQuery table called **example_table**. The table contains three columns called **Val 1**, **Val 2**, and **Date**. Let's create this table in BigQuery *without* defining any partition column:

```
CREATE TABLE example_table
(
val1  INT64,
val2  STRING,
date  DATE,
)
```

Now, we can access the table using the SELECT statement without any filtering:

```
SELECT *
FROM example_table;
```

By doing this, BigQuery will access all the columns and rows, as shown here:

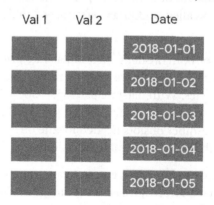

Figure 10.4 – Rows and columns accessed by BigQuery

Each dark-colored box shows that BigQuery is accessing the data in those particular rows and columns. From a cost perspective, the dark-colored boxes contribute to the total billed bytes that drive the BigQuery on-demand cost.

Let's say you access the table but SELECT only the **Val 1** and **Date** columns and then filter the date using a WHERE clause:

```
SELECT val1
FROM example_table
WHERE date = '2021-01-03';
```

BigQuery will access only the selected column and all the rows, as shown in the following diagram:

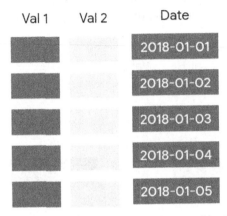

Figure 10.5 – Selected rows and columns accessed by BigQuery

Notice that, in this case, the **Val 2** boxes are light-colored. Jumping to the cost perspective, this means that the query cost is cheaper compared to the one shown in *Figure 10.4* because the total billed bytes is less:

- To improve the BigQuery cost even further, you can create a partitioned table by defining it in the CREATE TABLE statement:

```
CREATE TABLE example_table
(
val1 INT64,
val2  STRING,
date  DATE,
)
PARTITION BY (date);
```

- Now, let's run a query and only `SELECT` the `val1` column with a filter on the partition column date:

```
SELECT val1
FROM example_table
WHERE date = '2021-01-03';
```

Here, BigQuery will access the `Val 1` table and the `Date` columns. The `Date` column is included because it's used in the `WHERE` clause. But because we partitioned the table using the `date` column and used it to filter in our query, BigQuery will only access the rows in that particular partition. In our case, this is the 2018-01-03 partition. The following diagram shows this:

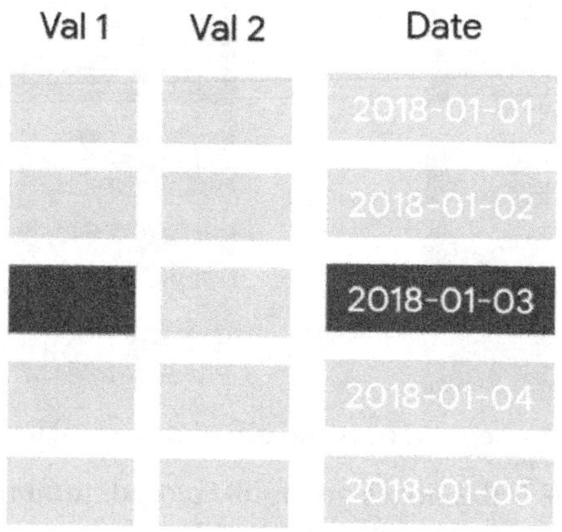

Figure 10.6 – Partitioned table

This will reduce a significant amount of cost compared to the non-partitioned table. For example, if the whole table is 1 TB and consists of 5 days' worth of data, then querying one single date will cost 200 GB (⅕ of the total size).

> **Note**
> One thing to remember is the partitioned table quota. The maximum number of partitions you can have in a table is 4,000. Check out the following public page to find the latest quota: `https://cloud.google.com/bigquery/quotas#partitioned_tables`.

If you store data daily, you will have 365 partitions each year, which means you can store around 10 years' worth of data.

Remember that you can partition your table per hour using integer columns. Always keep your quotas in mind when designing the table. For example, in the hourly partitioned table, you will have 8,760 partitions each year (365 days x 24 hours). This means that you can store only around 5 months' worth of data. This is useful for some use cases, but not for most.

Clustered tables

You can use a clustered table in BigQuery to automatically organize tables based on one to four columns in the table's schema. By **organizing**, we mean that BigQuery sorts the table records in the background using the specified columns.

Remember that BigQuery is a big data database, so it stores data in a distributed storage system. As an example, one large table that's 1 TB in size will be split and distributed into small chunks. Each chunk contains records from the table. In the data space, this chunk is called a **block**.

If you don't specify the clustered BigQuery table, each block will contain random sets of records. If we specify the clusters, the block will contain sorted records. Now, the question is, how can the sorted records help reduce the cost?

When a table is sorted by cluster, internally, BigQuery will know which blocks it should access specifically and ignore the irrelevant blocks. Take a look at the following diagram. The query has two filters, a date, and the Val 1 column equals 'frida'. It runs on a partitioned table, but it's not clustered:

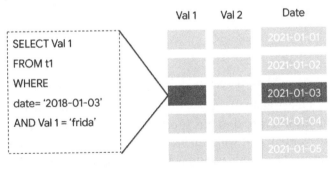

Figure 10.7 – A partitioned table without a clustered column

The query will access the whole partitioned table, as explained previously in the *Partitioned tables* section. You can improve the BigQuery cost even further by defining the clustered table in the `CREATE TABLE` statement, as follows:

```
CREATE TABLE example_table
(
val1 INT64,
val2  STRING,
date DATE,
)
PARTITION BY (date)
CLUSTER BY val1;
```

The `SELECT` statement query will access a small subset in the 2021-01-03 partition, as shown in the following diagram:

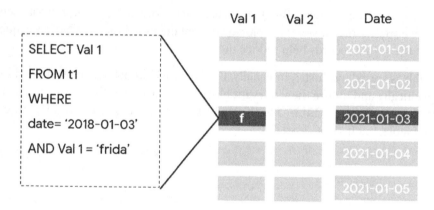

Figure 10.8 – The partitioned table with a clustered column

In this example, BigQuery will only access the **'f** block because it's the first letter of **'frida'**. BigQuery understands where to find this specific **f** block because the records on each partition are already sorted, so it will skip blocks **a** to **e** and won't look at blocks **g** to **z**. Back to the cost perspective, this way, you will optimize the cost not only to the date level but to the date and block level. This scenario will significantly reduce the total billed bytes from a large-sized table.

Note that the **f** block is an illustrative example. In reality, we won't know what data range is stored in a block. This is managed internally by BigQuery, and we, as BigQuery users, don't have visibility into BigQuery storage at the block level. What we need to do as a BigQuery user is make sure we define the cluster column whenever cost optimization is needed for BigQuery tables.

What we should consider when using a clustered table is which column(s) we should use for clustering:

- The first rule of thumb is choosing the column that is used the most by the user's queries. In our example, we use **Val 1** as the cluster column because the filter states **Val 1 = 'frida'**.

- The second rule of thumb is the number of columns and their order. We can use up to four columns in a clustered table. The order of the columns when we define them is important. For example, take a look at the following CREATE TABLE statement:

```
CREATE OR REPLACE TABLE t1
PARTITION BY DATE(date_column)
CLUSTER BY
    country, region, city, postal_code
```

We cluster the table using four columns as this is the best practice. The best practice is to put from the least to the most granular columns. In this example, the list of countries is less granular compared to the region. The list of regions is less granular compared to cities. Here, postal_code is the most granular.

Exercise – optimizing BigQuery on-demand cost

In this exercise, let's try to prove the concepts that we discussed previously as an experiment. For this experiment, we will create three tables. These three tables will be created from the BigQuery public dataset – specifically, the stackoverflow_posts table. We will run a query on the three tables and compare the total billed bytes. The fewer bytes that are billed, the better for us.

Follow these steps to run the experiment:

1. Open your BigQuery console and go to the SQL Editor.

2. Create a standard table using the following **data description language** (**DDL**) statement:

```
CREATE OR REPLACE TABLE `chapter_10_dataset.
stackoverflow_posts`
AS SELECT * FROM `bigquery-public-data.stackoverflow.
stackoverflow_posts`
WHERE EXTRACT(YEAR FROM creation_date) BETWEEN 2013 AND
2014;
```

3. Create a partitioned table using the following DDL statement:

```
CREATE OR REPLACE TABLE `chapter_10_dataset.
stackoverflow_posts_partitioned`

PARTITION BY DATE(creation_date)

AS SELECT * FROM `bigquery-public-data.stackoverflow.
stackoverflow_posts`

WHERE EXTRACT(YEAR FROM creation_date) BETWEEN 2013 AND
2014;
```

4. Create a partitioned and clustered table using the following DDL statement:

```
CREATE OR REPLACE TABLE `chapter_10_dataset.
stackoverflow_posts_partitioned_clustered`

PARTITION BY DATE(creation_date)

CLUSTER BY
   title

AS SELECT * FROM `bigquery-public-data.stackoverflow.
stackoverflow_posts`

WHERE EXTRACT(YEAR FROM creation_date) BETWEEN 2013 AND
2014;
```

5. Run the same query for the three tables and change the table names to the three tables from the previous steps:

```
SELECT DATE(creation_date) as creation_date, count(*) as
total

FROM `chapter_10_dataset.[THE EXPERIMENT TABLES]`

WHERE DATE(creation_date) BETWEEN  '2013-01-01' AND
'2013-06-01'

AND title LIKE 'a%'

GROUP BY creation_date;
```

To check the billed bytes, you can check the **MB processed** information under **Query results**. Take a look at the following screenshot:

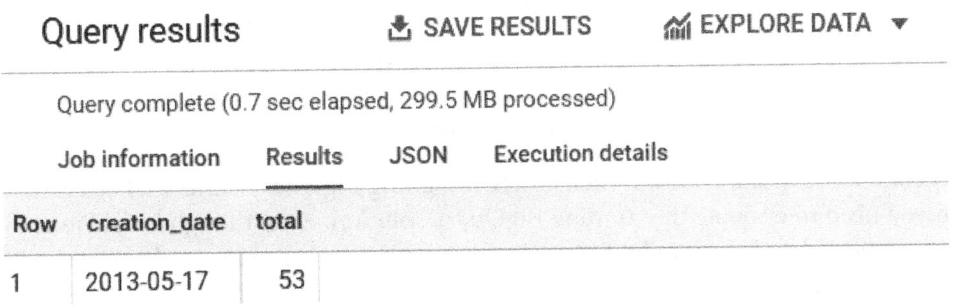

Figure 10.9 – BigQuery's Query results page showing processed bytes

In this example, the total billed bytes for this query is 299.5 MB. Run the query for the three tables and compare that number.

Finally, let's see the results in this table:

Table	Billed Bytes
Standard table	299.5 MB
Partitioned table	60.1 MB
Partitioned + Clustered table	57.2 MB

Figure 10.10 – BigQuery table types comparison based on Billed Bytes

As expected, the standard table processes the most bytes compared to the other tables, while the partitioned and clustered table processes slightly fewer compared to the partitioned table.

This result proves the general idea of the three approaches. The comparison ratio must be different case by case, depending on the table size, the partition size, the key columns that have been selected for the clustered tables, and the query. You must understand these possibilities to be able to improve your BigQuery cost, both directly when using the on-demand pricing model and indirectly when using the flat-rate pricing model.

Summary

In this chapter, we learned about two different things. First, we learned about how to estimate the end-to-end data solution cost. Second, we understood how BigQuery partitioned and clustered tables play a significant role in the cost.

These two topics are usually needed by data engineers in different situations. Understanding how to calculate the cost will help in the early stages of GCP implementation. This is usually a particularly important step for an organization to decide the future solution for the whole organization.

The second topic usually occurs when you're designing BigQuery tables and at a time when you need to evaluate the running BigQuery solution. Even though it's obvious that using partitioned and clustered tables is beneficial, it's not a surprise in a big organization as many tables are not optimized and can be improved.

Lastly, we performed an experiment using the three different tables. It proved that using the partitioned and clustered tables can reduce the BigQuery cost.

In the next chapter, which will be the last technical chapter, we will discuss a practice called **continuous integration and continuous deployment (CI/CD)**. This is a common practice for software engineers, but not that common for data people. Data engineers, partly as data people and partly as engineers, can benefit from understanding this practice to build a robust data pipeline.

11
CI/CD on Google Cloud Platform for Data Engineers

Continuous integration and continuous deployment (CI/CD) is a common concept for DevOps engineers, but most of the time, data engineers need to understand and be able to apply this practice to their development endeavors. This chapter will cover the necessary concepts of CI/CD and provide examples of how to apply CI/CD to our Cloud Composer example from *Chapter 4, Building Orchestration for Batch Data Loading Using Cloud Composer*. Upon completing this chapter, you will understand what CI/CD is, why and when it's needed in data engineering, and what GCP services are needed for it.

In this chapter, we will cover the following topics:

- Introduction to CI/CD
- Understanding CI/CD components with GCP services
- Exercise – Implementing CI using Cloud Build
- Exercise – Deploying Cloud Composer jobs using Cloud Build

Let's look at the technical requirements for the exercises in this chapter.

Technical requirements

For this chapter's exercises, we will use the following GCP services:

- Cloud Build

- Google Cloud Repository

- Google Container Registry

- Cloud Composer (optionally)

If you have never opened any of these services in your GCP console, open them and enable the necessary APIs. Make sure that you have your **GCP console**, **Cloud Shell**, and **Cloud Editor** ready.

You can download the example code and the dataset for this chapter here: `https://github.com/PacktPublishing/Data-Engineering-with-Google-Cloud-Platform/tree/main/chapter-11/code`.

Introduction to CI/CD

CI/CD is an engineering practice that combines two methods – continuous integration and continuous deployment:

- **Continuous integration** is a method that's used to automatically integrate codes from multiple engineers that collaborate in a repository. *Automatic integration* can be in the form of testing the code, building Docker images, integration testing, or any other steps that are required for integrating the code.

  The main benefit of CI is that you can integrate code changes from many developers as quickly as possible. With this practice, you can detect errors quickly and locate the issues more easily.

- **Continuous deployment** is a method that's used to automatically deploy the final code to the production applications. *Automatic deployment* can be in the form of pushing the built software to the production server, moving the necessary files to their destination, or any other steps that are required for deploying the final application.

The main benefit of CD is that you can deploy an application version as soon as possible to a production system. With this practice, when you detect an issue, you can handle the issue automatically; for example, a rollback mechanism.

Even though both CD and CI are highly correlated, it's not mandatory to implement both. For example, it's common that an engineering team decides to implement CI to automate a code error in their development environment. When deploying to production, they choose to do so manually because it's too risky to automate the deployment process.

In summary, CI/CD are steps. These steps are needed to check the developer's code and deploy it to the production systems automatically.

Understanding the data engineer's relationship with CI/CD practices

Now, the question is what does this mean for us, as data engineers? How much do we need to know about this practice? Which part of the data pipelines can use CI/CD?

First of all, I want to say that if you are already familiar and experienced with the CI/CD practice, you can focus on what tools can be used for CI/CD in GCP throughout this chapter. But if you are new to this practice, what you need to understand is the concept. In my experience, having met many data people, CI/CD is not a common practice in our space. If we compare ourselves to software engineers, the CI/CD practice is more mature in the software engineering space.

To start answering the previous questions, I will continue explaining the CI/CD practice using an illustration. I will illustrate it using an analogy from the culinary business. Imagine that you are very passionate about cooking pasta. You want to start making money from your passion. In this scenario, you have two options – open a restaurant and sell your pasta or join a big restaurant as a pasta chef.

In the first scenario, what you need to do is focus on perfecting your cooking skills and then sell them. In the second scenario, you are one of many chefs and other staff. What you need to do other than perfect your cooking skills is understand how a big kitchen works. In a big kitchen, there are many roles, including head chef, sous chef, waiters, and others. On top of that, there are systems such as cooking stations, receiving orders, food testing, and so on. These systems are there, and you need to follow them to deliver the pasta to customers.

Now, let's go back to our world – data engineering. What we've learned so far in this book is our process of perfecting our cooking. You've learned about all the important ingredients and components and how to use them. That knowledge is the core and the most important to any data engineer – the same as learning to cook the best pasta as a pasta chef.

If you are working on your data project by yourself or in a small team of typically two to three people, and you know that your data project is a short-term project (which means it won't have many updates in the long term), you don't need CI/CD. It is great to have it, but it's not mandatory. If you have a small restaurant by yourself, implementing a big kitchen system for your work would be great, but it's too much.

If you are working in a big organization that has a big and systematic engineering team, there is a higher chance that you will need to follow a system. And in engineering, the system is CI/CD. Now, also like the pasta chef in a big restaurant, what you need to do most of the time is follow the system. A data engineer rarely needs to create an end-to-end CI/CD system from scratch. The more common role that does this is the **development operations (DevOps)** team or sometimes the infrastructure team. What's important is to understand the concept, the components, and why they're there.

Let's go back to our original questions in this section. For data engineers, understanding CI/CD is not a must. It depends on where you work and what the practice is in that organization. But if you are working in an organization that uses CI/CD as a practice, you need to understand it.

In the data pipeline, any code-based applications can use CI/CD. For example, data pipeline code in DataFlow, Spark Python code in DataProc, Terraform scripts, Airflow DAG in Cloud Composer, and any other code-based data applications can use CI/CD as a practice. On the other hand, tools such as Data Studio that use a full UI can't use CI/CD.

In the next section, we will try to understand CI/CD by looking at GCP services.

Understanding CI/CD components with GCP services

There are some steps in the CI/CD practice. Each step may involve different tools or GCP services. To understand this concept better, let's take a look at the following diagram:

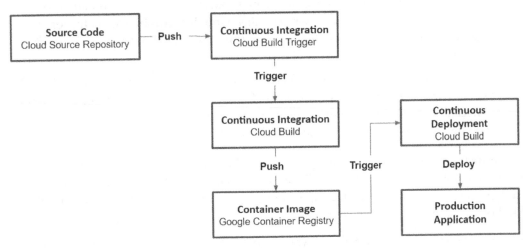

Figure 11.1 – The CI/CD steps and the GCP services involved

The diagram shows the high-level steps of a complete CI/CD. At each step, there is a corresponding GCP service that can handle that step. For example, the first step is **Source Code**. In GCP, you can create a GitHub repository using a service called **Cloud Source Repository**. Later, in the *Exercise – implementing continuous integration using Cloud Build* section, we will learn how to create one. For now, let's understand the steps and what GCP services are involved:

1. The CI process starts from **Source Code**. This **Source Code** should always be managed in a GitHub repository. It can be in GitHub, GitLab, or any other Git provider. As we mentioned previously, GCP has a service called **Cloud Source Repository**. When a developer commits and pushes a code change to the GitHub repository, the CI process is triggered.

2. The **Push** event on GitHub can trigger **Cloud Build**. **Cloud Build** is a CI/CD serverless platform on GCP. You can specify the steps in **Cloud Build** as per your needs. We will learn about it in this chapter's exercises.

   Cloud Build has an object or feature called a **Cloud Build Trigger**. We can configure the **Cloud Build Trigger** to detect events from **Cloud Source Repository**.

3. A **Cloud Build** run will start after being triggered by the **Cloud Build Trigger**. The **Cloud Build** run will run every defined step. These are the main CI steps and can include creating a Docker image, installing packages, testing code, or any other necessary steps.

4. One option with the CI step is creating and storing the container image. The term for this is **push**. But instead of pushing code, it's pushing the container to a container registry. GCP has a service called **Google Container Registry** for managing containers. Again, this step is optional; not all CI needs to build and push container images.

5. Once the container image has been created, we can trigger an event to start the CD steps. There is no specific CD tool on GCP, but we can utilize Cloud Build to do this. We can define how we want to deploy the image to the production applications. This will be the final step in the whole CI/CD process.

These are the five common patterns in CI/CD at a high level. At the lower level, you need to know about the common steps inside both CI and CD. But at this point, what you must understand is the high-level concepts. And in addition to that, you need to know what kind of tools are used for each step.

Using the services from GCP will give you advantages regarding serverless and seamless integration. For example, let's you want to create a CI pipeline for handling Cloud Composer code. In that case, you know that you need to use a service account, but that you also want the CI pipeline to be able to interact with Cloud Composer and GCS (remember that DAG in Cloud Composer storage in a GCS bucket). With Cloud Build, you know that it can interact with both Cloud Composer and GCS using a GCP service account.

After understanding all the concepts surrounding CI/CD and the corresponding GCP services, we will complete some exercises so that we understand each step. Note that if this is new for you, you should only focus on understanding the concept and what tools are used. You shouldn't worry too much about the detail of the code. For example, if you are not familiar with Dockerfile scripts, just making them work in the exercises using the provided example is good enough. You can always expand your knowledge when you face real requirements in your real working environment. Remember the pasta chef analogy – at this point, you don't need to think too much about *how a stove can convert gas and electricity into heat*; you just need to focus on knowing that a stove is needed to cook in a big restaurant.

Exercise – implementing continuous integration using Cloud Build

In this exercise, we will create a CI pipeline using Cloud Build. There will be four main steps, as follows:

1. Creating a GitHub repository using Cloud Source Repository
2. Developing the code and Cloud Build scripts
3. Creating the Cloud Build trigger
4. Pushing the code to the GitHub repository

Let's get started!

Creating a GitHub repository using Cloud Source Repository

First, let's prepare the GitHub repository. Follow these steps:

1. Go to your GCP console and find **Source Repository** from the navigation bar. It's located under the **CI/CD** section:

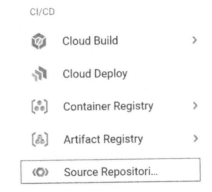

Figure 11.2 – The Source Repository menu in the navigation menu

2. After clicking the menu, a new browser tab will open within the **Cloud Source Repository** console. Click the **Get started** button on this screen to create a repository:

Cloud Source Repositories helps you privately host, track, and manage changes to large codebases on Google Cloud Platform.

Get started   View documentation

Figure 11.3 – The Get started button

Clicking this button will give you the option to create a new repository.

3. Choose **Create new repository** and click **Continue**. You will have two inputs when creating a new repository – the repository's name and the project's name:

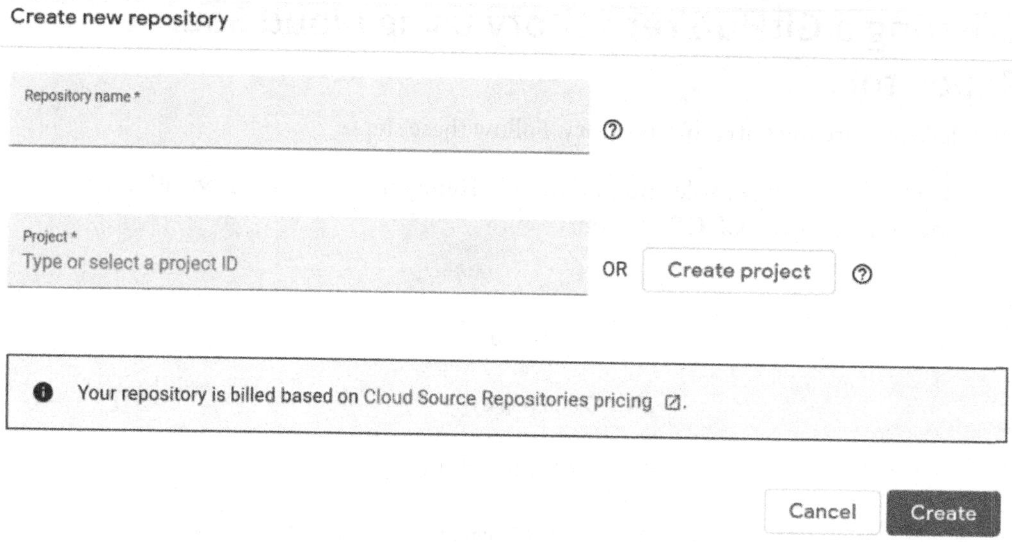

Create new repository

Repository name *

Project *
Type or select a project ID   OR   Create project   ⑦

ⓘ Your repository is billed based on Cloud Source Repositories pricing ☑.

Cancel   Create

Figure 11.4 – The Create new repository page

Choose a repository name. For example, mine is `packt-data-eng-on-gcp-cicd-example`. Don't use the name from my example.

For the project ID, I will use my GCP project ID, which is `packt-data-eng-on-gcp`. Make sure that you use your GCP project ID. Once you're finished, click the **Create** button.

At this point, you will have your new repository in Cloud Source Repository for CI/CD processes.

4. Now, go back to your GCP console and open Cloud Shell.

    We want to clone the empty GitHub repository that we just created to the Cloud Shell environment. To do that, call the following command from Cloud Shell under the `ci_example` folder:

    ```
    # mkdir ci_example
    # cd ci_example
    # gcloud source repos clone [your repository name]
    --project=[your project id]
    ```

    If this is successful, when you list the files (using the Linux `#ls` command), you will see that the repository name has been used to create a folder in your Cloud Shell.

    This is what it looks like in my environment:

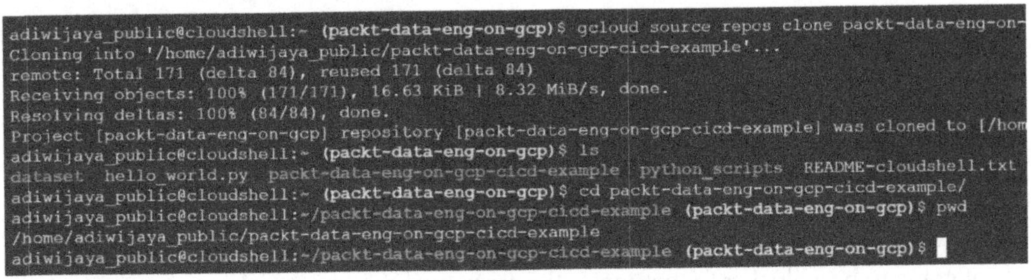

Figure 11.5 – Example of the expected commands and outputs

Now, we have a repository for our CI exercise. Let's continue to the second step.

Developing the code and Cloud Build scripts

In this step, we will use the following example code:

`https://github.com/PacktPublishing/Data-Engineering-with-Google-Cloud-Platform/tree/main/chapter-11/code/cicd_basic`

If you check this folder, you will see that there are three files and one folder. The main Python function is in the `calculate.py` file; there's another file called `Dockerfile`, and a `YAML` file called `cloudbuild.yaml`. The tests folder contains a Python unit test script that will be used for checking the function in the `calculate.py` file.

To be clear about the repositories, I will call this `GitHub` repository `packt github`.

Don't be confused with your self-created GitHub repository in **Cloud Source Repository (CSR)**, which I will call the `my CSR` repository.

The packt github repository refers to the *github.com* link that you can use for copying and pasting the code for our exercise. The my CSR repository refers to the CSR repository that you created in *Step 1* of this exercise.

What you need to do is copy all the files from the packt github repository to the my CSR repository. I won't give step-by-step instructions on how to do this; you can do this using any approach you like. You can copy and paste each file manually or clone the repository and copy it using Linux commands. Use any approach that you are most familiar with. For example, for me, after cloning the code from the packt github repository, inside the directory, I copied the files using the following Linux command:

```
# cp -r * ~/packt-data-eng-on-gcp-cicd-example/
```

The expected output is that your my CSR repository will contain the following files:

```
adiwijaya_public@cloudshell:~/packt-data-eng-on-gcp-cicd-example (packt-data-eng-on-gcp)$ ls
calculate.py  cloudbuild.yaml  Dockerfile  tests
```

Figure 11.6 – Listing the files in the directory

Let's quickly look at what these files are. As a heads-up before continuing to the code explanation, as we mentioned previously, you might get confused here. There are a lot of details that I chose not to explain in this book, such as containerization, Docker, and unit testing. I am not going to look at these topics in depth since they are huge topics. But that is not going to be a blocker for getting to the essence of this chapter about CI/CD for data engineers on GCP. Here, we will focus on understanding the high-level steps and what tools are involved. Now, let's look at the code:

1. The most important file here is the cloudbuild.yaml file. Pipelines in Cloud Build are defined under steps: in the YAML file.

    Let's take a look at the first step:

    ```
    - name: gcr.io/cloud-builders/docker
      id: Build Image
      args: [
          'build',
          '-t', 'gcr.io/$PROJECT_ID/cicd-basic',
          '.'
      ]
    ```

The goal of this Cloud Build step is to create a Docker image and give it a tag of `gcr.io/$PROJECT_ID/cicd-basic`. This tag will contain all the files from our `my CSR` repository.

First, let's understand the `name` parameter. The `name` parameter is not just a random name for an identifier. The `name` parameter is used to specify which Docker image or environment that you want to use to run that particular step. In this case, we want to use the publicly available image from `gcr.io/cloud-builders` that contain Docker libraries.

The `id` parameter is the step identifier. This value needs to be unique for each step.

The `args` parameter represents the arguments that you can define, depending on the image that you loaded from the `name` parameter. In this case, `args` are Linux commands for calling Docker pull requests. To see what's happening, we will run this step in a Linux virtual environment. The virtual environment will call the following Linux command:

```
# docker build -t gcr.io/$PROJECT_ID/cicd-basic .
```

Note that every value in the `args` parameter will be converted into Linux commands. For example, if you want to create a directory called `test_directory` in the environment, the `args` parameter will be as follows:

```
['mkdir','test_directory']
```

This will be used in every other step.

2. Now, continue to the second step. The goal of this step is to validate our Python code using the Python `unittest` package:

```
    - name: 'gcr.io/$PROJECT_ID/cicd-basic'
  id: Validation Test
  entrypoint: python
  args: [
    '-m',
    'unittest',
    'tests/test_calculate.py'
  ]
```

Notice that we set the name parameter to gcr.io/$PROJECT_ID/cicd-basic. This means we can use the Docker image from the first step and use and test the code that is already stored in that image.

There is an additional parameter here called entrypoint. The entrypoint parameter is used to change the default entry command in the environment. In this case, we are using Python. To illustrate this, we will convert the parameters we mentioned previously into this command and it will run in a container:

```
# python -m unittest tests/test_calculate.py
```

Note that this step can fail or be successful, depending on the unit test results. If it fails, Cloud Build will stop the process and won't continue to the next step.

3. For the final step, the main goal is to push the image to **Google Container Registry (GCR)**:

```
- name: gcr.io/cloud-builders/docker
  id: Push Image to GCR
  args: [
      'push',
      'gcr.io/$PROJECT_ID/cicd-basic:latest'
  ]
```

The last step is similar to the first step – that is, using the public Docker image from gcr.io/cloud-builders/docker. However, in this step, we will use the push command to push the image to our project container register.

To summarize this step, we need to copy all the code examples from the packt github repository to our repository. This step also explains the cloudbuild.yaml file. We've learned that to create a CI pipeline in Cloud Build, you must define the steps in the YAML file by configuring the necessary parameters. At this point, you don't need to change any code in this example.

Creating the Cloud Build Trigger

Now, go back to your GCP console and go to the Cloud Build console. You can find it in the navigation bar, under the **CI/CD** section:

1. There are four menus in the Cloud Build console – **Dashboard**, **History**, **Triggers**, and **Settings**. Let's choose **Triggers** by clicking the respective button:

Figure 11.7 – The Cloud Build Triggers page

Let's create one by clicking the **CREATE TRIGGER** button.

2. On the **Create trigger** page, input any name as the identifier.

   Take a look at the types of events that can invoke triggers. We can push to a branch, push a new tag, or pull a request, all of which are commonly available in GitHub or GitLab. Looking at these options will give you an idea of how automation can occur. Imagine that you and your colleagues change the code in a repository; every push or pull request will trigger a Cloud Build run.

   Keep all the inputs as-is except for the source repository. If you click **Repository**, you will see your GitHub repository from *Step 1*. In the **Branch** section, click the form and use **.* (any branch)** from the suggested input. Here is an example:

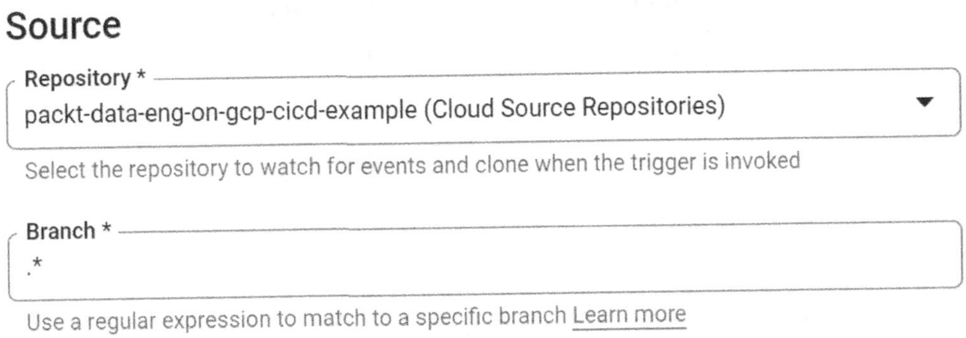

Source

Repository *

packt-data-eng-on-gcp-cicd-example (Cloud Source Repositories)   ▼

Select the repository to watch for events and clone when the trigger is invoked

Branch *

.*

Use a regular expression to match to a specific branch Learn more

Figure 11.8 – Configuring the Repository and Branch fields

When you're done, click the **CREATE** button.

Pushing the code to the GitHub repository

So far, we have three elements:

- A GitHub repository
- A Cloud Build trigger attached to the GitHub repository
- Code in the Cloud Shell environment

The final step is to push our code from the local Cloud Shell environment to the GitHub repository. Let's get started:

1. First, go back to your Cloud Shell.

   Inside the GitHub repository folder that you created in the second step, push the code using the following `git` commands:

   ```
   # git add .
   # git commit -m "initial commit"
   # git push
   ```

   If this is the first time you are committing using git from your Cloud Shell environment, you will see an error message stating **Please tell me who you are**. In this case, follow the instructions in that message by running the following two commands:

   ```
   # git config --global user.email "[Your email address]"
   # git config --global user.name "[Your name]"
   ```

   You will only need to do this once in every new environment.

   After running these commands, you can check the **Build history** page:

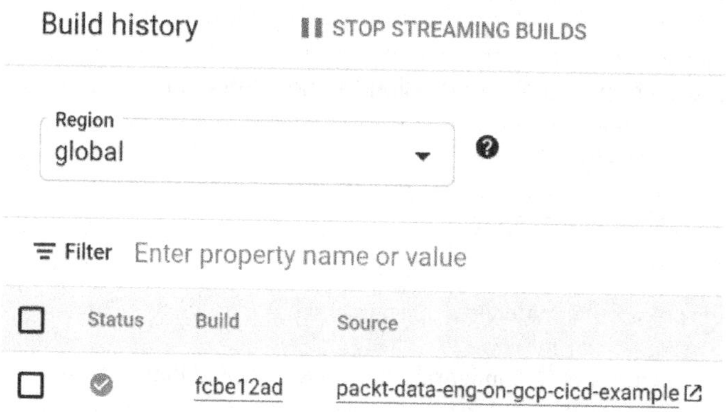

   Build history   ❚❚ STOP STREAMING BUILDS

   Region
   global   ▼   ❓

   ≡ Filter   Enter property name or value

   ☐   Status   Build   Source

   ☐   ✓   fcbe12ad   packt-data-eng-on-gcp-cicd-example ⬈

   Figure 11.9 – Example of a Cloud Build run successfully running

2. Check if the Cloud Build run has been triggered and is running successfully. After successfully pushing it, go to your Cloud Build console and open the **History** menu. You will see the **Build history** page. If there are no issues after running these four steps, you will see that a Cloud Build run is running in the build history.

   If you click the respective build ID (`fcbe12ad`), you will also see the steps that we learned about in the *Developing the code and Cloud Build scripts* section, when we discussed the `cloudbuild.yaml` file:

Steps	Duration
✓ **Build Summary** 3 Steps	00:00:18
✓ 0: Build Image build -t gcr.io/packt-data-eng-on-gcp/...	00:00:06
✓ 1: Validation Test python -m unittest tests/test_calculat...	00:00:01
✓ 2: Push Image to GCR push gcr.io/packt-data-eng-on-gcp/ci...	00:00:04

Figure 11.10 – Build Summary and the respective steps

Check if all the steps have run successfully.

3. Finally, we want to check the stored container. To do that, in the GCP console, find **Container Registry** from the navigation menu, under the **CI/CD** section. You will see that the image is there:

packt-data-eng-on-gcp

⇌ **Filter**   Enter property name or value

Name ↑	Hostname ❓	Visibility ❓
📁 ci-example	gcr.io	Private

Figure 11.11 – The Container Registry console

ci-example is the Docker image that is hosted in gcr.io, which is managed by Google Cloud. By default, the visibility of this Docker image is **Private**, which means that only you or any other users with the right IAM permissions can access this image.

For illustration purposes, let's try to make some unit tests fail intentionally. For example, I will change the calculate.py file, as follows:

```
result = arg_1 + arg_2
```

The preceding line of code will have the plus (+) icon change to a multiply (*) icon:

```
result = arg_1 * arg_2
```

I will commit and push it to the GitHub repository. As expected, Cloud Build will automatically trigger and start the Cloud Build run.

The result will be **Failed**. You can check this by clicking the Cloud Build step's log. For example, you will see the following logs upon clicking the **Validation Test** step:

```
1   Already have image: gcr.io/packt-data-eng-on-gcp/cicd-basic
2   F
3   ======================================================================
4   FAIL: testValue_sum (tests.test_calculate.TestSum)
5   ----------------------------------------------------------------------
6   Traceback (most recent call last):
7     File "/workspace/tests/test_calculate.py", line 7, in testValue_sum
8       self.assertEqual(calculate.sum_two_values(1,2), 3, "Should be equal to 3")
9   AssertionError: 2 != 3 : Should be equal to 3
10
11  ----------------------------------------------------------------------
```

Figure 11.12 – Example of an AssertionError in the Cloud Build logs

And that's it! The log shows you that the expected value is not correct. That's the power of CI. Imagine that there are tens of developers working in a repository and that there are hundreds of commits in a day. This automation will help your day-to-day life as an engineer.

In this exercise, I didn't mention or provide an example of CD because it only involves a few steps. You can create the CD steps in the same way that you perform CD using Cloud Build. And it also depends on what applications you have; the CD steps might be different. For example, to productionize our `calculate.py` file, we can deploy it as a web API. Learning how to deploy a web API is outside the scope of this book, so we don't discuss it here.

To summarize, in this exercise, you learned how to use all the GCP services to run a CI pipeline using Cloud Source Repository, Cloud Build Triggers, Cloud Build Run, and Google Container Registry. At the end of this exercise, you learned how automation can save you a lot of time while you're testing code when many developers are collaborating. However, you've also learned that the steps for creating automation are not easy. We have illustrated everything we've discussed regarding CI/CD considerations and the pasta chef analogy.

Exercise – deploying Cloud Composer jobs using Cloud Build

In this section, we will continue creating a Cloud Build pipeline. This time, I will help you get an idea of how this practice can be implemented in terms of data engineering. To do that, we will try to create a CI/CD pipeline for deploying a Cloud Composer DAG.

In this exercise, we will use the DAG from *Chapter 4, Building Orchestration for Batch Data Loading Using Cloud Composer*. Let's refresh a little bit on the exercises from that chapter.

In *Chapter 4, Building Orchestration for Batch Data Loading Using Cloud Composer*, we learned how Cloud Composer works. We learned that in Cloud Composer, you can develop DAGs to create data pipelines. These data pipelines can use Airflow Operators to manage BigQuery, Cloud SQL, GCS, or simple bash scripts. In those exercises, we practiced five levels of DAGs, with the level one DAG being the simplest one and the level five DAG being the most complex. To deploy a DAG, we can store the Python file containing the DAG in the Cloud Composer GCS bucket, in a specific directory named dags.

In this exercise, we will use the level one DAG from *Chapter 4, Building Orchestration for Batch Data Loading Using Cloud Composer*. We will use level one to avoid any complexity that is not relevant to this chapter, such as preparing the CloudSQL instances, BigQuery datasets, and the other long steps that were discussed in that chapter. However, the same technique that applies to this level one DAG can be applied to the other DAG levels. As a high-level summary, here are the steps that we will go through:

1. Preparing the CI/CD environment
2. Preparing the cloudbuild.yaml configuration file
3. Pushing the DAG to our GitHub repository
4. Checking the CI/CD result in the GCS bucket and Cloud Composer

You have two options for running this exercise:

- The first option is to recreate the Cloud Composer environment and deploy the DAG in the new Cloud Composer environment. In this case, you can use the new GCS bucket that's being used by Cloud Composer as the target deployment.

- The second option is to use the GCS bucket from your Cloud Composer environment from *Chapter 4, Building Orchestration for Batch Data Loading Using Cloud Composer*. Creating a Cloud Composer environment can be time-consuming (around 30 minutes) and can be costly. You can choose not to create the Cloud Composer environment and only use the GCS bucket as the target deployment.

Either way, what you need is a GCS bucket that we can use in our `cloudbuild.yaml` file later. Now, let's get started.

Preparing the CI/CD environment

The first step is preparing the environment, which includes doing the following:

- Creating a GitHub repository in Cloud Source Repository
- Cloning the empty GitHub repository to Cloud Shell
- Creating a Cloud Build Trigger and connecting it to the GitHub repository

I won't show you each step in this exercise. Practice going through them yourself by using your experience from the previous section, *Exercise – implementing continuous integration using Cloud Build*.

At the end of this step, your environment will be ready. For example, here is mine:

- Cloud Source Repository name: `packt-data-eng-on-gcp-cicd-cloud-composer`
- Cloud Build Trigger name: `cicd-cloud-composer-trigger`

In Cloud Shell, I have the following GitHub repository folder after using the `gcloud clone` command:

Figure 11.13 – The expected directory is inside the repository folder

Make sure you are in the right directory, which is inside the project folder. In the next section, we will prepare the `cloudbuild.yaml` file.

Preparing the cloudbuild.yaml configuration file

Now, let's prepare the `cloudbuild.yaml` file and the other necessary code. The example code for this exercise can be downloaded or git cloned from the `packt github` repository:

`https://github.com/PacktPublishing/Data-Engineering-with-Google-Cloud-Platform/tree/main/chapter-11/code/cicd_cloud_composer`

Notice the difference between this project compared to the previous exercise in the Python file. In the previous exercise, we have the `calculate.py` file as the main code, while this time, we have the `dags` folder containing the Airflow DAG.

The next thing you need to do is copy all the files in the example code to the GitHub repository that you created in the *Preparing the CI/CD environment* section. For example, this is what it looks like if I open the folder via Cloud Editor:

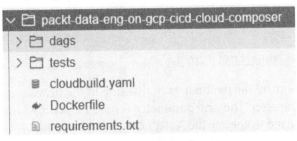

Figure 11.14 – Example code files in Cloud Editor

Now, let's look at `cloudbuild.yaml` and look at the necessary CI/CD steps:

1. The first step is using Docker to build the image from the Dockerfile:

```
- name: gcr.io/cloud-builders/docker
  id: Build Airflow DAGs Builder
  args: [
      'build',
      '-t', 'gcr.io/$PROJECT_ID/airflow-data-pipeline',
      '--cache-from', 'gcr.io/$PROJECT_ID/airflow-data-
  pipeline:latest',
      './'
  ]
```

If you open the Docker file, you will see that it involves installing Airflow, as stated in the requirements.txt file:

```
RUN pip3 install --upgrade --no-cache-dir -r
requirements.txt
```

This is important because we will need the Airflow Python package to unit test the DAG in the next step.

2. The second step is performing unit testing:

```
- name: 'gcr.io/$PROJECT_ID/airflow-data-pipeline'
  id: Validation Test
  entrypoint: python
  env:
  - AIRFLOW__CORE__DAGS_FOLDER=/workspace/dags
  args:
  - -m
  - unittest
  - tests/dag_tests.py
```

3. We learned about all the parameters in this step in the previous exercise, except for the *env* parameter. The env parameter is used for setting Linux environment variables. We need to specify the AIRFLOW__CORE__DAGS_FOLDER parameter so that Airflow knows where to find the DAG files. The dag_tests.py file will check your DAG and stop Cloud Build from running if there are issues in your DAG. The third step in Cloud Build is to push the image to GCR:

```
- name: gcr.io/cloud-builders/docker
  id: Push Image to GCR
  args: [
      'push',
    'gcr.io/$PROJECT_ID/airflow-data-pipeline:latest'
    ]
```

There is nothing new in this step compared to the previous exercise. This step is straightforward. But let's discuss why we need this image to be stored in GCR.

At this point, you know that you can deploy a DAG to Cloud Composer by uploading the Python file containing the DAG to a GCS bucket. We can't use Docker images to deploy a DAG. So, this third step is optional. The main reason we are performing this step is so that we can reuse it for the next run as a cache. Notice that in the first step, when we build the Docker image, we declared the `--cache-from` parameter, like this:

```
'--cache-from', 'gcr.io/$PROJECT_ID/airflow-data-
pipeline:latest'
```

The benefit of doing this is that we can make the Cloud Build runtime quicker.

4. Finally, we must deploy the `dag` parameter from the container to the GCS bucket using the `gsutil rsync` command:

```
- name: gcr.io/cloud-builders/gsutil
  id: Deploy DAGs
  args:
  - -m
  - rsync
  - -r
  - -c
  - -x
  - .*\.pyc|airflow_monitoring.py
  - /workspace/dags
  - [GCS bucket dags path]
```

Change [GCS bucket dags path] to your GCS path. For example, mine is `gs://us-central1-packt-composer--76564980-bucket/dags/`.

The `gsutil rsync` command will copy the files from the `/workspace/dags` directory to the GCS bucket. If you are not familiar with `rsync`, it's similar to copying the files, but only if the file does not exist in the destination folder.

You may also be confused about the -m, -r, -c, and -x parameters. They are all just additional parameters in `rsync` – for example, -m is used to make `rsync` to be parallel, or in other words, to be faster. You can check all the parameter descriptions and what `gsutil rsync` is by reading the public documentation:

`https://cloud.google.com/storage/docs/gsutil/commands/rsync`

To summarize, in this step, you must copy all the files from the `packt github` example to your GitHub repository in Cloud Shell. Then, you need to change `[GCS bucket dags path]` to your GCS bucket path.

Pushing the DAG to our GitHub repository

The next step is straightforward – you need to commit and push the code in your GitHub repository. For example, from inside your GitHub repository folder, use the following commands:

```
# git add .
# git commit -m "initial commit"
# git push
```

These commands will push your code to **Cloud Source Repository** and trigger the Cloud Build run.

Checking the CI/CD result in the GCS bucket and Cloud Composer

If everything has been successful, you will see the Cloud Build run in the CI/CD pipeline:

Steps	Duration
✅ **Build Summary** 4 Steps	00:01:31
✅ 0: Build Airflow DAGs Builder build -t gcr.io/packt-data-eng-on-gcp/...	00:01:02
✅ 1: Validation Test python -m unittest tests/dag_tests.py	00:00:01
✅ 2: Push Image to GCR push gcr.io/packt-data-eng-on-gcp/ai...	00:00:17
✅ 3: Deploy DAGs -m rsync -r -c -x .*\.pyc|airflow_monit...	00:00:03

Figure 11.15 – Cloud Build – Build Summary with four steps

The pipeline will check `level_1_dag` in the **Validation** step and the deployment will be done using the `gsutil rsync` command.

You can check your GCS bucket to see if the `level_1_dag.py` file has been copied to the correct path:

us-central1-packt-composer--76564980-bucket

Location	Storage class	Public access	Protection
us-central1 (Iowa)	Standard	⚠ Subject to object ACLs	None

OBJECTS   CONFIGURATION   PERMISSIONS   PROTECTION

Buckets ❯ us-central1-packt-composer--76564980-bucket ❯ dags 🗐

UPLOAD FILES   UPLOAD FOLDER   CREATE FOLDER   MANAGE HOL

Filter by name prefix only ▼   ⇂ Filter   level_1_dag.py

	Name	Size	Type
☐	📄 level_1_dag.py	681 B	text/x-python

Figure 11.16 – The Cloud Composer GCS bucket contains the DAG file

If it is, then congratulations! You have just created a CI/CD pipeline that manages Cloud Composer DAGs.

If you chose to create a Cloud Composer environment to practice this exercise, you can also check the Airflow UI to see if the DAG is running. However, if you don't have the Cloud Composer environment running, that's not an issue – whenever a Python file containing a DAG is uploaded to the `/dags` directory, it will automatically run in Airflow. If you are not sure about how DAG works in Cloud Composer and Airflow, you can always go back to *Chapter 4, Building Orchestration for Batch Data Loading Using Cloud Composer*.

To test if the validation step works, I'll try to intentionally make the DAG fail. For example, in the `dags/level_1_dag.py` DAG file, when we're defining `schedule_interval`, it should look like this:

```
schedule_interval='0 5 * * *',
```

The format for `schedule_interval` should follow cron expression syntax. I will change it to a normal string here, like this:

```
schedule_interval='This is wrong',
```

After pushing this change to the GitHub repository, this is what happened to the Cloud Build run:

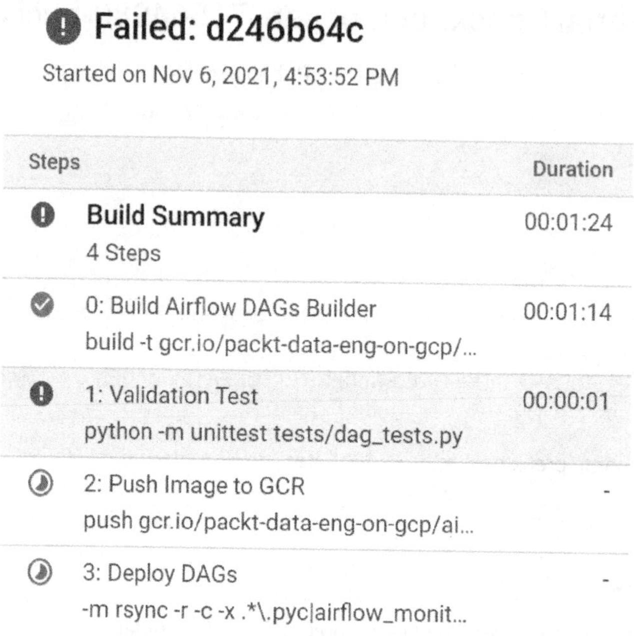

⊘ Failed: d246b64c

Started on Nov 6, 2021, 4:53:52 PM

Steps	Duration
⊘ **Build Summary** 4 Steps	00:01:24
✓ 0: Build Airflow DAGs Builder build -t gcr.io/packt-data-eng-on-gcp/…	00:01:14
⊘ 1: Validation Test python -m unittest tests/dag_tests.py	00:00:01
⊘ 2: Push Image to GCR push gcr.io/packt-data-eng-on-gcp/ai…	-
⊘ 3: Deploy DAGs -m rsync -r -c -x .*\.pyc|airflow_monit…	-

Figure 11.17 – The Cloud Build run failed the test

The Cloud Build stops at **Validation Test**. Here are the logs, explaining the error:

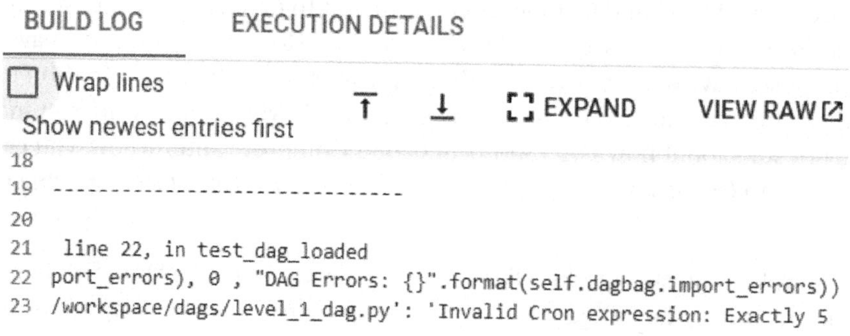

BUILD LOG   EXECUTION DETAILS

☐ Wrap lines   ↑   ↓   ⊏⊐ EXPAND   VIEW RAW ↗
Show newest entries first

```
18
19  ------------------------------
20
21   line 22, in test_dag_loaded
22  port_errors), 0 , "DAG Errors: {}".format(self.dagbag.import_errors))
23  /workspace/dags/level_1_dag.py': 'Invalid Cron expression: Exactly 5
```

Figure 11.18 – Example DAG error message in the Cloud Build logs

It says that `/workspace/dags/level_1_dag.py` : `Invalid Cron expression`. This is perfect! With this mechanism, if anyone pushes a failed DAG, the DAG won't be deployed to the GCS bucket. On top of that, we can use these logs to know which code has an issue and what issues it has.

With that, we've finished learning about CI/CD on GCP. Now, let's summarize what we've learned in this chapter.

Summary

In this chapter, we learned about how CI/CD works in GCP services. More specifically, we learned about this from the perspective of a data engineer. CI/CD is a big topic by itself and is more mature in the software development practice. But lately, it's more and more common for data engineers to follow this practice in big organizations.

We started this chapter by talking about the high-level concepts and ended it with an exercise that showed how data engineers can use CI/CD in a data project. In the exercises, we used Cloud Build, Cloud Source Repository, and Google Container Registry. Understanding these concepts and what kind of technologies are involved were the two main goals of this chapter. If you want to learn more about DevOps practices, containers, and unit testing, check out the links in the *Further reading* section.

This was the final technical chapter in this book. If you have read all the chapters in this book, then you've learned about all the core GCP services related to data engineering. At this point, I hope you've got all the confidence you will need to build a data project on GCP. The next chapter will be the closing chapter of this book, where we will revisit the content of this book in quiz format to boost your confidence and help you if you don't understand anything. I will also share tips on how to get the Google Cloud certification and how to take on the data engineering career path.

Further reading

To learn more about the topics that were covered in this chapter, take a look at the following resources:

- *DevOps practice*, by Google Cloud: `https://cloud.google.com/devops`
- *Containers on the cloud*, by Google Cloud: `https://cloud.google.com/containers`
- Updated blog post on software engineer testing: `https://testing.googleblog.com/`

12
Boosting Your Confidence as a Data Engineer

In this chapter, we will review and check our understanding of all the topics that have been covered throughout this book. We will do that by simulating the Google Cloud certification's question format. I'll start by talking about the Google Cloud certification so that you become familiar with it.

As the last part of this book, I will share my thoughts on what will be the future of Data Engineering. I hope that, by reaching the final section of this book, you will get all you need to have confidence as a data engineer working with **Google Cloud Platform** (**GCP**).

In this chapter, we will cover the following topics:

- Overviewing the Google Cloud certification
- Quiz – reviewing all the concepts you've learned about
- The past, present, and future of Data Engineering
- Boosting your confidence and final thoughts

Let's get started!

Overviewing the Google Cloud certification

Let's start this final chapter by talking about the Google Cloud certification. In my opinion, taking the certification is important. I highly recommend that you take it – not only to get the certificates on paper but also to validate how much you know about the topics that are needed to be a Google Cloud professional. The experience that you get while preparing for the certification is the most important part of your journey. Regardless of whether you pass or fail the exam, I believe that you will get new knowledge along the way.

Google Cloud provides a list of official certifications that you can use to validate your expertise with the Google Cloud technology. There are three main categories available:

- Foundational

- Associate

- Professional

Foundational is intended for anyone with no hands-on experience with Google Cloud technology. *Associate* is recommended for anyone who has 6+ months of Google Cloud experience. Finally, *Professional* is recommended for anyone who has 1+ years of Google Cloud experience, with 3+ years of industry experience.

My suggestion is to take the certifications based on your experience. However, in terms of Data Engineering, there is only one certification available at this time. This is under the *Professional* category and it's called **Google Cloud Data Engineer**. I highly recommend that you take this one. Please check out the public information about the Google Cloud Data Engineer certification at

`https://cloud.google.com/certification/data-engineer.`

The other relevant certifications that can support your Data Engineering skills are Cloud Architect, Cloud DevOps Engineer, and Machine Learning Engineer. They are not the core of Data Engineering, but if you plan to expand your knowledge, they are good candidates.

In this chapter, I will focus on discussing the Data Engineering certification. I will share the preparation tips, example questions, and their relevance to the content of this book. My sharing will be based on my experience passing the certifications two times, in 2019 and 2021. There might be changes in the future or when you read this book, but hopefully, there won't be many. As a disclaimer, note that everything that I have shared in this book, and especially in this chapter, is purely my personal opinion based on my own experience. For the official and most updated information from Google Cloud, you can always go to their public website.

Exam preparation tips

First, let's talk about *whether you should prepare for the certification.* My answer is yes, you should! This doesn't only count for beginners – even if you already have enough hands-on experience with engineering data in Google Cloud, you should start preparing.

There are a lot of questions that are very detailed and cover edge cases. For example, some questions might be asked about **Google Cloud Storage (GCS)**, which you probably already have good knowledge and experience of using due to the exercises that were presented in this book. In the exam, there might be questions such as the following:

What is the best storage class in Cloud Storage if the user intends to access the data less than once every quarter?

- **Standard**
- **Nearline**
- **Coldline**
- **Archive**

The answer to this question is **Coldline**. If you are not sure what this means, take a look at the following screenshot, which shows creating a GCS bucket:

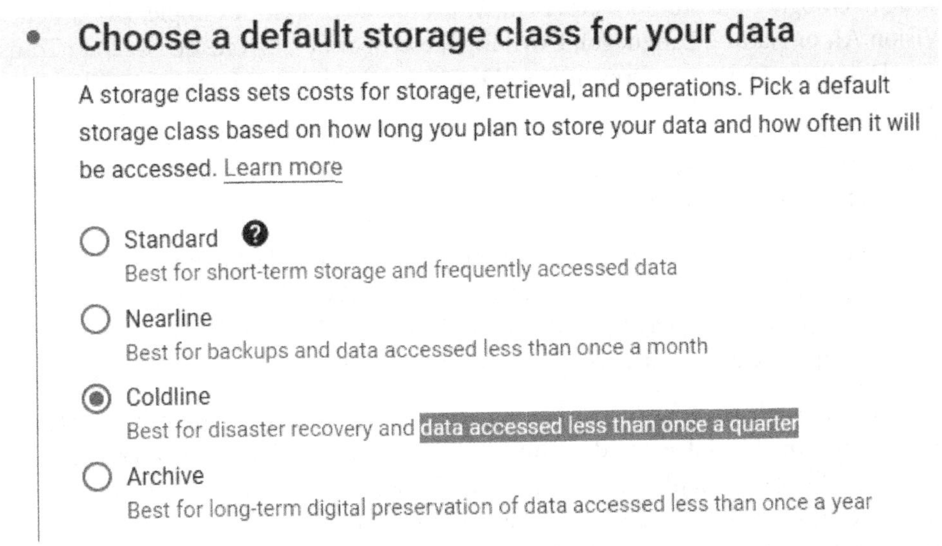

- **Choose a default storage class for your data**

  A storage class sets costs for storage, retrieval, and operations. Pick a default storage class based on how long you plan to store your data and how often it will be accessed. Learn more

  ○ Standard ❓
     Best for short-term storage and frequently accessed data

  ○ Nearline
     Best for backups and data accessed less than once a month

  ● Coldline
     Best for disaster recovery and data accessed less than once a quarter

  ○ Archive
     Best for long-term digital preservation of data accessed less than once a year

Figure 12.1 – GCS bucket storage class options

Sometimes, you need to remain aware and remember the detailed information about each of the technologies. So, make sure you are prepared and practice a lot.

Now, let's talk about what is covered in the exam. There are four sections in the Data Engineer exam:

- Designing data processing systems
- Building and operationalizing data processing systems
- Operationalizing machine learning models
- Ensuring solution quality

Each section will validate your knowledge of all the GCP services related to Data Engineering. You can cross-check the Google Cloud public website to make sure the list is still the same and check the more detailed sub-topics.

Compared to what we've learned in this book, the exam topic area is broader. Remember that the goal of this book is to help you narrow down the most important knowledge that's required for you to be a Data Engineer that can use GCP. On the other hand, the exam checks your knowledge very broadly. This means you need to expand a little bit from what you've learned in this book.

The GCP services that might be included in the exam are as follows:

BigQuery, Google Cloud Storage, Cloud Composer, DataProc, DataFlow, Pub/Sub, CloudSQL, Google Data Studio, Vertex AI, AI pre-built APIs (for example, Document AI, Vision AI, or Natural Language), IAM, BigTable, Spanner, DataStore, Data Transfer Service, DataPrep, **Data Loss Prevention (DLP)**, and Stackdriver Logging or Cloud Logging.

To compare and summarize what we've learned in this book, here is the list of GCP services that we used in our exercises:

BigQuery, Google Cloud Storage, Cloud Composer, DataProc, DataFlow, Pub/Sub, CloudSQL, Google Data Studio, Vertex AI, AI pre-built APIs (for example Document AI, Vision AI, Natural Language), IAM, Cloud Shell, Cloud Editor, Cloud Build, Google Container Registry, Cloud Source Repository, and Terraform.

Based on these two lists, we've learned about almost all of the topics mentioned. However, some topics haven't been discussed in this book, including BigTable, Spanner, Datastore, Data Transfer Service, DataPrep, DLP, and Cloud Logging (or Stackdriver). These are important technologies that are available on GCP, but I decided not to create dedicated chapters for those technologies in this book. In the next section, I will briefly talk about them and point out the common questions that are related to those technologies.

Extra GCP services material

In this section, I will list all the other GCP services that might be part of the Google Cloud Data Engineering certification's questions. The information that will be provided here is not the most complete resource to learn about the technologies but a very generic explanation for you to at least be familiar with the terminologies and their positioning.

Cloud Logging

Cloud Logging is an out-of-the-box service on GCP that logs all of your GCP services. This is useful for checking errors, warnings, or historical usage of users. You can find Cloud Logging in the **Navigation** menu on your GCP console. What is important about Cloud Logging regarding the certification is that you know that Cloud Logging captures logs from GCP services, as we mentioned previously. You can also export Cloud Logging to other storage options, such as Cloud Storage, BigQuery, and Pub/Sub.

Bigtable, Spanner, and Datastore

These three services share a common positioning in the technology architecture. They are highly scalable application databases. Please review *Chapter 2, Big Data Capabilities on GCP*, the *Service mapping and prioritization* section, for more information.

It's important to know how to choose between these three application databases. The following diagram provides an overview of them in the form of a decision tree:

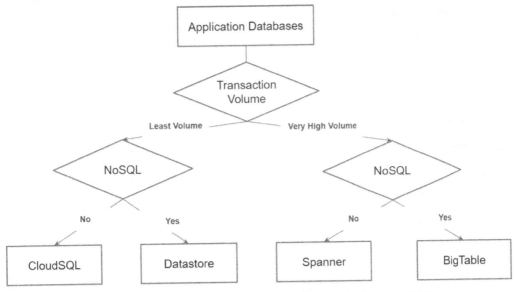

Figure 12.2 – Decision tree for choosing application databases on GCP

The preceding diagram shows a highly simplified decision tree for choosing between four GCP services for application databases. I added CloudSQL here because this service is also an option for application databases. The first consideration is the data volume. If there is a requirement to handle a very high volume of data, such as more than 1 TB a day, that's a good indication to use either Spanner or BigTable. On the other hand, if the data to handle is less than 1 TB a day, you should choose either CloudSQL or Datastore.

The second consideration is whether it requires SQL or NoSQL databases – or in other terms, a structured or unstructured database. On the left-hand side of the diagram, if the requirement is to handle structured data, choose CloudSQL. Otherwise, you can choose Datastore. Datastore is a NoSQL database with a document data model. On the right-hand side of the diagram, for very high volumes, Spanner is the best option for structured and semi-structured data. BigTable is the best option for unstructured data. BigTable is a managed wide-column NoSQL database.

There are many other aspects to consider when you need to decide between these GCP services, such as high availability; the replication method – zonal, regional, or global replication; price; available expertise; and other aspects. But for the certification's purposes, you need to know their high-level positioning. There might be questions such as the following:

Your company needs to choose a database to handle data that is more than 10 TB in size. The data is generated from sensors that should be handled in a NoSQL database. The end product is a real-time application that requires high throughput and low latency. Which service should you use?

- **Cloud SQL**

- **Datastore**

- **Spanner**

- **BigTable**

The answer is **BigTable**. The data volume is high, and it requires a NoSQL database.

Regarding these four services, there will be more questions regarding BigTable compared to the others. We'll talk about this in the next section.

BigTable

As we mentioned previously, BigTable is a Google Cloud managed wide-column NoSQL database. BigTable is a very scalable technology that has very high throughput, low latency, and provides high availability.

BigTable is highly correlated to an open source product called Apache HBase. BigTable supports the Apache HBase library for Java.

BigTable works well for use cases such as storing time series data for real-time applications, storing transaction histories, stock price histories, and IoT. The key difference between BigTable and BigQuery use cases is the real-time aspects. Even though BigQuery is capable of handling real-time data ingestion using streaming ingestion, it's not suitable as a database that serves real-time data for low- latency applications. On the other hand, BigTable is not capable of handling Data warehouse use cases that require a lot of JOIN operations.

There are many ways to optimize BigTable. One of the easiest ways to improve performance is to switch from using HDD as the underlying storage to SSD. Another way to make sure that performance is optimal is by choosing the right key on each table. BigTable performance can be very badly affected by key hotspots. For example, some bad key examples are the website domain name and the timestamp. Some good key examples are random numbers, timestamps combined with other columns, and reverse domain names. Check the public documentation from Google Cloud regarding this topic:

`https://cloud.google.com/bigtable/docs/schema-design#row-keys-avoid`.

Another important aspect of BigTable is that the service is highly available. If a node in a BigTable cluster is down, you don't need to worry about the data. Data in BigTable is separated from the compute, meaning that if one of the nodes goes down, then the data won't be lost.

Data Transfer Service

This service is required when a company migrates its data from outside to inside GCP. Many approaches can be chosen when you're moving data to GCP, and the common pattern is moving data to Cloud Storage.

One of the main considerations when moving data to Cloud Storage is the data's size. If you're transferring data that's less than 1 TB in size, you can use the `gsutil` command. We used this command in some of our exercises. However, if you need to transfer more than 1 TB of data, you can use a service called **Storage Transfer Service** on GCP. Finally, if you need to transfer more than 100 TB of data at once, you need Transfer Appliance. Transfer Appliance is a physical appliance for moving offline data that can be used for more than 100 TB of data.

Data Loss Prevention (DLP)

Data Loss Prevention (DLP) is a tool in GCP that helps Data engineers handle **Personally Identifiable Information(PII)** data. DLP has sets of different actions that can help you detect and remove PII data, such as in a scenario where you store data in Cloud Storage and the files are in CSV format. You know that one of the columns contains free text information. You need to detect whether there is a name, phone number, and credit card number in the free text before loading it into a BigQuery table. This is a use case example where DLP can help.

Dataprep

DataPrep is a tool that's used for data preparation and is developed by Trifacta. Data preparation can include analyzing data to understand its distribution, finding outliers, data cleansing, and data transformation. The difference between using DataPrep and our approach of using Cloud Composer and BigQuery operators is the expected user experience. In DataPrep, a user can do data preparation using a **Graphical User Interface (GUI)** and require no code. This is a good option when there is no one in an organization that can code but the organization needs to do data analytics.

Now, let's use the knowledge we've gained in this section and all the chapters in this book for the next section's quiz.

Quiz – reviewing all the concepts you've learned about

In this section, I will give you examples of what the Google Cloud Data Engineer certification's questions look like. There are 12 questions in the exam that are grouped into 4 categories.

I will list all the questions first; the key answers will be provided in the next section, after the twelfth question.

Questions

Each question has four options and you need to choose the correct answer.

Designing data processing systems

Please choose one answer for each of the questions in this section:

1. Your company runs a variety of Spark jobs on an on-premises cluster. You are planning to migrate to GCP quickly and easily. What kind of deployment would you recommend?

    A. Deploy a Cloud Dataproc cluster to run the Spark jobs.

    B. Run Spark and Hadoop jobs in Cloud Dataflow.

    C. Migrate HDFS files to Cloud Storage. Load data from Cloud Storage to BigQuery. Convert all the Spark jobs into BigQuery SQL.

    D. Run new jobs on a custom Spark deployment in Compute Engine but run legacy jobs on a Cloud Dataproc cluster.

2. Your company needs to be able to handle log streaming data. The logs come from multiple devices and you need to be able to process and store them. The final output will be used for data analytics purposes. What services should they use for this task?

    A. Stackdriver, Cloud Dataproc, and Cloud Spanner

    B. Kubernetes Engine, Cloud Dataflow, and Cloud Datastore

    C. Cloud Pub/Sub, Cloud Dataproc, and Bigtable

    D. Cloud Pub/Sub, Cloud Dataflow, and BigQuery

3. Your company is planning to choose a managed database service in Google Cloud. The database will be used to serve a web application that handles product catalogs. Your database is 500 GB in size. The data is semi-structured. Which storage option should you choose?

    A. Cloud Bigtable

    B. Cloud SQL

    C. BigQuery

    D. Cloud Datastore

Let's continue to the second section.

Building and operationalizing data processing systems

Please choose one answer for each of the questions in this section:

4. Your company has multiple systems that all need to be notified of orders being processed. How should you configure Pub/Sub?

    A. Create a topic for orders. Create multiple subscriptions for this topic, one for each system that needs to be notified.

    B. Create a topic for orders. Create a subscription for this topic that can be shared by every system that needs to be notified.

    C. Create a new topic for each order. Create multiple subscriptions for each topic, one for every system that needs to be notified.

    D. Create a new topic for each order. Create a subscription for each topic that can be shared by every system that needs to be notified.

5. Your company has multiple MySQL databases on CloudSQL. You need to export all the data into Cloud Storage and BigQuery for analysis. Once the data has been loaded into BigQuery, you need to apply multiple data transformations for the business users. You need to repeat all these processes every day at 5 A.M. How should you approach this?

    A. Use Pub/Sub and Dataflow to process and schedule the required transformation.

    B. Create a Cloud Composer environment. Develop DAGs that extract data from CloudSQL and load them into Cloud Storage and BigQuery. Apply the transformation using BigQuery operator and schedule the DAG as per the requirements.

    C. Configure a DataProc Spark job to load the data from CloudSQL and schedule the job using Hadoop.

    D. Configure a compute engine to create Python scripts to handle all the processes. Use crontab to schedule the scripts' execution daily.

6. Your company is implementing a data and analytics ecosystem using a Cloud Storage bucket and BigQuery. There are three different types of users: data administrators, data providers, and data readers. What should you do to make sure each user gets the required permissions?

    A. Assign IAM roles for each user to Cloud Storage predefined roles and BigQuery predefined roles on both Cloud Storage and BigQuery individually.

B. Assign a primitive Owner role to the administrator at the project level and the primitive Editor role to the data providers and the data readers.

C. Create three custom IAM roles with the appropriate policies for the access levels needed for Cloud Storage and BigQuery. Add these users to the custom roles.

D. Assign a primitive Owner role to the administrator at the organization level and the primitive Editor role to the data providers and the data readers.

Let's continue to the third section.

Operationalizing machine learning models

Please choose one answer for each of the questions in this section:

7. You need to quickly add a new feature to your web application that will allow it to process uploaded user images, extract any text contained within them, and perform sentiment analysis on the text. Your company doesn't have any machine learning experts. What should you do?

A. Use the Cloud Vision API and the Natural Language API.

B. Use the Cloud Vision API and Cloud AutoML Natural Language to build a sentiment analysis.

C. Build and train models for text detection and sentiment analysis with TensorFlow and deploy them with Vertex AI prediction.

D. Use the Cloud Vision API. Build and train a sentiment analysis model with TensorFlow and deploy it with Vertex AI prediction.

8. You would like to create a model to predict a tree's height in the future based on some known parameters and labels from the historical data. What type of learning algorithm would you choose?

A. **Principal component analysis (PCA)**

B. Linear regression

C. K-Means

D. Logistic classification

9. You are building a machine learning model. You have found that the model is performing very well on training data, but very poorly on new data. What is the potential issue in this case?

   A. There is not enough data in the training set

   B. There are insufficient infrastructure resources assigned to the model

   C. There is not enough data in the validation set – the model has been overfitted

   D. There is not enough data in the test set – the model has an implicit bias

Let's continue to the fourth and last section.

Ensuring solution quality

Please choose one answer for each of the questions in this section:

10. Your company uses BigQuery to store data for more than 1 year. Some queries need to access the full historical data, but most of the queries only need to access the last 10 days' worth of data. Over time, the cost of the queries keeps rising. What can you do to optimize the queries' cost?

    A. Use integer range partitioned tables.

    B. Create a new table every 10 days. Use `JOIN` statements to conduct long-term analytics queries.

    C. Make sure that the BigQuery table uses `DATE` partitioned tables and the partitioned column that's used in the queries.

    D. Use Cloud Composer to automatically archive the data that is more than 10 days old in Google Cloud Storage.

11. Your company is considering using BigTable. What will happen to data in a Bigtable instance if one node goes down?

    A. Lost data will automatically rebuild itself from Cloud Storage backups when the node comes back online.

    B. Data will be lost, which makes regular backups to Cloud Storage necessary.

    C. BigTable will attempt to rebuild the data from the RAID disk configuration when the node comes back online.

    D. Nothing, as the storage is separate from the node compute.

12. You are using Data Studio to present a report that uses live user interaction data from BigQuery. One of the business users has found that the data in the report is not up to date. What should you recommend to them?

    A. Contact the infrastructure team to check if there are any issues with the Data Studio instance.

    B. Click the **Refresh Data** button on the Data Studio report to clear the BigQuery cache.

    C. Recreate the underlying BigQuery table.

    D. Clear browser cookies and reload the Data Studio web page.

Answers

Here are the key answers. Check if you answered the questions correctly. For each key answer, I have mentioned the relevant chapter from this book.

1. The correct answer is *A*. Pay attention to keywords such as *Spark jobs* and *quickly and easily*. DataProc is the best technology in GCP for running Spark jobs. The other options are possible, but they require a lot of unnecessary effort. Review *Chapter 5, Building a Data Lake Using Dataproc*.

2. The correct answer is *D*. For streaming data, we can use Pub/Sub to handle ever-increasing amounts of telemetry data. Pub/Sub can't process data, so we need Dataflow to process it. When it comes to analyzing the data, BigQuery is the best option. Review *Chapter 6, Processing Streaming Data with Pub/Sub and Dataflow*.

3. The correct answer is *D*. There are three key points as requirements in the question – a database for serving web applications, the database's size is 500 GB, and the data is semi-structured.

   BigQuery won't be suitable for serving web applications. BigTable is suitable for data above 10 TB. Cloud SQL can't handle semi-structured data, so Cloud Datastore is the best option. Review *Chapter 12, Boosting Your Confidence as a Data Engineer*, in the *Extra Materials* section.

4. The correct answer is *A*. Remember that a Pub/Sub topic can handle multiple publishers and subscribers. So, you only need one topic. The multiple systems need to be notified individually so that you can create multiple subscriptions – one subscription for each downstream system. Review *Chapter 6, Processing Streaming Data with Pub/Sub and Dataflow*.

5. The correct answer is *B*. Cloud Composer is the best option for orchestrating multiple steps of tasks from multiple GCP services. Cloud Composer is also able to handle scheduling. Review *Chapter 4, Building Orchestration for Batch Data Loading Using Cloud Composer*.

6. The correct answer is *A*. Granting permissions to users for specific GCP services is recommended compared to doing so at the organization or project level. And if possible, using predefined roles is simpler compared to custom IAM roles. Review *Chapter 9, User and Project Management in GCP*.

7. The correct answer is *A*. The Cloud Vision API is the quickest way to extract data from user-uploaded images. The Natural Language API already has a built-in model for sentiment analysis. Using TensorFlow or AutoML needs someone who understands machine learning. Review *Chapter 8, Building Machine Learning Solutions on Google Cloud Platform*.

8. The correct answer is *B*. The tree's height is a numerical value. Linear regression models attempt to predict a numerical output based on the known parameters and historical data. Review *Chapter 8, Building Machine Learning Solutions on Google Cloud Platform*, and additional resources from the public internet about basic machine learning models; for example, `https://www.datasciencecentral.com/profiles/blogs/how-to-choose-a-machine-learning-model-some-guidelines`.

9. The correct answer is *C*. The model has been too well trained on the training data and will fit it too closely, so it will perform badly when it's exposed to real-world data for predictions. Increasing the amount of data can help to reduce this overfitting. Review *Chapter 8, Building Machine Learning Solutions on Google Cloud Platform*, and additional resources from the public internet about basic machine learning models; for example, `https://towardsdatascience.com/what-are-overfitting-and-underfitting-in-machine-learning-a96b30864690`.

10. The correct answer is *C*. In BigQuery, using the `DATE` partitioned tables can reduce the cost of queries based on the date filters, which in the given question is 10 days of data. Review *Chapter 3, Building a Data Warehouse in BigQuery*, and *Chapter 10, Cost Strategy in GCP*, the *Tips for Optimizing BigQuery using partitioned and clustered tables* section.

11. The correct answer is *D*. In BigTable, storage and compute are separate. This topic is not discussed in depth in any of the chapters in this book, so please check the extra materials in *Chapter 12, Boosting Your Confidence as a Data Engineer*.

12. The correct answer is *B*. There is a **Refresh Data** button in Data Studio that can be used to clear the BigQuery cache and refresh the data. No additional action is needed. Review *Chapter 7, Visualizing Data for Making Data-Driven Decision with Data Studio*.

I hope this gives you an illustration of what the exam questions look like and that you can summarize what you've learned in this book. Remember that this book is only one tool for you to be prepared. Check the official website and other resources to be 100% ready to take the Google Cloud Data Engineering certification exam.

In the next section, I will share my opinion on the future of Data Engineering.

The past, present, and future of Data Engineering

The Data Engineering practice has been around since the early internet era in the 1990s. Going back to *Chapter 1, Fundamentals of Data Engineering*, in the past, data engineers were mostly ETL developers using specific tools. Most of these tools were proprietary tools and located on-premises. The term *data engineers* itself didn't exist; the more common terms used to be data modelers, database admin, and *ETL* developer (*ETL* references the proprietary ETL tool's name). Each of the ETL tools had the necessary expertise and best practices surrounding them.

Now, in the present, Data Engineering has evolved into a more mature and singular role. This means that the practice has a lot more common principles, concepts, and best practices. This is due to two reasons – the rapid improvement in the technologies supporting the practice and the fact that Data Engineering has become a critical and central role to organizations.

"Data engineer was the fastest-growing job in technology with a 50% year-over-year growth in the number of open positions" – 2019, reports from *Burning Glass's Nova* platform. The platform analyzes millions of active job postings. Data engineer remains the top tech job, with a 50% year-over-year growth. I have to say that the present day is the best day for anyone who wishes to become a data engineer.

The words big data and the cloud are no longer considered as the future – they are the present. If you are looking for jobs in Data Engineering, you must have strong knowledge of both of these. If you are a representative from a company that is looking for data engineers, you must ask the candidates about these two words. This is unavoidable and has become a new norm because it's the present.

Now, what does the future look like?

There are two aspects that I can think of. The first is the technology aspect, while the second is the role aspect:

- From a technology perspective, now, in 2022, the adoption from on-premises to the cloud is still happening. It's still an uptrend, and it's still far from the peak. When it reaches its peak, traditional companies such as banking corporations and the government will have adopted the cloud – not only in certain countries but globally. The advancement in data security, data governance, and multi-cloud environments are essentials. As you may already know, the regulation of data has been maturing in a lot of countries in the last few years. The data and cloud technologies need to keep adapting to these regulations, especially when it comes to financial industries. And on top of that, the capabilities to integrate data and technologies across cloud platforms and with on-premise systems will become more mature.

- The second aspect is the data engineer role. I think this role will go back to being a non-singular role. There will be clearer and more specific roles compared to the *data engineer* role. Companies will start to realize that the data engineer role can be broken down into more granular roles. It will be easier for them to find good candidates for specific needs.

One other thing about the role is who will write SQL queries. In the past, and still, in the present, data engineers are the ones who take full responsibility for writing SQL queries to transform business logic into answers. It is starting now and will occur more in the future that non-engineers will be SQL-savvy people. Non-engineers can include the marketing team, the human resources department, C-level, or any other role. They are the best at understanding the business context and gain the most benefit when they can access data directly via databases using SQL. For data engineers, this means that the role will be more focused on shaping the foundation. In terms of ELT, the extract and load process will still be handled by data engineers, but the majority of the transformation process will probably be taken over by non-data engineers. Going back to what I mentioned previously, data engineers will need to be more focused on designing and developing data security and data governance as a foundation.

Boosting your confidence and final thoughts

One thing that I hope you have after reading this book is more confidence – the confidence to design and develop a data pipeline and, more importantly, the confidence as a data engineer using Google Cloud Platform.

I will quote the definition of the word *confidence* from the physiological aspect by the *American Psychological Association*:

"Confidence is Self-assurance: trust in one's abilities, capacities, and judgment."

By following all the chapters throughout the book, you've learned about the important GCP services related to Data Engineering and tried them out in your environment by completing the hands-on exercises provided. You've tried 19 new technologies from GCP, including BigQuery, Google Cloud Storage, Cloud Composer, DataProc, DataFlow, Pub/Sub, CloudSQL, Google Data Studio, Vertex AI pipeline, Vision AI, Translate AI, AutoML, IAM, Cloud Shell, Cloud Editor, Cloud Build, Google Container Registry, Cloud Source Repository, and Terraform.

These are your new abilities, and I have to tell you that these abilities are in very high demand! I suggest that you start implementing your data projects using these technologies, outside of what we've tried in the exercises.

Back to the definition of confidence, the capacities are correlated to your experience. Depending on how much experience you gained when reading this book, if you are someone who is just starting the journey, always remember to start small. You've learned that the topics in terms of *Data Engineering using Google Cloud* are very wide. Adding those topics to the number of other materials that you need to learn about for the Google Cloud Data Engineering certification might be discouraging if you are new in this space. My suggestion is don't be discouraged!

The broad landscape of Data Engineering is there for many data experts to collaborate. Depending on how big an organization is, it's very common that a data engineer can focus on one aspect of Data Engineering. For example, there are many roles in the market that require you to only know about BigQuery, just Hadoop (DataProc), or the other specific tools. If you just started, I suggest that you start with those roles as a small step, and then build and grow your capacities. Then, one day, you won't realize you know most of these things.

Finally, believing in your judgment is also part of gaining confidence. I have to say that good judgment in Data Engineering is highly dependent on the first two factors: abilities and capacities. But on top of that, most of the time, you need to go back to the fundamental principles. For example, in this book, we talked about some principles such as the principle of least privilege, the data modeling principle for Data warehouses, and ETL versus ELT. My suggestion is to go back to the fundamental principles whenever you're in doubt.

Summary

In this chapter, we concluded everything we've learned throughout this book. We started the chapter by overviewing the certification options from Google Cloud. There, we covered most of the GCP services that are part of the certification. But for those that weren't covered, I suggest that you take a look at those services by looking at other resources.

In the next section, we looked at some quiz questions to help you gain a better understanding of the types of questions that will be asked and the format of the certification. I highly suggest that you review the other chapters if you missed some points from any of these questions.

Finally, I shared my thoughts on the past, present, and future of Data Engineering. Do remember that big data and the cloud are the present. You, as a data engineer, are and will be the center of it. Today is the best era for Data Engineering and I'm 100% confident in this. I hope that you enjoyed reading this book and have a great Data Engineering journey with Google Cloud Platform.

Index

C

`Packt.com`

Subscribe to our online digital library for full access to over 7,000 books and videos, as well as industry leading tools to help you plan your personal development and advance your career. For more information, please visit our website.

Why subscribe?

- Spend less time learning and more time coding with practical eBooks and Videos from over 4,000 industry professionals

- Improve your learning with Skill Plans built especially for you

- Get a free eBook or video every month

- Fully searchable for easy access to vital information

- Copy and paste, print, and bookmark content

Did you know that Packt offers eBook versions of every book published, with PDF and ePub files available? You can upgrade to the eBook version at `packt.com` and as a print book customer, you are entitled to a discount on the eBook copy. Get in touch with us at `customercare@packtpub.com` for more details.

At www.`packt.com`, you can also read a collection of free technical articles, sign up for a range of free newsletters, and receive exclusive discounts and offers on Packt books and eBooks.

Other Books You May Enjoy

If you enjoyed this book, you may be interested in these other books by Packt:

Data Engineering with Python

Paul Crickard

ISBN: 9781839214189

- Understand how data engineering supports data science workflows

- Discover how to extract data from files and databases and then clean, transform, and enrich it

- Configure processors for handling different file formats as well as both relational and NoSQL databases

- Find out how to implement a data pipeline and dashboard to visualize results

- Use staging and validation to check data before landing in the warehouse

- Build real-time pipelines with staging areas that perform validation and handle failures

- Get to grips with deploying pipelines in the production environment

Data Engineering with AWS

Gareth Eagar

ISBN: 9781800560413

- Understand data engineering concepts and emerging technologies
- Ingest streaming data with Amazon Kinesis Data Firehose
- Optimize, denormalize, and join datasets with AWS Glue Studio
- Use Amazon S3 events to trigger a Lambda process to transform a file
- Run complex SQL queries on data lake data using Amazon Athena
- Load data into a Redshift data warehouse and run queries
- Create a visualization of your data using Amazon QuickSight
- Extract sentiment data from a dataset using Amazon Comprehend

Packt is searching for authors like you

If you're interested in becoming an author for Packt, please visit `authors.packtpub.com` and apply today. We have worked with thousands of developers and tech professionals, just like you, to help them share their insight with the global tech community. You can make a general application, apply for a specific hot topic that we are recruiting an author for, or submit your own idea.

Share Your Thoughts

Now you've finished *Data Engineering with Google Cloud Platform*, we'd love to hear your thoughts! Scan the QR code below to go straight to the Amazon review page for this book and share your feedback or leave a review on the site that you purchased it from.

https://packt.link/r/1-800-56132-6

Your review is important to us and the tech community and will help us make sure we're delivering excellent quality content.